The Zephyrs of Najd

JAROSLAV STETKEVYCH

The ZEPHYRS *of* NAJD

The Poetics of Nostalgia in the Classical Arabic *Nasīb*

THE UNIVERSITY OF CHICAGO PRESS *Chicago & London*

Jaroslav Stetkevych is professor of Arabic literature in the Department of Near Eastern Languages and Civilizations at the University of Chicago.

The University of Chicago Press, Chicago 60637
The University of Chicago Press, Ltd., London

Printed in the United States of America
02 01 00 99 98 97 96 95 94 93 5 4 3 2 1

ISBN (cloth): 0-226-77335-3
ISBN (paper): 0-226-77336-1

Library of Congress Cataloging-in-Publication Data

Stetkevych, Jaroslav.
The zephyrs of Najd : the poetics of nostalgia in the classical Arabic nasīb / Jaroslav Stetkevych.
p. cm.
Includes bibliographical references and index.
ISBN 0-226-77335-3. — ISBN 0-266-77336-1 (pbk.)
1. Qasidas–Themes, motives. 2. Nostalgia in literature. 3. Arabic poetry—History and criticism. 4. Pastoral poetry, Arabic—History and criticism. 5. Poetics. I. Title.
PJ7542.Q3S74 1993
892′.7104309—dc20 93-14631
CIP

♾ The paper used in this publication meets the minimum requirements of the American National Standard for Information Sciences—Permanence of Paper for Printed Library Materials, ANSI Z39.48-1984.

To the memory of

Sir Hamilton A. R. Gibb

As I watch'd where you pass'd and was lost in
the netherward black of the night

—Walt Whitman

CONTENTS

Acknowledgments ix
Preface xi

ONE

Arabic Lyricism and Its Structure: The Nasīb *within the* Qaṣīdah 1

1. The Poem as Rhetorical and Epideictic Strategy 6
2. *Ut Musica Poesis:* The *Qaṣīdah* as Sonata—The *Nasīb* as Sonata Form 16
3. Toward the Ternary Archetype 26

TWO

The Nasīb*: From Archaic Tears to Spiritual Pilgrimages* 50

1. The Tolerance of the Archaic Vision 50
2. The Freeing of the Metaphor: Ḥassān Ibn Thābit 59
3. Toward the Courtly Idyll with Abū al-ʿAtāhiyah 64
4. The Stylizing Imagination: Silences and Voices of the Desert from Dhū al-Rummah to Ibn Khafājah 74
5. The Delicate Balancing of a Stubborn Structure: Ibn al-Fāriḍ 79

THREE

Names, Privileged Places, Idylls 103

1. When Toponymy Becomes Poetry 103
2. Najd and Arcadia: The Topology of Nostalgia 114

FOUR

Meadows in the Sky 135

1. Of Pastors and Their Dreams: A Digression into Common Grounds 135
2. Toward a Cosmic Pastoral Space 142

FIVE

In Search of the Garden 168

1. On the Periphery of Autochthony 168
2. Spaces of Delight: Perceived, Lost, Remembered 180

Appendix of Arabic Texts 203
Notes 235
Bibliography 299
Index 319

ACKNOWLEDGMENTS

THIS BOOK HAS BEEN many years in the making and during those years I had to test the patience, indeed the credulity, of three esteemed colleagues and deans of the Division of the Humanities of the University of Chicago. In the first place, therefore, I would like to express my gratitude to Karl Joachim Weintraub, who many years ago took such an active interest in the early version of my manuscript and gave me his unflagging and generous support. Thanks are due, too, to Stuart M. Tave, who likewise afforded me the encouragement and research time necessary to bring the present version to completion. Finally, during the last editorial stages of the book, Dean Philip Gossett has followed the magnanimous tradition of his predecessors in granting me the time needed to bring the work to publication.

To my wife and closest colleague, Suzanne Pinckney Stetkevych, for her inestimable help I give unmeasured thanks.

PREFACE

CLASSICAL ARABIC POETRY, together with the Qur'ān, has traditionally been considered by the Arabs themselves the preeminent accomplishment of Arab-Islamic culture. The continuation in that tradition of a single dominant poetic form—the tripartite *qaṣīdah*—from pre-Islamic times to the early decades of our own century produced a poetry turned in upon itself in such a way as to achieve a most rigorous form-consciousness and within it a degree of subtlety of expression not easily apprehended, much less appreciated, by Western critical and poetic sensibility. The Arabic *qaṣīdah*'s integrated polarity of lyricism and formalism—two properties which in Western genre-theory, still strongly Romantic-indebted, are virtually incompatible—remained baffling to Western aesthetic norm and sensibility. To challenge this state of affairs, this study takes as its main subject the *nasīb,* the lyrical-elegiac opening section of the *qaṣīdah,* which is also the section most sharply displaying a modal-formalist polarization. Quite intentionally, the study, too, is both polarized and integrated. When it approaches classical Arabic poetry from Western literary perspectives, it does so with two goals in mind: first, to demonstrate that the rigorous formal tradition of the classical Arabic *qaṣīdah,* far from producing the constraint and artifice that Western readers have expected and, indeed, read into it, was able to generate a vibrant and delicate lyrical mode; and second, through a comparatist approach, to integrate the classical Arabic lyric into an enlarged understanding of lyrical poetry as category of genre and as experiential quality. Before choosing any Western—or what we should term "modern"—optic, however, no effort has been spared and no level of experience shortchanged to give the poetic text—qua Arabic poetic text—its fullest primacy. So, too, have classical Arabic critical considerations been taken into account, albeit implicitly more often than explicitly. Also on the implicit level, allowing for the intimate ring of things that are culturally and historically self-understood, hearing has been given to the interpretive voices of the Arabic poets' own (invariably implicit) readings of the messages of their tradition.

The Zephyrs of Najd is thus addressed equally to readers in the fields of European literature, comparative literature, and literary theory and to specialists in Arabic literature.

With the elucidation of the *nasīb* as the main objective, the book's five chapters should lead the reader in a methodologically circuitous but progressively tightening manner from questions of containing structure (the *qaṣīdah*), to the pursuit of the historicity of the lyrical immutable (the *nasīb*), to the Arabic equivalent of Celan's *Niemandsrose* of lyricism, the never-temporal, or pretemporal, Ruinous Abode (the *ṭalal*).

Thus Chapter 1, "Arabic Lyricism and Its Structure: The *Nasīb* within the *Qaṣīdah*," presents, in a manner that is introductory to the book as a whole, three theories of structure of the tripartite *qaṣīdah:* the rhetorical, the modal, and the mythopoeic-anthropological. All three, however, are shown to be structural refractions that are interdependent. Chapter 2, "The *Nasīb:* From Archaic Tears to Spiritual Pilgrimages," illustrates how the pre-Islamic poetic lamentations over abandoned abodes evolved historically into expressions of the spiritual nostalgia of Arabic mystical poetry. Chapter 3, "Names, Privileged Places, Idylls," treats the elegiac uses of idyllic place-names, and on that basis establishes an analogy between the highlands of Najd in Arabic poetry and Arcadia in the European tradition. In Chapter 4, "Meadows in the Sky," with the recognition of the pastoral element in the Arabic lyric, a ground for comparison with European pastoral is established. The chapter then proceeds to the more specifically Arabic motif of "the pasturing of the stars." The final chapter, Chapter 5, "In Search of the Garden," provides a more explicit localization of the pastoral-paradisal archetype by turning first to medieval Arabic prose, such as al-Maʿarrī's and Ibn Shuhayd's visits to the literary Parnassus/Paradise and the *Thousand and One Nights,* then to the elegiac *nasīb* imagery of the abandoned encampments of the pre-Islamic Arabian desert, and ultimately to the ruins of the palace city, al-Zahrāʾ, in al-Andalus. With this, the argument of the book, which is the survival of the Arabic symbolic optic in the life of the *nasīb,* is brought to its theoretical closure.

In light of the variety of approaches to the translation of classical Arabic poetry, I think it proper to clarify my own stance. In the present book, I have aimed not at producing literal translations, which at best would serve instructional purposes, but rather at capturing in the English literary idiom the meaning and, above all, the poeticality of the Arabic originals. For the reader of Arabic the original poetic texts appear in the appendix of Arabic Texts keyed to the English translations.

ONE

Arabic Lyricism and Its Structure: The Nasīb within the Qaṣīdah

IN ITS EXTRAORDINARY FORMAL CONTINUITY, the *qaṣīdah*,[1] the preeminent form of Arabic poetry up until recent times, has maintained the most rigorous observance of the canon ruling its content. All through the main creative periods of Arabic literary history, the *qaṣīdah* underwent a crystallization of theme and meaning and an accumulation of formal solemnity. This crystallization of meaning in a very limited number of structurally determined themes and the formal solemnity of their succession and interplay have sustained, over time, an almost ritualistic power over poet and audience. The submersion in the process of the expected in the Arabic *qaṣīdah* was inseparable from its "experience." It is also because of this peculiarly charged crystallization that Arabic poetic form-elements may be studied as abstractions; and even more: they must be perceived as abstractions, as quintessential conventions wherein every bit of thematic congealment and stylization harbors—almost to the degree of reductionism—an underlying symbol. There we may even suspect elemental filtrations of ancient concerns of nation and race. Furthermore, as so quintessential a form, the *qaṣīdah* gives Arabic poetic expression a great sense of inner control and self-containment. It draws a precise horizon, reducing a comprehensive aesthetic vision to a microcosm. From this microcosm, as a pattern of the mind, a habit of thought, or a mode of vision, it then seems to fulfill a need for a comprehensive synthesis of an entire culture's view on world, life, and historical experience. The emergence of this poetic form within the historical process of transition from antiquity to the Middle Ages is in itself significant: synthesis was the mold of thought and expression at the cultural threshold between antiquity and the new age. The Arabic culture of the Jāhilīyah (the "Age of Ignorance," or rather of zeal, impulse, and pretheological "agnosis") may be viewed as a geographically marginal culture in itself, but having been born in the shadow of two formidable inheritors of Hellenistic antiquity, Byzantium and Sassanid Persia, it could not escape involvement in the process of gestation which finally produced what we call the medieval man and the medieval mind. It is in the meaning of the main sections of the Arabic *qaṣīdah* that some faded features of that remote man and that elusive mind have to be sought—and also in the implicit reasoning behind the structuring of those main sections into the *qaṣīdah* as a formal whole.

The sections of the *qaṣīdah* are obvious. In its sequential thematic structure there are three main thematic nuclei: (1) the theme of loss and yearning (*nasīb*); (2) the travel or "setting out" theme (*raḥīl*); and (3) the themes of praise of self (*fakhr*), praise of others (*madīḥ*), and the reverse of praise, the invective (*hijā'*), in the satirical alternative to the "straight ode."[1] To gain a cohesive view of Arabic poetry and above all of the lyricism of the *nasīb,* we must first turn to the *qaṣīdah* as framing structure and poetic vehicle. Even this preliminary phrasing of intention, however, presents us with some of the problems of a "formal" inquest: the distinction of a specific "vehicle" of meaning and of lyricism has been made, a structure suggested, and the somehow unique name ascertained. Furthermore, in so invoking "form" and "name," we have opened the door to the abstract dichotomy of form and content.

We shall address ourselves first to this dichotomy. Arabic poetry has fared particularly badly in the debate over form and content. It is true that Arabic poetic theory has not been very helpful in providing an alternative to the utilitarian, rhetorical approach to poetics as craft. There is little one can say in behalf of Arabic poetics after reading al-Jāḥiẓ's (d. 255/868) opinion that poetic content (*al-maʿānī*), which is also terminologically equivalent to poetic ideas, lies scattered all over the road, and that the business of poetry is to choose from it and to put it in order. "After all, poetry is a craft, a sort of weaving, a kind of figural design."[2] Qudāmah Ibn Jaʿfar (d. after 329/932) then speaks with added "Aristotelian" precision. To him *al-maʿānī* as poetic ideas are the given raw matter, and the craft of poetry consists of imposing on that matter a specific form.[3] In this he also sees an analogy with every other kind of "craft." Abū Hilāl al-ʿAskarī (d. after 400/1010) uses the analogy of the body and its attire: one is the meaning; the other, the word.[4] To go no further, Ibn Ṭabāṭabā al-ʿAlawī (d. 322/934), in his *ʿIyār al-Shiʿr,* gives us a step-by-step procedure for the nonpoet on how to make poetry, how to put all the ingredients together and "shake well."[5]

In these uninspired postulations of the chief problem of all aesthetic thinking, however, Arab rhetorical theorists are, in the post-Aristotelian sense, perfectly neoclassical. There is not very much to differentiate them from the whole belated European neoclassical tradition.[6] It is only in the instances where the Horatian simile *ut pictura poesis* shows its semblance that form and content seem to unite more closely under the general intention of mimetic function. In Ibn Rashīq (d. 456/1065 or 463/1071) such references are reduced to mere hints, as little more than somebody else's happy phrasing.[7] In ʿAbd al-Qāhir al-Jurjānī (d. 471/1078), they will become his many personal theories of the *maʿānī,* often reiterated but without the lapidary force of formulation.[8]

And yet the separation of form and content, which certainly drops all its pretenses in medieval critical writings, should perhaps be reconsidered. In the philosophical atmosphere of the age, there were two roads to choose for the setting of aesthetic premises: the Platonic and the Aristotelian. As suggestive as the Platonic idea of unity of form and content may appear to us, it is of a limited, turned-against-itself effect in literary practice. Within Platonism a poet would at best aim at achieving a phantom of an image of an ideal reality. If this phantom was obtained by imitation, that imitation itself had as its model a secondary object. The direct vision of the ideal remained as yet restricted to the realms of prophetic revelation and mystic contemplation. From the first realm poetry was most emphatically excluded, while in the second it was a stepchild and a subterfuge. The lack of faith in poetry as statement may have its origins in the Platonic incompatibility. And poetry's self-defense is then, understandably, psychologically true to itself in its use of irony and paradox: "In poetry the most mendacious is the truest" will be the Arabic maxim,[9] and the self-assured poet al-Buḥturī (d. 284/897) will answer succinctly:

> You imposed on us the strictures of your logic—
> In poetry, its lie is uttered unmindful of its truth![10] [1]

Shakespeare phrases this somewhat less epigrammatically:

> Audrey: I do not know what poetical is: is it honest in deed and word? is it a true thing?
> Touchstone: No, truly: for the truest poetry is the most feigning. . . .[11]

To Vico, man the dreamer, wanting to become man the creator (poet), searches for self-realization not so much in the lie as in the paradox of poetry, "the credible impossibility."[12]

The Aristotelian pragmatism of mimesis, where object and means are clearly defined, is thus most welcome. In an age where the symbolic dimension of poetic creativity as yet evades the conscious conceptual grasp, the concretizing principle of mimesis may itself be understood as a methodological middleground, or protosimile. Mimesis, thus, comes close to the very essence of the prime poetic principle by which the poet is allowed to hang onto his realm of reality and truth. It is of concern to the pre-Romantic and presymbolic poet not whether he achieves the visionary unity of form and content but whether his form and content are as closely united as possible without losing themselves conceptually. To base one's understanding of Arabic aesthetics and creative mechanics, however, on the stereotype of a form-content dichotomy is, to say the least, inadequate. The definition of poetry given by standard Arabic criticism as "measured and rhymed speech"[13] is always and only preliminary. It is a first, external, descriptive statement that precedes, and predates, critical opinion. An Arab critic would have to have been blind and deaf and otherwise insensitive not to have noticed what is so obvious. Beyond this first glance, Arabic critical sources and poetic confessions display a sufficiently representative diapason of emotive "Platonic" statements on the sources, nature, and effects of poetic feeling. The lack of a *corpus* and the many internal contradictions in such statements are a sign of the times rather than a peculiarity of Arabic aesthetic attitudes.

Then too, instead of looking for signs of dichotomy of form and content, one could, with equal ease, reverse the lens and see in Arabic poetry the closest possible—or the will to the closest possible—marriage between form and content, precisely because that poetry is so highly "formalistic." Actually, in instances where form becomes its own content, a sui generis unity becomes perfect, as may be seen in the arabesque. Such a structure brings content in a material sense much closer to form than loose, outstretched panels or discourses of an epic nature. In the formal unit of the Arabic poetic line, for instance, content is under a closer control by form than it is in practically any type of European poetry. The subdivision of the Arabic verse into hemistichs invites a further sectioning of content, and the highly characteristic "formal" phenomenon of parallelism of meaning between two hemistichs incorporates, in an almost ingrown way, the so-called content into form. All these elements, together with the meter and, to a much lesser degree, the rhyme, could not possibly or reasonably be considered to be simply superimposed upon the content from the outside. No content in abstract would survive a similar rod of iron. Instead of succumbing under the constraint of form, however, we must admit that poetic content not only survives but flourishes, albeit in unaccustomed ways, and extracts out of its predicament a strange power and solidity of imaginative impact.

Cohesiveness of form and inner harmony of structure preoccupied the ancient theorists and their Arab and European successors quite markedly. Horace begins his *Ars poetica* with the example of a mixed species, a woman with the neck of a horse, some odds and ends of arms and legs, feathers of different colors, all this tapering off into a slimy, discolored fish. After laughing at this, and more like it, he gives the aspiring poet a master's advice: "In short, be the work what you will, let it at least be simple and uniform [*denique sit quod vis, simplex dumtaxat et unum*]."[14] To al-Jāḥiẓ, "the best achieved poetry should be a free-flowing, cohesive unit. This way one knows that it was also smelted and cast all in one."[15] Abū ʿAlī al-Ḥātimī's (d. 388/928) assertion that "the *qaṣīdah* is created like a human body" engages the critical imagination with an even greater ease, but then, too, it no more than reflects its culturally idiosyncratic sense of form. The perfectly harmonious organism which in al-Ḥātimī's mind is the *qaṣīdah* does not relinquish its irredentist structural characteristics as we know them or as a critic such as Ibn Qutaybah knew them[16]—that is, as a sequential, but for the most part drastically paratactic, arrangement of a *nasīb,* then a *raḥīl,* and then a *fakhr/madīḥ*. This was al-Ḥātimī's "organic" form, and the biological human body was its analogue. At best, his equation is a metaphorization of what we choose to call biologically paradigmatic, and, in the end, we must accept the fact of a "conditioned" sensibility and of a deeply rooted, unflinching cultural habit.[17] Remarks concerning general aesthetic principle, however, especially inasmuch as they touch upon the structure of the *qasīdah* and exceed the bounds of the dominant rhetorical preoccupation, have run their course almost as soon as they are issued. Most of all, one must not carry them over into poetic practice. As much as the mimetic principle applies to the handling in Arabic poetry of subject, theme, and motif, a presumption in it of the Romantic "organic" concept of form and structure strikes a discordant note with basic Arabic ideas of form.

When the Greek lyrical poet Alceus left us a fragment now referred to as the *Maiden's Complaint,* he seems to have posed to classical literary criticism a problem. In the poem, the opening verse is concerned with the maiden's complaint about some great sorrow, yet the next subject is the belling of a stag. "No one has satisfactorily explained this connection," remarks Albin Lesky.[18] In the Arabic lyrical tradition, where the easily dismissed Greek anomaly is the norm, the riddle nonetheless stands out glaringly. The structural-thematic elements of the *qaṣīdah,* in their abrupt changes, contrasts of subjects, and reversals of moods, have not been "satisfactorily explained" either.

In what follows, three theories, or rather three faces, of the *qaṣīdah* will be outlined: the first one will lay bare the structure's rhetorical and epideictic strategies; the second one will tie the sense of structure to the conversion of thematic interdependence into an interdependence of moods and the conversion of the verbal order of meaning into the tonal order of music; and the third one will reach one level farther yet, to the ternary archetypal prelogic, or the anthropology of harnessing the flow of vitality into a cycle of experience.

1. The Poem as Rhetorical and Epideictic Strategy[19]

The rising zeal to discover unity in the classical Arabic *qaṣīdah* and the further notion that a story told from its beginning to its end evinces a form's unity have led to attempts to understand the Arabic *qaṣīdah* as a story told or to view it structurally as a hollowed-out mold into which a poet may pour his poetic matter and in which that matter will organize itself both into story and into formal unity. Such an approach is too obviously simplistic, and its validity is at best that of a preliminary strategy. If such a paradigmatically molded "story" of the *qaṣīdah* is retold here, it is only for the sake of subsequent reference. Thus we first meet the poet pensive and suffering in the abandoned encampment scene. His memories of the beloved have been awakened. There follows an almost cinematographic change of scenery, a flashback, and in it the beloved herself appears. The daydreaming and erotic fantasizing flare up brightly and then end with the poet's regaining self-control. He mounts his camel and rides forth. The journey is difficult, but his bravery is great and the qualities of his riding beast are formidable. So the poet reaches what proves to be his real goal: his proud, warring tribe or the court and presence of his king or benefactor. The subsequent appearance at court with a eulogy is the final major theme, which, however, may also be followed by an excursus, such as the poet's expression of self-esteem or a string of epigrammatic maxims to serve as the poem's closure.

The above elucidation of the Arabic ode corresponds in form and, to a large extent, in spirit to the critiques dating from what we should call the Arabic neoclassical critical period (third to fourth centuries H.). Its neoclassicism rests on the fact that the compositional evidence from which it draws its rationalizations is not only of its own time but also, more selectively, of the autochthonously classical Jāhilīyah as paradigmatically represented in the collection of seven *qaṣīdah*s called the *Muʿallaqāt*. In a more direct way, however, the above elucidation owes the most, both in what it understood and in what it misunderstood, to Ibn Qutaybah's (d. 276/889) descriptive account of the ternary structure of the *qaṣīdah*.[20] To him the *qaṣīdah* was a formally highly distilled paradigm, and he proposed to make clear its functionality. His critical stance is to be viewed as reflecting the mode and the circumstance of that paradigm's being "in place." Its place, as Ibn Qutaybah saw it, was well delineated. It was the courtly and, broadly speaking, public forum. The necessary mode operative in that forum was the epideictic one. His further intent, however, was to capture the elusive moment of a formal classicism of the Arabic poem/ode. Ibn Qutaybah achieves this generalizing effect mainly through the use of an artfully insinuated past tense—as if suggesting that his poetics is based upon the literary practice of a canonic past, which in the Arabic case is always that of the poetry of the Jāhilīyah. In the strictest sense, however, Ibn Qutaybah's model applies only to the Arabic *qaṣīdah* when it had acquired its self-consciousness in its Umayyad phase and then became the vehicle of Abbasid courtly panegyric.

Ibn Qutaybah thus assigns to the *nasīb* the mission "to dispose favorably, attract attention, and exact a hearing—because rhapsodizing a beloved touches souls and clings onto the hearts." Then, he explains, "assured of being heard, . . . he [the poet] followed up, impressing his entitlements"; and after punctuating the hardships of the *raḥīl* (journey), "knowing that he had thus duly obligated his patron to fulfill his claim and expectation," the poet commenced with the solemn main theme of the panegyric.[21]

What we derive from Ibn Qutaybah's definition of the *qaṣīdah* in the first place, is thus the realization that this Abbasid critic is talking to us of a structure that functions *rhetorically:* it has an inherent message and is meant to influence.[22] Thus every approach to the *qaṣīdah* as a structure with such a rhetorical function must also, by the sheer intrusiveness of analogy, engage in some kind of associative poetics with respect to other forms and genres produced by the rhetorical imperative, that is, such other epideictic structures as the oration and the epistle. Arabic rhetorically based literary criticism must have been aware of this even before Ibn Qutaybah's time, although the first explicit reference to the similarity between the *qaṣīdah* and the *risālah* (missive, epistle) appears to be that of Ibn Ṭabāṭabā.[23]

According to Ibn Ṭabāṭabā it had been said of poetry that it was "bound epistles" (rhymed and metered) and of epistles that they were "unbound poetry," which, viewed analogically, extends also to the poem (*qaṣīdah*) and the oration (*khuṭbah*)—the difference being one of medium and circumstance of delivery rather than of structure. What is more, because of the intrinsic orality of the delivery of epideictic poetry, the analogy between oration and ode can be drawn even more closely.[24]

Speaking of the way in which the fourth-century Athenian Sophist Himerius might have delivered an oration, George A. Kennedy calls up a scene that ought to fit effortlessly into the Arabic genre context: "Himerius," he suggests, "should probably be imagined delivering it in an elevated chanting tone, with carefully planned gestures. His audience would have been made up of connoisseurs who would appreciate the rhythms. The speech is to the fourth century what the poems of Pindar were to the early classical period."[25] What Kennedy means is that in the Greek cultural-historical context the epideictic oration has at this point replaced the archaic epideictic ode, and that it has become more stylized in texture and structure—but without losing its essential rhetorically dictated form. It thus continues to effect "many of the functions earlier performed by poetry, and many epideictic orations, including encomia, epithalamia, and celebrations of the gods, are hymns in poetic prose."[26]

We could say similar things of the dialectic between the Arabic *qaṣīdah* and the *khuṭbah* and *risālah*—only that in the Arabic case that dialectic still remains a matter of internal tension even within the epideictic *qaṣīdah* itself, in the manner in which that form served as paradigm to Ibn Qutaybah, for instance. Thus even the manner of the formal delivery of the *qaṣīdah* tended to remain in its "archaic" ceremonial context, where the courtly Arab poet, wanting to affect ancient seriousness, would deliver his ode standing erect as he grasped his bow planted in the ground before him.[27]

It is within the rhetorical context that the ceremonial aspects which accompanied the delivery of both the archaic Arabic ode and its courtly Abbasid offspring—as described by Ibn Qutaybah—should be viewed. In the eyes of Ibn Qutaybah, what the Arabic courtly poet thus delivered was a form of missive. It was natural for him, or for that matter for any other rhetorically predisposed Abbasid critic, to have translated this analogy-based perception into the outline of an epideictic scheme for the *qaṣīdah*.

If we thus accept that from the high Abbasid period onward a rhetorical notion of structure was assuming increasingly clear contours in the minds of poets as well as critics, and that that tendency may have been aided by a concurrent dissemination of Hellenistic rhetorical theory, we may be prepared to understand the Arabic critical bias and to see in the structural whole of the *qaṣīdah* elements which may be integrated functionally into a coherent rhetorical design. A rhetorical theory of the structure—that is, the rationale behind the rhetorical organization of the poem, not the rhetoric of discrete, decontextualized figures of speech,—is what is thus needed if we are to understand the epideictic functionality and theoretical defensibility of the Arabic *qaṣīdah* as the age of Ibn Qutaybah knew it.

Thus, to start with, the very word *qaṣīdah* (intended/intending: as purpose or goal) could be explained with an almost flippant ease as signifying "missive" or as the "rhetorical intent" implicitly present in the poem. Also, if we keep in mind the mechanics of persuasion inherent in the Hellenistic, Ciceronian, and early medieval European rhetorical genres of the epistle and the oration, they will lead us to the actual structural makeup of those genres—precisely to the extent conveyed by the descriptive terminology which Greek and Latin rhetoric had developed for them. We have to go no further than to trace the respective structures through their three, or eventually four, constituent parts: (1) the exordium, (2) the narration, (3) the argumentation, and (4) the conclusion; even though we observe that in the Ciceronian forensic speech structure the "narration" is further modulated through a "digression," while "argumentation" develops into the dialectic of "partition," followed by "confirmation," and "refutation." Furthermore, already in its Ciceronian understanding, the purpose of the "exordium" was essentially that of "rendering the audience attentive and well-disposed."[28] The further eagerness to clarify the rhetorical intent implicit in the exordium then makes medieval epistolary theory equate it with *captatio benevolentiae*.[29] Ibn Qutaybah's remark "so as to dispose favorably, attract attention, and exact a hearing" is so much like the Ciceronian "rendering the audience attentive and well-disposed" as to allow for a functional equation between the *nasīb* and the exordium. The Arabic *qaṣīdah* theorist's "knowing that he had thus duly obligated his patron to fulfill his claim and expectation," although still identifiable with the post-Ciceronian *captatio benevolentiae,* will tell us, however, that in Ibn Qutaybah's *qaṣīdah* theory the "journey section" (*raḥīl*) is, in its rhetorical intent, indistinguishable from the exordium, even though stylistically it may already be a *narratio*. It tells us something else besides: namely, that the *nasīb* and the *raḥīl* in the Arabic *qaṣīdah* are of one and the same voice or poetic "persona," and that together they form the subjective part of the poem. This fact has to be kept in mind not only because it is relevant to the understanding of theories of the *qaṣīdah* other than the rhetorical one, but also because within the rhetorical theory of the Abbasid period it will help explain the progressive and progressively easy dispensing with the *raḥīl* section altogether, without taking the poet's own voice, and self, out of the poem and without depriving it of its rhetorical exordium-tied effectiveness, now dependent entirely on the *nasīb*.[30]

The philosopher Ibn Sīnā (d. 428/1037), whose theoretical interest in rhetoric frequently led to critical observations on poetry, notices that the exordium is not the exclusive property of the rhetors but of the adept among the poets as well. To this he then adds that such an analogy may be drawn especially between "adversarial oratory" (*al-khuṭab al-khuṣūmīyah*) and the epideictic *qaṣīdah,* especially the *qaṣīdah* of praise.[31] In pointing to the Abbasid courtly panegyric with its rhetorical characteristics of "missive," Ibn Sīnā implies the existence of a shared rhetorical intent and actual formal indebtedness between it and the adversarial genres such as invective (*hijā'*), satire, and blood vengeance (*tha'r, taḥrīḍ*), which, with the fullest rhetorical explicitness, introduce their "message" segments with a fixed repertory of specific stylistic "signals." Ibn Sīnā, it seems, knew of the formal genre dependence between "adversarial oratory" and the *qaṣīdah* in at least one of its manifestations—even if he turned the sequence of formal dependences around, for, according to the Arabic chronology of the emergence and development of genres, it was the adversarial prose oration which came on the coattails of the pre-Islamic Arabic adversary *qaṣīdah,* stylistically as well as structurally, and not vice versa.

With great sensitivity for semantic modalities, Alfred Bloch[32] has brought together a representative repertory of the stylistic devices which signal the presence of a missive in the early *qaṣīdah,* proceeding from there to the proposition that the term *qaṣīdah* itself should originally have been applicable to the missive alone, and that such a missive, with its prevalent adversarial characteristic, would be not only a *Gedicht* (poem) but, even more cogently, a *Schmähgedicht* (invective), similar to the archaic Arabic genre-meaning of *qāfiyah* as "verse of invective" first and only later as "rhyme."[33]

The stylistic "signal" of the missive in these primarily adversarial poems is of direct interest as far as a closer identification of genre is concerned. Thus we notice that a missive is most readily introduced, or at times recapitulated as topical closure, by way of the Form IV imperative *abligh* (convey, inform) or by its dual *ablighā* or by the equally available Form II variant *balligh,* as well as by the interrogative formula *man mublighun* (who will convey?).

Bashāmah Ibn ʿAmr is thus unambiguous as he dispatches his missive of remonstration:

> If I die without reaching them,
> To the notables of Sahm then *convey* a message.[34] [2]

Equally clear is Zuhayr Ibn Abī Sulmā:

> Now, to the confederates—and to Dhubyān—
> *Convey* from me a message:
> "Have you so sworn every solemn oath?"[35] [3]

And after the battle of Uḥud, the Meccan champion ʿAbd Allāh Ibn al-Zibaʿrā (d. after 23/644) sends out his defiant message of victory—his uncontainable verse—to the Medinan champion of the defeated party, Ḥassān Ibn Thābit (d. ca. 40/661):

> *Convey,* you two, my message to Ḥassān,
> For gnawing on verse soothes the sufferer
> of burning thirst.[36] [4]

The expanded opening formula *alā man mublighun* is familiar to al-Nābighah al-Dhubyānī,[37] and the Form II imperative *balligh* is found in the *mukhaḍram* poet Kaʿb Ibn Zuhayr,[38] but it becomes clearly favored by the Umayyad poet Mālik Ibn al-Rayb. Thus in Ibn al-Rayb's moving elegy for himself, the missive is signaled at first by the archaic threnodic invocation *yā rākiban* (O rider) and then made explicit by the emphatic imperative *ballighan:*

> So, too, O rider, should chance afford it, *convey*
> To Banū Mālik and al-Rayth that we'll meet no more,
>
> And to my brother ʿUmrān deliver
> my cloak and my loincloth,
> And to my old woman *convey,* this day,
> that we'll be near no more.[39] [5]

Within this firmly established style, the poet then closes his elegy with a restatement of the entire rhetorical intent of the missive:

> O, *who shall convey* to Umm al-Ṣarīkh a message,
> Telling her of me, though I be far?[40] [6]

Such stylistic signals[41] facilitate an almost mechanical recognition of the rhetorical intent of a fair portion of the earliest Arabic poetry. Furthermore, they ought to lead to an ultimate identification of genre—to the *qaṣīdah* in its explicit rhetorical function, both epistolary and oratoric. In his approach to the *qaṣīdah,* Alfred Bloch may well have presupposed all this, even though his overruling historicist interest leads him to the subsequent postulation that the *qaṣīdah,* defined strictly thematically as missive and confirmed in that definition by the etymology of its name and term (*qaṣīdah*), antedates the formation of the complex, multithematic ode—and that only this "missive"/*qaṣīdah* can claim terminological appropriateness. Thus Bloch's criticism addresses itself only to one obvious thematic unit in early Arabic poetry: the one announced by the stylistic signals *abligh,* etc. It avoids the confrontation with any problem arising out of possible structural complexity. His is a process of historicist regression toward a hypothetical "first" knowledge that precludes a movement toward the historically equally legitimate knowledge of the fullness of form.

Having isolated the rhetorical impulse of the *qaṣīdah* as missive and having become alerted to that missive's stylistic signals, it is therefore necessary to take into account the functional existence of early missive *qaṣīdah*s of the complex kind, for it is only through them that we will be able to establish an analogical connection with the great formal tradition of the Arabic poem.

There is a sufficiently large number of *fully structured* early Arabic *qaṣīdah*s that are explicitly missives to persuade us of the validity of the *qaṣīdah* as a rhetorically functioning form—or rather of its suitability to function as such. Thus, Imru' al-Qays will easily begin a poem with an elegiac *nasīb* (vv. 1–9) of *diyār* (abodes) and *aṭlāl* (ruins) and plunge into the intoxicating reverie of recollection of the tribe's departing maidens, only to change abruptly to a celebration of his travel-hardened she-camel in a shorter but clearly defined *raḥīl* (vv. 10–14). It is after this that, with the signal *abligh,* he will introduce the message itself as an expression of his self-assertion, *fakhr* (vv. 15–21).[42] Such a *fakhr,* however, may then not be devoid of the characteristic, and at this early stage rather obligatory, adversarial tone.

This structural and stylistic pattern becomes particularly clear in two *qaṣīdah*s by Bashāmah Ibn ʿAmr [al-Ghadīr], contained in the *Mufaḍḍalīyāt* as nos. 10 and 122. In both poems we have an elegiacally tinted *nasīb* opening, followed by a richly articulated camel journey in no. 10 and a highly compacted one in no. 122. In both, the message section is signaled by the unmistakable *abligh.*[43] With equal rhetorical clarity a variant of this signal in a poem by al-Nābighah al-Dhubyānī—his much acclaimed "Yā dāra Mayyata" (O abode of Mayyah!)—refers to the poet's she-camel as the mediator of his message: *tuballighunī* ([a she-camel] delivers me to . . .) and ***fa tilka tuballighunī*** (and such a [she-camel] delivers me to . . .). The missive, however, is something the poet intends (at least as a conceit) to deliver himself. It is meant to be his oration, and even his plea—almost, as it were, before a court of law. Formally, therefore, the poet's oratory in this case may approximate forensic oratory in tone and form. Beyond being an illustration of this variant, al-Nābighah's poem has indeed become quite genre determining as the paradigmatic ode of royal praise and forensic apologetic plea (***iʿtidhār***). In it, too, we have an elegiac ***nasīb*** (vv. 1–6), followed by a thematically complex ***raḥīl*** (vv. 7–19), and ultimately by the longest (vv. 20–50) and most artfully intertwined courtly (***madḥ***) and forensic (***iʿtidhār***) missive/oration that comes introduced by the formulaic signal (v. 20) "A fa tilka tublighunī al-Nuʿmāna?" (Will it be such a [she-camel] that takes me to Nuʿmān?).[44]

With the advent of the Umayyad period, the structural and stylistic pattern of the epideictic ***qaṣīdah*** becomes even more firmly established, due largely to the growing role of poetry in courtly convention. With this development, too, the traditional ***qaṣīdah*** structure becomes less oblique in its function and formally more schematic. Poets begin to give the impression that their sense of form has acquiesced fully to the rhetorical imperative—this despite the undiminished pervasiveness of the full repertory of archaic ***qaṣīdah*** elements.

Among the poems best suited to illustrate and sum up the configuration of the "missive ***qaṣīdah***" at this point is the philologically and critically tradition-honored *Malḥamah* (Battle Lay) of ʿUbayd Ibn Ḥuṣayn Ibn Jandal, known better as al-Rāʿī al-Numayrī (d. 96 or 97/714 or 715).[45] This poem, which consists of no fewer than eighty-six verses,[46] is fully structured into a ***nasīb*** (vv. 1–4); a ***raḥīl*** (vv. 5/6–29/31); and a missive of complaint, caliphal panegyric, and apologetic self-praise as motif components of the concluding section (vv. 30/32–86/92). It is also important to notice that the missive section is ushered in by the familiar signal of ***abligh,*** and that it is precisely by way of this complex thematic "mounting" of the missive that the poet hopes to convince the Umayyad caliph ʿAbd al-Malik Ibn Marwān of his unflagging allegiance to him and of the unsubstantiated nature of his previous declaration of fealty to the caliphal pretender ʿAbd Allāh Ibn al-Zubayr or of having embraced any other heresy. We may, therefore, have here another example of a poem in the form of a plea (***iʿtidhār***). However, the poet in this ***iʿtidhār*** is no longer merely an individual suppliant at court but a solicitor for his tribe. This gives the whole poem the political character of a brief or tract presented at the now "imperial" caliphal court. And yet, at the same time, the poet remains a tribal spokesman according to the most archaic traditions of his craft and his society.

An important structural and rhetorical tightening up of al-Rāʿī al-Numayrī's *qaṣīdah* occurs already in its opening section, which, on the basis of its diction and place in the poem, calls for a first identification as a *nasīb,* but one that upon closer analysis reveals adjustments to a specifically epideictic function:

> Why this restless tossing in your bed?
> Is there a mote in your eye,
> or is journey on your mind?
>
> When she saw my sleeplessness
> and long vacillation
> Through that evening and into the night,
>
> Khulaydah said: "What befell you?"
> And yet she was not
> One to question when grave matters struck.
>
> O Khulaydah, two cares were guests
> of your father's pillow.
> One spent the night there by its side;
> within, the other.
>
> Both made their nightly call,
> for such are cares—
> I'll lull them with young camel mares,
> some pregnant, bent like bows,
> some yet to pair. [7]

As a first step, we ought to be alerted to the distinct connection between al-Rāʿī al-Numayrī's "*nasīb*" and a specific thematic section in a *qaṣīdah* by the pre-Islamic poet al-Aʿshā that begins:

> My daughter says, when imminent is the journey:
> "I look at us as through an orphan's eyes."[47] [8]

In itself, however, the complaint of al-Aʿshā's daughter represents only a version of the otherwise well attested and defined motif of the *ʿādhilah* (censuress), which, in the hands of Ḥātim al-Ṭāʾī, was transferred to the opening section of the early *qaṣīdah.*[48] In al-Aʿshā's poem it introduces the final theme, which in many respects resembles the melancholy topos of *ubi sunt,* but which in the context of the Arabic *qaṣīdah*'s thematic framework of the *ʿādhilah* is only one of the possible arguments leading to the poet's self-assertion, or to an ultimately defiant stoicism. We may thus understand why it was possible for the still firmly Jāhilī Ḥātim al-Ṭā'ī to transfer his potentially melancholy theme all the way to the elegiac *nasīb,* and ultimately why it was so poetically felicitous for al-Rā'ī al-Numayrī to turn to al-A'shā for his own poem's opening. What has happened in the opening line of al-Rā'ī al-Numayrī's *qaṣīdah* is the legitimation, through references to motifs that fall outside the *nasīb,* of an important inversion of roles: it is not going to be the "beloved" of the poet who, as *ẓa'īnah* (woman traveling in a litter), is going to depart, leaving the poet-lover behind to pine over a desolate encampment, but rather the poet himself who must travel, driven onward by two "cares," quite personified, that come to him at night as it were from two directions, one from within and the other from without. There is much ambiguity in these two cares, which are not only the poet's internally consuming anxieties but also his active "concerns"[49] that point toward the road he must soon travel. On the one hand they thus belong to the *nasīb* turned-upon-itself, while on the other hand they already enunciate the *raḥīl.* In their *nasīb* epiphany, however, these cares are also part of another metaphor, that of the "nightly phantom" (*ṭayf al-khayāl*) that troubles the despondent lover.[50] It is such topically evocative personifications that the poet chooses to see as his cares/concerns; and it is they whom he will receive with obligatory Bedouin hospitality (*aqrīhimā*), either slaughtering for them his most precious riding animals or offering those animals to them as mounts that will carry them auspiciously to their destination. The larger metaphor that leads up to the journey has thus been established. The subsequent expatiation on the journey's mounts as supremely pedigreed she-camels, together with episodes of the crossing of the desert, constitutes the *raḥīl* section of the *qaṣīdah.*

The metaphor of the rhetorical structure comes to its culmination when the message itself is ushered in with the appropriate "signal":

> To the Commander of the Faithful
> this message *convey:*
> "An unanswered complaint to you
> of grief and lament,
>
> From one who is far off, with many a care
> to lay before you,
> If he finds to you a way!" [9]

The key word *sabīl* (way), however, allows the poet to exploit further the rhetorical possibilities of the journey section: he dwells digressively on the length and arduousness of his efforts to reach the presence of the caliph, that is, on his eagerness to purge himself of his erstwhile political obliquities. Only then does the form of addressing the caliph become direct,[51] while the style of the exposition of the argument contained in the missive—now more clearly an epistle—adopts forensically discursive and even narrative characteristics. It is thus only in this rhetorically paved approach to the final argumentation and implied plea that al-Rāʿī al-Numayrī achieves an eminently political discourse, and with it an eminently political poem. In the classical Arabic perception of form which the Umayyad poet represents, this happens precisely due to the retention of the vestigially archaic semiotic ingredients of an "introductory" lyricism (*nasīb*), followed by an agonistic *raḥīl,* and ultimately leading up to the explicitly epideictic argumentation and plea. In trying to penetrate the formal rationale of the *qaṣīdah,* it is erroneous to regard such a structure's concluding section alone as a formally sufficient missive—that is, as a kind of uncomplicated, economical oration or epistle—that has become somehow inexplicably encumbered by "subsequent" structural accretions, and in which the eventual opening of *abligh,* or its variants, is meant to signal merely a more specific adversarial stance (*stasis*?). If there is an epideictic rhetoric of form in the classical, or classicist, Arabic *qaṣīdah,* it must indeed be that of the functionally complex structure, and the explanation of its model must ultimately take Ibn Qutaybah's all-too-fragile definition into account.

The above structural model, however, motivated as it is by the rhetorical efficacy of the *qaṣīdah* as form, may not tell us enough about the nature of poetic structure itself and thus leave us with the uneasiness of further, unresolved, if not unsuspected, formal riddles for which rhetorical criticism has neither ear nor answer.

2. Ut Musica Poesis: *The* Qaṣīdah *as Sonata—The* Nasīb *as Sonata Form*

When the verbal order of the poem is perceived as stepping across its cognitive contours and as leading to intimations of another sphere of meaning—such as the tonal order of music—what then takes place is a transposition of poetry's concretizing cognitive property, that is, of its case-hardened semanticity, into what Goethe saw as poetry's "liquid element,"[52] the deconcretizing sphere of mood that yet so tenaciously clings to some form of cognition. Sensing this much, we would, in our Arabic case, no longer feel the need to take refuge in an analogy with the mediating Platonic "language of the souls," where music must yet affect through "language," almost as if it were in fear of any further rarefication and did not trust the ability of mood to articulate on independent cognitive levels.

Since it is above all the structuring efficacy of mood in Arabic poetry that presently concerns us, it is out of this concern that an alternative to another critical near-axiom is necessary, namely a corrective reformulation of Horace's *ut pictura poesis* into *ut musica poesis*—now clearly understood as not aspiring to be a Platonic analogy.[53] Our Arabic concern to arrive at an equation of poetry with music thus ought to gravitate toward apprehending the specificity of the poetic mood as it hierarchically rules the poem's subjects and themes and determines their integration into the structure of the poem. Ultimately, in the Arabic case the analogy to be established—if that is the objective of formal criticism—is between the structural function of mood-determined themes in both music and poetry.

If in matters of aesthetics explanations fail, comparisons must never do so. Thus, as regards the structure of the Arabic *qaṣīdah,* it will be helpful if, pursuing the postulation that "as music is so is poetry," we realize that it is particularly the structured, paratactical contrast of moods in the *qaṣīdah* which brings it close to one of the most cherished artistic conventions in the West, namely, to the form of sonata/symphony in European classical music. There, too, the movements are independent units, and the sequence of the "tempi" obeys no immediately evident inner logic but claims to be based on tradition, placed as it were outside the sphere of semiotic and aesthetic self-consciousness or at least presuming the inappropriateness of such a self-consciousness.[54]

Thus, after the opening "allegro" in this taken-for-granted structure, there ought to follow a sharply antithetical "adagio" or "andante." The third movement should once again be antithetical and fast, closing the ternary form, or it may instead be a "minuetto" as a distinctly courtly statement of mood, which is then only heightened or, in musical terms, accelerated into a "presto" or another "allegro" of the "finale." What thus comes about formally is the late classical structure of the four-movement symphony or of the equally late developments in the string quartet and in other characteristic small (chamber ensemble) forms. However, if we compare this later four-movement structure as it is epitomized by Mozart's Symphony No. 41, for instance, with those classical sonatas, concerti, and symphonies that are ternary, we realize that one of two things appears to have occurred in the four-movement variety: either the third movement is an insertion that is structurally assimilable because of its affinity to the tempo that it anticipates in the finale, given that it itself, especially when it is a minuetto, fails to produce a closure, or else the way to understand the apparent anomaly of a fourth movement in the Mozartian symphony, and thereafter, is to see in the finale, not in the third movement, merely a formal accretion of a predominantly mechanical and ancillary nature that enlarges the volume of the form without significantly changing its structure.[55] Whichever way one views the addition of a fourth movement to the ternary structure, one ought not, however, to confuse the results of such an addition (which is principally an expansion of the ternary structure) with the slow-fast-slow-fast, strictly binary, Baroque *sonata da chiesa.*

Romain Rolland describes the classical sonata felicitously and above all very pertinently for our argument, which revolves around mood but deals ultimately with structure:

> The whole structure obeys not merely the fundamental laws of each particular genre but the still more imperative laws of the society to which the work is addressed, — laws of discretion, of good taste, of both technical and moral equilibrium between the various parts. Whatever the emotion or the humor that possesses the artist, he must not wholly abandon himself to it; he stands before a select public, and his first duty is to speak for this before speaking for himself; he must conform to the rules of good company. The first of these is, "*Ne quid nimis!*" Do not insist too much! . . . It is for this reason that in the order of succession of the several movements care is taken that the mind shall taste of everything without being overborne by anything. . . . Learned yet not pedantic, sensitive yet not doting, gathering at its choice the flowers of feeling but lingering over none of them, this exquisite art is for the lovely butterflies of the salon and is made in their image.[56]

Unquestionably, Ibn Qutaybah's summary view of the accomplished poet and his well-wrought "courtly" product is close to Romain Rolland in phrasing and spirit:

> A felicitous poet is one who takes this course and balances these parts. He does not let any one of them dominate the composition, neither going to such length as to bore the listeners nor cutting short while in their souls there is still thirst for more.[57]

If the eighteenth-century pre-Beethoven sonata thus offers a specific analogue in form and spirit to the "exquisite art" of the Arabic courtly *qaṣīdah,* it also corresponds to, and even accentuates, the essential characteristics of the *qaṣīdah* as a generic form even as that form had crystallized in pre-Islamic times.[58]

Continuing with our formal parallelism between the different tempi of the sonata and the themes of a schematized *qaṣīdah,* we notice that, with regard to the emotional curve in both, the only difference is that in the structure of the sonata, or symphony, the slow and lyrical andante movement[59] comes after an initial allegro, whereas in the *qaṣīdah* the sad and emotional themes of the abandoned encampment and of the parting of lovers precede the allegro of the journey section with its dramatic wilderness episodes. As for the third movement, which, especially in the quantitatively expanded structure of the symphony, may be the minuetto, it is as much a courtly tempo and theme as the *madīḥ* and the poet's genuflections of polite excuse and supplication. The final presto of a scherzo or rondo is thus to be viewed as parallel to the signing-off of the *qaṣīdah.*

At this point we should also notice that in the Baroque sonata it is the slow movement which precedes the fast one, the core sequence of tempi thus being slow-fast, which, when repeated, produces the enlarged structure of slow-fast-slow-fast. The Baroque sonata is thus essentially binary, *A-B,* and its rhythmic curve is ascending. Since the "speed" of rhythm in music also equals mood to the extent to which it is not easily separated from the thematic and melodic factors, which, in turn, determine the choice of key and mode—to that extent the basic ascension of what emerges as the Baroque rhythmic curve is also an ascension from elegiac lyricism toward the playful, the festive, or the heroic. It is only with a further amplification of this musical structure that the "classical" order of tempi comes about, namely, through an anteposition of a movement that is contrasting, therefore fast, to the formerly opening slow movement. The new opening tempo is thus fast by rhythmic determinism as it were, with the slow tempo remaining intact while yet allowing the structure to end on the surviving fast tempo, providing for an ultimately ascending rhythmic curve. Within the ternary structure of the sonata/symphony thus obtained, it is the first movement (fast) which now assumes the "privileged" position as far as attention to its internal structure is concerned.[60] It becomes its own, terminologically somewhat confusing, "sonata form"—essentially a song conceived in its total sonority as instrumental. Furthermore, being the first movement of a comprehensive ternary structure, it is ternary in its own internal structure as well, beginning with (1) the *exposition* of the main theme in the tonic key and moving on to the secondary theme in the likely, harmonically kindred, dominant key; proceeding then to (2) the *development,* where the secondary key will ultimately lead back to the main key; and, in conclusion, rounding off the relationships between theme and key (tonic) with (3) the *recapitulation*. Such, then, is the (for the present purpose highly schematized) structure of theme and key of that song without words called the sonata form as it gives further internal terseness to the containing structure (sonata/symphony). As such it is not necessarily limited to the first (fast) movement, however, for it may reappear as the organizing factor of the second (slow) movement as well.

Awareness of this further articulation of the sonata structure is then what impresses upon our sense of form a second level of analogy. We note that of the individual sonata movements it is especially the first movement with its "sonata-form" structure which, when placed opposite the internal logic of the arrangement of motifs in the first section of the *qaṣīdah,* will suggest in both forms a correspondence of parts that ultimately may be structurally binding for reasons that range all the way from formalism, through psychological surface responses, to distant archetypal notions. This analogy can thus tell us as much about the sonata as it does about the *qaṣīdah*.

Here, too, the opening section/movement of the Arabic *qaṣīdah* will provide us with the necessary formal analogue to the sonata form as a paradigmatic opening movement. Thus, applying sonata terminology to the *nasīb,* we are introduced first to the "tonic key" of the opening theme/motif of the abandoned encampment (*aṭlāl*). The Arabic poet may dwell on that theme for as long as does Labīd in his *Muʿallaqah* (11 verses)[61] or for only two lines, as in the *Muʿallaqah* of Ṭarafah.[62] What is formally important is that a distinct tonic key of the "main theme," translated poetically into the obligatory elegiac mood, has been enunciated. Out of this "tonal" first theme/key/mood, or against it, there is introduced the secondary theme (or countertheme) with its own characteristic key, which is nevertheless harmonically and modally dependent on the key that generated it (tonic → dominant). In the classical Arabic *nasīb* this "leap of a fifth" into the "dominant" key is the evocation, also elegiac in tone, of the scene of the departure of the poet's beloved with her entourage (*ẓaʿn*), as in Labīd's *Muʿallaqah* (vv. 12–15),[63] where it is closer to being a continuation of the bittersweet idyll of the preceding *aṭlāl* pastoral, or as in Ṭarafah's more abrupt change from the abandoned encampment of Khawlah to the distant perspective of a caravan that like ships at sea disappears in dune-crested desert sands (*Muʿallaqah,* vv. 3–5).[64]

This countertheme in the *qaṣīdah* constitutes the thematic, and modal, analogue to the "development" in the sonata form, since it, too, is a development out of its own secondary key, which is the *ẓaʿn*. It is also a development in the strictest semantic sense, for in it the poet foreshortens his perspective, bringing his beloved ever closer into view, almost to the point of making the vision graspable and present both spatially and temporally—that is, he turns memory into reverie. It is only at this point and as a flight from the reality of melancholy into the irreality of reverie, that eros makes its appearance; but we would lose all formal clarity if in this thematic modulation of the *nasīb* we saw nothing more than what traditional *qaṣīdah* criticism calls "the description of the beloved." As a "development," the flight into reverie, and into eros, is usually quite perceptibly set off from the *ẓaʿn* of the "exposition." It may either be relatively succinct, as in Ṭarafah's *Muʿallaqah* (vv. 6–10)[65] and in ʿAntarah's (vv. 13–19);[66] or else it may acquire proportions that would suggest its special importance within the overall design of a specific *qaṣīdah*. Thus in the *Muʿallaqah* of Imruʾ al-Qays (vv. 10–42)[67] this "development" is uncharacteristically long for the *qaṣīdah* form, while at the same time it pertinently reflects, or perhaps even establishes, the literary-biographical character of that particular poet.[68]

The return to the main theme and to the tonic key as "recapitulation" has its analogue in the closure of the opening movement of the *qaṣīdah*, where, in its own return to the tonic key, the structure of the *nasīb* requires that the mood of reverie be followed by an abrupt awakening to the true present of sorrow, and that the indulgence in the illusion of a regained past be halted. The tonic key of the *nasīb* thus reveals itself once again as necessarily evocative of the poet's mood when he first stood over the desolate "abodes." It is elegiac and melancholy, even if this time the elegiac spell does not remain a spell for long, turning into conflicting desires: between self-loss and redemptive purposefulness. Like so many other important transactions of theme and mood in the classical Arabic *qaṣīdah*, this recapitulative turn, too, is normally introduced by its own highly conventionalized signal, which may either be that of *humūm* (cares) or of *himmah* (determination, endeavor).[69]

The dark gem of pre-Islamic poetry, Imruʾ al-Qays's brooding evocation of nights of despondency—if not despair—(*Muʿallaqah*, vv. 44–48),[70] furnishes the most proportionately articulated example of the end of reverie and of return to the "tonic key" and to the sense of loss that characterizes the classical Arabic poem's "first theme":

Many a night, like a surging sea,
lowered its veils upon me
To try me with varied cares.

To it I said when it stretched its trunk,
Then reared the rump and heaved a heavy chest:

Break, O long night, break into morn!
But in your morrow there's no greater boon . . .

Oh, what a night, as if its stars
Were tied to Mount Yadhbul with every
 well-wound rope,[71]

As if the Pleiades in their stations hung
 From impassive boulders
 on fine flaxen ropes. [10]

Al-Muthaqqib al-ʿAbdī's exquisite *Nūnīyah* (ode rhyming in the letter *nūn*)[72] gives us another formally persuasive example of a recapitulation. In the case of this *qaṣīdah,* however, one should stress that the theme sequence in its *nasīb,* even as it observes the structural pattern established by the *aṭlāl* mood, does not contain the *aṭlāl* as its opening ("main") theme and "tonic key." These are provided by the motif of the beloved's rejection, which is, of course, ultimately a motif of loss as well. The recapitulation in such a structure will thus have to take the specific opening variant into account.

The sonata-form analogy in the case of the *Nūnīyah* would thus identify the *nasīb*'s four opening lines as the "main theme" establishing the "tonic key," after which there comes a distinct enunciation of the *ẓaʿn* as the "second theme" and as the "dominant key's" deflection of mood (vv. 5–9). There now follows the transition into the descriptive, erotically charged and actualized "development" of the *ẓaʿn* in verse 10, which in turn ends when the poet sees the *ẓaʿāʾin* (departing women) no longer in a false, reverielike light of "presentness" but rather as signifying separation after all. This, then, is the "recapitulation" or re-echoing of the mood that had marked the *nasīb*'s opening and that is now its closure (vv. 16–19):

Now rising upon a hilltop,
 now sinking into a vale's fold,
And not a moment ever
 for a noontime rest.

To one of these I said, my saddle
 girded fast,
My forehead facing head-on
 the scorching midday-hour:

Were you ever to sever our bond,
My soul and I would yet
remain a pair.

So rid yourself of care
on a she-camel, sturdy,
Its head like a smith's hammer raised. [11]

Of further note is here al-Muthaqqib al-ʿAbdī's use of the signal *al-humūm* (cares), which he places at the end of his recapitulative motif. As such, the occurrence of *hamm/humūm/himmah* also signals the imminent transition into the structural section of the journey, which, in sonata terms, should be a transition to a new (second) "tempo."

Examples of recapitulation without the "signaling" occurrence of *hamm/humūm/himmah* are not entirely rare either, however. Thus in a *qaṣīdah* by ʿAbīd Ibn al-Abraṣ the opening *nasīb* motif is that of transhumance and dispersal of Bedouin tribes and clans (*bāna al-khalīṭu*). Here the *ẓaʿn* is therefore the first theme, followed by the evocation of old, happy days as the second theme and by a development that adheres to the characteristic tone of reverie. In the end there is a return to the *khalīṭ/ẓaʿn* image (and mood) of the poem's beginning in the form of a recapitulation (vv. 16–17):

And I continued sending in their wake a rueful eye,
The pupil drowning in its flood, still reaching out.

But all who meet must also go apart,
And all who live will one day be embalmed.[73] [12]

In this manner the poet also obtains a stylistically deliberate "closure" of the *nasīb*.

Similar in thematic sequence to the above *nasīb* section by ʿAbīd Ibn al-Abraṣ is a *nasīb* by Bishr Ibn Abī Khāzim. In it, too, that poet dispenses with the *hamm/humūm/himmah* signal in the recapitulation (vv. 15–19):

I spent the night awake, not able to find sleep,
As if the wine were seeping through my joints,

My watchful eyes up in the sky on Ursa's brood[74]
As they turned round like a herd of antelope
that comes about,

And as the Pleiades unyieldingly clung on long
into the still of night,
With neighboring Capella in their wake.

For if well-tended camels took them to distant parts
As distant abodes did with pledged-away hearts

Still, we and they once had our fleeting days,
Until war made us travel different ways.[75] [13]

The analogy between the *nasīb* viewed as "movement" and the sonata form defined structurally by its sequences of themes and keys has already necessitated, if only in passing, our repeated references to the stratification of poetic time in the opening section of the classical Arabic poem. In closing this studiedly formalist argument, it then appears necessary to tie together whatever loose ends of the *nasīb*'s poetic time still remain, and to which the model of the sonata form offers us its strong analogue and procedural impulse.

In approaching poetic time in the *nasīb* by way of the structure of the sonata form, we find the classical Arabic poet initially establishing in his poem a point in time that is placed as far in the past as his overall thematic design will permit him. The poet's clearly archetypal point of regression into the past is that of the "absolute" past of the *aṭlāl* (ruins). Another, more personal temporal vanishing point—that of the *diyār* (abodes), also ruinous—no more than subjectivizes that absolute past. Otherwise, the point in time may not go any further back than the still quite graspable recollection of the seasonal dispersal of the transhumant clans (*al-khalīṭ*). Even then, however, within the overall design of the *nasīb* as sequential time, it stands as the anchoring point of the poet's recollection. In the terms of our sonata analogy, this time is thus the time of the *nasīb*'s first, or primary, theme—and of its tonic key.

From such a radical point, or against it, poetic time in the *nasīb* progresses as if in a perspective of foreshortening: in the ensuing *ẓaʿn* scene the poet's memories bring him to the moment of his beloved's abrupt farewell and to the recollected vision of her gradual, miragelike absorption into the receding landscape. In sonata terms we are here in the *nasīb*'s second theme and in its dominant key. In terms of such a poetic time, which, as we realize by now, also agrees with mood, we have progressed to a closer plane of recollection. Poetic time is now personal and is drawing closer along the lines of what resembles perspectival foreshortening—except that the flow of time projects from the distant vanishing point rather than streaming toward it.

What now takes place is the arrival of the poet in his recollection—and of the *nasīb*'s poetic time—at the most highly foreshortened plane of the false actuality of reverie. At this point memory re-creates its visions entirely in the present tense. This translates itself poetically most easily into a style of pictured, descriptive immediacy, for a "picture" exists primarily as a fact of the present rather than as a "story" of the past. Such then is the nature of this imagined immediacy that it never ceases to be a recollection of the beloved's departure, even though it *develops* both psychologically and formally into the erotic daydream of her presence.[76] Still in pursuit of the analogy between the sonata form and the *nasīb,* we note that the "development" out of the poet's past into his state of false present has its thematic and modal point of departure in the second theme (*ẓaʿn*), characterized modally by the dominant key, rather than in the first theme (*aṭlāl/diyār*), with its tonic key. It also becomes quite clear how false the presumption in the *nasīb* of the present as point in time is when we follow the classical Arabic poet to where he leaves his reverie behind and awakens to the reality of the *pastness* of his states of happiness.

At this point the poetic time of the *nasīb* becomes once again explicitly that of the past—indeed of the radical past of loss, which takes the poet back to the brooding mood of the poem's beginning. Such a return in poetic time is thus a recapitulation, easily understood through the analogue of the sonata form.

If we were to represent poetic time graphically in the *nasīb,* we would draw a curve that begins in the radical past, rises to the plane of the subjective past, and from there continues rising steeply to the psychological present of memory as reverie, only to drop from there precipitously to the original level of the past as radical loss. If poetic time at the vertex of the curve thus seems to take us out of the past into its own realm of the present, that realm is nevertheless irredeemably swallowed up by the ultimate-and-original reality of loss, whose realm is the past. Furthermore, the correct understanding of poetic time in the *nasīb* is essential in order to clarify the obdurate critical confusion that surrounds the so-called erotic description within the *nasīb* and the use of the term "erotic prelude" as applicable to the entire *nasīb.* Both terms imply the "presentness" and tarrying concreteness of the erotic encounter. Such a level of reality is simply alien to the classical *nasīb,* which is always elegiac and "has a function only in relation to the *qaṣīdah*."[77] The failure to understand this prevents us from correctly differentiating between the *nasīb* in its precise formal confines (*qaṣīdah*) and the separate genre phenomenon of the so-called urban Umayyad *ghazal,*[78] whose poetic time is not that of the elegiac past but rather of a narratively actualized, dialogued, and quasi-dramatically "projected" present—a pretense of direct witnessing.

3. *Toward the Ternary Archetype*

We are already well familiar with the ternary structure of the Arabic *qaṣīdah* both on its rhetorically functional epideictic level and as a sequence of moods or states of sensibility analogous to the moods and tempi of a musical form such as the sonata or symphony. If the rhetorical-epideictic interpretation of the *qaṣīdah* structure is all too forcibly explicit in the deterministic singlemindedness with which it links structure to functionality, the musical analogy that converts mood into meaning only to return to mood as its own poetically sufficient realm may be too remotely inferential and discreet or too unconcerned with its own formal self-justification. Both theories, or rather both uses of one and the same radical structure of the poem, in order to be conducive to a compatible critical understanding must therefore be capable of revealing their point of intersection of meaning—which may also be their common denominator.

"If a number of things occur in succession," writes Prosser Hall Frye, "the human mind is bound to make a series of them."[79] We shall redirect these steps of the human mind back to their prearticulate state, however, where that of which the human mind has made a series is still a number of things that occur in succession. To come to the point, we readily admit that we are accustomed to seeing the Arabic ternary *qaṣīdah* as a man-made series when, in effect, we should also allow for the inductive return to the point of departure, or the "beginning," of that form, where we are faced once again with only the "number of things that occur in succession." In brief, we have to trust the form of the *qaṣīdah*.

The "succession of things" in the *qaṣīdah* on the primary level, from where only intimated similitudes reach the glossy storied surface available to Ibn Qutaybah, is in itself as much on the surface as to be in danger of being overlooked—indeed it has remained overlooked even past the point at which modern criticism ought not to have shown much patience with major oversights. In the first section of the *qaṣīdah* the poet halts, stands, and remembers. It is his remembrance, however, that introduces all the ultimately important things in their "occurrence in succession," or rather in their presence in his mind in that order. The poet's first, supposedly visually concretized but in a true sense still mental, image is that of the ruinous remains of habitation, which, as *ṭalal,* a word of implicitly archaizing overtones, presents a frame of time of the utmost remoteness, where there is only an evanescence of objects. As such it is coupled with the psychological frame of some great personal loss. There follows an image, still more the creation of the remembering mind than of direct visual apprehension, of the emerging reality of desolation and emptiness, in which the airy figment of the *ṭalal* becomes the personal lost "circle" of perfection, the abode as *dār*. Also, the *dār* as the circle of erstwhile habitation changes into, or is placed within, the seasonally more specific lyrical quadrature of the lost springtimes of *rabʿ*, the pasture ground that once was green; and then lost loves appear in a realm that hesitates between dream and reverie only to disappear again there where those other memories, or wishes, of the past lie buried. These are the things that happen at various levels of remembrance as the *qaṣīdah* opens. Then the poet's journey begins—sometimes with a clear statement of resolve or purpose (*himmah*), sometimes out of a need to erase from the mind what the passage of time has failed to accomplish physically. Such an impulse to act, the poet confesses, is one of sorrow, care, and buried concerns (*humūm*): it leads out and yet not beyond the self, but in the process it changes the self nonetheless; or else it is a wish to remain within the circle of bondage, to try to overtake and seize the point of departure of that time which has become memory. For whichever reason the journey is undertaken, as experience it is always an unqualified break with everything that has come before. It is an "act" after, and out of, a "state." The harsh effect of differentiation is also an effect of separation, and nothing stresses this more clearly than the formal juxtaposition of those two sections of the *qaṣīdah:* their jarring, often complained about parataxis.

Certain things occur to the poet on his journey, or rather, once it is undertaken he enters into a very strictly defined realm. His "mediator" in this entry is the she-camel, a mount whose species and gender are both canonically specified.[80] The desert he enters is inclement, and the hours of his journey stress that inclemency: they are either when the sun is approaching its zenith or when the night is the most haunted by sounds instilling awe. Other animals appear as further mediating similes of access to the journey's true realm. The journey may then end with the hazardous itinerary in high prominence and the purpose clearly fulfilled, or it may stop abruptly, with nothing lingering in the sensibility but the imprint of the desert's awesomeness and the she-camel's paradoxically diffused singularity—one that is diffused even further by similes of animals that are closer to being some built-in intuition of the desert itself rather than of its conqueror, the she-camel.

The journey has ended, or was merely stopped, and now, in the final section, it is time to praise and boast: the king and ruler is praised, so is the tribe; and within the praise of the tribe, or tangential to it, there may be room for the glorious euphoria of boasting or for the confessed or unconfessed anxiety of self-justification. Little is explained further beyond what comes in the language, or the semiotics, of act and image. All along, as "things were occurring in succession," the poem was meant to have spoken for itself, that is, to have ordered itself into a significant series.

At this point we are groping for understanding. What significance might have come "formally" together? Certainly there is something other here, too, besides Ibn Qutaybah's mildly intriguing rhetorical game lurking with studied conspicuousness behind the lines of a storied conceit. Nor is it just the apotheosis of the rhythms and moods of lyricism, for even it seems to have tried to speak of things outside itself. A temporally prior series, or one composed of a succession of time not *of* the events but *inherent* in the events, seems to be involved: the time of life, its rhythm—thus, too, an archetypal time or a model of time. It is in this ordering of time then that the ternary quality of the *qaṣīdah* begins to acquire its reality and that its jarring parataxis of structural sections gains its formal justification. The emerging three levels of time in the *qaṣīdah* become in that respect and to that degree a formal differentiation of life's otherwise cognitively unharnessed, even unobserved, flow; and the *qaṣīdah* displays a triptych of the knowledge of the self on yet entirely prepsychological levels, a kind of primal formulaic anthropology. Thus, in the *nasīb,* there is the time of loss with its recollective projection into a past in which the sense of the personal will loses itself in something so remote as to be no more than an unarticulated wish, a figment of the transpersonal, the ancestral and the preancestral, and always an understanding of lost time as lost happiness.

In the *raḥīl* the time is one of breaking away, of a desire to change, and, even more, of the inevitability of change. In it all that *was* is to be challenged or suspended in its efficacy. The past, too, is to be traversed as though it were another dimension of the desert if the poet is to emerge out of the time of the journey, which, being "transitory," is also real and dimensional. Unlike the other times of the *qaṣīdah,* that of the *raḥīl* does not stand still but leads to where transitoriness is supposed to exhaust itself in fulfillment. There it ends, and another time in another structural place of the poem begins. But as long as the time of the journey lasts, it is its own self-contained world of realities—physical, psychological, and above all emblematic and iconographic-symbolic. Being largely a world of signs and of encoded, circuitous significances through which the poet moves in a highly ritualized manner, the world of the journey is a prescribed and circumscribed space-time dimension of adventure, trial, and quest, and a medial zone between what is lost and what is not yet gained, or regained. In the ultimate consequence of poetic vision, the ***raḥīl*** is the poet's self-view in a moment of crisis—of his undoing and of his becoming. During the process, however, the poet does not "speak" as he will in the final section of the ***qaṣīdah,*** nor is there any longer room for the internalized language of memory as in the prior section. He introduces us to the main reality of his journey—which is his she-camel—and from there on abandons us to that language of images, signs, and emblems. We must ultimately understand that the poet speaks of his she-camel—and through her of all else in his journey—only in terms in which he may ***not*** speak of himself, of his encoded extreme experience. Her journey, her run, are his; her substitute images are his too; and so is the hardiness, the pathos of loneliness, and the ability to gore with the deadly horns of the oryx cow or the oryx bull; and so, too, is the earthiness given to her by the ever-gregarious wild ass.

The time to praise kings, rulers, the ties of tribe and blood is a time of arrival and once again of stasis. The stasis that was the ***wuqūf*** (halting) over the past of the ***nasīb*** has to reenact itself in that new ***wuqūf*** of arrival. The cycle must complete itself. Because the ***nasīb*** was all "past," its contemplative remembrance had to be abandoned when the time had come to "travel," or just because the time had come—not unlike the Roman fate-defining ***navigare necesse est.*** Now, in the fullest sense of the "now" of time, the poet stands in the present and in the presence not of what was lost but of what is found, and not found again, but new with each arrival, as each journey was capable of changing all things.[81] A magnificent poetic image and symbolic emblem of this new ***wuqūf*** is the apotheosis of the hunt- and battle-horse as it stands statuelike in the ***Muʿallaqah*** of Imru' al-Qays.[82]

Unquestionably, an archetypal series of significant time has come together in the kind of human time that is both singular and communal. In its beginning it offers a very archaic backdrop (***ṭalal***) of aggregation and belonging that, out of the "pastness" of its loss, reemerges only as memory and evocation. Then, having passed through the process of a carefully encoded agonistic individuation (***riḥlah***), it reaches its conclusion, or issue, in the more easily concretized social moment of arrival or "return." As a model it may also serve the poet in the most varied and richly stratified ways, for a model is itself a paradoxical meaning-producing polarization: it facilitates, but in equal measure it restricts. By thus developing a particular form that in a kindred and vital sense is the form of man's other domains as well, the Arabic ternary ***qaṣīdah*** has secured for itself an inherent yet paradoxical potentiality and vitality—and its otherwise unexplainable durability. It became a "form" because on levels preliterary but not necessarily pre-poetic there already was such a form. The *qaṣīdah* never was a pieced-together construct that was somehow all at the same time willful and incomprehensible. If we fail to understand that, we may just as well abandon all further *qaṣīdah*-connected critical pursuits, as well as invalidate all foregoing ones. We know that in the *qaṣīdah* we have a poem structured much more vitally in the sense of human time (although not "organically" in any pseudobiological Coleridgean sense) than whatever may have been revealed at first glance, and that the poem's parataxis of sectional structuring is itself an expression of the radical character of the changes that take place as the poem moves from one section into another. The semiotics of structure thus bespeaks not only the significance, but also the agony, of change. It is not surprising therefore that the sharpest, or the most dramatically felt, break in the poem should be that between the *nasīb* and the *raḥīl*. Nevertheless, it is precisely here that the archaic poet is most likely to signal to us that his state of suspension from the edge of his "past" time's fragile reality is no longer bearable and that his resolve to break away, whether it be as *humūm* or as *himmah,* must forthwith be translated into the poem's decisive structural leap—all this provided that we are attuned to observing such verbal gestures.

On the other hand, there may be no comparable one-word signals to prepare us for the leap from the *raḥīl* into the section of the new *wuqūf.* Nevertheless, the drama of the journey and the solemnity of the arrival and the "presence" translate into kindred styles and moods that allow sharp syntactical parataxis and seemingly disparate semanticity to function in accordance with the poem's overriding formal logic by achieving structural compatibility on the level of the symbol. Thus, for instance, the image, in itself apotheotic, of the victorious oryx, as well as that of the wild ass on a promontory overlooking the vastness of the surrounding desert, transcends symbolically even the sharpest thematic disconnectedness between *raḥīl* and *fakhr/madīḥ.*

Having dealt with such formal considerations, it ought to be of further hermeneutical usefulness to see in the formalized wholes of the classical Arabic *qaṣīdah,* with their constraints of relationships that are ultimately the constraints of symmetry, the basic Lévi-Straussian structural conditions of myth formalization.[83] In this sense, the structural configuration of the Arabic *qaṣīdah,* too, lodges in the semiotics of its form the myth of Arabic poetry. Its "dissymmetrization," that is, its "freedom" from symmetry, would also be—and indeed historically has been—its deconstruction.[84]

Maintaining the formal symmetry without fear of excessive reductionism, we may now proceed to isolate the symbols or, in a more figurally representative sense, the "icons of structure" of the Arabic ternary *qaṣīdah*. The first is the "ruinous abode"—*dār* as *ṭalal* and *ṭalal* as *dār*—which in its iconic sense stands for the *nasīb*. The following two lines, which the great antiquarian-anthologist Abū ʿAlī al-Qālī (d. 356/967) places in the context of attributions to Majnūn Laylā (the exemplar of the lover, himself more icon than flesh and blood), reflect the sensibility of the Umayyad period and are in many respects a hermeneutic threshold out of the archaic poetic matter as well as back into its very core. Through their own "glass darkly," these lines give us an insight into this iconic *nasīb:*

I looked as through a bottle's glass
At the abode that faded
as drops of water fade.

My eyes at times in tears drowned,
I stood blind, then again,
Too faint to see, too spent to cry,
I had sight.[85] [14]

This "ruinous abode" of poets both pre-Islamic and Umayyad is of great mutability visually and symbolically. Its meaning moves across levels, or layers, of the reality of place and time, not unlike the "abode" or "abodes" of the Taoist earthly paradise. This shared sense of a central symbol (as chapters 4 and 5 of the present book will show more distinctly) is evidenced in the Arab poet's own archetypally distant but still symbolically obliging understanding of his abode, which, as ruin, is both empty and replete. It is a paradise that has come closer to archetypal memory by being a "lost paradise," or a paradise of poetic imagination. In Taoist terms, too, this abode appears as the "abode of fancy" or, as Joseph Campbell calls it, "the enclosure of poetic intuition"; as the "abode of vacancy," an unadorned "vacuum into which the imagination of the beholder can pour"; and also as the "abode of the unsymmetrical," that is, of mutability and movement.[86]

The she-camel, *al-nāqah,* is the undisputed structural icon of the *raḥīl*. As such it stands out with monumental splendor in the *Muʿallaqah* of Ṭarafah and in a later poet's, Abū Tammām's, epigrammatic succinctness that renders a single verse's associative totality of meaning hermeneutically compelling:

Amber she-camels,[87] care, the deep of night, together,
A triad forever by one harness bound.[88] [15]

In the *qaṣīdah*'s third section it becomes less obvious which one is the commanding icon of structure of either the other-directed panegyric that is the *madīḥ* or the praise of self and tribe that is the *fakhr*. Thus *al-ḥimā* (consecrated tribal precinct), one such possible icon, albeit much more frequently implied and ideated than textually elicited, carries within itself symbols of ancestral belonging and leads to the roots of autochthony, where arrival is also return after danger incurred. It is the ideal place that is both past and future, unlike the *dār* of the *nasīb,* which, in a primary way, because of its placement in the *qaṣīdah,* takes us into the past because its matrix, the *nasīb,* is itself the past. This *al-ḥimā* toward which the Bedouin poet's she-camel aims her mysterious homing sensitivity is in the end, however, too richly saturated with substances of uncompromising lyricism, the kind of lyricism that in successive literary-historical stages will have homed in its own sensors ever so strongly back toward the kindred regions of the *nasīb,* never to leave them thereafter.

But even as the poet al-Ḥuṭay'ah is about to close the chapter of the Jāhilīyah, he affords us a major interpretative insight that helps explain the later migration of *al-ḥimā* into the semiotically kindred realm of the *dār,* for already through his verse we perceive the presence not merely of the possibility but of the symbolic requisite of an iconic link between the *qaṣīdah*'s opening and closure, that is, between its first and third sections. This link results from the association, on the one hand, of *al-ḥimā* as the poet's affirmation of active communal "belonging" and, on the other, of the abode that has fallen into ruin, with its accolade of encroaching nature:

> The spears of Banū Saʿd secured
> as *ḥimā* for their men
> Pastures of wild asses, of ostriches,
> and wide-eyed oryx cows.[89] [16]

Here the poet still refers himself to the *ḥimā,* which was soon to become abolished as a tribal institution by the new rule of Islam. Thus, for instance, in a *ḥadīth*-phrasing, *al-ḥimā* turns with relative ease into a preserve "of God and his apostle" precisely because it had previously been a no less interdicted place of either votive consecration of singularly meritorious riding- or milch-camels[90] or privileged pasturage conquered or usurped by a tribal lord. Ultimately—either religiously, socioeconomically, or politically—*al-ḥimā* enjoyed the aura of unapproachability and, even more, of autochthonous sacrality. It was symbolically both inclusive and exclusive, a tribe's property that was unapproachable even to the tribe itself. Thus its institutionalized privileges were inclusive only to the degree to which they stressed exclusion.

What is interpretively significant about al-Ḥuṭay'ah's verse beyond this broad scope of meaning of *al-ḥimā* is that, just as in the *nasīb* the *dār* is relinquished to "nature," so in the tribal *fakhr* the pastures of the wild animals—those that otherwise invade the *dār*—are taken over as *al-ḥimā* by "culture." Wholly within his symbolic right, al-Ḥuṭay'ah thus proceeds to reclaim in the tribal *fakhr* what Labīd cannot retain in his *nasīb*.

In the theme, or structural section, of the pre-Islamic tribal *fakhr*, there is also room for a referentially polarized, and thus hermeneutically more effective, reappearance of a symbolically construable *dār*, thus bringing that vestige of the *nasīb* close to the meaning of *al-ḥimā*. In its substitute poetic locale, *dār*, too, then becomes the repository of ancestral tribal glory and authority, of heritage and lineage. These qualities are spelled out clearly in ʿAbīd Ibn al-Abraṣ's tribal *fakhr:*

> Ours is an *abode* to whose age-old might
> We're heirs from both paternal and maternal side.[91] [17]

On the other hand, Labīd's preference for calling such an edifice a *bayt* rather than a *dār* in a verse that in its *qaṣīdah* context is otherwise close in meaning to the verse of ʿAbīd Ibn al-Abraṣ contributes additional semantic and semiotic clarity to both words, *dār* and *bayt*. Labīd's use of *bayt* evokes the other ancient, or ancestral, abode, which is the "ancient house" itself: the Kaʿbah as *al-bayt al-ʿatīq*. Thus Labīd, after cryptically referring in verses 83 and 84 of his *Muʿallaqah* to an ancestral "lord" (*al-malīk*) who is a "divider" of endowments and lots, speaks in verse 85 of the tribe's lofty communal house:

> For us he built a house of lofty reach,
> And to it rose men of full age and lads.[92] [18]

Such a solemn "house of council" is also the communal-tribal "noble house" of the earlier Jāhilī bard Ṭarafah, to which he "ascends" for council as well as for another no less ritually and communally significant purpose, the knightly-heroic, and also "courtly," banquet:[93]

> And if the whole tribe in assembly meets, you find me
> High in the noble house to which all flock,
>
> My boon-companions bright as stars, a songstress slave-girl
> In striped cloak or shift to serve us.[94] [19]

Ritually and socially more readily definable as *buyūt*—not the geometrically primary and archetypal *dūr*—are also the noble high-poled tents of Ḥassān Ibn Thābit's elders of the clan[95] and of Zuhayr Ibn

Abī Sulmā's much eulogized tribal lord, Sinān Ibn Abī Ḥārithah al-Murrī.[96]

Another worthy icon of structure in the final section of the pre-Islamic *qaṣīdah,* more richly indulged in as image and more carefully encoded as symbol, is the horse, which serves as a locus, especially in the heroic *qaṣīdah*s, for the blending of the purposes of individual and tribe. In its emblematic salience and brilliance, the horse is the poet's manifest pronouncement of belonging to the tribe. Here, as already noted above, the *wuqūf* of Imru' al-Qays's horse in that poet's *Muʿallaqah* is the supreme emblem. Lank and fiery (v. 56/53), it is yet suggestive to eye, touch, and nostrils of finer, feminine erotic graces (v. 60/56), while not ceasing to be the potent stallion (v. 61/66). It stands statuelike before the poet's admiring eye as it remains through the night in full readiness, unaffected by previous exertion (v. 70/58):

> Saddle and bridle remained upon him through the night,
> And through the night he stood before my eyes
> ready, not lax.[97] [20]

Especially according to the poem's redaction in Imru' al-Qays's *Dīwān,* it is after the gallant chase that ensues that the static image of the horse is brought back as the theme's closure; and just as in the image above (as v. 58 of that redaction) the reference to the bridle alerted us to the frontal visual angle, so now the eye is allowed to rest on the animal's magnificent tail as it "falls down straight, almost reaching the ground" (v. 66). The "statue" has thus been seen in the round.[98]

With no lesser sense of pride in something that is not merely possessed, Imru' al-Qays's literary and chivalrous rival, ʿAlqamah Ibn ʿAbadah, exhibits his horse—this time a mare—before his tribe. The effect of the emblem is preeminent here too:

> Oft before the tribe I lead a long-bodied mare
> Preceded by a lineage to the tribe well-known.[99] [21]

There are other symbols equally strongly linked to the image of the horse, such as those of fertility, water, the night's end and the breaking of dawn, and the light that is *ḍaw'* (ultimately the sun, or "light upon light," opposite which is *nūr,* or "light within darkness"). All these contribute to the total effect of the signs of meaning that enter into the third section of the *qaṣīdah.*

At this point, for reasons that go beyond mere consilience and comparison of seemingly unrelatable literatures and genres, the example of two poems by Chrétien de Troyes may be profitably introduced. They are his *Yvain* and *Erec.*[100] In both, the narrative falls into three parts. In both, the hero is introduced as winning his beautiful bride; in both, however, the happiness of love-union is soon lost seemingly forever. It is for us important to note that these events occur as the respective poems' section I progresses and passes into the opening of section II, thus giving in section II each respective hero cause for self-trial and adventure or journey. Both poems conclude with a reconciliation in section III that in one breath equals return and new arrival.

Specifically in *Yvain,* as discussed with a comforting sense for structure by Jean Frappier,[101] we find in the first section the structurally defining great exploit at the "spring of life." The symbol thus introduced is that of birth of life and the early idyll of life, both translatable mythopoetically into "paradise." The second section is thematically that of Yvain's wasteful adventure followed by a redemptive adventure: a year of purposeless and selfish tourneying that leads to disgrace and madness is followed by acts of penance and service to the weak. In an act of gallantry, this transformation is symbolically sealed in Yvain's combat with Gavain. In its third section, the poem's theme-as-structure represents the knight's "reintegration" on levels both factual and symbolic.

Having been helpful in the above schematization of the Yvain story, Jean Frappier comes even closer to illustrating much that is pertinent to our concern with the workings of ternary structures in his analytically arrived at summation of the story—and structure—of *Erec.* In that poem he recognizes more clearly three thematic stages, or an organization "as a triptych"—that is, as separate thematic panels that may even be viewed as not possessing "a real conjointure." *Erec,* too, is seen as consisting of three "acts." Its first act (*le premier vers*), which, as we shall duly take notice from our vantage point of the *qaṣīdah,* is "preparatory." In it Erec displays all his courtly and knightly qualifications. He is "courteous, generous, but proud, a little secretive and quick to take offense, reluctant to owe anything to anyone"—all of them virtues and poses that are as proper to the French medieval context as they are to the Bedouin-yet-courtly context of the Arabic *qaṣīdah.* Furthermore, Erec is also "moved by a deep and imperious love for his beautiful bride." Altogether, the mood of this *premier vers* is one of idyll and springlike freshness, which, however, is soon to be disturbed by what Frappier calls "an emotional crisis." Once again, to a reader sensitive to the inflections of mood and theme in the classical Arabic *nasīb,* such a "crisis" is easily perceived as a variant of the "transitional" signal of *humūm,* for it, too, has a transitional structural function in the French poem.

In its theme, the second *vers* of *Erec* is devoted to the hero's "adventures"—his exploits as a knight. Having tested himself, the hero reaches the untroubled moment of reconciliation with his beloved. This turn of the "story" Frappier recognizes as the section's "conjointure" or even as the poem's possible closure. Admitting the stark externality of comparison, the identification of such a conjointure/closure in *Erec* nevertheless leads us to the formal problems in the classical Arabic *qaṣīdah* presented by the use of the term *takhalluṣ*[102] to mean both transition between structural sections and closure.

The third leaf of *Erec*'s triptych opens upon the chivalric exploit of the "Joie de la Cort," which Frappier identifies in its broader sense as "bringing joy to a king and his people."[103] To those who would consider the poem structurally and thematically ended after the "turn" (or *takhalluṣ*) at the end of the second section, this "episode" may appear external to the core of the poem; and yet, especially because of our experience with the classical Arabic *qaṣīdah,* we may not only tolerate it at this point in the "story" merely for the festive brilliancy of its motifs but even insist on the necessity of such a conclusion, provided the semiotic dictates and internal complementarity of the ternary structure are accepted and each of its sections fulfills its self-validating role. Thus viewed, the third section in *Erec* is in its main, and particularly in its conclusion, a magnificent courtly pageant that culminates in the hero's apotheotic coronation at Nantes under King Arthur's aegis and attended by the flower of Angevin knighthood. To be noticed here, however, is that in Chrétien's *Erec* the heroic knight is himself the one who is apotheotically raised, not his sovereign or "patron." The return to the fold in the third section is thus, in this respect at least, a return to the "self." In the Arabic formal sense, therefore, Chrétien's poem ends on a *fakhr* that is first personal and then implicitly communal, embracing all of knighthood. It does not end on a *madīḥ*. Furthermore, it is to be noticed that this third "act" or leaf of the "triptych" is symbolically a redemption and restoration of the kingdom as "wasteland." In this it lags behind *Parceval* only in symbolic apparel and narrative explicitness—which the "language" of structure is trying to make superfluous.

The ternary structure of such courtly heroic poems as *Yvain* and *Erec* thus sums up for us the form-inherent nature of the conception of the stages of heroic time. Because of its great simplicity, however, the role of this essential structural characteristic is easily overlooked. Only beyond all storied simplicity do we recognize that in the first structural section of such ternary forms there prevails the static air of things as they either had been in their distant, irretrievable past or as they turned out to be once they reached their state of repose in the presumption of an arrested present that is locked in within itself, lacking the sense of the passing moment which could be its dynamic "outlet." It is closed and, as "time," too, it is thus tantamount to a state "accomplished," as much as the "past" itself. It is in this bivalent realm that happiness had once been obtained, consummated, and lost. If there is an exit out of the closed time frame of this section, however, it is through the only door open, which is that of the awakening to the sense of loss.

The second structural section represents the time and condition of the heroic search or quest, which is necessarily a time of becoming from within, expressed through external acts that, like "adventures," must be "pointless" if they are to be symbolically and psychologically part of the heroic becoming. Here again the ternary poem merely insinuates times and tenses, leaving room for a sense of their antinomy and dialectic. If there is a story told in the second section, the "grammar" of its narration implies its own temporal mode. We may thus still be in the "past"—in a sequential but not necessarily historical time—the exit out of which is by way of a progression through it: it is a tunnel that must be followed to wherever it leads. This is the most obvious, and important, difference between the first and second sections. But the traversing, or the "passage," is not necessarily horizontally traceable, with a clear beginning, middle, and end. Rather it is a temporally and even contextually extrapolated series of *actuations,* of smaller "presences," states, or merely signs of awareness, whose time is no longer that of the process of experience within the pastness of narrative but the captured moment of the consciousness of experience. Such time is change itself in the instance of awareness or seizing. In the ternary poem's second section the characteristically disjointed series of smaller thematic panel-insertions—perilous encounters, adventures, chases, crossings of bridges, vignettes from animal life— function to foreground the instant of perception through a time-liberated presence of narrative-turned-image and to propel it into an extrapolated presentness. There is ultimately no "narrative," therefore, only pictorially conceived projection. This is also what happens with an especially persuasive stylistic clarity in the case of the second section of the classical Arabic *qaṣīdah.* What takes place temporally in the second ternary section is thus never a single "state," not even a narrative, but the obligatory enactment of an allegorized "passage" of the heroic time of experience. And the "settings-out" and "adventures" in Chrétien de Troyes's poems as well as the journey in the classical Arabic *qaṣīdah* are such allegorized "passages."

The return to stasis and to a new, closed time frame is accomplished in the third section in Chrétien de Troyes's ternary conception of the poem—as it is in the classical Arabic *qaṣīdah.* Restitution, homage, celebration, and apotheosis, all are acts fully described and qualified by the act and temporal moment of arrival as a "present" out of which, at least in the poem, there is no further exit. That is why the poem, too, must end upon it. It is a present that needs the timelessness of apotheosis, for even if it were seen as future, it would still have to be a future without development or change, the paradoxical, no longer textual duration beyond the point of closure of poetic time.

After a measure of form analysis that is mainly form description, we must still arrive at a more schematic postulation of the argument of ternary *qaṣīdah* structure as form and formula all in one. Here too, however, we shall proceed inductively, as has been our method thus far. First, we shall stop at one further validating stage and review crossgeneric, but in its own way structure-specific, literary evidence of the ternary principle. This procedural skirting of a formulary conclusion of the ternary argument will be conveniently facilitated by Harry Slochower's application of the principles that govern ternary structure to as broad a form-determining concept as mythopoesis, which he views as a restructuring of primary heroic experience (myth) into civilizing literary creativity (mythopoesis).[104] The distinct merit of Slochower's application of the ternary formula lies both in the theoretical cogency of the approach and also in the critical flexibility which allows it to reflect the nature of complex literary texts in their structural totality and inclusiveness. His examples of literary mythopoesis are the Book of Job, Aeschylus' *Prometheia,* Sophocles' *Oedipus,* Euripides' *Medea* and *The Bacchae, The Divine Comedy, Don Quijote, Faust, Hamlet,* and several modern works.

Each such work of mythopoesis emerges in its structure as a "Drama in Three Acts with an Epilogue."[105] Act I offers a remote mythical backdrop, as it were, an insinuation of "Creation or Eden." However, it preserves no more than a nostalgic memory of that backdrop. Act II represents the hero's homeleaving, or expulsion, and his subsequent quest. The *journey,* which is here the requisite experience, is then a descent either into a narratively concretized mythic Underworld or into a symbolically deconcretized "dark night of the soul"—or the former as metaphor of the latter. In pre-Renaissance mythopoesis the journey still has its "fixed goal." Thereafter it may take on an "indefinite character." Altogether, however, the mythopoeic journey is that experience capable of releasing "the ageless springs of human creativity."[106] In act III the cycle closes with the "re-creation" of the hero. As *process* it has already unfolded in act II. Now it is accomplished as "homecoming" or as "destiny." As such it is, or it aspires to be, a *state*. Even where there is an epilogue with its own potentially or incipiently antithetical place in the closing of the structure, there is ultimately no strictly structural way of separating it from act III. There may occur, however, an opening of the structure that points beyond the confines of storied textuality. Due to this ambiguity concerning the ternary structure's "epilogue," we may assume that the mythopoeic "cycle" is not necessarily a true "circle" but rather an open-ended spiral with unresolved antithetical tensions as part of the structure's potentiality or variability. Thus, turning to Slochower's textual examples that speak for themselves the most, we find in *The Divine Comedy* a clear third act "of homecoming in the divine kingdom," while in *Don Quijote* the epilogue, which indeed puts the hero's reintegration in question, remains nonetheless an integral part of the third act.[107]

Conceding the sharp differences of genre, style, and sheer expansiveness between the textual examples on which Slochower relies and such paradigmatically ternary classical Arabic *qaṣīdah*s as, for instance, *The Ode of Exculpation* (rhyming in *dāl*) by al-Nābighah al-Dhubyānī[108] or the *Muʿallaqah* of Labīd,[109] it is nevertheless not only surprisingly easy but outright unavoidable to recognize in Slochower's formula of mythopoesis the same sequential rigor in the structuring of "heroic" experience as is in evidence in those classical Arabian odes. What is more, the Arabic paradigm of the *qaṣīdah* ought to be seen as the formal case in point that most directly validates the mythopoeic ternary sequence of "acts" and comes the closest to the very substance of experience in them.

Thus, in its own first act—the *nasīb*—the "drama" of the classical Arabic *qaṣīdah* introduces us to what must once have been a state of "communal harmony" as presupposed by the mythopoeic scheme; and, just as in mythopoeic structure, that initial state of harmony or blissfulness no longer exists but is only a nostalgic memory or a meditation. The *qaṣīdah,* through its *nasīb* section, conveys the sense of loss of that premythopoeic—that is, mythical—backdrop of a time of fulfillment that seemed to have stood still. It provides a framework for a "first mythopoeic act" that is more explicit and certainly more structure-rooted than the form-flexible and thematically "open" examples available to Harry Slochower.

The "second mythopoeic act" has an even more explicit analogue in the *qaṣīdah*. In the Arabic case it is the *journey* itself—always and necessarily—not the metaphor of it. It is the concrete *raḥīl* extended to encompass the mythopoeic requirement of structure, and it is then also that specific dimension of experience that ultimately had to fashion for itself a structure. Even the bivalency of the semiotic clues that announce the journey—*humūm/himmah*—is, as it were, a contraction of multiple possibilities of language into two ultimately interdependent semantic focal points of the mythopoeic quest. As the central formative experience of the mythopoeia of heroic beginning and individualization, the journey is given in the *qaṣīdah* its formally equilibrating position. In its claim to experiential reality, too, it offers an ingeniously explicit, mediating obviousness of points of departure and arrival, of an in-betweenness flanked by cause and purpose. It is a departure and a severance from things which themselves, at one end, may not have any clarity save the clarity of loss planted anywhere between the instantaneous and the archetypal and, at the other end, may offer an arrival at that which is still only a potentiality or a wish—that is, the future. The true becoming that is also the true being is the journey.

Within this ternary sequential logic of mythopoesis, the third section of the *qaṣīdah* can once again be easily recognized as almost a formulary rendering of Slochower's "larger" variants of "homecoming" as restoration to grace and gratification and to "harmony, peace and unity . . . on a higher, more complex level," where "the bad authority is converted into a good authority."[110] The total effect of the *qaṣīdah*'s "third act," whether it is phrased as a panegyric or as a collective tribal exultation, is, as mythopoesis in its own right, a proclamation and rhetorically enhanced celebration of *arrival*.

In all simplicity, however, the application of the form-dynamism of myth to mythopoesis and of mythopoesis to literary structure lightly veils a ternary schema that is of an even more recessed provenance. This schema is Arnold van Gennep's anthropological model of the "ritual dynamics" and "ceremonial patterns" of *separation, transition,* and *incorporation,* which, together, represent the full cycle of any implicit or explicit, concerted or spontaneous, communal or individual enactment of significant change of status. This process van Gennep terms the "rites of passage."[111]

It is important to stress that, even terminologically, this triadic model is thus centrally and comprehensively determined by the semiosis of the "passage." We obtain further insight into the theoretical core of van Gennep's structural construct if we keep in mind the unfailing terminological intent with which he insists that the "scheme of rites of passage theoretically includes preliminal rites (rites of separation), *liminal* rites (rites of transition), and postliminal rites (rites of incorporation)" (my italics).[112] There is thus affirmed not only the passage itself as the center-absorbing while at the same time formally "mediating" experiential focus of the whole model but also the deeper specificity of that segment: its *liminality*. Through this affirmation, too, the liminality-related and liminality-dependent existence and experiential validity of that which preceded the passage and that which followed it acquire full dimensionality. The realm of the passage lies "outside," across the threshold, in what might also be called a limbo—the in-between zone which Patristic theology (itself a liminal venture) had placed between Heaven and Hell and which to the archaic Arabian poet was the time, space, and state of mind that oscillated *bayna al-raghbah wa al-rahbah* (between desire and awe). In a powerful paradox, van Gennep's terminology thus tells us that the "limit" is his ternary experiential model's true "core," the access to all other understanding of formalized or ritualized sequential behavior, and that, as a structure, it is thus never to be understood as static.[113] It turns and centers around its element in motion: the passage.

In his own foreword of 1908, Arnold van Gennep issued an interesting invitation to "the reader" at large, which might as well have been a challenge especially directed toward Arabic *qaṣīdah* criticism: "I invite the reader to check it [the demonstration] by applying the conceptual scheme of *The Rites of Passage* to data in his own realm of study."[114] His conceptual scheme is no longer in need of validation in anthropology, where "the rites of passage," although still a technical term, has long since acquired the currency of common usage. Literary-critical domains, however, remained much less receptive to theorizing built on the ternary structure of whole works.[115] Instead, within the broad epigone spectrum of structuralism à la Lévi-Strauss, the infatuation with binary structure, forever more receptive to fragmentary analysis short of the totality of form, enjoyed its magisterial moment of near-monopoly. Otherwise, as in the case of Harry Slochower, ternary analysis of the wholeness of structure had begun acquiring new names and new interpretative slants—this despite their intrinsic, but muted, van Gennepian parentage.

The critically most unflinching and, in the best sense, "orthodox" literary-structural application of van Gennep's ternary model of the rites of passage came, none too soon, in an act of poetic justice as it were, out of Arabic *qaṣīdah* criticism and that criticism's search for ways to solve the riddle of its chief poetic structure's radical triadism. The Belgian anthropologist's "challenge" was picked up by Suzanne Pinckney Stetkevych in 1980 and then pursued in a series of essays—all centrally van Gennepian in their theoretical premises.[116] Thus, through its awareness of the literary-critical validity of van Gennep's "behavioral" paradigm, Arabic *qaṣīdah* criticism not only has found pivotal answers to the most unrelenting and cross-grained among its structural questions but has also added a strong, textually scrupulously validated literary dimension to a potentially reductionist van Gennepian anthropology. In her access to and full usufruct of the structural model of the rites of passage, S. Stetkevych has furthermore availed herself of van Gennep's especially liminality-oriented followers. Of these, Victor Turner[117] and Mary Douglas[118] contributed in a particular way to her thematically sound readings and structurally disciplined understanding of the *qaṣīdah*'s *raḥīl* section as "the passage itself" with its co-terminal liminality.

Just as in van Gennep's terminologically infectious interplay between the notion of liminality and the three respective stages of the passage, in the ancient Arabian *qaṣīdah,* too, the ternary sequential process is, explicitly or implicitly, present in the very nature of structure—or in what may be called its deep structure—even if the concrete textual reality of a specific *qaṣīdah* should fail to display a clearly wrought and balanced triadism of form. Here van Gennep himself is prompt to issue the warning not to insist too rigidly on the quantitative symmetry of the structure of his model; the whole scheme always implies three stages in their obligatory sequential order, but to the extent to which it is a scheme of progression and development, not of static binarism, in "specific instances" any one of those stages may not necessarily be found "developed to the same extent by all peoples in every ceremonial pattern."[119] Neither is it necessary that, in a strictly formal sense, there be in the *qaṣīdah* in each textual instance a sufficiently apparent, or actually "given," normative balancing of the sequenced thematic and modal triad. Only one or two of its "normative" segments may thematically constitute a "sufficient" poetic text capable of safeguarding the sense of the wholeness of a subtextual awareness of form. Even in such cases the ternary pattern thus remains in force as the ultimate form-validation—the Goethean *Formgefühl.* This is demonstrated by S. Stetkevych's identification of the structure of the so-called brigand (*ṣuʿlūk*) poem, in which the passage as a tripartite structure of "developmental" stages is truncated in one decisive way: the third section of the *qaṣīdah,* its thematic segment of "incorporation" or "reaggregation," is by the very nature of the *ṣuʿlūk* identity and the *ṣuʿlūk* experience missing in the *ṣuʿlūk* poem. Such a "passage" is thus, by both behavioral and formal necessity, manqué.[120] As an outcast, the *ṣuʿlūk* poet will remain a prisoner of the behaviorally as well as formally "medial" liminality stage of the passage itself.

On the other hand, but still entirely analogically, we may then view the forlorn ʿUdhrī poet, behaviorally as well as formally, as a prisoner of the first section of the *qaṣidah,* its *nasīb,* only that even then a strengthening of the effect of arrested liminality claims for itself, as it were, the van Gennepian "preliminal" stage, at which "separation" should occur and after which the formative "passage" should ensue. What takes place in the ʿUdhrī poem, therefore, is only the awareness of the poet's inability to break out of that which is, or should be, a left-behind *state* in the sphere of his "past." As a result, such a poet's would-be *qaṣīdah* does not seem to be capable of breaking out of its *nasīb*—or at least it is forced to compensate for that inability by allowing that which ought to have been preliminal to usurp the full behavioral and formal function of the liminal. The memory-cocooned, nostalgic "state" that might have been the *nasīb* thus turns into a turbulent contradiction of form and purpose, acquiring a paradoxical full liminality within the confines of a static, presumably preliminal, structure. The agony of form thus confirms form rather than denying it.

In a more paradigmatic *qaṣīdah* structure such as, for instance, the already-referred-to ode by al-Nābighah al-Dhubyānī or the *Muʿallaqah* of Labīd, van Gennep's behavioral model and the classical Arabic *qaṣīdah* harmonize formally, in their general outlines, to a degree that can only be viewed as a mutually illuminating coalescence of an archetype. Furthermore, beyond this level of accord between what is behavioral and what is poetic in structure, there are in the *qaṣīdah* as well as in the anthropological conception of the rites of passage also levels of coalescence of structural brick-and-mortar that sharpen and refine the initial delineation of archetypes into effective forms. Van Gennep, and especially those cultural anthropologists who subsequently took upon themselves the task of developing further the notion of liminality, had, from their end, identified a rigorously structured repertory of attributes and types of ritualized behavior that, respectively, would characterize the three stages of the "passage."[121] Within its own formalized sphere of archaic, or archaizing, Bedouin poetic expression, the *qaṣīdah,* too, reveals its respective repertory of "behavior" in the form of its three thematic stances as these stances themselves are divided into and articulated through rigorously structure-determined and structure-characterizing motifs and images, down to a scrupulously adhered-to, discriminative repertory of the lexicon.

Thus preliminal motifs in the classical Arabic *qaṣīdah* must conform, explicitly or implicitly, to a concept of time that is primarily not of duration but of evocation of loss: a *state* of emotively indwelt pastness. Such time-as-loss must also be one of absence of happiness, whether as love or as innocence. For the conveyance of such a state of mind as poetic intent, the Bedouin poet may want to reach to a past as remote as his oldest legendary lore will permit him:

> Whose are the abodes at the mountain-top of al-Ḥijr,
> Turned desolate over years and ages? [22]

In this opening verse of a *nasīb* by the pre-Islamic bard Zuhayr Ibn Abī Sulmā,[122] we may, without much hesitation, follow the "suspicion" of the early scholiast Abū ʿAmr Ibn al-ʿAlā' (d. ca. 154/770) that the poet's al-Ḥijr is none other than the Ḥijr of the legend-clad Thamūd and that through such an avenue of induction into a state of poetic melancholy we have thus made contact with autochthonous layers of remote and tragedy-nurtured myth. So, too, al-Nābighah al-Dhubyānī will add elegiac depth, and concomitant melancholy, to his own sense of loss by allowing it to share in the archaic myth of Luqmān, which is a myth about the failure to arrest time. It is also at this point, therefore, that this poet's *nasīb* must end and his "journey" begin.[123]

Besides these echoes of an archetypal, conceivably mythical remoteness, there is in the inweaving of most of the motifs of the classical *nasīb,* and in the whole texture of its diction, a highly detailed repertory of references to stages of time and experience that have come to a close and that have been irrevocably consummated. What testifies to this in the *nasīb* with characteristic poetic efficacy is, paradoxically, the poet's willful false reality of reverie, of the insistence on an illusory present in a denied past. Ultimately, however, such an escape has to end, and what ensues is the jarring alternative of rupture with a closed episode of life: the departure and the journey. Indeed, the structure-conscious thematic perspective of the larger part of the present book will be one of illustration upon illustration of the Arabic lyrical awareness of the preliminality of the elegiac stance of the *nasīb.*

If the repertory of motifs and diction in the *nasīb* is itself clear and unmistakable in its capacity to generate precise structure-dictated resonances of semiosis, what the classical Arabic poet sees, hears, smells, thinks, feels, or otherwise experiences in the *raḥīl* is even more structure-determined and structure-revealing. This determinism and semiotic precision begin with that poet's riding beast, which, being a she-camel, is with the utmost strictness differentiated in its gender from the male camel upon which the poet's beloved, the *ẓaʿīnah,* has journeyed off and estranged herself.[124] His time of departure and hours of journeying must also be different from those of the *ẓaʿīnah,* for his are always the hours of danger and inclemency, in the dark of the night or in the scorching heat of the zenithal hours. He will hear around him dark foreboding echoes of the owl's voice; his riding animal will show agitation as though a mysterious, catlike *qarīnah* (female devil) were cleaving to its side;[125] during his journey he will encounter none but brackish water.[126] Not only is the poet in heightened contact with nature, but through a series of mediating similes and conspicuously extended pseudothematic panels drawn from the "untamed" animal world, he turns into an agent of that untamed nature which he must otherwise traverse and conquer.

The Bedouin poet's liminal self-view becomes more explicit, even quite declarative, when he is a *ṣuʿlūk* (brigand). Then, in his "arrested" liminality, he is linked much more directly to the nature and the ethos of the desert. Since he is condemned not to undertake the journey to the outside of his liminality, he dispenses even with the mediating presence of the she-camel. Instead, he invokes the brotherhood of the desert's predators and scavengers: the hyena, the leopard, the viper, and especially the wolf.[127] Moreover, as traveler in the liminal desert, even a poet who is not a *ṣuʿlūk* may not refuse to give hospitality to that other liminal "passenger," the wolf.[128] Other characteristic symbols of the liminal passage in the *qaṣīdah* are the darkness of the night and its silence broken only by the hooting of the owl, and then the polarization of that liminal time, the noontime hour, its mirages and chameleons prostrate as if crucified on the sand.

The third part of the *qaṣīdah* falls into a thematically much broader and much more accommodating framework than either the *nasīb* or the *raḥīl*. It can be an "other-directed" panegyric, which, as a structural unit, will then constitute the poem's *madīḥ* section, or it can be an expression of personal "boasting," which for the most part leads up to a communal/tribal affirmation of value, valor, and honor. As such it will be known terminologically as *fakhr*. In respects impersonal as well as personal, this section is to be characterized as clearly postliminal and reintegrative. Still a "passenger," the poet has now arrived beyond the time and place of marginality. He is now past all "formative" uncertainty. The realm of symbols and semiotics that engulfs him must therefore reflect his integration into the ethos of the community even when in his boasting he yet seems to stress his erstwhile (liminal) singularity and his individuality (personal *fakhr*).

As we already know, the horse is one of the most emblematically fixed motifs of the Bedouin poet's reintegration. It is the obverse of the strictly liminally mediating she-camel. The *chivalrous* hunt, followed by the communal banquet, is one of its semiotically valent appearances. For instance, the *mukhaḍram* poet ʿAbdah Ibn al-Ṭabīb gives us a structurally fully coherent sequence of the passage in his ode that figures as no. 26 in the *Mufaḍḍalīyāt*. It begins with a relatively brief *nasīb*, passes into a well-articulated she-camel journey, and then emerges out of the journey's pronounced liminality, throwing the poet into a chivalrous hunt (vv. 60–65), which is preceded by a "signaling" reference to fecundating rainfall (v. 57) and by an idyllic, in its quite consciously nonliminal quasi-pastoral picturesqueness, *tableau vivant* of desert nature (vv. 58–59) that might easily have been derived from the *nasīb* of Labīd's *Muʿallaqah*. Out of that deceptive idyll, and after the chivalrous hunt,[129] the scene of the banquet occurs, which is strong enough thematically and structurally to take up the remainder of the *qaṣīdah* (vv. 66–81). Linked evocatively to the theme of the horse and the chase through its opening phrase, "Wa qad ghadawtu wa qarnu al-shamsi munfatiqun" (Oft I set out with the morning, when the sun's horn broke through the dark),[130] this "courtly" and exuberant banquet scene evidences its character of integration.

On the other hand, ʿAlqamah, Ibn al-Ṭabīb's elder by approximately three generations, sets a different order in the sequencing of his postliminal themes and motifs of personal, and also communal, *fakhr*. In one of his odes he places the festive banquet panel (vv. 39–45) before a concluding, semiotically unmistakable assortment of motifs of measured prowess and station-conscious generosity. Here, too, he does not exclude the motif of the horse (vv. 52–54), although battle (v. 46), not chase, is on this poet's mind.[131]

In another thematic conjointure of postliminality and integration, illustrated by the ode "*Ṣaḥā al-qalbu ʿan Salmā*" (The heart sobered after Salmā) by Zuhayr Ibn Abī Sulmā,[132] a distinctly iconic "still" projection of the motif of the horse (vv. 9–11) blends skillfully into the dynamism of a chivalrous chase (vv. 12–29), only to lead, in a manner well understandable to us now in spite of the obviousness of the seams and sharp edges of parataxis, to the objectivizing and culminating theme of integration, which is the panegyric (vv. 30–45).

Similar contexts are given stability and become more explicit in their semiotics of reintegration in the *Muʿallaqah* of Labīd, where the exit out of the liminality of the *raḥīl* is effected—almost tentatively and, in the formal sense, "transitionally"—by means of a vauntful, self-assured banquet interlude (vv. 58–62). The ground thus well prepared, the poet proceeds with the surest logic of reintegration. In a semiotically compacted manner he proclaims himself the champion of his tribe (v. 63):

> And often I protected the tribe
>   on a fleet courser bearing my full armor.

Its reins as cross-shouldered sashes,
I set out into the breaking day.[133] [23]

The first signal is here that of ***ḥamaytu*** (I protected), which necessarily brings to mind the tribal autochthony and inviolability of ***al-ḥimā***.[134] This verb is then followed by ***al-ḥayy*** (the tribe),[135] clearly the pivotal Bedouin reality—and notion—of social integration. The warrior-poet in such a role, or posture, is explicitly nonliminal. Not unlike the Greek hoplite,[136] he is a warrior in full armor (***shikkah***). He is also mounted on a fleet mare, and in his "setting out at the break of day" (***idh ghadawtu***) he implicitly partakes of the knightly gallantry of the chivalrous huntsman. In only one verse we are thus given semantic directness and the connotation of the burden of mature heroic responsibility accentuated by the concrete "hoplite" staidness of a warrior's full armor, the pride in knightly horsemanship, and the exhilaration of the "setting out" for battle as much as for chivalrous hunt. All these are strong integrative, postliminal characteristics and values that are then further expanded and elaborated in what remains of the closing section of Labīd's ode (vv. 64–83).

The wholly other-directed panegyric, especially of the "royal" variety, which in the ***qaṣīdah*** represents a personal "arrival" or "homecoming," is most consistently characterized by its recourse to the semiotics of sovereign power, with the assurance of that power's cyclic vegetative renewal. In its symbolic core, this arrival/homecoming is radically different from the associations with "hearth" and "womb" that characterize the ***nasīb*** with its regressive reverie and dream of merging and blending with one's own having-once-been. Hearth and womb as feminine and maternal symbols contrast sharply with the symbols of power in the ***madīḥ;*** these are not only masculine but also essentially paternal. The symbolic polarity between the ***nasīb*** and (especially the royal) ***madīḥ*** explains a further important aspect of the polarity of the semiotics of pre- and postliminality in the ***qaṣīdah***'s ternary structure. Thus the panegyrist al-Nābighah al-Dhubyānī, in trying to regain the favor of the king of al-Ḥīrah, al-Nuʿmān Ibn al-Mundhir, and reenter the court, uses in his ode "***Yā dāra Mayyata,***" as the culmination of his praise, the image of the water-rich and storm-lashed Euphrates—its destructive fury as well as its promise of fertility. Both the king's unbounded exercise of power and his proven generosity toward those whom he favors are thus symbolized. The king, who in the poet's representation surpasses even the Euphrates, is the water of life. He, the sovereign stream, is also the sufficient manifestation of the state. The presence of a ship in this metaphor/allegory of all-embracing power is, therefore, not a reference to the polity/community or the state but rather to the fragility of the fortunes of the individual who navigates in the "stream" of royal power and who, as the oarsman/helmsman, "after fatigue and sweat" finds his course and, inferentially, his access to royal favor.[137]

When Kuthayyir ʿAzzah, of the Umayyad period (d. 105/723), directs a panegyric to Caliph ʿAbd al-ʿAzīz Ibn Marwān, he adopts the same archaic metaphor but with the Nile taking the place of the Euphrates. The burden of the metaphor's meaning then necessarily—and with an intentional display of flexibility—shifts from power to fertility and bounty, thus abiding by the characteristically Egyptian river-symbolism.[138]

In each variant of the metaphor, the eulogized king, and with him the point of reintegrative arrival, is nature itself. The king not merely secures fertility and prosperity, he is their personification. Thus once again, al-Nābighah al-Dhubyānī, when speaking of his benefactor al-Nuʿmān Ibn al-Mundhir, here surnamed Abū Qābūs, expresses himself entirely archetypally:

> Were Abū Qābūs to die, the springtime of mankind
> And the Holy Month of sanctuary, too, would die,
>
> And after him we'd hold but what is left of life,
> Emasculated, humpless.[139] [24]

Here the vegetation symbolism of kingship, of an Arabian Fisher King, as it were, combines the clarity of the archetype with the concrete Bedouin condition of camel breeders. So, too, the much later poet Sibṭ Ibn al-Taʿāwīdhī (d. 583/1187) will address Caliph al-Nāṣir li Dīn Allāh on the occasion of his enthronement as the "annihilator of the enemy hosts" by the epithet *mubīd al-ʿidā,* which could also be implicitly construed as meaning "he who destroys—or removes—stone slabs that cover wells." He then rounds off the epithetic invocation: "O you, whose dew vanquishes barrenness!" (*yā qātila al-maḥli nadāhu*).[140]

Ultimately, within the symbolic range of the classical Arabic panegyric, the triadic structural cycle inclines to close, explicitly or implicitly, with an echo of the poem's beginning reverberating in the equation or comparison of two abodes: the first being the "lost" one of the *nasīb,* and the final the "regained" one of the *madīḥ.* With his characteristic conceptual and stylistic poignancy, Abū Tammām expresses this structural interdependence almost as economically and effectively as he coined his "formula"—or epigram—of the *raḥīl.*[141] He says of his eulogized patron, the commander of the caliphal army, Abū Saʿīd:

> Sweet and delightful was his eulogy.
> It soared above the abodes' description
> and love's rhapsody![142] [25]

The poet's arrival is thus complete, for it has succeeded in overcoming even the archaic sense of loss that was the burden of the *nasīb*.

TWO

The Nasīb: From Archaic Tears to Spiritual Pilgrimages

1. *The Tolerance of the Archaic Vision*

FEW THINGS IN ARABIC LITERATURE raise such polarity of feelings as the *nasīb*. On the one hand, it is the nucleus and the pervading, enduring life force of Arabic lyricism. It has perhaps most strongly determined the whole formal nature of the lyrical genre in its expression through the *qaṣīdah*. As such it had to be an eminently conservative force. Given the tenacity with which the *qaṣīdah* imposes itself upon the entire Arabic lyrical genre, its key element, the *nasīb*, becomes itself like a vestige of the past endowed with some special power. This in turn provokes a certain critical ambiguity. Whenever traditional aspects in poetry are to be praised, the *nasīb* receives the lion's share of positive, sympathetic attention. Whenever tradition is under attack, however, the same *nasīb* will appear as the root of all evil. Even its lyrical validity will then be questioned, as it will be accused of standing in the way of poetic truth and experience. It is therefore not surprising that the several thematic and formal revisionist attempts in the history of the Arabic *qaṣīdah* were in a direct or indirect way concerned with the problem of the *nasīb*. In an ever more accentuated way, the critics of the *nasīb* considered it a relic which somehow lingered on and had to be tolerated and, if the critical necessity arose, identified by way of external topical description: it was meant to speak of abandoned encampments, of empty abodes, courtyards, tribal enclosures, of departures, tears, memories, things entirely archaic, Bedouin. A query from outside the formal tradition as to the place and the role of such things and moods in a late, entirely non-Bedouin poem could easily produce an almost reflexlike critical alienation. The verdict would be that such things are of other times and of other places and have little or nothing to do with the times and places of any poet not fully Bedouin and not unquestionably pre-Islamic.

The practicing poets of the *qaṣīdah* before al-Mutanabbī, however, as well as those who later would not follow him, knew better.[1] It is true that to them the Bedouinity of the *nasīb* meant other times and other places as well; but those Bedouin times and places were of a texture different from what was apparent on the surface and what the critics of the *nasīb* chose to see in them. They were now transposed to a different plane, closer to the

> Altri monti, altri piani,
> Altri boschecti et rivi
> Vedi nel cielo et più novelli fiori

of Sannazaro,[2] or maybe not quite. But they had certainly developed their own symbolic mode of being.

When a severe earthquake struck Syria in A.D. 1157, causing general ruin and destruction, among the afflicted was one of the most gallant knights of the lands of Islamdom and one of the finest poets of his generation, Usāmah Ibn Munqidh (d. 584/1188). Loss of family and property and the view of the desolation left a deep imprint on that chivalrous and sensitive soul. The memory of the disaster appears to have haunted him for years, for as late as 1172, in between knightly pursuits, he finished the compilation of a rather remarkable anthology, entitled *Al-Manāzil wa al-Diyār* (Campsites and Abodes). As the poet-anthologist tells us in a highly personal, directly felt introduction, the work is an act of loyalty to the memory of those places that had been his true home:

> What moved me to compile the present book was the ruin which had visited my country and my home. Time, in all its arrogance, seemed to have made it its design to efface them by every means. Everything came to be as if it had never existed. Those courtyards, formerly so full of life, were now turned desolate. When I reached home, the fury of the earthquake had already passed. Thus I saw the extent of what had happened to that earth which was the first thing to touch me in my life. I did not recognize my own house, nor my father's or my brothers' houses. . . .
>
> My only solace I found in the compilation of this collection, as I made it from my tears over my home and over those I loved.

> I know it is too late for help or benefit now, but all the same, in it goes all that I have.[3]

And indeed, Usāmah Ibn Munqidh put into his anthology a great effort, but also something more. The hundreds of pages of poetic lamentations, all grieving over lonely Bedouin campsites and abodes, are a filtration of deep personal experience. The experience goes even further than Usāmah Ibn Munqidh himself. It embraces a very basic manifestation of the deepest sensibility of a nation or people, and it goes further than a single historical disaster of the magnitude of an earthquake. Collected into one volume, not as signs of writing or verses but as feeling, it seems to contain a whole people's historical reservoir of sorrow, loss, yearning—above all, of yearning—and this reservoir seems not to have any historically precise source in some concrete poetic theme of Bedouin beginnings. Everything appears to blend into a feeling that is entirely ahistorical, where concrete points of reference are transformed into symbols. It is nonetheless important to remember that Usāmah Ibn Munqidh converted all this generic sorrow of a culture into his personal outpouring of pain over very real ruins and very sincerely lamented friends and relatives. It is quite clear that to him the literary theme contained in the *nasīb,* which in turn is part of a rigidly structured *qaṣīdah,* was pregnant with intimate, but not determinate, meaning. This fact alone should move *qaṣīdah* critics to reconsider issuing their sterile, formalistic but yet form-alienated, and pointedly historicist value judgments regarding the entire formal tradition of the *qaṣīdah.* If one part of the *qaṣīdah* can have such lyrically essential "presence" and such symbolically active ambiguities, then perhaps literary tradition has its own secret dimension—secret to the critics but open to poets who, without knowing it, may even be prisoners in just this one dimension or may have an increasing dialogue with their poetic tradition on a symbolic level deep enough to enable them to transcend the actual historically registered point of the birth of that tradition. Such communication then becomes archetypal. In it the time-bound, denotative references and metaphors open up to new and ever different poetic uses.

Usāmah Ibn Munqidh not only compiled an anthology of a poetic archetype but also wrote some of the most thoughtful and delicate verses of that anthology. His own poetic tradition is still that of the Bedouin *nasīb.* His language and his imagery do not try to hide it, and yet it is a tradition which has already become freed for new, unlimited poetic use:

You are not the first one whose abode is far.
Why then this fire in the heart?

To forget, to die—
There will not be a third choice.

Yours was a day. Don't hope for more.
Quite as in night and day, none truly meets for long.

So here you stand, a gesture of farewell:
These are the litters carrying your love,
    the empty abode there.

Contain your tears, for as much as now they swell,
They will forsake you first when separation truly comes.

After long absence the tide of tears will ebb away,
Unless from deepest depth it stirs.[4] [26]

Poetry like this speaks not of antiquarian things, not of "traditional" images and motifs; rather it establishes its very own, although frail, communication with dimensions of feeling and mood in old words and in timeless visualizations. There is no room for the fireworks of novelty in such poetry. The poet has to tread softly on very ancient ground:

Tread softly! What seems the skin of our earth
Is of these bodies made.[5] [27]

These words by the blind poet from Maʿarrat al-Nuʿmān could be written over the gates of a tradition.

For the Arabic poet to speak of eternal questions, not divinely eternal but eternally human, of a mindless fate, of a restless life, and of a hope which does not want to go to waste but clings on in endless agonies of nostalgia—in brief, of the essence of human existence—what could be more natural than to speak in those other distillates of wise, ancient poetic tradition, where so few words are needed to express so much. Thus the Abbasid courtly poet al-Buḥturī does not hesitate to use the old idiom, drawing deeper analogies for his own feelings out of the archetypal well. His are also among the verses which Usāmah Ibn Munqidh later finds in the same well—almost as his own:

Slowly, O wheeling stars! Which one do you hold
Prepared for me: plunder or death unavenged?

. . . .

Riders along stations are we, fated to arrive
And to depart,

With such long hopes spun over
Such short lives.[6] [28]

The poetic theme of melancholy desolation, loss, and sorrow, which most strongly characterizes the *nasīb,* has been in evidence since the very earliest remembered and recorded Arabic poetry. Remembered, because Imru᾽ al-Qays, one of the first recorded poets to cultivate the theme, recalls in a verse of his own how somebody else before him used to intone a similar song:

Stop at the ruins of yesteryear,
There to intone our lament Ibn Khidhām's way![7] [29]

Today we can hardly say that we know more of Ibn Khidhām than what this fleeting homage by Imru᾽ al-Qays chooses to tell us. Perhaps there remains a verse, or at the most two, which could be attributed to that poet. Aside from that, he is only a name of disputed pronunciation, one of the host of potentially important figures who crowd every literary-historical limbo.[8] As a forerunner of Imru᾽ al-Qays, Ibn Khidhām would belong to the earliest generation of named pre-Islamic Arabic poets. In fact, he may have lived as early as the first half of the fifth century.

It is entirely unlikely, however, that Ibn Khidhām, or any poet of that immediate time, could have initiated the important theme of the abandoned encampment. A better known poet of the same period, remembered now mostly by his rhetorically spellbinding, runic elegies, Muhalhil Ibn Rabīᶜah, already betrays a complete awareness of the traditionality of that theme. Indeed, we see him struggling against the overbearing power of the *aṭlāl* theme, as we shall refer to it from here on, rebelling against what is quite obviously already the burden of a tradition. The theme wants to impose on the poet its air of melancholy reverie, the luxury of another type of elegy, in which mere memories of loss, mere forlornness in vague thoughts of elusive happiness, of withered places, or of encounters and separations, can grant the poet a respite, a genteel catharsis. But Muhalhil's elegy must be different. His beloved brother Kulayb has been killed. The blood is not yet dry. It demands immediacy, the response of passion:

Chide your eyes for tears over ruins shed—
In the heart, over Kulayb, there is a burning thirst to quench!

In the heart there is a need which shall remain wanting
As long as doves upon the branches coo.

How shall he weep on faded ruins who pledged himself
For now and ever to fight mankind![9] [30]

In these verses by Muhalhil we notice an objective distance from the *aṭlāl* theme. The poet may intone it, but only with the divided vision of a secondary reflection which intrudes upon the primary image. He tries to disassociate the two. In a poem like this we are struck by the realization that this early poet possesses the distance and the perspective with which to see himself. He knows he is about to follow the custom of intoning a song, a poem, the way such things always are, and he feels, as it were, the wrong tears coming, the wrong song issuing. He cannot help himself: a song is a song, a poem is a poem. But he can see himself, and he can feel the other song stir inside, one of war and blood, not tears. His real song is different, because it is one of urgency, of the unfinished business of blood and not one of remembrance of the past. The final poetic statement thus is a clash between the pathos of blood vengeance and elegiac melancholy. The vision which comprises both is obtained through the objective stepping out of one perspective into another. It is thus closely related to the objective nature of poetic irony.

This very early example of poetic irony, however, ought not to be extended to mean a precocious awareness of the formal rigidity of the *qaṣīdah*. The pre-Islamic poet's objective view here is of himself and of his issuing mood rather than of his "form." When already in the Umayyad period the poet al-Farazdaq suddenly interrupts the recitation of a poem by his fellow poet ʿUmar Ibn Abī Rabīʿah, exclaiming, "By God, this is what the poets had in mind, but they took the wrong turn and wept over abodes instead,"[10] we seem to be overhearing the acknowledgment that an unaccustomed poetic sensibility is making itself felt—and that there may even be appearing a patently new sense of form. ʿUmar Ibn Abī Rabīʿah's poem, which so intrigued al-Farazdaq, was the one that begins:

Love's counsel hastened between me and her,
And on the day of Stoning brought me close to death.

She stirred up ardor in my heart, her very nearness
Twined the rope of bliss into my rope.

If ever a thing I forget, I shall not forget
When in the deep of night we stood, she and I,
there where the palm-grove slopes,

For, when we stopped there, I knew that what was in her
Was quite as what was in me, measure for measure.[11] [31]

It was a new poem, quite unencumbered by the *nasīb*'s structural functionality within a complex *qaṣīdah*, and ʿUmar Ibn Abī Rabīʿah was writing at a time when a whole school of lovelorn desert poets, assisted decisively by the lively urban school of which ʿUmar himself was the leader, was issuing the first major challenge to the *qaṣīdah* form. The challenger is the new kind of poem called *ghazal*, especially the "true" *ghazal* of the school of ʿUmar Ibn Abī Rabīʿah. Inasmuch as both the *nasīb* and the *ghazal* may legitimately share the same themes, they have been fated to suffer from constant confusion, especially since later developments in the *nasīb* itself tended to obscure all formal differences between the two. At the time of al-Farazdaq, however, the difference was quite obtrusive. The poem he was hearing from ʿUmar Ibn Abī Rabīʿah was precisely the new *ghazal*. But his comment—or rather critical statement—came as late as the eighteenth verse into the recitation. It seems that al-Farazdaq interrupted the recitation at exactly this point because there was clearly no further possibility of a reversion to the classical features of the *nasīb*. Up till this point the poem appears as little more than a lively chit-chat between the poet, his beautiful paramour, and her discreet confidantes. Then, at the appropriate moment, with the wisdom of good company (v. 18),

They rose, letting know one of alert wit,
That what they were about to do was for my sake. [32]

One can indeed imagine the charming scene: like butterflies the observant damsels disperse, leaving the lovers alone. Everything is playful and quite explicit. But precisely here lies the difference between this new *ghazal*, which operates on an as yet unaccustomed surface of sensibility, and the internalized, symbolic nature of the true *nasīb*, with its wasting abodes and campsite ruins. There, nothing that concerns meaning is explicit.

Moreover, the poem which caught al-Farazdaq's attention exemplifies the formal peculiarity of Ibn Abī Rabīʿah's *ghazal*—its stylistically tantalizing, although ultimately not altogether novel, tendency to structure an argument or a story into dialogues.[12] This "dramatization" of the subject matter of a poem, even if employed for narrative purposes, produces an overall quickening of pace and a new kind of subjectivized immediacy which stands in strong contrast to the remoteness of the archetypally objectivizing symbolism of *diyār* and *aṭlāl* evocation.

The alternative to the *qaṣīdah,* or at least to the structured *nasīb,* which Ibn Abī Rabīʿah's *ghazal* seems to offer, did in the long run lead to the legitimization of a formal fragmenting of the complex ode structure. By independently developing only one aspect of the *nasīb,* however, it could not aspire to being an all-encompassing alternative to the traditional "great" form. Formally at least, it was bound to remain an unfinished, if charming, development, like every other formal development in Arabic poetry that was not the *qaṣīdah.*[13] The Andalusian *muwashshaḥah,* which in a way is an outgrowth of the *ghazal* as well, is too marginal a phenomenon, with too many ambiguities and half-measures. In the end it is unable to free itself from the gravitational pull of the *qaṣīdah* and falls into compliance with the dominant form's complex structural pattern. The *ghazal* in all its many consequences is thus more like a tangential complement to the *nasīb,* rather than an alternative to it. Unencumbered by the *nasīb*'s elegiac outlook, the *ghazal* provides more amply for the development of the erotic element. This was enough to blur the form-perception of Arabic neoclassic *qaṣīdah* theory.

Muhalhil may have had his moment of objective distance within the poetic tradition; al-Farazdaq may have vaguely realized that there was the practical possibility of an alternative not only to the *nasīb* but through it to the whole notion of the traditional poem: he noticed critically that ʿUmar Ibn Abī Rabīʿah *was* different, but whether Ibn Abī Rabīʿah the poet actually—critically—wanted to be different, we are nowhere told. The historical honor, if not always the aesthetic merit, for wanting to be different belongs to the court poet of Hārūn al-Rashīd, the man of many epithets, Abū Nuwās (d. ca. 198/810):[14]

> Talk of effete ruins is an affair for the dull.
> Your epithets must fit the daughter of the vine![15] [33]

Irony—the irony which was objective distance in Muhalhil—becomes in Abū Nuwās a parody or, even more precisely, a travesty. He is capable of seeing only the risible in the old ways of intoning a poet's song. And yet the very fact that he cannot forget the old mold altogether but again and again turns to the antiphrastic distortive device in beginning his own poems should alone suggest to us the formal vacuum in which the poet was bound to find himself the moment he discarded the traditional theme. That theme proved to be inseparable from the poetic mold of the *qaṣīdah,* which, after all, was a neoclassic Abbasid poet's only true aesthetic horizon and his final frame of reference. The poet is thus left with his own paradox: rejection without change. This in essence is how travesty comes about and functions. It may suggest new ideas, new contents, but in terms of literary form a travesty is quite purposefully an imitation of what is being rejected, of the serious or "pathetic" mold. It would lose itself if it suggested a new form.

Thus, a characteristic pseudo-*nasīb* by Abū Nuwās sounds all too different to be unfamiliar:

Many an abode the gleeful company forsook
 and rode into the night,
And what remained were traces fresh and faint:

Trails left by wineskins drawn along,
Sweet myrtle's bunches fresh and dry.

There I detained my company,
 and I renewed their pledge—
For only such a company I keep.

So what if none of them I knew
 beyond the testimony
Of those desolate abodes east of Sābāṭ? [16] [34]

Such a poem has to adhere with great strictness to the accepted form of the opening theme of the *qaṣīdah,* the way it was understood to be the norm in the days of Abū Nuwās. It is thus in one sense perhaps more stringently imitative than an uninhibited, non-ironic poem would be—with the difference that it has lost, or pretends to lose, the old symbol carried by the *nasīb.* Muhalhil takes the form seriously, even when he sees himself outside it. Abū Nuwās, on the other hand, imagines himself entirely independent. He tries to assert his independence by means of laughter at the expense of a form that proves to be strong enough to make his laughter possible. In a historical sense, from the present perspective of the consummated formal tradition of the *qaṣīdah,* it becomes quite clear that in the end the ironic object became the true ironist. Deeper and enduring changes in the *qaṣīdah,* and especially in the *nasīb,* were not achieved by defiant mockery of the misunderstood *nasīb* themes. The chief mistake of Abū Nuwās—if one wants to take his challenge to the *nasīb* seriously—was his literalist approach to the archaic thematic archetypes. Yet his proposed alternative with respect to *nasīb* themes did not mean merely a substitution of an antiquated realism by an updated realism, not a change from a Bedouin vision of physical environment to a courtier's vision of a duly metamorphosed setting. He did not realize that he was replacing a very broad sense of reality that had already been absorbed into a symbolically and mythopoetically active imagination with a very narrow reference of fact—the ideal with the real and the symbolic with the concrete. Therefore even his close parody of the *nasīb* missed the point. In fact, he was ridiculing something which the *nasīb* was not, or which it had long since ceased to be, which ultimately brings to mind Lessing's maxim that "Not all / Are free who mock their chains."[17]

2. *The Freeing of the Metaphor: Ḥassān Ibn Thābit*

For truly meaningful and enduring changes in the entire tone of the *nasīb* and in Arabic poetry as a whole, we ought to turn to an earlier poet, the contemporary of the Prophet, Ḥassān Ibn Thābit (d. before 40/661). His purely traditional *nasīb* is characteristically short: two or three verses, followed by an equally short section of disengagement from the *nasīb* and of transition to the following substantive section of the *qaṣīdah*.[18] Thus he will start by musing over the muteness of the traces of a long deserted encampment, perhaps intending to lose himself in nostalgic reveries. But then comes the awakening and the transition:

> But leave aside the abodes and recollections
> of every virgin pearl,
> Fair, of pleasing discourse,
> of round and youthful breasts.
>
> To God lament your cares and what you see
> of mankind's angry pack![19] [35]

This abrupt termination of a Bedouin theme and transition to the novel theme of religious preoccupation reflects the just awakened religious zeal in a poet who begins to feel the tension mounting between his new spiritual life of Islam and the traditional poetic molds which were meant to contain the old urges of the Bedouin soul. In their autochthonism, on certain ineffable levels, those poetic molds were perhaps not wholly unrelated to the new "codes" of the spirit. Viewed ideologically, however, they came to be perceived as "heathen." The sorrows of life must no longer be poured out over insensitive "abodes" and "ruins," those customary repositories of all tears. Now these tears must go to God. They must be converted into prayer, or else, would one not fall into idolatry? Perhaps the poet would not go so far, but how clearly, without being explicit, he voices the conflict with the old form, which, at this crucial point, still asserts its validity! There is no victor at the end of this conflict. Ḥassān Ibn Thābit himself achieves the harmonization of both. The result is a characteristically medieval mode of compatibility in which old modes are retained through a metaphorization of what is believed to be the old content or through infusion of an allegorical meaning.

At first the poet seems to be passing through an intermediate stage of such harmonization, but this is also the point at which true change occurs. The framework and the idiom of the traditional mold are used to contain and express or to comment on an immediately contemporary historical event. The mood and state of mind which accompany the event are thus quite definite too. In this way, in a poem composed on the occasion of the battle of Badr, what is structurally recognizable as a *nasīb* becomes a song of sorrow over the fallen companions. The use of the word *qawm* in the first line sets the tone—they are the Bedouin fighting men:

> O *men*, can what is decreed be stopped?
> Can the good life that is no more return?
>
> I remembered a time long gone,
> and my anxious thoughts
> Rushed down upon me, and my tears burst forth.
>
> My passion's throes brought back to mind
> thoughts of those I loved—
> And those in battle fallen:
> Rāfiʿ and Nufayʿ,
>
> And Saʿd—all now in other Gardens,
> while here
> Their campsites are in desolation, the land
> a waste.[20] [36]

What follows is a eulogy of the men who fought and reached for martyrdom, and of the Prophet. What is important and what is new about the poem, however, is the manner in which nothing of the old poetic formal sense is lost while the poet speaks of entirely innovative things; for at this point the old content and language of the *nasīb* are already "form" for metaphors and allegories of things to come.

Thus we find that what was previously the characteristic mood framework for only one part of the poem may now be extended to the whole of the poem. In this way the new poem does not become just an extended *nasīb*. It is an altogether different poem. As we shall presently see in Ḥassān Ibn Thābit, precisely because of the *nasīb*-specificity of its mood, the resulting poem may be a tightly knit elegy; or, as we shall see later in Ibn al-Fāriḍ, it may be a sublimated abstraction of mystical experience. What then are the ruins and which are the traces over which Ḥassān Ibn Thābit weeps at the death of the Prophet?

At Ṭaybah[21] there remain the Prophet's
relics and a luminous
Encounter place, while other relics fade
and waste away.

Indelible are the signs of that inviolate abode,
Where the Guide's pulpit stands on which he used to mount.

It stands so clear, the contours firm—and there
His precinct with a prayer-place and mosque.

There his chambers are, there
The Lord's light found its repose,
to give him light and warmth—

Signs which will not be effaced as time goes by,
Finding renewal in each decay.

There I recognized the Prophet's traces
and where I saw him last,
A grave in whose dust he, hidden, lies.[22] [37]

And then, after a long series of verses which do not depart from the surface theme of the *aṭlāl* in language but apply it to an immediate elegiac poetic object in a mixture of praise and sorrow, the poet returns even more forcefully to the essential *aṭlāl* theme (vv. 29–32):

The holy places lie in empty patches
For want of the live prophecy
which once they knew,

A desolation but for the life which is the tomb
Which hosts the one lamented
by Balāṭ and by Gharqad,[23]

His mosque, and all that's lonely in his loss—
Ravaged the place he stood, the place he sat.

And at the Great Jamrah[24] waste
Abodes and courtyards, vernal camp
and natal ground.[25] [38]

The poem then continues with an apostrophe, the poet calling upon his eyes to weep for the Prophet—thus for another fourteen verses.

Even though this poem, being an elegy in the Arabic generic sense, would normally not enter into our discussion of the *nasīb* as it is structured into the *qaṣīdah* ode, nevertheless we have to pay it particular attention, for it crystallizes the phenomenon of theme transformation from the classical ode with the Bedouin *nasīb* to the subsequent form of the ode where not only an archetypally symbolic but an immediately figurative understanding of the *nasīb* becomes possible.[26]

To assess properly the distinct power of the *nasīb* to confer meaning, it is extremely important to notice that it is through the use of a particular motif in the *nasīb* that that motif acquires a symbolic value which is permanent, like an additional symbolic dimension. The *nasīb* is like a catalyst or like a filter through which new aspects, or purer filtrations, are achieved. It is through this realization, or one may say discovery, that we may begin to understand the genesis of symbolic language in Arabic poetry: everything that touches the *nasīb* becomes a symbol. In his definitive liberation of the Bedouin *nasīb,* Ḥassān Ibn Thābit represents a decisive point in the genesis of Arabic symbolic language. Through his use of the archetypal mood of loss and yearning and the concomitant theme of ruin and wasteland to express the full weight of contemporary events, he converted tangible things of measurable time into transcendent poetic symbols. These were—above all in the literary realm—the symbols of an integrative culture that insisted on its own idiom.

It is important to apprehend critically the moments of these decisive filtrations of values from one mold into another, and from the religious realm into the literary-cultural realm. In Ḥassān Ibn Thābit we may seize one such moment. But we must never forget that we move in the realm of specifically Arabic poetry, where a characteristic quintessential condensation of expressive means and of symbolic molds has developed and remains unbroken. Everything that enters into the Arabic poetic sphere has to undergo a similar condensation in order to become a poetic symbol. Ḥassān Ibn Thābit shows all the poets who follow him how this is done. Only with Ḥassān Ibn Thābit in mind will it be possible to develop a whole symbolic scheme of references for Arabic mystical poetry. These references will invariably be anchored in what we consider to be the traditional *nasīb* mold. Without this reference, one must say, the reading of Arabic mystical poetry is of no truly *poetic* experiential value. An authentically mystical poet like Ibn al-Fāriḍ only heightens the symbolic abstraction and transcendency of feeling which the form-conscious Ḥassān Ibn Thābit has already sketched out in its essential terms. Arabic mystical poetry as poetry and as part of one uninterrupted poetic tradition begins thus, oddly enough, with Ḥassān Ibn Thābit. Its branches may be in one paradise, but its roots are in another.

Soon after Ḥassān Ibn Thābit, other poets, too, will begin to introduce into their still very Bedouin *nasīb* themes objects and references belonging to the new times and the new culture of Islam. Even a purposefully archaic poet like Dhū al-Rummah (d. 117/735) invokes his two Bedouin companions (*yā ṣāḥibayya*) and commends them to Paradise and to the comfort of its broadly spreading shadow, where—in another poem—they may share the company of the Prophet on the Day of Judgment. In still another *nasīb* opening, the poet finds the encampment in ruin and desolation, save for pegs to tie riding-beasts and for poles used to support what was once a mosque.[27]

To the courtly Abbasid poet Abū Nuwās, whenever he is not half-mocking, half-imitating the *nasīb*, the motifs of the mosque and of other recognizably urban landmarks become his more intimately familiar elegiac setting:

> Muṣallā is no more, desolate
> the dunes which saw me once,
> The square of Mirbad, of Labab,
>
> And the great mosque which once combined
> such gallantry and worship—
> Withered and gone its courts and vast concourses.[28] [39]

In Abū Nuwās such a new modality of the elegiac spirit, however, does not extend beyond the *nasīb* as formal entity. This is precisely its significance, or its difference, with respect to the pure elegy of Ḥassān Ibn Thābit. What is obtained is only a transformation of motifs. The broad metaphor of the *nasīb* theme remains intact as regards its formal function and delineation. After it has been developed, the poet feels free to move on to another theme—in this case to the favorite theme of wine. The development of the basic *nasīb* in this new fashion, however, is significant. Remaining formally, or let us say externally, intact, the *nasīb* has acquired an inner plasticity and metaphoric adaptability to whatever new variations of the elegiac mood the poet's own experience or the convention of the evolving culture may suggest as the new "concrete" reference. Thus the evocation of the ruins may now point to the urban landscape of Basra, as in the above ***nasīb*** by Abū Nuwās. The ruins themselves are fully internalized. The poet does not try to tell us that the city itself lies waste. It is his youth and his happiness in that city which are in ruins. If a poet like Abū Nuwās is perhaps rarely serious in his feelings, his metaphors and his poetic intentions may be so nonetheless. His melancholy may even be as short as the lingering in the mind of his ***nasīb*** metaphor. After that, life, wine, and a different kind of poem may go on. As in the present poem, however, one soon notices that even with the change of theme—from melancholy to wine and revelry—the reversal of mood only tries to regain that which was lost at the outset. Thus a reversal becomes a reaffirmation, and in effect, the ***nasīb*** never fully disappears from the poem.

A solution like this is part of a new type of courtly ***nasīb*** and of courtly melancholy which experience their full development in the high Abbasid period and of which Abū Nuwās is a leading representative. The metaphoric openness of the old ***aṭlāl*** theme now permits the sophisticated courtly poets to indulge in more or less vague feelings of elegant melancholy in the recollection of old places and old friends, in a bittersweet mixture of elegy and idyll. In this type of courtly ***nasīb*** the role of the boon-companions becomes especially prominent. Abū Nuwās in particular would not be found without them, as the pride of his own courtly life had been to have figured among the boon-companions of Caliph Hārūn al-Rashīd. But by now the courtly transformation of the ***nasīb*** is a nearly accomplished process, and Abū Nuwās is by no means the only agent in this change.

3. *Toward the Courtly Idyll with Abū al-ʿAtāhiyah*

Before this transformation could acquire its new semblance, however, certain initial adjustments in motifs had to take place. One motif transformation, or rather transposition, which helped to give the courtly ***nasīb*** its character was the change of the traditional Bedouin travel companions who used to assist the poet in his moments of sorrow into boon-companions whom the poet no longer addresses but rather whom he remembers as part of the melancholy landscape of his soul. The entire ***nasīb*** now becomes a recollection, and the poet addresses himself, in the form of an apostrophe, to his own past.

The motif of the boon-companion, or companions, had its place outside the ***nasīb*** in some of the most representative of pre-Islamic poetry, however, and we must assume that that is its direct line of descent. We may further assume that it comes down directly from sources such as the *Muʿallaqah* of Ṭarafah, where it occurs in verse 48:

> My boon-companions are fair as stars,
> and a singing girl
> Joins us, half in striped robe,
> in a saffron bodice half.[29] [40]

But we must also notice the lack of connection within the poem between this motif and the *nasīb,* as well as the immediate context of the verse. Thus the preceding verse introduces us to a markedly "courtly"[30] scene, where the tribe is assembled and where the poet occupies, either by right or by presumption, the seat of honor. The setting is thus not an average one. It is that of the banquet preceded by an implied council, and as such it is directly conducive to later courtly interpretation and assimilation.

On the threshold of the Islamic era we find the motif of courtly companionship, and thus of the "banquet," already comfortably incorporated into the *nasīb*—even though as yet only in what might be called the "development" of the *nasīb*. Ḥassān Ibn Thābit, whose free and highly original treatment of the *nasīb* mold we have already observed, introduces us to this more traditional *nasīb* variety as well when he lets the archaic melancholy produced by the abandoned encampment develop into a cheerful recollection of carefree times:

> What frolic, O Umm ʿAmr, have I been privy to
> Among some fair-skinned, dainty beauties, stately-robed,
>
> With boon-companions of clear countenance and noble,
> Who wake up only after Arias sets.[31] [41]

Melancholy is here, and in the verses which follow, fully compensated for. Once again there is happiness in remembrance, and the melancholy itself proves to have been but light. It will take later poets to develop a fully courtly *nasīb* in which the air of melancholy is maintained throughout. Ḥafṣ al-Umawī, a poet capable of great delicacy who spanned the later Umayyad and the early Abbasid periods, seems to have captured the tone of the *nasīb* as it would be cultivated with increased frequency throughout the Abbasid and the Andalusian periods. He retains the archetypal metaphor of loss and the resulting desolation, but both are converted entirely into inner states. They are poetic, lyrical states, as though of some remote participation rather than of the immediacy and trenchancy of direct experience. Furthermore, they presuppose a refined, controlled sensibility which knows how to play the higher game of discretion and which respects the accepted conduits of self-expression. The *nasīb* becomes a very sensitive and responsive tool for such a game. The opening verses, as in Ḥafṣ al-Umawī, may be very traditional in image and diction: the empty abode, the wind weaving its mantle of oblivion, the apostrophe and invocation of clouds, tears, memories of calflike, tender maidens. Then, however (vv. 4–6), a more delicate tone of melancholy softens the traditional, Bedouin framework for poetic feeling, of which the *dār*, the abode, has to be the expression:

How many a time in its wide courtyards
    I was enravished
By its air's redolence and forgot
    the time of night in conversation!

Those were the days without fear of ever parting,
Without thought that anything might ever
    fall apart.

For a time it seemed we could stand fast,
Till our peace was broken,
    our life of ease dispelled.[32] [42]

The development of a fully courtly *nasīb* in a fully courtly *qaṣīdah* becomes perhaps most clearly realized—at still an early stage—in the poetry of Abū al-ʿAtāhiyah (d. 210/825), a contemporary of Abū Nuwās. He, too, had experienced all the pomp that was Baghdad and the caliphal court at their apogee. If his name is today so often associated with poetry of epigrammatic sententiousness, asceticism, and somewhat spasmodic bouts of piety, he was also a man about court, capable of new subtleties in the old poetic craft of the ode. Unlike Abū Nuwās, to whom the theme of wine and ribaldry is the reverse of the coin of the forlornness of the poet in the *nasīb*, Abū al-ʿAtāhiyah's changes of mood within the poem are not capricious reversals or parodies. A memory of happiness, regardless of how well it is cocooned in the *nasīb*, is only a memory, and the idyll is never entirely separate from the elegy. At least in one ode of this general character, Abū al-ʿAtāhiyah develops an extended metaphor of this idyllic-elegiac tension, a metaphor that should be seen as an allegory and that contains, and represents, the whole poem. The first verse of the poem will tell us where the poet's reveries of recollection begin, perhaps what brought them about; the second verse will tell us something about the true meaning of such an evocation of the past, which now is more a state than a time; and the third verse will introduce us to a whole theme of elegant, refined, courtly delight, perhaps the only form of delight the poet could truly imagine, even if he should imagine himself in Paradise. The final six verses of the poem obey the canon of the *qaṣīdah*. They introduce, succinctly develop, and hastily, but not without elegance, close the two remaining sections de rigueur—the travel theme and the panegyric:[33]

1. Where is the fleeting while we spent
   between Khawarnaq and Sadīr,
2. In Heaven's ethereal chambers,
   in a sea of joy afloat?
3. Amidst a brave lot, falconlike,
   a firm grasp on fate's reins,
4. None but the valiant in passion's face,
   none faltering before it.
5. They pass around a golden wine,
   a nectar fresh:
6. Of virgin grape—reared by a beam of sunshine
   in noontime's fruitful heat.
7. A wine pristine, a maiden noble—
   by hearth, cauldron, grease untouched.
8. Before the company an artless fawn
   in courtly tunic walks.
9. But oh, how craftily his cup extracts
   a minute secret from a discreet mind!
10. Shining, pearly, starlike, in expert hand
    around it goes,
11. And leaves the wit not knowing
    here from there.
12. Then maidens slender, in the still of night,
    will leave their sheltered alcoves,
13. Their buttocks plump, their waists
    a ring could brace.
14. Veiled the lucent faces, tamed the glance,
    but still so black the eyes.
15. The bliss of Paradise is theirs to revel in,
    the richest perfumes to indulge,

16. And feast the eyes in triple pageant:
    of grace and beauty, of intimacy's lure, of silken pomp.

17. The sun they see but rarely, and then
    through curtains' pleats.

18. But now that times so falter, let us our refuge take
    where God has placed His trust:

19. To reach him we have strained
    our mounts by night and day.

20. Their necks in capricious arch,
    on eagles' wings they glide

21. Over soft vale and rugged ridge,
    in darkness mantled,

22. To bring us lastly to the lord
    of palaces and cities,

23. Robust and wise when yet
    too tender to be weaned.[34] [43]

This entire poem, we soon realize, is in effect an allegory of Earthly Paradise, and even the somewhat cursory treatment of the ***raḥīl*** and the ***madīḥ,*** which was duly noticed by medieval criticism as falling short of the norm, may be viewed as a purposefully subordinate development in the structural sense, at the service of the poet's design of one cohesive allegory of lost happiness.

As the poem begins, we observe a marked change in the elegiac landscape. The Bedouin ruins of campsites and abodes, so entirely presupposed by the very language of the ***nasīb,*** have disappeared entirely from this new landscape. Instead, the poet recalls other ruins, not seasonal, not yearly ruins of ephemeral nomad tents pitched against the desert wind, but ancient ones, historically aged, and possessed of that palpable sublimity of the monumental and the legendary. Such vision belongs to those who have learned how to dwell upon "ruinous perfection."[35] The poet's elegiac evocation brings back the days spent in the shadows of the old palaces of Khawarnaq and Sadīr. Concerning Sadīr, neither trace nor historical certainty exists. Khawarnaq, we must assume, once marked the outskirts of the Lakhmid capital of al-Ḥīrah, close to the poet's own birthplace. It was in the poet's days enwrapped in a legendary aura, which proved so productive, first in the Arabic poetic imagination and later, increasingly, in the Persian. Its charming representation even in relatively late Persian miniatures shows how strong the legendary-poetic vitality of the object must have been.

There, in quintessentially elegiac shadows, the poet had once spent a memorable time, a time forever marking the elusive point in life which is then remembered as youth. Such a time and such a place could only have been one thing to the poet—they must have been in that heaven of which the qur'ānic messages speak with such enticement. But there is something ecstatically vague and unreal about that happiness, something pagan as well. The second hemistich of verse 2 has a decidedly Dionysiac halo. It is akin to that most poetic of all ancient Greek pictorial representations of reverie, Dionysus afloat in the sea of delight, signed by Exekias around 540 B.C. But the Dionysiac motif is not introduced capriciously.[36] On the contrary, it signals the main tenor of the theme of past happiness as it is developed in the larger part of the poem. In verse 3 we are then sure that what the poet has in mind is to let us participate in a memorable courtly garden party or outing. Here we begin to enter into the factual circumstance of the reverie. Not that the other circumstances are not equally important, the circumstance of the setting and that of mood. It is through the specific recollection of the happy events, however, that we may also understand better how the poet chooses and sees his setting. Suddenly we feel very close to the genre itself, to the idyllic-elegiac spirit in its almost timeless manifestations and metamorphoses, but always allowing for parallels within certain basic, culturally analogous situations. We may thus easily let our imagination roam over all the idyllic "marble wildernesses"[37] and culturally imprinted landscapes which have ever been part of the elegiac feeling: over Titian's Bacchic scenes and allegories placed in nature, over Poussin's Arcadies and somehow unduly sad, antiquarian classicist landscapes, over so much of Claude Lorrain, only to come back to Giorgione's *Fête Champêtre,* and then once again close the circle with our poet at Khawarnaq and Sadīr.

Our poet's pleasures are truly worth celebrating. They have been celebrated and nostalgically bemoaned—and this may have been their most lasting form of celebration—for as long as man thought that he had to seize the day, the moment, because their enjoyment was too volatile, and, for the most part, even unconscious. Such celebrations are creations, inventions, art. The reality of our present *nasīb* must therefore not be the question—especially as the form of the *nasīb* in itself already contains an allegory. What the poet has to do is to make this allegory his own. The form itself does not demand from him the whole truth. But then, wouldn't the whole truth be so much less than what the form permits? The only valid reality is that the poet once was happy and that he is now only recalling, in the full etymological sense he is calling back one important moment. This is what the *nasīb* has to perform for him. The poet's boon-companions, perchance, are real. But they have no faces, only wings, falconlike. The grape is a virgin. Is it pure, or does it offer purity? It is half reared by the sun, incubated in noontime's womb, possessed of the sun's cosmic quality, and half a Bedouin flower of the jealous, mollifying luxury of the tribal aristocratic tent, known only to Imru' al-Qays. But then, in its effects, this wine can play such games. The virgin grape is no more. Everything is lively ferment, bubbles, volatile substance capable of every mischief. What a contrast when such substance comes from the hand of so artless a fawn of a cupbearer. Or is it? Aren't all contours, profiles, limits too blurred by now?

Such games are played when the shadows are lengthening, when evening is falling. With the full cover of night, in the still of it, a voluptuous motion can be perceived. Are these the maidens of the tribe who come out in pageant? Were then the caution and the hard-won conquests of the ancient Bedouin poets all a wasted effort? Is everything different now, in the shadow of Khawarnaq and Sadīr? Yet the language of the senses has not changed. Every word, it seems, could have been heard where dunes and tribal enclosures formed the inviting horizon of the lovers. The wisdom of ancient form, of the *nasīb,* interrupts our reveries at this point and reminds us that so far we may not have left its confines, its particular horizon of dunes. We need this reminder, because the theme of the poem suddenly changes. If we accept verse 18 as being one of transition, we are left with only five verses for a hurried, yet quite dramatic, run through what might formally have been two major sections of the poem. Had the poet run out of things to say precisely at the point which could have risked the alienation of the poem's caliphal recipient? Critics may have felt so, but it seems that the caliph did not. The poet's dramatic flight over a landscape wrapped in darkness must not have escaped him. Furthermore, the poet referred to him as the lord of palaces and cities. But the cities are also al-Madā'in, the Ctesiphon of the once mighty Sassanid Empire, and the palaces could have also been those of the now legendary Persians, like the renowned Īwān Kisrā of Ctesiphon or the equally famous Khawarnaq itself, and Sadīr, even if the last may have been little more than a name then or ever. The real castles and the real cities of the great Abbasid Empire are self-understood but may not necessarily be the main reference of what is not so much a direct statement as a metaphor. One symbolic reference demands another. The caliph al-Hādī is here being given wholly mythical attributes. His maturity and robustness before the age of weaning, rather than being the usual poetic hyperbole, are signs of a quite special nature. Such signs are signals of higher destiny, shared only with legendary world conquerors, saints, and mythic dragon killers.[38]

This closure, with its reference to heroic kingship, however, makes us necessarily think back (as all formally compelling closures do) to the beginning of the poem, for there is unquestionably something compelling to the lingering presence throughout the poem, even to its very end, of the evocative names of Khawarnaq and Sadīr. Of a palace by the name of Sadīr we know close to nothing outside its recurrences in poetry. Khawarnaq, however, has a much stronger claim to historicity, even though that historicity, too, loses itself in the mists of legend.[39]

The legend tells us that Khawarnaq was built for the youthful Sassanid prince Bahrām V (A.D. 420–438) by the vassal king of al-Ḥīrah, Nuʿmān I. In that palace Bahrām, also known by the epithet of Gūr, grows up under the tutelage of Nuʿmān, or of his son Mundhir I, to become the legendary hunter of lions and wild asses. Furthermore, we know of Bahrām Gūr that, as king, he defeats the king of the Huns and dedicates the crown of the vanquished enemy to the sacramental temple of Iranian kingship at Shīz in the mountains of Azerbaijan.

This latter act ought to bring us back to Bahrām Gūr's fabled palace of Khawarnaq, for the symbolic act of offering a crown as a votive gift to the temple of Shīz—probably by suspending it under the temple's dome—is an act of affirmation of the royal Iranian *khvarne*,[40] the same *khvarne* that in a symbolic way went into the "building" and naming of the palace that Nuʿmān of al-Ḥīrah supposedly erected for his Iranian suzerain's, Yazdigird's, offspring and intended successor, the boy Bahrām Gūr. The word *khvarne* which we recognize in Khawarnaq despite Ibn Jinnī's "little hare" etymology (*khirniq*), Nöldeke's rabbinical Hebrew "arbor" and "plantation," and Niẓāmī's "sun-splendor" (*kwor-rawnaq*, which, in spite of being a characteristic example of neo-Persian syncresis, comes at least tangentially close to part of the original meaning)[41] represents the most central concept of ancient Iranian (and perhaps in a culminating fashion Sassanid) power, glory, and, symbolically most distinctly, kingship. It was *khvarne* that was sacrally present in the royal temple of Shīz. It was then also the *khvarne* immanent in Bahrām Gūr's palace that fated upon the child-prince a special destiny. Iranian legend of heroic kingship understood it and transmitted it ultimately to Niẓāmī, bypassing Ferdowsī only as far as reference to Khawarnaq is concerned. The name Bahrām Gūr itself provides the symbolic ingredients of heroic kingship. Bahrām (red) connotes the king of the "red planet," which in color and astrological significance was linked to the astral lion image. In contrast to the leonine image of contained power, that of Gūr (onager, stallion) is the symbol of carnal impetuousness. Thus the name Bahrām Gūr encompasses the symbolic polarization familiar to us from medieval European heraldry as that of the Lion and the Unicorn.

The occurrence of the palace Khawarnaq in Arabic poetry prior to Abū al-ʿAtāhiyah is well attested. The pre-Islamic instances from al-Munakhkhal al-Yashkurī[42] and al-Aswad Ibn Yaʿfur al-Nahshalī[43] come to mind primarily, but also those of Ṭarafah Ibn al-ʿAbd,[44] al-Mutalammis (ʿAbd al-Masīḥ Ibn Jarīr),[45] ʿAmr Ibn Umāmah,[46] ʿAdī Ibn Zayd (who was himself of al-Ḥīrah and in whose poem there is a reference to al-Sadīr as well),[47] and the late pre-Islamic al-Aʿshā (who establishes an elegiac analogy between Khawarnaq and the castle Ablaq "built by Solomon" and endowed with all the trappings of a "lost" *locus amoenus*).[48] Of these, al-Munakhkhal's reference to Khawarnaq (and Sadīr) at the end of a poem presents obvious structural and thematic difficulties. It hesitates between a pseudo-*nasīb* that is in reality the motif of the "blamer" and between a *fakhr* that leads the poem backward to motifs that are *nasīb*-like but that here, since there is no longer a *nasīb* framework to contain them, are closer to *ghazal* eroticism. Then, as if in spite of it all, the poem returns to a mood of sadness that can only come with a "structural" awareness of the thematic constraint of the *nasīb*. In this general context, the reference to Khawarnaq and Sadīr introduces the poem's anticlimactic—or rather its anti-*fakhr*— closure: when inebriated, the poet sees himself the lord of Khawarnaq and Sadīr; when sober, he owns only a few sheep and camels (vv. 21–22). His final admission is that he is no more than a captive of love, a shackled prisoner (v. 24). The context of the motif of Khawarnaq and Sadīr in al-Munakhkhal's poem is thus ultimately that of a structurally inverted *nasīb*. No wonder that other poets, such as al-Aswad Ibn Yaʿfur al-Nahshalī, should have placed the motif in the actual *nasīb* with a full sense of formalist propriety. So, too, did Abū al-ʿAtāhiyah. Once "restored" to the *nasīb,* the motif also becomes imbued with that structural section's prevailing mood of melancholy. Here the question arises, however: Would the pre-Islamic poet have had such feelings about palaces that in his day ought still to have radiated all the splendor of time-defying royal majesty? This is the question that forces itself upon the reader of al-Aswad Ibn Yaʿfur al-Nahshalī's poem especially. Ibn Rushd in his *Middle Commentary on Aristotle's Poetics* understood too well the formal and thematic tradition of the classical Arabic *qaṣīdah* for any problem of mere anachronism to have troubled his mind. To him al-Aswad's Khawarnaq and Sadīr are as elegiac as the Bedouin ***aṭlāl***.[49] Questions of textual authenticity thus come to the forefront.

In this context it is also important to note that in the majority of the Khawarnaq and Sadīr poems, or verses, the prevailing meter is the ***kāmil***, and specifically the ***majzū' al-kāmil***. This includes the poem by Abū al-ʿAtāhiyah. Unquestionably, we have here the tradition of a motif within which Abū al-ʿAtāhiyah represents the courtly Abbasid reformulation and gives some of the ancient meaning back to the time-worn, name-locked symbol of kingship that belonged to Khawarnaq. Outside the literary context, but firmly within the symbolic one, one might note the survival of Khawarnaq in the name given during the Arab historical period to the truly unsurpassable temple complex of Karnak, which, too, is connected to the succession and symbolic legitimization of sovereignty.[50]

It is through such substructural conduits that Abū al-ʿAtāhiyah thus manages to maintain a steady symbolic tension as far as a possible ultimate reference is concerned. The elegiac motif at the outset is archetypal but also revealing of the new courtly development of sensibility. It is followed, and strengthened, by an unequivocal qur'ānic reference to heavenly Paradise. This reference is then repeatedly confirmed by the treatment of the wine, the courtly heavenly cupbearer, and the Bedouin-heavenly pageant of black-eyed damsels. In his memories of the past, the poet had actually never left Paradise. It is only when the dream of the past is extended and shows signs of becoming the daydream of the future that the wish to regain Paradise arises. This is what leads the poet to a benefactor who is a caliph; but more than a caliph, within the poem, he is another mythic figure, whose cities and castles are none other than the ones in whose shadow the poet's dream of the lost Paradise was first dreamt. The circle is thus closed, the poem ended—and completed; and, if the total structure's formal ***madīh*** is conspicuous for its shortness, the ***nasīb*** in its harmonic effect played out in counterpoint is, in fact, also the poem's ***madīḥ***.

Before making our way to another major stage of theme transformation and progressive symbolic and formal opening of what had once been the Bedouin ***nasīb***, a stage perhaps best illustrated in the poetry of Ibn al-Fāriḍ, we might obtain further critical clarity by looking into some characteristic instances of ***nasīb*** enrichment through heightened internalization of the elegiac landscape, observing also how a new recourse to descriptive facets of pre-Islamic verse produces an assimilation of "objective" motif-references into the "subjective" elegiac framework.

4. *The Stylizing Imagination: Silences and Voices of the Desert from Dhū al-Rummah to Ibn Khafājah*

Already in Umayyad times there was in evidence a new poetic response to the landscape, an inner lyrical view of the surroundings. The "Platonizing" ʿUdhrī poets of the desert were beginning to sing in unison with the inanimate world of objects. But the ʿUdhrī poets, too, were moving away from the *nasīb* of the things of the desert toward a *nasīb* whose center of poetic reference was the "beloved," and whose formal development was toward the *ghazal*. It is therefore perhaps more important to find a traditional poet of the desert like Dhū al-Rummah gaining an internalized, lyrically subjective sense of communion with nature through the Romantic paradox of "poetic solitude."[51] Thus, in the course of an extended *nasīb* which begins with the customary invocation of desolate places ("O you fading campsite, stay well!"), the poet suddenly feels compelled to confess:

> The lonely place I love, for there
> I sing of her the purest tune.[52] [44]

Is this the same loneliness through which other poets sought to achieve concentration or seclusion in the hermetic world of Art? The poet Jarīr, Dhū al-Rummah's contemporary, was known to have stuck his head under a blanket for hours in composing his poems. D'Annunzio and Proust would lock themselves up in soundproof, cork-paneled rooms. No doubt, Freudian interpretations of the matrix of poetic creation are possible and applicable in such cases. Salvador Dalí's return to the eggshell should have something to do with Jarīr's blanket. Neither was meant merely to keep the noise out. The hermetic world of the artist is in the main a world of the inner voice. But this is not the creative solitude of the romantics, nor is it that of later Arabic poetry, which is a solitude of many voices and of wide horizons. Romantic subjectivity, the Romantic poetic monologue, always claimed to be only a harmonization of those other voices which live around the poet in the many silences of nature. And the silences of the desert were beginning to be discovered by the new, already half-courtly brand of Umayyad poets who were purposefully seeking out the desert less as landscape and more as a poet's milieu. This internal vision of the desert was unfortunately also to entail much artificiality, because the poet in the desert, as we shall see, is always the lover of the *nasīb*.

Not until the high Abbasid time, however, does all this become quite true and does the poet learn to sustain a vision in the heart when his eyes have to turn from the poetic object:

I did once pass by their abodes,
Their ruins a prey in decay's grip.

And I halted till my jaded mount reared restively,
And the company beset me with blame.

My eyes then turned away.
The ruins were no more—and then
my heart looked back. . . .[53] [45]

These verses are by al-Sharīf al-Raḍī (d. 406/1015), a poet who more than most Arabic poets of the period sees with the heart; but other poets, too, like the *qāḍī* Abū Muḥammad ʿAbd al-Wahhāb Ibn ʿAlī Ibn Naṣr, know the agony that persists in the heart after the last good-bye has been said:

I shan't forget the one to whom I bade farewell
at dawn upon the strand,
With the drivers intoning their singsong,
the riders in haste.

There we were: one bound for distant lands,
The other remaining in body,
when the heart had left.[54] [46]

And once again al-Sharīf al-Raḍī, bending his heart to the pastoral metaphor, exclaims:

O gazelle, you who graze in willow groves,
May it well become you, now that my heart is your pasture!

Water, let the others drink it all.
Only my weeping eyes will quench your thirst.[55] [47]

And then he heaves that sigh of poets which so well bridges the cleft between pastoral artifice and romantic pathos in European poetry as well:

Heaven's bliss, hell's torture,
How sweet to the heart, how bitter! [48]

The poet in the desert, as we noticed earlier, figures now increasingly as the lover. His Bedouinity, formerly clearly profiled in its ethos, is entirely transformed. Even being a poet-lover becomes markedly a cultural attitude or pose. The old ruinous abodes, and indeed the entire desert, turn into a stylized landscape through which only poets roam. Such a desert exists only in the mind. Thus, Mihyār al-Daylamī (d. 428/1036), a poet whose sensibility developed under the compelling influence of al-Sharīf al-Raḍī, leans to a *nasīb* which is itself an ode to the desert as the abode of lovers. In his invocations, the abode of Umāmā becomes a mystical place devoted to the memory of a mystical beloved. It could just as easily have been the *qubbah* of a saintly anchorite. It receives the life-giving rain of clouds carried by the luxuriant south wind; it is drenched in lavender by the gentle easterly breeze. Other places may remain forever abandoned or visited but rarely. But of this most privileged of all the ruins in the desert, the poet assures:

> Love decreed that you become
> Travel station and abode
> to lovers all.[56] [49]

Dār Umāmā is thus no longer a ruin in the desert but an analogy for the other sacred places of pilgrimage and devotional retreat. This is the decree of Love, and we may imagine here an allegory which could lead us to other, now chronologically quite close allegories in the nascent European lyric: of Venus with her bower of Love and of the Rose with her enclosure sought by lovers.

The sacred reverberations of the language of the *nasīb* continue and grow in intensity. One of the finest lyrical talents of al-Andalus, Ibn Khafājah (d. 533/1137) of Alcira, near Valencia, makes the mystic air of this desert of the lovers even more rarefied. In a delicate mixture of references to the rites of holy pilgrimage, to obligatory Muslim prayers, and to the now wholly mythologized religion of love of the mad lover of the desert, Majnūn Laylā, the poet from the distant Spanish shores kisses with a pilgrim's fervor the traces of the abandoned abode. In revering them even in their emptiness, he is like one who has to perform his ritual prayers in a waterless desert: to him a symbolic ablution with a handful of sand is also purifying (v. 14). The camels of his caravan, too, are referred to as *rikāb,* a term which now carries its own allusion to the rite of pilgrimage. Everything around the poet becomes impregnated with irresistible, communicable yearning, even his mounts, those which could have been bound for Mecca (v. 15):

> The camels in plaintive unison moaned too,
> as passion awakens passion,
> And soon the whole wide desert knew
> none but the pining lover.[57] [50]

Here the first reference is to Majnūn's sorrow at Laylā's death and to the participation of the entire animal world of the desert in that sorrow.[58] Ibn Khafājah, however, adds some further imaginative overtones. Everything in the desert is now by love possessed. The lovers who inhabit the desert will seemingly roam it forever. They are "enslaved by love." On the one hand we may have here a "typical" poetic hyperbole; on the other, however, the idea of a desert full of wandering lovers, which is the next image to come to mind, is similar to the image it evokes subsequently—that of the desert full of anchorites. Such deserts, teeming with colonies of anchorites, were not mere inventions of Byzantine iconography or figurative, topical exercises of Renaissance painters. As the biblical hills were traversed by roaming bands of prophets, as the hills of early Christian Ireland were swarming with marauding saints and sorcerer-poets, as the desert of Sinai had always been irresistible to those who sought some form of escape or salvation, so also the lovers as poets had forever wandered about their own landscapes in their own poetic ways, imagining the world either as cosmic solitude or as a sympathetically vibrating community of other lovers. The shepherds of the idylls and pastorals, a pristine race of poets in spirit, were perhaps the clearest exponents of this poetic paradox of solitude within a spiritually harmonious community. Hence the hills of the Renaissance and Baroque Arcadies were full of solitude-seeking shepherds.

In general, one may say that by the eleventh century A.D. the symbolic openness of the *nasīb* themes has gone a long distance since Ḥassān Ibn Thābit, and the growing stylization of the topical poetic conventions and of the entire formal medium has heightened the objective quality of the *nasīb* as art. Stylization in Arabic poetry is a lengthy historical process indeed. After its pre-Islamic classicism, Arabic poetry was at a loss for an alternative, culturally integrated mode of aesthetic vision which could be called style and which would express the progression of time and the change of sensibility. Thus the history of Arabic postclassical poetry, however rich in sovereign moments, runs the danger of being seen only as the record of a constrained, limited search after an integral vision of the cultural self, the history of syntheses of stylizations rather than of antitheses of styles. This, however, may be a question too complex to be even tangentially proposed, let alone decided; and above all it ought not to be treated as a basis for value judgment.[59] If nothing more, however, the history of the *nasīb* as form and as vehicle for important cultural archetypes shows a continuous stylizing effort which is not purely decorative—as many critics have so glibly and so often maintained. The drawing anew and the reformulation of the symbolic correspondences in the *nasīb* meant each time a due readjustment of the poet's vision to his culture's changing imaginative and conceptual horizon. How large or how small the change was, and how rapid its process, remains another question.

As we saw earlier, in the development which took place between the pre-Islamic poet Ṭarafah and the Abbasid Abū al-ʿAtāhiyah, the motif of the boon-companions had found its way from a courtly interlude occurring in the middle of a *Muʿallaqah* into the heart of the idyllic-elegiac musing of the new *nasīb*. Such transfers of motifs, particularly from the more highly acclaimed and culturally assimilated instances of the classical poetic heritage, become quite characteristic of the traditionally ever more self-conscious "late" *nasīb* poets. It is those poets who display the most insistently stylizing imagination too. As we shall see in an example from the Andalusian Ibn Khafājah, however, a motif transplantation in the *nasīb* redraws, colors, and modulates that motif. Thus, in a melancholy elegiac poem, so full of the old yearning which more and more finds its new home in al-Andalus, Ibn Khafājah appears to sum up his mood with a motion, a gesture:

> I turn my gaze about the sky; perhaps I shall divine
> Rain from that distant lightning flash.[60] [51]

The verse catches our attention, yet in its mood, motif, and diction it at first appears in no way unusual among the other verses of the poem. What is intriguing about it, however, are certain familiar but nonetheless unsettling echoes. We know that the poet is on a voyage, a long way from home, and that he yearns for his native Valencia. The entire poem has only this one theme, and the mood is thoroughly subjective. The poet does not just see the "concreteness" of a landscape. The echoes that we perceive in the above verse are of a different coloring. A critical second thought tells us that in some part it owes its image and diction to four verses out of Imruʾ al-Qay's *Muʿallaqah* (vv. 71–74). We have, therefore, an influence, perhaps an imitation. Very much the way tradition-sensitive generations of postclassical poets used pre-Islamic, or in general terms classical, images and diction, Ibn Khafājah takes over the four verses of Imruʾ al-Qays and reduces them to only one of his own—with a difference, however: whereas Imruʾ al-Qays is concerned with a natural phenomenon and with its description within a larger semiotically decisive context, the Andalusian poet is not. Whereas in the *Muʿallaqah* the lines introduce the final theme and image of a lengthy and complex *qaṣīdah*, whose *nasīb* section has long since been left behind, in Ibn Khafājah's poem the "imitative" verse forms part of what would normally have been the *nasīb*, had the poet chosen to structure his *qaṣīdah* fully. Perhaps Ibn Khafājah does not even imitate his nonetheless recognizable classical model. What is it that he does? Something very significant has now happened to the classical poetic heritage. Almost as a whole, as a cultural entity, it has acquired a "charge" of meaning, of a different meaning mostly, of a sense of yearning for the old scenes, places, people, names, and *words*—above all, words. As echoes, these old things sound different now, and they sound only as echoes. Nothing is simple and direct. These are approximations of things irrecoverable. Direct imitation of even the greatest of models no longer offers its validating objectivization. The poetic view turns personal, its perspective is inverted, and within it description becomes a wish for a landscape, for an experience, not the landscape itself. If there is "imitation," it is not what the motival and lexical components say it is. The Andalusian poet, and any other post-classical poet if he is a poet at all, does not necessarily imitate within the rigid literalism of a neoclassicist style. Rather he lets himself respond to old tunes. But all ancient tunes may easily sound sad now. So he takes stormy skies out of the old "objective" scenery and lets the natural phenomenon befit the requirements of his sensibility: perhaps the flashes of lightning which used to guide an ancient Bedouin gaze over the spread of the horizon will now direct homeward his longing soul. Such changes are brought to pass, poetically, in the facilitating framework of the *nasīb*.

5. *The Delicate Balancing of a Stubborn Structure: Ibn Al-Fāriḍ*

By the time of Ibn Khafājah, the *nasīb* has assimilated everything there is to assimilate. It has proven its symbolic efficacy with every traditional motif and subject matter that had come within its reach. Nonetheless there is an ultimate consequence yet to draw—namely, the obtaining of complete formal equivalence between the *nasīb* as theme and the *nasīb* as poem. Such an equivalence, as we already know, had been achieved previously in the case of the *ghazal* offshoot of the *nasīb*. Many a pseudo-*nasīb* by Abū Nuwās, too, could, and actually did, stand as an independent poem. Above all, however, the poetry of such Andalusians as Ibn Khafājah produces something formally very nearly approaching the severance of the umbilical cord of the new lyrical poem. But even in formally very obvious cases of this kind, it is nevertheless possible to conceive of a structured *qaṣīdah* as lurking somewhere in a theoretical formal limbo past the closure. The tension of the *qaṣīdah* has not disappeared entirely. A residual sense of form seems to bring back to mind that which was left out on purpose. We are therefore free to speak of a formally implied *nasīb* section even when we speak of a poem that in its entire structure has already become a *nasīb*.

It is in the poetry of the Egyptian mystic Ibn al-Fāriḍ (d. 632/1235) that further formal solutions to the new *nasīb* emerge and are put to the test in a major way. On the one hand, Ibn al-Fārid epitomizes the trend toward a self-referential *nasīb* poem and toward its disengagement from the structured *qaṣīdah*. On the other hand, however, he manifestly "regresses" into the *qaṣīdah* by internally structuring the formally secured "total" *nasīb* that his poem has become into its own ternary form that is fully analogous to the archaic *qaṣīdah* paradigm. As far as the theme and the mood of the resulting poem are concerned, Ibn al-Fāriḍ, who lived one hundred years after the time from which our last example by the Andalusian Ibn Khāfajah was drawn, has been justly named, for his poetry, the Prince of Lovers. Love was a constant word on his lips and, indeed, the permanent state of his soul. But it was love as yearning for the remote experience of the desert as pilgrimage, the love of the holy places of his now only recollected, poetically conjured mystic states. What on the surface might thus appear to owe its language to the "erotic" part of the *nasīb*-turned-*ghazal* is actually only a metaphor of another metaphor: the theme of loss and desire in Ibn al-Fāriḍ is closer to the archetype of the *aṭlāl* than it is to the surface metaphor of the beloved. His loss is always of a once-possessed sense of paradise, and his desire is an even more clearly aimed arrow. An almost retrogressively obvious *nasīb* poem of his begins with the Bedouin apostrophe:

> Stop at the abodes and greet the withered
> vernal camping grounds! . . .[61] [52]

only to end with a fully personal sigh (v. 14):

> O paradise, which my soul loathed to leave!
> But for the solace of Abode Eternal,
> of sorrow would I die. [53]

As suggested earlier, Ibn al-Fāriḍ represents a development out of the symbolic matrix of Ḥassān Ibn Thābit.[62] He is also less intrusively affected by the Umayyad *ghazal* school than is his contemporary Ibn ʿArabī (d. 638/1240), the great mystic conceptualizer, but lesser poet. Indeed it is difficult to say when Ibn ʿArabī as poet escapes the literary commonplace. His resourcefulness in poetry is ramblingly eclectic, rarely achieving a compelling submersion in the symbol, and even then the symbolic atmosphere may be quickly dispelled by a poetically awkward, declarative explicitness:

Just as I have lent clothing to branches,
Moral qualities to gardens, smiling lips to lightning.[63] [54]

Ibn al-Fāriḍ, on the other hand, achieves a stylistically characteristic—and one could say personal—economy of basic themes and diction. Everything means what it means as it takes its place in the poem. Traditional motifs and diction undergo a symbolic change in substance, an ultimate abstraction or reduction to a highly condensed poetic matter that is given a totally new "specific gravity."

There is, however, a sense of the paradox in this ultimate condensation of the symbolic meaning of the *nasīb,* which in its basic motif structure always consisted of a very small nucleus of verses. A three-verse *nasīb* is an early formalistic development. If now, on the opposite extreme of the developmental trajectory, there is to be achieved a maximal theme condensation together with an expansion of the *nasīb* nucleus into a poem all its own of twenty, thirty, or even forty verses, such a formal paradox is bound to subject the resulting new poem to great inner stresses. Ibn al-Fāriḍ's solution to the problem is, at least on the surface, a quantitative one. He relies on reiteration. A poem becomes like a cumulative scheme of serially reiterated symbolic equivalences which in their totality form a dizzying, narrowing vortex of the quintessential—subtextual or, rather, supratextual—*nasīb.* The all-engulfing yearning surfaces under the names of remote Bedouin personifications of beauty: Laylā, Salmā, ʿAzzah. Are there differences among the three? Are they more than symbolic emblems? One could just as well ask whether the three Graces were ever truly meant to be separated, or what happened when, in wanton mythopoesis, the self-indulgent Paris chose among Hera, Athena, and Aphrodite. The many place-names in this new *nasīb* poem are equally fluid, dreamlike. They move between remote dunes, hills, and valleys where ancient, pre-Islamic abodes once stood abandoned, from which so many tribal caravans departed, and those newer places, with their newer names and echoes, full of the sweetness of ritual, of faith, of ineffable gnostic essences, of loss in the fold of the Mother of Cities. The levels of symbolic consciousness never stand still. It becomes difficult to apprehend the difference between Tūḍiḥ as Imruʾ al-Qays saw it and Khayf, the slope of Minā, where the Prophet once stood. The poet wants both. There is a way in which he remembers them together—and also Laʿlaʿ, Ḥimā, Salʿ, and ʿĀlij; Ḍārij and ʿĀmir; ʿUdhayb, Ḥājir, and Zamzam; and ʿArafāt, Mecca, the rugged Ḥijāz, and the high Najd. There is a way in which he has seen all that he has loved, and then known its absence, everywhere. The cumulative effect of these series of symbolic apprehensions soon ceases to be quantitative. A new, vertical dimension of experience appears, as deeply anchored in the recesses of tradition as it is freely soaring into the spheres of pure appetite of the soul. Within this dimension, too, the poem is simultaneously the maximally condensed ***nasīb*** and the open form of seemingly unlimited verse series, repetitively heightened in a crescendo effect of symbolic insistence. To provide an illustration, only a whole poem will have the sufficient eloquence of the form:

1. Did lighting flash from far-off vale,
   Or did veils lift from Laylā's face?
2. Was the tamarisk aflame, with Salmā in its grove,
   Or was this light the gleam of tear-filled eyes?
3. The scent of lavender, perhaps
   or Ḥājir's balm,
   Or in the Mother of Cities
   ʿAzzah's languid redolence?
4. Would that I knew! Does Sulaymā tarry still
   in the valley of Ḥimā,
   Where one lovelorn roams?
5. Did rolling thunder rend the sky at Laʿlaʿ,
   And did the generous cloud let down its load?
6. Shall we surely reach the sweet waters
   of ʿUdhayb and Ḥājir,
   As surely as the morning
   scatters the phantoms of night?
7. And are our valley's hills
   still green and fertile,
   And shall we regain there what we once had?
8. And in the hills of Najd, in Tūḍiḥ,
   is there someone
   To bear to Naqā my bosom's pain?
9. At the sandbars of Salʿ, at Kāẓimah,
   does someone ask there
   About one in love's bondage,
   what yearning does to him?
10. Are flowers plucked from tender myrtle,
    And do acacias in the Ḥijāz
    come to full bloom?

11. And in the valley's folds,
    do tamarisks bear fruit,
  And are the hostile eyes of fate aslumber?

12. Are the shy, doe-eyed virgins of ʿĀlij
    faithful to their oath,
  Or is all lost?

13. Will the gazelles of the meadows
    yet linger after us,
  Or will they too disperse?

14. Will maidens lead me in the glen
    to happy springtime pastures?
  Those joyous grounds!

15. Does the lote-tree east of Ḍārij
    still cast its shade?
  Weren't my tears enough to water it?

16. Is the mountain pass of ʿĀmir
    still traveled after us?
  Will it once again join parted loves?

17. Are they headed to the house of God,
    O ʿUmm Mālik,
  The beloved Arabs, to whom
    I owe so much?

18. And the riders from Iraq, have they stopped
    at ʿArafāt?
  Was custom followed,
    did each one find his tent?

19. Did the she-camels run briskly through the passes?
  How must the white-canopied litters
    have swayed and clashed!

20. Will someone help us reunite at Jamʿ?
  Will my own life buy back our nights at Khayf?

21. Has Salmā hailed the stone on which we vowed,
  On which our fingers met in clasp?

22. And has she sucked the breast of Zamzam?
  Oh, may its sweetness
    be forever hers!

23. Perhaps in Mecca a dear company
    will with Sulaymā's name
  Allay my bosom's fire,

24. Perhaps sweet nights cut short
will soon return
To still the longing:

25. So once again the sad one may rejoice,
the lovelorn live,
The yearning one find peace,
the one who hears the song
in it delight![64] [55]

There are six poems in the *Dīwān* of Ibn al-Fāriḍ that are closely related in theme and mood, and that are structured out of a *nasīb* nucleus. Among them the above poem emerges as the most formally smooth and compact. It is characterized stylistically and rhetorically by clusters of repeated patterns encountered with great frequency in Arabic elegiac poetry. In broad terms, the grouping of verses within a poem into series of reiterations may be technically defined as parallelism. In a poetic art as highly refined as that of Ibn al-Fāriḍ, however, parallelism acquires a syncopated sinuosity which escapes the oftentimes burdensome effect of cumulative, rigidly parallel statement. Furthermore, reiterative parallelism in Ibn al-Fāriḍ's present poem is a preeminent structural element. Through it we may easily distinguish three structural clusters of verses, the first one (vv. 1–3) hinging on a series of interrogative alternatives (*a* — *am*), the second (vv. 4/5–22) on a stream of simple questions (*wa hal* — *wa hal*) which swells with the force of a prolonged crescendo, and the third (vv. 23–24/25) on a hopeful "perhaps" (*laʿalla* — *wa ʿalla*). The differing closing line of the poem does not disrupt the third cluster, since it constitutes an enjambment within a poetic phrase which began with the displaced caesura of the preceding line. We do not obtain stanzas this way, but we do obtain three separate varieties of cohesive locution, each one with a distinctive structural function within the poem.

Thus in the first series of three verses the poet expresses his perplexity and hopeful wonder over a sign in the sky, a nightly glimmer of remote campfires, a bestirring scent in the air. The type of questioning in these three verses is based on a parallelism of alternatives. It is not a purely rhetorical device, however. The resulting "either-or" has its tension between a physical phenomenon and a thought, a name, a desire. The poet does not see or smell with the senses alone. His senses are invariably associative with what totally occupies his heart and mind. The transfer of meaning is a process which for him is contained in the external phenomenon itself. One could call this the conviction of the metaphor. When there is a light over the horizon, the poet's first thought is: the beloved! When there comes a breath of perfume, the poet's sense of smell knows only one response: the beloved! The alternative questions, as far as the poet's feelings are concerned, should even be reversed. The poet actually asks himself: Are these the apparitions of my beloved or are they but deceptive physical phenomena? Such a reversal of the question has its own pathos and also a certain sadness. Thus the dissolution of his wish for an apparition contained in the initial questions comes in the fourth verse. "Would that I knew!" the poet exclaims, and this exclamation is valid as much for the first cluster of questions, which it concludes, as for the succeeding, much larger cluster, which it opens.

Here we observe another shift, aside from the one that takes place in the type of questioning and in the parallelism. So far the poet has wanted to seize his own present moment. The flash of lightning, the remote glimmer of fire, the lavender in the breeze, the thought of the beloved—these are things of the instant, of the present. Beginning with verse 4 all the way to verse 22, the poet reaches into his past, into his memories: "Do acacias in the Ḥijāz come to full bloom?" "Does the lote-tree east of Ḍārij still cast its shade?" These memories are unconstrainedly produced by those first things the poet saw and smelled and by the phantomlike illusiveness of the beloved names. At the end of the poem, in the concluding cluster of the hopeful "perhaps," another change of time occurs. We have moved to the poet's future. Thus what started as an apparition of the present instant and then evoked a stream of desire projected into the past, into memories, reverses its direction toward pure hope, which is the future. The three clusters of parallelism have lost their merely rhetorical surface effect and have become integral structural sections.

This initial structural overview should help us understand why Ibn al-Fāriḍ's poem represents one aspect of the evolution of the *nasīb*. The three opening verses of the poem represent a motif highly favored by Ibn al-Fāriḍ. Other poems in his *Dīwān* begin in like fashion, with verses that come mystifyingly close to being copies of each other.[65] Within a *nasīb* this motif is quite obviously a variety of the "nightly apparition" or "visiting phantom" (*ṭayf al-khayāl*) type. Already Jarīr had exhibited a veiled, but poetically effective, preference for it at the expense of the more archaic *aṭlāl* theme. His use of the word *ṭalal* with a double meaning—as "looming form," "looming figure," and, more important, as "campsite ruin"—is fully intentional:

Is it the phantom of Khālidah
        coming through the night?

No looming shape [campsite ruin] should I see dearer
than such a nightly vision.[66] [56]

Ibn al-Fāriḍ's own version of the motif has a close antecedent in the poetic manner of al-Buḥturī, who is considered one of the most eminent cultivators of the nightly apparition ***nasīb:***

Is it a phantom's nearing,
a lover's greeting,
A lightning's glare, a fire's blaze?[67] [57]

But Ibn al-Fāriḍ also fits into the mode which we had observed in the Andalusian Ibn Khafājah, in the crucible of whose ***nasīb*** ancient motifs were given new pliability. Indeed, Ibn al-Fāriḍ's poem would not be excessively distorted if it was preceded by the verse of Ibn Khafājah discussed above.[68] The coincidence of meter and rhyming consonant is almost inviting—as though Ibn al-Fārid began his ***nasīb*** poem where Ibn Khafājah left off.

Perhaps more than a casual similarity of motif produced from a common topical fund is Ibn al-Fāriḍ's opening of the poem that echoes the beginning of the famous *Al-Mu'nisah,* "the poem of solace in solitude," by Majnūn Laylā:

From Thamdīn we could see Laylā's fire,
And by the grove of tamarisks we spurred on
our fleet mounts.

The one among us with the most piercing eyes exclaimed:
I see a star,
A solitaire from Yemen set against
the black of night.

But I replied: Oh no,
'tis Laylā's fire burning,
Its light rising on high to shine for me![69] [58]

The open sharing of the topical pool of distinctly ʿUdhrī deposition becomes even more apparent if one reads Ibn al-Fāriḍ's verses 5 and 6 together with verses by the Valencian Ibn Saʿd al-Khayr (d. 571/1175):

O you, who ask the riders,
did dew fall over Laʿlaʿ,
As once its evenings were dew-laden, mild,

Did they arrive and halt
at al-ʿUdhayb's sweet waters

That exhale redolence when greeted
by soft breeze's palm?[70] [59]

Not unlike the traditional *nasīb* when it opens with the nightly apparition motif, Ibn al-Fāriḍ's poem, too, reverts to the mood of melancholy memories. The illusion of the phantom lasted but an instant. The memories it evoked may have to last as long as there is life.

It is in the main section of the poem that the spirit of the archetypal *nasīb* is recaptured. Everything is phrased as a question. Memories operate in a field of tension between the consummation of time, the projection of desire, and the impossibility of apprehending the moment. Is everything in the realm of happiness still as the poet had left it, as he had once experienced it? Through question after question the past struggles to become present in an effort which in all its insistence only strengthens the melancholy realization that what the poet is actually asking about is where his past has gone. This is then the main part of the poem, and this is where the poem does not depart from the *nasīb*. The motifs, which could have made so many a *nasīb*, are here multiplied, exploded within one poem.

But the veins of the classical poetic tradition run in still another way through this poem whose structural layers we thought we had already explored. The tradition of the formal *qaṣīdah* structured primarily by its sequence of themes once again demonstrates its formidable pervasiveness. Thus the three identifiable verse clusters of the poem reveal more than just a strain of analogy with the trisectional structure of the fully developed *qaṣīdah*. Either by their theme or by the eliciting of a distinctive mood, they achieve an identifiable correspondence with the normal sequence of *qaṣīdah* sections.

The presence of the opening *nasīb* (vv. 1–3) has already been established. No peculiar complexities are to be expected here. The theme of this *nasīb* within a *nasīb* is the series of previously discussed nightly apparition motifs.

The middle part of the poem (vv. 4–22) presents at first a problem of identification. Once identified, however, it lays bare a structural and thematic tension which gives the poem its form-definition, for this section of the poem, in spite of the fact that it operates entirely with the mood, the motifs, and the idiom of the *nasīb,* has nevertheless a stronger, deeper thematic affinity with the second section of the *qaṣīdah,* which is the *raḥīl*. But how different this late mystic poet's travel theme is from its archaic Bedouin antecedents! The road along which this *raḥīl* progresses is studded with evocative names that one would not expect to find except in a *nasīb,* names charged with unmistakable, warm nostalgic feeling that can lead only back into memories, names to which one *returns* in thought rather than journeys to in fact. Beyond that, however, these names are also the poet's travel stations along one road, the road of pilgrimage to Mecca. Another road of pilgrimage studded like this with pilgrims' stations but leading west to the remote Santiago de Compostela was known in Ibn al-Fāriḍ's time as the Milky Way. His so very Arab road of the soul, however, has to be one that takes him along stations in the desert where countless "dear abodes" might have, could have, must have stood in the wind and then vanished, as now there are countless *aṭlāl*.

The poet's *raḥīl* is thus a vision of the past. He asks, wonders, and wishes, but he himself is not there any more. Those participating in the *raḥīl*, those on pilgrimage, are the desires of his soul, his poetic messengers, the "beloved Arabs" (v. 17). But this *raḥīl* is also rich in *nasīb* motifs, as in verse 19. There the departure of the women of the tribe in their camel-borne litters is part of the soul's pilgrimage. It is also the expression of the poet's reawakened yearning. Thus, while sharing in the central mood characteristic of the *nasīb*, it also drives the poet on toward the goal of his pilgrimage as though in a *raḥīl:* he would give his life for the nights on the slope of Khayf (v. 20), at Minā, with the other cherished places around Mecca so near.

And finally there lies Mecca, at the end of the soul's road, and in Mecca there is the memory of the bond sealed with Salmā as their fingers locked in a clasp of union, intertwined over the black stone, the single witness. But for the mystic the dearest place and the sweetest, the warmest and the richest, is the breast of that Mother of Cities, the well of Zamzam. Did Salmā suck of it, drink of it? Because only there is the poet's assurance that she lives, that his entire spiritual journey, too, may still be relived. Only a mother's breast, life's milk, will deliver such visions from the realm of memory into the realm of hope. This is also the end of the journey, the culmination of the soul's *raḥīl*.

What follows is the concluding section of three verses, where the poet actually feels hope stirring in his heart. Within the formal *qaṣīdah* structure this section allows a variety of themes, the most common among which ought to be that of eulogy, as suggested by the term *madīḥ*. But madīḥ rarely appears without an underpinning of specific motives. It presupposes or is introduced or followed by the poet's plea for patronly favor: for pardon, for distinction at court, or for stark monetary compensation. The prevalent mood in the *madīḥ* is therefore one of expectation, of hope; and, as we observed in following the development of the *nasīb*, the structured sequence of moods defines a *qaṣīdah* as much as does that of themes. The mood of the concluding section of Ibn al-Fāriḍ's poem is therefore not unlike that of any concluding (or third) section of a structured, classicist ode, even though, as far as the general thematic flow of motifs is concerned, at the end of the poem we are still in the sphere of the *nasīb*. Within these interdependences, the final, almost jubilant change from thoughts of the past to hope for the future once again reaffirms Ibn al-Fāriḍ's subtle sense for the tradition of the ode as it reaches, through him, its consummate formal as well as symbolic abstraction.

The language of hope also proves to be the most direct one. All meaning is now contained in one word quite clearly and explicitly. No images are necessary. The word is "Mecca"—the name and its symbolic content are one. It is as if other symbolic connotations have now receded into the background, now that the goal has been reached. There the pilgrim-poet's memories lie hidden, waiting, and from there new joy may once again come. Verse 24 especially rings like a trill escaping. It has the quality of the *zaghārīd* of weddings and victories, and of hallelujahs: *wa ʿalla al-luyaylāti allatī* . . . ! There is a double caesura in this verse, one after *taṣarramat* (were cut short, elapsed) and then another after *yawman* (soon, some day). But after that the verse does not stop. The rhyme means nothing. The verse runs over into the following verse, rushing toward the closure of the poem. The poet must have taken a deep breath before it, or he must have hastened in hopeful, breathless exultation. When the last word is said, there is nowhere left to go, nothing more to feel. By his hope the poet has laid himself wide open. He must not speak of the past again. No more memories. No more memories? Have we ever left the *nasīb*? But the poem is finished, and through it the poet may have recaptured something. In his final outburst he may have wanted to say that he has felt, if not the experience itself, at least the hopeful, disturbing nearness of an experience. If he has not retained the mystic state, at least he knew it was there, a possibility, a dimension to reach out to.

So far we have seen Ibn al-Fāriḍ's poem through its structure. Its symbolic and mystical intimations have emerged as so many translucencies of a stained glass window, running over the dividing ribs of the lead strips and forming larger planes of time, theme, and mood. In the poem's inner maze of individual semantic components, some of the translucency may nonetheless turn opaque. This may occur because of the poet's willful design, but also because we no longer possess a key to every lock in that maze.

A reader of thirteenth-century Arabic mystical poetry is bound to envy the critical certainty with which Émile Mâle can say in regard to European art of the same period that "symbolism has too large a place in medieval art to leave room for the fancies of modern interpreters."[71] We perceive with the true empathy of historical attunement how large a room symbolism has in Ibn al-Fāriḍ's poetry, but this empathic attunement soon turns into apprehension when we realize that there may be no way to avoid a "modern" interpretation. Arabic poetic symbolism, especially in its mystical stage, is (in spite of efforts to the contrary by medieval commentators) still mostly a symbolism that has to be interpreted rather than "decoded." European medieval symbolism, on the other hand, develops toward a visible, decodable surface. That surface is largely translatable into various types and levels of allegory, the key to which is to be found in a series of culturally seminal literary, philosophical, and theological writings of Late Antiquity and the Patristic period. This heritage, with its strong link to the earlier classical Platonic matrix, is, in Erich Auerbach's words, "the cloudy syncretistic Neo-Platonism merged with Christianity, for which we have coined the term 'vulgar spiritualism.'"[72] Within the essentially idealizing atmosphere of this "vulgar spiritualism" all allegoric interpretation and figural assimilation[73] of the remains of both classical and biblical antiquity take place. C. S. Lewis may then refer to the whole cultural substance which resulted from this process as "the discarded image,"[74] but in the Christian Middle Ages this image was the model of all intellection of what was considered to be objective reality.

Inseparable from this reality was the world of symbols to which this image was the key. When the image was discarded, there arose also the danger that the key to the medieval world of symbols would be lost. In effect, if to the art historians of the early nineteenth century the Gothic cathedrals had appeared at times hieroglyphically obscure, this was because, as regards the arts, during the centuries of classicist infatuation the preceding cultural image had lost its validity. Also lost seemed the key to the medieval world of the symbol, of which the Gothic cathedrals were the supreme repository. At that point it was only natural that "modern"—which had to be synonymous with subjective—interpretations of medieval symbolism would be undertaken. When subsequently, due to arduous scholarly effort, the "key" was recovered, medieval symbolism once again became the open book it had originally been, even though the façade of a Gothic cathedral was now no longer the *Biblia pauperum*,[75] legible to all credulously open eyes in unmitigated possession of "the image." Modern *pauperes* had long since gone for instruction to other sources, and only an erudite minority remained in possession of the old symbolic writ.

In whatever hands, the key to decoding European medieval symbolism was, and remains, operative largely because of the allegoric nature of that symbolism. An allegory, which is basically an extended—or only insinuated in its extension—metaphor, gravitates toward the telling of a "story." An allegoric personification has symbolic validity because behind that personification there is a phenomenon which is also a happening and a "story." Allegoric symbolism, therefore, aims at the kind of personification in the background of which there is at least the suggestion, if not the outright explicitness, of a circumstance. In artistic representation such symbolism is most conveniently translated into iconography, the meaning of which becomes condensed by reason and requirement of the art form in question. Individual symbols or images may be linked into iconographic chains of sustained allegory as much as they may be considered in isolation. As far as the symbolic idiom is concerned, there is little difference between a sustained, cumulative allegorical context and the more circumscribed context that gives validity to each individual iconographic allegorization. A remarkably precise, rather antisymbolic frame of descriptive external reference is necessary to bring such iconographically coded allegory to life. Thus medieval European allegoric symbolism demands as its key a vast repertory of philosophical, theological, and generally encyclopedic writings which together constituted the disseminated knowledge of the age. Boethius's *De consolatione philosophiae,* Martianus Capella's *De nuptiis Mercurii et Philologiae,* St. Isidor of Seville's *Etymologiae,* the *Bestiaries,* Vincent of Beauvais's *Speculum majus,* these and many more were the tributaries, as they are presently the roads of access, to the maze of allegorical-symbolic perception and representation of one part of the medieval world of the spirit—and of artistic imagination.

Faced with Arabic literary symbolism in the particular instance of Ibn al-Fāriḍ, we realize how comparatively little we are able to draw on if we look for an extraliterary repertory of equivalences in a symbolic reading of a poem like the one we have before us. The main allegory of the poem, as we already noticed, did not even seek expression through a directly transferable idiom of equivalences with what could be called an objective circumstance. Its expression came rather through form and structure, through eminently literary avenues. If the question of a quid pro quo symbolic code arises nonetheless, it should perhaps not be taken outside the Arabic medieval literary tradition of the closely literal, atomistically analytical commentary. In that type of commentary a verse of poetry is explained word for word chiefly on morphological, syntactic, and lexicosemantic levels, after which there usually follows a brief paraphrastic elucidation of general content. A commentary on a symbolic-mystical verse differs from such a standard philological approach only in that it supplements the semantic explanation with an additional, eventually quite elaborate, listing of symbolic equivalences for all pertinent "external" connotations of the lexicon, after which the paraphrase of the content becomes a recapitulation of the mystic intention.

A very elaborate example of a symbolic commentary comes from the great mystic and hermetic symbolist Ibn ʿArabī, who (supposedly under stress, but undoubtedly also as his own afterthought and further search for meaning) provided his otherwise poetically undistinguished lyrical collection, appropriately entitled *The Interpreter of Desires,*[76] with a fastidiously detailed quid pro quo "interpretation." But his commentary appears trapped in its own hermeneutic logic, detached and esoteric. His poetic text would hardly have been served by anything else, however, if the modest amount of mystical substance contained in it was to be salvaged and the general symbolic pretense maintained. In brief, the result is that the commentary develops largely its own sphere of content, treating the poetry merely as a "point of departure," and the poetry, going its own traditional ways, never quite manages to warrant the flights of the symbolic imagination of the commentary. Ultimately, such a commentary is not even quid pro quo. Ibn ʿArabī's chief interpretive method combines philologically rooted etymology with a symbolism of formalistically—but not always psychologically—motivated association of concepts to the exclusion of sensory perceptions. He thereby obtains a hermeticism that is dense in symbolic texture but restricted in experiential scope. Verse after verse ends up meaning the same thing, even if suggested by capriciously differing means. Almost wholly unconnected with the possible levels of reading of underlying verses and even contrary to their mood, words of important classical-cultural, poetically imbedded connotation are reduced to mystic states or theological concepts. Thus Bedouin ruins (*ṭulūl*) refer to divine names in the hearts of the gnostics,[77] to appearances of forms, to rain or dew, and to tears,[78] only to retain in another verse a semblance of their poetically current meaning but at the same time coming to mean a "natural sign, a mark" or what remains thereof,[79] etc. No doubt the richness of the lexical meanings and connotations of the word *ṭulūl* warrants a broad diapason of mystical "equivalences," but in each case, or rather as a precondition, these ought to have been derived from within the poem as true imagist and symbolic resonances that are in harmony with their poetically activated semantic base. Otherwise, a mystical-symbolic commentary that refuses to be bound by the poem that has engendered it degenerates into an exercise in capricious mystical hermeneutics entirely at the expense of its primary semantic matrix, which is the poem.

It is a pity that such a dissociation should characterize the mystical commentary of Ibn ʿArabī, for as a hermeneutical procedure applied to a poetic text, it represented a distinct novelty on the Arabic philological-exegetic scene and might have served as a much needed imaginative contribution to the creation of an Arabic poetic "higher exegesis," or a poetic "*ta'wīl.*" As such it ought to have been allowed to cross the barrier of the closely delineated sphere of the commentary (*sharḥ*)—which in classical Arabic editorial practice was, and still is, no more than a philological reading aid—into textual interpretation as an essential ingredient of Arabic literary criticism. There it would have offered a refreshing alternative to the cheerless single-mindedness of established rhetorical criticism and classificatory theorizing. Ibn ʿArabī was indeed in possession of the interpretive idea, if not altogether of the method, with which to achieve precisely such a breakthrough. His unflinching reliance on etymology as a hermeneutic avenue to the poetic text, in this case his own, was capable of producing something that at times approached critical-interpretive essays in "reading." Ibn ʿArabī the poet, however, almost always disappears from that reading as soon as Ibn ʿArabī the interpreter emerges. And then the interpreter is no longer his poetry's retainer. Instead, he gives all of himself in a perverse sort of way to the tangential becoming of a different textuality—the textuality of the activated, but now self-formulating, mystical compulsion. Quite correctly, Ibn ʿArabī calls the effect of this "The Interpreter of Desires," for in it the "desires," or the "yearnings," are those of the mystic, irrespective of the always "independently" existing, as if objectively detached, poetic text. The end result is that the etymological method of Ibn ʿArabī, although in a purely theoretical sense marvelously refreshing and replete with critical possibilities, once having gone astray in its original application, was ignored by subsequent Arabic literary critics and mystical exegetes alike.

A further example of the mixed effects of Ibn ʿArabī's etymological method is his textually extrapolated understanding of the word *shiʿb,* which ordinarily means "a mountain pass" and which is also a place-name. It becomes for Ibn ʿArabī "a road to the heart," and because the word implies the circumstance of the mountains, it also comes to denote a "permanent mystic state," as opposed to "transitory" state.[80] Here the final association is with the epithetic denotation of mountains as *rawāsin* (firm, firmly anchored, fixed ones).

Much more felicitous poetically, as well as mystically-experientially, is his etymologizing triggered by the place-name Laʿlaʿ, which can mean "glimmer" or "mirage." It comes to signify a mystic state of bewilderment and perplexity, but also of infatuation (*tawalluʿ*),[81] of which we later learn that, as "incandescence," it is also a "state of mystic passion."[82]

On the whole, the interpretive language of a symbolism like Ibn ʿArabī's has the tendency to become totally hermetic, thus depriving the reader of a modicum of an objective frame of circumstantial cultural reference—particularly since mystic hermeticism in poetic interpretation was never meant to enter into the formal critical tradition of Arabic poetry. It simply availed itself of the technical externalities of that poetry's critically least involved tool, which was the philological commentary. Even this aspect of the critical tradition, however, after narrowly philological objectives have been satisfied and exhausted, has the capacity to uncover, or at least not distort, a poem's layers of immediate as well as remote meaning; and this is where, in the traditional critical perspective, the realm of poetry truly lies. On the other hand, in poetry that is hermetically "totally" interpreted, the symbolic codification of the poetic lexicon breaks the harmonizing interdependence between mood and image and their emotional and sensory conveyance. Words run the danger of appearing like denuded, uprooted stems, leaving the imagination at best in amazement. Grouped into what we call "poetic language," such words lack contact with each other as well as penetrability to the reader. They have lost all sense-projection, plasticity, and dimensionality. What the understanding of purportedly mystical poetry through hermetic commentary achieves is a theology of mysticism, an abstract scheme for extrapoetic ideas. The mysticism which is experience, which also ought to be poetic experience, escapes this conceptualizing entirely. Not unlike the Christian symbolizing figural interpretation, which in its effect upon actual events, in the words of Erich Auerbach, "dissolved their content of reality, leaving them only their content of meaning,"[83] this kind of symbolic reading *into* poetry rather than *of* poetry imposes an aesthetically unbearable rigidity on everything it touches.

How in the parallel Christian context "reality" is turned into an abstraction by the figurally denatured medieval eye may be illustrated by a passage from *De bestiis et aliis rebus,* for a long time attributed to Hugh of St. Victor, in which a description of a dove affords little else than a composite figure of meaning out of a disembodied world where things seem to exist only to the extent to which they aprioristically "mean":

> The dove has two wings, even as the Christian has two ways of life, the active and the contemplative. The blue feathers of the wings are thoughts of heaven; the uncertain shades of the body,

> the changing colors that recall an unquiet sea, symbolize the ocean of human passions in which the Church is sailing. Why are the dove's eyes this beautiful golden color? Because yellow, the color of ripe fruit, is the color too of experience and maturity, and the yellow eyes of the dove are the looks full of wisdom which the Church casts on the future. The dove, moreover, has red feet, for the Church moves through the world with her feet in the blood of the martyrs.[84]

In a like manner of detachment from the object, the peacocks in Ibn ʿArabī's commentary become the spirits of the inward and outward actions which are carried toward the highest level of aspiration. They "are the spirits of those actions, for no action is acceptable or good or fair until it is conveyed through a beautified spirit or a lofty aspiration. These he [the poet] compares to birds inasmuch as they are spiritual, and he also refers to them as peacocks for the variety of their beauty."[85]

Often the only virtue of excess is that it is eminently illustrative. Returning to a middle ground—even if it be one of classical proportion and clarity—inevitably means a relinquishing of some of that illustrative eloquence of single-mindedness. So too, returning from Ibn ʿArabī's *Interpreter of Desires* to Ibn al-Fāriḍ's poem is like facing the ambiguities of real literary problems after the unproblematic, glossed-over tolerance of the exemplary.

To begin with, in the absence of Ibn al-Fāriḍ's own commentary, a reading of his poetry allows a much higher degree of interpretive freedom, even if we realize that some form of code of mystic equivalences would not have been alien to the poet's consciousness. Critics must, however, be cautioned not to accept the authority of an annotated mystical edition beyond the same bounds and within the same hierarchy of marginality as they accept the discreetly helpful presence of standard commentaries on the classics or on any poetry of significance. One such edition of Ibn al-Fāriḍ's *Dīwān* most often referred to is that of Ḥasan al-Būrīnī (d. A.D. 1615) and ʿAbd al-Ghānī al-Nābulusī (d. A.D. 1731),[86] whose combined commentary reflects what had become the definitive formulation of Islamic mystic concepts spun into and out of the surface meaning of the language of the *nasīb*.

Thus regarding verse 1 in our poem, we learn that "a flash of lightning" is the "manifestation of divine being"; that the valley or "low ground" is "the innermost part of man, in which there is a heart infused with divine spirit"; that "the (lifted) veils" are "the things which perish in the manifestations of the divine face." In verse 2 the "tamarisk tree" is "the world of potentiality." In verse 3 "the scent of lavender" is once again "the manifestation of divine being," while the place-name Ḥājir, which is rich in etymological possibilities (wall, dam, refuge, prohibitive; and other possible etymological associations, like protection, bosom, mind, stone, etc.), is explained as "the absolute absence, hiddenness," which in turn in Arabic mystic terminology signifies "divine essence inasmuch as it may not be visually apprehended."[87] The Mother of Cities, which is recognizably Mecca, is also "the heart of the perfect gnostic submerged in the contemplation of divinity"; and so forth.[88] From there a paraphrase of the first three verses in the mystic sense, with appended concrete poetic references (italicized), could read as follows:

Verse 1. Was it the manifestation of divine being—*lightning-like*—illuminating the depth of my heart, infused with divine spirit—*coming from the depth of far-off vale*—or has all that perishes disappeared in the luminous manifestation of the divine face—*like veils lifted from Laylā's*[89] *face?*

Verse 2. Was it the subtle substance made incandescent by divine presence in the dark world of potentiality which God's word can bring to be—*was it Salmā and the flame of the tamarisk*—or is the redness, that which the parted lips in a smile show, the redness of weeping eyes fearing the sudden loss of divine presence—*was it yet Salmā's smile through tearful eyes?*

Verse 3. Was it divine being manifested, emanating, or was it the presence of the absolute hiddenness of divine essence as it reveals itself in the beauty of its names at Mecca, which is the heart of the perfect gnostic submerged in contemplation of divinity—*was it lavender spreading, or balsam out of Ḥājir, out of the Mother of Cities*—or was it the divine presence unreadable to the mind's faculties, the one apparent to true gnostics only—*spreading abroad like ʿAzzah's redolence?*

If Arabic philological and interpretive commentaries on poetry suffer on the whole from patently unpoetic formulation, the Būrīnī-Nābulusī commentary being no exception, this does not mean that their lack of poetic sense ought to be read into the glossed verse or poem itself. It does, however, mean that there was a certain externally observed sobriety in the medieval critical attitudes toward "meaning." This sobriety, which at the hands of generations of philological commentators had maintained its separate mode of being, one could say almost its own style of "functional" antipoetry, may have also reflected the ever-present paradox of the levels of existence of medieval poetry. Medieval critical distrust of poetry as itself possessing meaning, as a complex of values with a self-contained aesthetic mode of existence, had complacently welcomed all the accusations leveled against poetry as a chiefly deceitful device. Much critical effort was therefore exerted to somehow neutralize the attractive illusoriness of the externality of poetry, concentrating subsequently, with an even more unchecked zeal, on the rationally obtainable and meaningfully usable elements in poetry. Much critical energy was expended over all the minute definitions of meaning as mere formal denotations, and unflagging attention given to such handicaps as the completion of statement (meaning) in a verse (*al-ma'nā al-mufīd*) and other forms of functional interdependence between rhetoric and logic.

When finally, with the appearance of the mystic-symbolic strain in Arabic poetry, the scales of poetic values were reversed, poetry suddenly became overtly a vehicle of maximal symbolic meaning. But it still remained a vehicle only. Meaning could not easily have been perceived by tradition-bound commentators as residing in poetic expression itself—or even less in the formal language of poetic structure. The only level of meaning accessible to commentators was the superimposed system of poetically external symbolic equivalences. Even while knowing that the poetry of mysticism was somehow the message itself, that it was fully legitimized as bearing meaning, a commentator could not rid himself of the old concept of poetry as being in its essence determined by the dichotomy between form and meaning. Earlier he had trusted the form and distrusted the meaning, while now it was the other way around. But his old trust in form had not been fair either. He had known all the time that form was deceitful, that the poetry of the first reading, of the aesthetic reading, that is, was only a beautiful lie. Faced presently with a poetry which so eminently wanted to be one of meaning, his awareness of a chasm between form and content became even more acute. If poetry in its manner of being was a lie, then whatever meaning, or truth, it contained had to be detachable or abstractable, because truth could only coexist with nontruth as long as it could preserve its separateness. Such an understanding of truth and meaning in symbolic poetry offered a cogent argument for the further polarization of form and meaning.

The reading of commentaries on medieval Arabic mystical poetry is still our straightest route of access to these questions, which should otherwise have found their place among the major topics of Arabic literary theory and criticism beyond the narrow "genre" of the commentary. As we have seen in the case of Ibn 'Arabī, however, not even a symbolist mystic poet in commenting on his own poetic work manages to escape being confined to the philological, dichotomy-based tradition of commentary which aims at a construction of meaning through extrapoetic equivalences. After such a construction—or supra-position—of "true" meaning has been achieved, the commentator-critic ceases to show interest in the formal presence of the poetic "lie" itself. What has made symbolic interpretation possible thus precludes the further step into literary criticisms.

An even clearer illustration of this paradoxical existence of poetry both as falsehood and as carrier of truth can be obtained from the allegorizing experience in the poetry of the Latin Middle Ages, which is wholly contemporary with the growth of Arabic-Islamic poetic symbolism. Thus in *De planctu naturae,* Alan of Lille (d. A.D. 1202) makes Dame Nature say of poetry the following:

> Poetry's lyre rings with vibrant falsehood on the outward literal shell of a poem, but interiorly it communicates a hidden and profound meaning to those who listen. The man who reads with penetration, having cast away the outer shell of falsehood, finds the savory kernel of truth wrapped within.[90]

Here, too, the savoring of the "kernel of truth" seems only possible at the expense of casting away "the outer shell of falsehood." If we keep in mind that this is the poet himself speaking—not even the commentator—we realize the extent to which the medieval "symbolist mind," to use Père Chenu's fitting term,[91] was free of self-consciousness with regard to the discrepancy between the stubborn fact of the existence of poetry in an intellectual atmosphere of disenfranchisement and the perception that "the soul's" and "the seeing heart's" truths, in their evasiveness and volatility as states of experience and cognition, yet demanded the power of verbalized concrete presence. To try to contain them with poetry was to affirm the paradox, like the proverbial fighting fire with fire. The medieval poet, particularly the poet of the "symbolist mind," stood facing his increasingly complex poetry in amazed innocence. He saw it coming on him and passing by him like a river. He could drink of it, fill his small vessels from it or send them down to sea, but he knew that that river was treacherous, that he had no real control over it and that, as he ran his hand through its water, it was escaping his grasp.[92]

It was precisely in this atmosphere of ambiguity with regard to poetry, in this prepsychological love-hate relationship, that symbolism could develop, reach so deeply, and spread so widely with so very little ballast of general critical concern and even less of theoretical rationalization of the creative poetic process.

A certain process of rationalization was going on nonetheless. In fact, it had been lingering in the background since Plato presented theoretic literary criticism with the paradox of admitting poetry into his own world of thought while denying poets access to the social realm of his ideal state. It was Plato's rationalized distrust of poetry as a weapon that is likely to fall into the wrong hands which was then transmitted to the Church fathers—like Jerome and Augustine—only to come to its full "theoretical" flower among the Platonizing poet-theologians of twelfth-century Christian Europe.[93]

But the resulting accentuation of poetic ambiguity failed to be taken into account. Perturbing on unexplored levels, the intrusion of the poetic phenomenon into the serene sphere of the mind and the spirit, or rather of opinion and faith, was only explained away, rationalized away. The easiest way to do this was to restrict criticism to the formalistic level of a neatly presented dichotomy, with the poetic aspect as the form and the conceptual one as the content, after which a clear and rigid hierarchy of values would place the poetic aspect into due subordination. In this guise poetry was confirmed in its usefulness, and the paradox, never solved, appeared dormant.

The antipoetic bias that is not to be entirely separated from Plato's attitudes is also apparent in Muḥammad, the Prophet and also the initiator of the Arabic tradition of the Platonic paradox. The Sūrah of the Poets as a whole, not only verses 224–26, is an indictment of carriers of false messages, who throughout the cyclic history of prophetic messianism were the antagonists of every rightful messenger of each cycle. It is only in Muḥammad's own cycle that the explicit term "poets" is given to the antagonists. Poets, therefore, are not harmless, and their means of persuading "those likely to be led into error" have certain traits in common with the means employed by the true messengers. This becomes clear in the confrontation between Moses and the Egyptian sorcerers. In fact, Moses uses the means of the sorcerers. The result is quite simple: the stronger magic wins. The confrontation of the final cycle is only implicitly postulated: it takes place between the Prophet and the poets. Here, too, the stronger of the antagonists will win, and the poets will eventually bow down before him, not unlike the Egyptian sorcerers who prostrated themselves before Moses (vv. 45–47). If the differing means which make up the magic aspect of persuasive argumentation in both cases allow only a metaphoric analogy, the emerging metaphor nevertheless converges on the point of the special nature of the magic-poetic act.[94]

It is through this magic-poetic act, however, inasmuch as it is a claim to knowledge of the nature of things, that representations endowed with their own reality may come to exist in the mind—supposedly representations only, imaginary things, but the product of a creative process nonetheless. And it is through this claim that this magic-poetic act approaches most closely the religious realm of reality as interpreted—creatively represented in human terms as it were—by the prophets. In the end the claim is to what is real, and the contention, too, is for what is real. The contention becomes less pointed and purposeful as soon as the religious articulation of the vision of the real turns into theological conceptualization assisted by a philosophy living off its own self as logic. Here the resulting separation of idiom reaches to the roots. The theologically logical argument loses its commonness of idiom with the poetic act. The hostility of alienation now takes the place of what had once been the hostility of contention. Furthermore, as Herbert Reed would probably want to say, to the extent to which poetry retains—in particular, through the idiom of the symbol—its original grasp on the creative act of the spirit and the imagination, theology and philosophy will be with respect to poetry in the ex post facto relationship of the commentary.[95]

There is no denying that a mystic understanding of Ibn al-Fāriḍ's poem is possible. More than that: one must concede that without such an understanding, or such a reading, what is experientially real in the poem would lack its full dimensionality. The poem's intensity of experience would dilute itself too much in the aestheticist vagueness of very traditional tropes and topicality. The poem's hope would still be an awareness, like Wordsworth's in *The Prelude,* "Of words in tuneful order," to be found sweet "For their own *sakes,* a passion and a power."[96] Or, as in Dante's famous canzone, the poem should be able to say to us: "Consider at least how beautiful I am!"[97] But the delicately balanced formal structure, held together by the mystic quest of the poet's soul, would cease to be quite so self-explanatory. The poem would revert to being a diffused conglomerate of powerful but unrelated *nasīb* elements. However much one may therefore try to remain unaffected by the forced, schematized transcendentalism of mystic theology as it emerges from the poem's interpretive commentaries, and however much one should shun the pitfalls of the artificial rigor of quid pro quo mystic equivalences, Ibn al-Fāriḍ's poem is, to the very recognizable extent to which it is a self-contained artistic whole, also a record of an emotive response to certain stirrings of a soul bent upon regaining its own self through a transcending leap or gesture. As a poem, however, and particularly as an Arabic poem that has grown out of a very precisely defined tradition of form and genre, it imposes on itself a harness of definitiveness and of patterned articulation.

These confines, then, are also the true horizon of the available poetic vision in the literary-historical sense. And, after all the explorations into the background of the historically definable tensions in the poetic idiom, into the conflicts between message and means, and into the detached dimensionality of a superstructure of rarefied mysticism that wants to transcend both poetic meaning and means, what remains is once again the poem itself: possibly enriched, certainly more complex, but still the poem itself. As such it guides us back to the main problem that has concerned us throughout, but whose peripheries always appear so rich in entanglements. This problem in perpetual evidence is the existence within the Arabic lyrical genre of essential structural elements that are archetypal and whose presence in a poem is that of anchoring, meaning-bearing symbols; and it is furthermore the fact that every such symbol is expressed in quintessential theme condensations. The archetypal nuclei provide Arabic poetry with its only organically valid repertory of symbolic references, but they also lie too deeply immersed in the poetic matter to have been consciously apprehended in an age which had its eyes set on other critical targets.

These symbols pointed to the main concerns of Arabic poetry in all its ages and in all its stages of development. The condensations of themes which crystallized around these archetypal symbols enabled a poem to be constructed, thus presenting a semblance of cohesiveness and expansiveness in what was basically a symbolic statement. The poem's texture was what medieval commentators and theorists had foremost in mind, which they thought could be explained away as form after the meaning had been salvaged. The fact that the meaning itself is not separable by a code of equivalences from the other two levels, that it was conceived and made in the poetic texture and not in the afterthought of any precise mystic doctrine, and that, if forcibly separated, it could only become something other than what the poet meant to say—this did not enter into the medieval theory of the symbol as derived from the mystic commentaries.[98] The interpretation based on an imposition of word-for-word mystical equivalences is fallacious when applied to poetry such as Ibn al-Fāriḍ's. Whatever symbolic effectiveness of meaning survives this process does so only insofar as it draws upon the central symbolic archetypes which underlie all Arabic poetry. Mystic equivalences as the sole substitute for the poem's meaning produce not only a nonpoetic but also a nonsymbolic paraphrase. All symbolic energy still dwells in the poem, and mysticism as experience needs that energy, because without it it turns into mere theology of mysticism, a scheme imposed from the outside.

If now we are left with Ibn al-Fāriḍ's poem again, we realize that we have come full circle, back to the problems first raised by the growing symbolic permeability of the classically rooted *nasīb*. This *nasīb*, as we have learned, demands, critically, a constant renewal of interpretation even as it is constantly renewing itself in the alchemist's forge of a poetic vision which filters through historical changes in new moods and preoccupations. The poetic vision of the mystic Ibn al-Fāriḍ was one of seemingly irreconcilable contradictions. In it a passionate exaltation of sense-bound experience is contrasted in a highly charged polarity with the need to transcend matter, to achieve a total release, an abstraction, of the spirit. Such contradiction, unavoidable in transcendentalized mysticism (in opposition to a mysticism of pantheist symbiosis), could find a particularly fitting embodiment precisely in a *nasīb* that had become all-dimensionally flexible: that could be sense-bound to the point of being earthy, emotive and musing to the point of being sentimental, but that could also abstract itself from the realms of object and feeling alike and open avenues of intimation of mystic progressions and self-transcending unions. The symbolic dimension that allowed such intimations—all three avenues, in fact—had its beginning in the poem, and the poem had its beginning in the *nasīb,* and the *nasīb* had its beginning in very ancient yearnings. This is what Ibn al-Fāriḍ affirms unequivocally in his own poem, and this is what makes it possible to view it critically, and indeed interpretively even in the mystic sense, within the great tradition of Arabic poetic forms and archetypes. The understanding of the poetic work that this tradition facilitates is, in a critically controlled sense, more objective than what all the impersonal theology of mystic codes and equivalences supplies. In it words retain their texture even when they are diaphanous symbols of transcendencies; and where such texture still exists, there is no need to overstep the ancient internal-symbolic wealth of the *nasīb* in search of external codes and keys. A live poetic form is its own guide and key, and the *nasīb* is still alive in Ibn al-Fāriḍ. Indeed, within the historical logic of the whole process of its development as a repertory of symbols, the *nasīb* in its present translucency has evolved to its highest form of life or measure of poetic efficacy. At the same time, however, it has reached the outer limits of a development that had run its full course.

THREE

Names, Privileged Places, Idylls

1. *When Toponymy Becomes Poetry*

IN THE ARABIC POEM, and particularly in the *nasīb,* there are never-ending recurrences of certain words which have come to be regarded as key elements of the Arabic poetic lexicon. These words are names: names of mountains, dunes, rivers, wells, stretches of desert, tribal grounds, regions. There are equally unending insistences on motifs of arrivals at abandoned campsites, of departures from the tribal grounds, of sorrow over such arrivals and departures and over the emptiness that always lies before and after them, and of the glimpse of happiness in between—just enough happiness to reduce everything else to unceasing yearning. The place-names are seemingly self-explanatory. One could assume that they are meant to bring everything within an objective perspective of a landscape, particularly since they occur most often in conjunction with those other, less objective but equally often repeated motifs of arrivals and departures, of short happiness and long yearning. To assume only a concrete, objectivizing function for the numerous place references in the Arabic poem, and particularly in the *nasīb,* would, however, be hasty at best. Poets may make use of the mood of the *nasīb* to give strength to their personal and immediate feelings. Sensitive poets do precisely that. Regardless of references to actual localities, however, the ancient metaphor locked in the *nasīb* is never far away—even if a given poem, or fragment, is truncated and deprived of the full structural context of the *qaṣīdah.* Thus there is little doubt about the provenance of the mood of the lines by al-Qāḍī al-Fāḍil (d. 596/1200), the poet who, as a young boy, drank from the water of the Nile and remained faithful to it for life. While following Saladin to the shores of the Euphrates, he has thoughts only for his beloved Nile:

> By God, tell the Nile from me
> That Euphrates' waters
> could not quench my thirst.
>
> Many a Buthaynah you left there, O heart,
> While here I invoke your patience
> not to falter.[1] [60]

The poet's thoughts of his adopted river flow over into the essential imagery of the *nasīb,* where they join the stream of the old elegiac mood which is more lingering and insinuating than that which the verses in their surface meaning would be capable of depositing in the imagination. As part of the *nasīb* feeling, his immediate mood of sadness and yearning thus issues into a broad sea of kindred harmonies of experience, striking echoes of a distant archetypal nature.

This characteristic *nasīb* framing of a concrete place-name reappears even more pronouncedly in another poem by al-Qāḍī al-Fāḍil, in which he allows his yearning to take him back to his native Syria (al-Shām):

> Shām alone on earth is all-surpassing,
> So speak no more of other horizons!
>
> O wind that comes from Shām, O messenger,
> Bearing the pains of lovers' want,
>
> When your breeze visits my armor's tunic,
> It is an embrace soothing to the heart.
>
> So let my tears be yearning's runways,
> Then speed along like the noblest steeds!
>
> My eyes have hoarded such stores of tears:
> Take pains, O cares, to spend them
>
> Where dew is like the enchanter's spittle,
> The rustle of the breeze as though a sorcerer's spell.
>
> Hail, then, to the nights gone by
> From one tormented by the nights to come.
>
> After the loss of Shām, I'll yet remember it,
> For there with yearning turns my heart.

Memory so limned it to my eyes
That now, as though through gardens,
    I walk in the pupils' round.

May silver clouds not keep from it their salutations
That garb the bough with leaves' finest brocade,

And may God visit upon distance the torments of distance,
And give to separation of its own bitter taste![2] [61]

It is in a rare instance only (and significantly enough at a point in time when Arab history had justified the replacement of the profound elegiac melancholy of the classical *nasīb* by a self-satisfied, forward-looking idyll) that new, contemporary place-names are introduced into *nasīb*-like openings of poems with the ultimate intent to praise rather than to bemoan. The formal result of such inversions becomes then a new, primarily descriptive (*waṣf*) pseudo-*nasīb,* and as such objective rather than subjective. Manṣūr al-Namarī (d. ca. 193/809) of the golden early-Abbasid moment, illustrates this development toward a new, descriptive poetic optic:

Baghdad, what rich diversity it holds,
What wonders to grace creed and state:

Of dewy narcissus between Quṭrubbul and Karkh,
Of beds of gillyflowers, eglantines.

There souls live diffused in perfumed breath
And silently stir in sweet basil leaves.

May blessings rain down on those towering mansions
And on their wide-eyed does in human guise!

There the Tigris blithely flows,
And you see dark-coated ships like horses heaving,

Loggias with doors flung open,
Gracefully trimmed and decked,

Castles that wing their eager way
Carrying visitor to visited,

Each one a true fire-ship,
A castle rising from the deck, colonnaded, tall.[3] [62]

Nevertheless, a more form-conscious level of analysis will in this case, too, reveal the poet's compelling dependence on the model from which he tries to depart.[4] Thus not only are his *diyār*-evoking references to Baghdad, Quṭrubbul, and Karkh precisely where place-names in the *nasīb* ought to occur (vv. 1–2), but his "wonders" (v. 1) of the present moment, too, can only be the obverse of the coin of the antiquity and desolation of his formal model, the "ruinous abodes." The bringing into the picture of the "wide-eyed does" (v. 4) is then followed by what ought to be recognized formally as a pseudo-*ẓaʿn,* in which refined ladies of Baghdad are seen seeking recreation on festively arrayed pleasure-barks (vv. 5–8).[5]

Even this poet, however, is more likely to seek poetic recourse to traditionally attested place-names of *nasīb* provenance. Among the favored ones is always al-Ḥimā, with its meaning of "hallowed precinct," and when such a name is wrested from the past, it makes the poet hesitant about the light mood of pure idyll and ready to return to elegy, the mood that owes its melancholy to its formal indebtedness to the *nasīb:*

> Many a halting place was yours at al-Ḥimā
> When there the tribes in medley throngs,
>
> When short the days there
> And long the joy,
>
> When stars of good fortune ascended
> And ill-boding stars declined,
>
> When Mālikīyah and youth,
> When songstress and cool wine. . . .[6] [63]

Arabic *nasīb* lyricism may also quite comfortably mix contexts and interlace its references to poetic places old and new, symbolic and concrete. Thus Ibn ʿUmayrah al-Makhzūmī, a seventh/thirteenth-century poet from al-Andalus, will talk of his sorrow over the loss of Valencia by first invoking ancient Bedouin passions of the heart (vv. 1–2) and that heart's yearning for its autochthonous place of repose, the distant Najd of Arabia (v. 3). Only then may he give himself the poetic license to elicit the concrete place-name of Valencia (v. 7), for such a Valencia will now be endowed with the poetically validated, elegiac quality of a "lost Paradise" (v. 10):

> O heart, you who proclaim this ardent passion,
> Must love's intemperance be so manifest?
>
> But can a lovelorn one hope to forget
> Love's agony of thirst, rejection's awesome jolt?

He yearns for Najd, but all in vain!
The adverse turns of time have doomed him never to return.

O mountain of water-sated verdure, like none I knew,
How time's ill turns of fortune slighted your spring.

And O you people that I love—but events now exact
That I stand alone, apart from those who merit love—

Will pleasure one day be bared of desire,
When to us it bodes denial at all times?

After the woe that befell Valencia,
Will beacons in the heart still shine with secret candescence?

People hope for shields against afflictions
That transfix them with their pliant spears.

Yet would that I knew, will she once more rise,
Will her star return as it once was?

Or did the sons sin their fathers' sins
And bring upon themselves expulsion from Paradise?[7] [64]

For the most part, due precisely to the need for a tone-setting elegiac validation, the landscape of the *nasīb,* or of *nasīb*-related verse, expands around names of places which are symbolic denotations only. Such places may have existed—indeed, many may still be geographically identifiable—but poetically this is no longer important. We do not even know whether the place-names in the most ancient Arabic odes were ever more than evocative moorings for those entirely ethereal effusions of loss and yearning which form the mood of the *nasīb.* With some certainty, albeit poetic certainty, we may thus assume that, at least within the *nasīb* proper, references to places are for the most part of an indirect, symbolic nature, and that particularly in post-Jāhilīyah poetry their metaphorization and symbolic saturation become fully consummated. Furthermore, the recurrence of those ancient Arabian references increases in those outer fringes of Arabic poetry which in time and geography had grown the farthest apart from the matrix of Bedouin time and place. There those names, those words, become purely poetic entities. No other reality is demanded of them. Indeed, too abrupt a concretization would rob them of their poetically magnetic, evocative aura.

Marcel Proust describes his youthful daydreams of distant places that had meaning to him because they had names which in themselves were magic words—Florence, Parma, Pisa, Venice—all glorious evocations of hope, close to the sense of touching the semblance of Paradise. Such an illusion, "and the same readiness of our dreams to be magnetized by place-names," comments Maud Bodkin, "has given to these a distinctive value and power in poetry."[8] But Proust goes so far as to insist on the preference for vagueness over certainty and for the remotest intuition that such places exist over precise description and qualification. He reveals the whole magic of the matter by telling us so charmingly that although his response of exultation at the prospect of experiencing those Italian cities "had as the basic motive the desire to enjoy artistic delights, yet, more than by books on aesthetics, it was nourished by travel guides and, even more, by train schedules."[9]

Proust's magic names, which were symbolically most effective when divested of their concretizing circumstance, had become the special topography of his imaginative, or poetic, state. As John Stevens observes in his discussion of that world of the imagination that is medieval romance, such a transformation of places into names necessarily occurs at the expense of a real, or material, link with concrete time and space, which are rendered poetically subordinate, or even irrelevant, through the internalization of vision. Thus he notes that "to a large degree the greater importance of images in romance results from the lack of a sense of space and time," allowing the heroes of romance to live, move, and act in a "faceless landscape," which is, however, "*not a nameless one* [emphasis mine]; but the names themselves are liable to tell us more about the spiritual adventures of questing knights than about a countryside (Le Chastel de Pesme Aventure, Le Pont de l'Espee, and so forth)." Such a landscape should not yield to "precise geography." Everything in it takes its meaning from the "experience being conveyed."[10]

The Arabic lyrical ear will easily register at this point modal congruities with the pronounced tendency toward "interiorization" in the Abbasid *nasīb*. In ʿAlī Ibn al-Jahm's (d. 249/863) *nasīb,* for instance, all place-names become internalized visions. Like echoes of remote, reawakened passion, they are what the poet "knows and does not know":

Does' eyes between Ruṣāfah and the Pont
Ushered in passion—whence I know
 and I know not.

Back they brought the ancient longing,
 though I had not forgot,
And threw embers upon embers.[11] [65]

The dreamy eyes of oryx-cows draw here a trajectory of longing across the River Tigris between two topographically easily identifiable points and early landmarks of caliphal Baghdad. But then, al-Ruṣāfah, which in this image seems to echo the poet's sighs of longing, sending them toward, or across, the Pont (al-Jisr), is not merely the residential and recreational palace on the left bank of the river built originally by al-Manṣūr (the caliph who founded the round city of Baghdad)[12] that was once the pride of Hārūn al-Rashīd and then gave its name to a populous suburb rich in noble mansions; nor is it quite the memory of the Ruṣāfah of Hishām, that older, now ruinous, recreational lodge of a preceding dynasty that was still Bedouin enough to have sensed and sought out nostalgically the existential and symbolic contrast of desert and water,[13] for, as a word alone, not necessarily as a place-name, al-Ruṣāfah allows for rich, lyrically effective visualizations. On the one hand it implies the compactness and firmness of stone; but that stone is necessarily associated with water, *mā' al-raṣaf* being "rock-water." Furthermore, it brings to mind the idea of the building of a pier or embankment. As such it carries imagist sensibility to the very edge of that which is its semantic opposite. From there, too, it implies the anticipation and the longing for the other bank of the river. Al-Ruṣāfah, in brief, was to the poet a name and a word that implied semantic tension and yearning for its opposite.

Such etymology will also explain the poetic nexus that exists in Arabic between al-Ruṣāfah and al-Jisr and their appearance together in contexts of mutually reinforcing elegiac yearning. In its plain meaning, the latter is a strong insinuation of the former, and even more than that, it allows us to understand the other correctly in its poetic function. Thus *jisr,* with its Aramaic and Arabic etymologies, can mean "embankment" or "dam" quite explicitly, whereas al-Ruṣāfah only points to this etymologically. Furthermore, in a poetically more commanding way, *jisr* means a bridge that spans and crosses, just as *jasara* as a verb means not only "to build a bridge" but also "to cross as one crosses a stretch of water or a desert." Poetically indispensably, too, *jasara* also means "to dare," "to venture upon something (an adventure?)."

What we thus obtain in the two *nasīb* lines by ʿAlī Ibn al-Jahm is not so much a landscape or a topography of caliphal Baghdad as a complex metaphor built out of internalized *loci* where yearning occurs, or where it is possible. Between al-Ruṣāfah and al-Jisr there comes into being a "pont" unlike that of the adventure of the sword in Chrétien de Troyes (*Lancelot,* vv. 680–82) but rather one capable of lyrically transforming adventure into the trajectory of the sigh. In this it does not name itself as does the Venetian Bridge of Sighs. Instead it adheres to the aesthetically much more efficacious option of deconcretization within a metaphor. It thus avoids the danger of the banality of lyrical long-windedness and explicitness to which even admittedly poetic names may fall victim.[14]

As much as we are entitled to take for granted the Arab poet's appreciation of the lyrical efficacy of place-names, we must not necessarily expect comparable sensitivity from medieval Arabic literary critics, for these critics acted primarily as textual authenticators and exegetes. They sidestepped the poetic implications of the massive presence of toponymy, especially in the pre-Islamic *nasīb,* and saw in it no more than its lexical-philological materiality. With ease, poetic place-names could subsequently be reduced to "textually" validated entries in geographical lexicons and compendia. The ubiquitousness of place-names in the early Arabic *nasīb* could also move critics to bemused irony as well as to irony that was not bemused, but aggressive and mordant. The latter was the case with the Ashʿarite theologian and inveterate dabbler in literary criticism al-Bāqillānī (d. 403/1013), who took issue with Imruʾ al-Qays's *Muʿallaqah,* which is the *locus classicus* of pre-Islamic *nasīb* toponymy:

> Halt, let us weep, you two and I, as we remember
> beloved and campsite
> At the winding dune's crest, between al-Dakhūl
> and Ḥawmal,
>
> Then Tūḍiḥ, then al-Miqrāt, its impress not erased
> By what the winds weaved south and north.[15] [66]

In al-Bāqillānī's view such a geodetic "recording of places and naming of localities" fails to serve a useful purpose, since a more limited reference to the locale that witnessed the poet's sorrow would have sufficed. Imruʾ al-Qays, however, "was not content with one specification but went so far as to make it four specifications, as if he wished to buy the campsite and was afraid that, if he made a mistake in one of the demarcations, the purchase would be void and its conditions invalid."[16] In its sociologically curious alienation from autochthonous Bedouinity, al-Bāqillānī's banalizing wit has thus transformed Imruʾ al-Qays's ancient tribal campsite into an urban real estate prospect. Falsely objectivized as a target of irony, such a place is thus rendered lyrically inoperative. Since al-Bāqillānī's motivating impulse was extra-literary to the extent to which he was championing the exclusivist proposition of the inimitability of the Qurʾān (*iʿjāz al-Qurʾān*),[17] he was, of course, essaying his prowess more in diatribe than in literary analysis and more in apologetics than in criticism. To him the dialectical battle lines drawn in the Sūrah of the Poets were still bristling with combat readiness.

Imru᾿ al-Qays's place-names, however, suggested the quadrature of an elusive geography of a kind quite alien to a "land surveyor" like al-Bāqillānī. The toponymy does not confer geographical location but serves rather to situate the privileged space, the poet's *siqṭ al-liwā,* in the memory and in the imagination.

Indeed, the first line of Imru᾿ al-Qays's ode does not yet speak of an actual arrival at the place described as *siqṭ al-liwā*. It is a call to halt as if at a distance, to remember, and to weep over what once was a beloved's campsite—"over there," where the crested dune curves (*bi siqṭ al-liwā*). The actual arrival takes place only in verse 3 ("There stopped my companions"), that is, after having imaginatively entered the inner space of the quadrature. If we continue along this line of interpretation, our questions about the special circumscription of privileged places in the classical Arabic *nasīb* are bound to lead us to entirely archetypal answers—or to further entirely archetypal questions—such as why there are four rivers mentioned as flowing out of the Garden of Eden (Genesis 2:10ff.), since those rivers do not concretize the geography of that garden; nor are they meant to be guides that will lead all desirous pilgrims to that place that was lost only to be yearned for ever since.[18]

To sample further the lure of place-names in Arabic poetry, we can choose almost at random. For instance, we notice that certain river-names in the *qaṣīdah,* such as the Euphrates, experience various degrees of metaphorization. Their abundance of water becomes an expression of generosity, their strong currents an attribute of power, the goodness of their water an echo, both qur᾿ānic and pre-qur᾿ānic, of al-Kawthar, the stream of Paradise. These metaphors can mix or become comprehensive symbols, but a river like the Euphrates, especially if used poetically outside the *nasīb,* may nevertheless return to its physical dimensionality within an identifiable landscape.[19]

One particular river in the Arabic poetic tradition, however, has consistently reappeared in contexts of landscape and mood which are symbolic beyond a merely functional metaphoric applicability. This river, or rather this river's name, is the ʿAqīq. Contrary to what textual commentary would suggest, little about its geographical identity, as well as its appearance in literature, is clear or certain. It may not even be a true river, but a riverbed which lies dry for the greater part of the Arabian year. It might have been first the ʿAqīq near the city of Medina, but that is certainly no waterway worthy of capturing a nation's poetic imagination over generations and centuries, or it may have been another semidry riverbed of that Arabia so empty of things and so full of names. And yet, in both the East and the West, old and not-so-old Arabic poetry has clung to the ʿAqīq as one of its most permanent motifs.[20] And that is what it is: a motif, not merely a name or a metaphor that has to be construed in each new poetic instance. As motif it is part of the poetic idea embodied in that peculiarly suggestive landscape that may be called pastoral, idyllic, or, in an archetypal way, a vestige of man's dream of the earth when it was good. It is a metaphor of sweetness, joy, and garden surroundings, too, and it is a poetic convention. But like all conventions which sprout near cultural roots, it holds within itself its central meaning, its etymology of symbolic memory; only thus could it have achieved poetic survival.

In its earliest appearance in the pre-Islamic *qaṣīdah* the ʿAqīq seems to be but one of the many topographic references to the elegiac landscape of the *nasīb*. Even then, however, its place in the key verses that are the bearers of the elegiac mood begins to be recognizable. Thus in a poem attributed to Imruʾ al-Qays, a reference to the ʿAqīq concludes the *nasīb* and reinforces the sense of distance suggested in the preceding verse:

> And after them I sent my gaze, when already
> There stood between us
> dunes crested with aloes and myrtle:
>
> In the wake of a tribe bound for a distant land,
> Then settling at the ʿAqīq—
> or at the pass of Muṭriq.[21] [67]

In the *Muʿallaqah* of al-Ḥārith Ibn Ḥillizah it occurs in an analogous position of ascending feeling in the *nasīb,* just before the verse of transition to another theme:

> Hind lit a fire for you to see
> At evening time, to beckon from the heights.
>
> She kindled it between the ʿAqīq and Shakhṣān,
> With aloes-wood, bright as daylight.[22] [68]

In a poem by Durayd Ibn al-Ṣimmah it is part of the scenery in an opening verse as the only elegiac vestige in an otherwise truncated *nasīb* which has to accommodate itself to the subsequent tone of satirical reproach:

Whose ruins are these at Dhāt al-Khams,
of but yesterday,
Swept away between the ʿAqīq and Baṭn Ḍars?[23] [69]

It is in the later periods of urban and courtly poetic refinement that the motif of the ʿAqīq achieves the fullest symbolic crystallization, passing through a transformation from the Bedouin elegy to a courtly elegy and finally to a nostalgic idyll. Thus in al-Buḥturī (d. 284/897):

I beseech the rain its morning clouds to empty
Over the ʿAqīq, although abodes lie there in desolation,

A place upon whose days days smile, and
On whose nights smile nights.[24] [70]

So, too, in the finely tempered lyricism of al-Buḥturī's contemporary ʿAlī Ibn al-Jahm:

This is the ʿAqīq, rein in
The amber camels in their rush![25] [71]

Or in a lesser poet:

We passed by the banks of the ʿAqīq,
And alive with grass became the torrent beds
drenched by our eyelids.[26] [72]

Until in remote al-Andalus, with most abandon, it acquires its full idyllic aura, and thus a semblance of dislocation from the old Bedouin context. To the Cordovan poet Ibn Zaydūn (d. 463/1071), the ʿAqīq appears with a bridge. It is certainly not the remote riverbed of Arabia. Now it is the river epitomized, in which poets everywhere take delight. Physically it may be the Guadalquivir, or any other of the known rivers of the broad Arab domains. As a symbol, however, it will always be the ʿAqīq:

On many an encounter
by the ʿAqīq, at the bridge,
We sat on flowers red and yellow,

My gazelle-fawn pouring
of its wine the best.[27] [73]

Another pristine lyricist of al-Andalus, Ibn Khafājah (d. 533/1137) of Alcira, near Valencia, wishes gentle breezes to carry his greetings to where love has gone, to cast a lingering glance upon the ʿAqīq, to roam for awhile in its "memorable places," and then, between al-Kathīb and al-Ḥimā, between "the dune" and "the sacred tribal enclosure," to deposit kisses over the tracks of those who have left.[28] Here, too, al-Kathīb and al-Ḥimā have long since ceased being anything but place-names. Such references are thus no longer obscure rivers, places of ancient habitation, memorable dunes, and hallowed tribal grounds, not even when philologically minded commentators insist on designating them as such. Suspended in poetic tension between primary meanings with their reverberating etymologies and place-names, they are fully imaginary locations which are nothing and nowhere—if the poet were asked to explain himself—but which are everything and whose places are clearly felt as "the abodes of the hearts" (*fī al-qulūbi manāzilu*) of al-Mutanabbī, never seen by the poet, having no contours, only presence.

The poetic power of these ancient names expands and embraces everything. When the above-mentioned Ibn Khafājah turns in an elegiac apostrophe to his companions, asking them to talk to him of youth, which, as we hear later in the poem, is mostly the memory of a night at the elusory al-Liwā (v. 9), he addresses them rather mystifyingly by calling them Ḥimyarites:

> Stirred to passion by narcissus' fragrance
> As it met the coolness of the eastern breeze,
> I said:
>
> Friends, Himyarites, speak to this graying fellow
> Of the nights of youth![29] [74]

To Ibn Khafājah the ancient southern Arabian Ḥimyarites were legendary at best. Although his companions may have been of southern Arabian lineage and his own genealogical identity through the tribal name Khafājah as a branch of Kindah was purportedly southern Arabian too, all the poet really wants here is the sound of those ancient and remote names. His mood of nostalgia and melancholy absorbs all distant echoes especially avidly—distant in time and distant in place but racially close and intimate as heritage, not at all in need of an externally validated context.

2. *Najd and Arcadia: The Topology of Nostalgia*

Aside from the numerous, diversified, and often seemingly incidental occurrences in the *nasīb* of place-names which are either difficult to identify or which should not be identified, Arabic poetry also delights in reveries over entire regions of the Arabian Peninsula, like Tihāmah, the Ḥijāz, and, above all, Najd. These broader elegiac musings or idylls are post-Jāhilī, thus of a later age in the overall chronology of theme and motif developments of the *nasīb* and its offshoots.[30] By and large they are datable within that early Islamic (late seventh to early eighth century A.D.) revival of Bedouin lyricism which culminated in the passionate, sentimental, and idealizing poetry known as ʿUdhrī, named after the tribe of the poet Jamīl, the lover of Buthaynah. As designation, the term "ʿUdhrī" was then used more broadly for a whole school of self-immolating poets of the central Arabian Desert. Their poetry, together with what it engendered of biographical and explanatory notations (*akhbār*), which in some cases form veritable romances approaching those of the Hellenistic period, well merits being seen as an Arabic corpus of *erōtika pathēmata* ("stories of erotic suffering").[31] The *erōtikon pathos* of Majnūn Laylā, the only wholly legendary figure among those poets, is quite paradigmatic in its fictionality as well as in its archetypal quality.

To place this exaltation of poetically favored regions squarely into the aesthetics of a school such as ʿUdhrism is valid for our discussion mainly because it helps identify an early focal point of a type of Bedouin yearning which will soon spread, finding for itself a particularly fertile emotional soil in the outlying provinces of the sprawling new empire of Arabizing Islamdom. There it will live on as a desire to seize the autochthonous symbol.

The concentration of the idyllic-elegiac effusion in Arabic poetry on such regions, easily observable toward the end of the Umayyad period, may have had various causes. Ṭāhā Ḥusayn properly notices the air of melancholy and yearning for the idealized Najd among the poets of the ʿUdhrī school. Inasmuch as he relies on a vaguely formulated sociology of rising expectations, however, his interpretation of the phenomenon is one-sided. In his view, the now Islamized Bedouin poets had been influenced by the idealizing and refining factors in their new faith, but they did not join in the new civilization and its benefits. Thus, in isolation and facing the frustration of their awakened material expectations, these poets turned inward, complaining and idealizing, their complaint being aimed at the present conditions and their idealizing at the past, presumably before Islam, when life was better or when those new expectations did not exist.[32]

On the other hand, changing our perspective and allowing it to comprise the later centuries of Arabic cultural attitudes, we notice most strongly perhaps the presence of a centrifugal movement in the political and social life of the Arabian Peninsula, a movement which also begins to threaten the old cultural moorings of the Bedouin poet.

The staunchly parochial Bedouin, in spite of his seasonal restlessness, had been only marginally aware of the world outside the region of his pendular nomadic movement. Within that region he knew every stretch of desert, every abandoned and possible campground, every marking of the trail. The region as a whole, however, he saw only from within. Only the inner discrete space had strong objective contours and imaginative validity. The whole was not yet visible, at least not from the outside, where it would offer a surface to the imagination and, as a rounded poetic entity with its own name, would conjure all the symbolic magic of possession. The Bedouin poet thus began possessing Tihāmah, the Ḥijāz, and, above all, Najd when he stepped out of them; and when he had lost these regions in the dispersion of the empire,[33] these places, these names, then possessed him. Such possession implied the awareness of loss through the great paradox of the nostalgic seizing of time—of time one once had and also of that much larger time to which one's soul feels a compelling affinity, to which it must return because it itself is possessed. The end of the nostalgic process is always the return of all the waters to the sea.

Among the numerous instances of the early manifestation of this regional nostalgic spirit is the poetry attributed to Majnūn, who seems to have been invented precisely to accommodate such feelings. It celebrates to an equal degree the beloved Laylā and Najd:

> As nights go by, even as I despair of ever returning,
> I yearn for Najd.
>
> Were there no Laylā and no Najd, admit
> That you'd forsake all till Judgment Day.[34] [75]

And again in a line given to Majnūn but also to the flesh-and-blood poet Ibn al-Dumaynah (d. 143/760), whose lyricism is that of Najd even if his provenance is traced to other regions of Arabia:

> O East Wind of the highlands,
> when did you stir from Najd?
> You journey through the night
> and passion upon passion add![35] [76]

Majnūn speaks of Najd and the Ḥijāz together:

> I long for the land of the Ḥijāz, and of the tents in Najd
> is my want—too far for eyes to reach.
>
> My gazing toward Najd indeed may be in vain,
> and yet for this I look the more![36] [77]

Even more representative of the early elegiac treatment of Najd are the two fragments, or short poems, contained in the *Ḥamāsah* attributed to the Umayyad poet al-Ṣimmah Ibn ʿAbd Allāh al-Qushayrī. One is a pristinely nostalgic elegy:

> Pause, say farewell to Najd and to those
> who dwell on sacred tribal grounds!
> But who of us can ever say farewell to Najd?
>
> My life I'd give for this land, its hills so comely,
> So good its grass both spring and summertime!
>
> The evenings of those native pastures
> shall not return,
> But let the tears run freely, let them. . . .[37] [78]

The second song to Najd carries the "genre" one step further. It is significant that Friedrich Rückert clearly recognized the character of this poem when he gave it the descriptive title "Farewell to Idyllic Highlands."[38]

> To my companion I say, while amber camels rush
> with us downslope:
>
> Delight in the fragrance of the oxeye of the Najd,
> for come the night it will be gone!
>
> O lovely breezes from the Najd,
> perfume of meadows after nightfall!
>
> O happy people when there the tribe sets camp,
> and you are carefree, and all is well!
>
> Months pass, yet we heed not how quickly
> full moons are dwindling.[39] [79]

This is pure idyll. As landscape, Najd has become transformed into an arrested poetic vision. It is the desert abloom in the poet's memory long after the rain of spring is lost in vaporous figments of mirages and long after the desert has reverted to its nearly year long inclemency. It is all the poet chooses to remember and to live by. To say that this particular poet's Najd never existed does not invalidate the vision. His and every true poet's Najd existed when it was retained poetically as a chosen moment. The merit of al-Ṣimmah's idyllic poem is that we, too, are experiencing Najd as a moment that will become unforgettable as our own *et in Arcadia ego.*

Other, later poets will reduce the Najd motif to its purely abstract, symbolic value. It will be the aim and the road of all yearning. Thus, with his usual high sense of drama, the blind Syrian Abū al-ʿAlāʾ al-Maʿarrī lets natural forces yearn, strive, and despair in pursuit of Najd. In only two verses he gives us a characteristic Arabic poetic quintessence of the elegiac, the pastoral, and perhaps the mythic:

> A rain cloud rife, how seaward it drove its mounts;
> And when their thirst was quenched,
> yearning betook it toward Najd.
>
> Against it with his host rose the eolian king.
> He tore it asunder—without will or whim.[40] [80]

And to a poet of remote Valencia, too, Najd and Tihāmah are above all exquisite, rarefied mental images of roads never traveled, goals never attained:

> O tents in Najd! But before Najd lies Tihāmah,
> And there are highlands and roads in the night
> to stride and amble.[41] [81]

The mystic Ibn al-Fāriḍ appears to carry this poetic yearning beyond the point where it functions as an unequivocal expression of archaic Bedouinity. At least he addresses our consciousness on a level that is less at the mercy of intrinsic *nasīb* ambiguities. Thus in one of his best achieved poems of spiritual peregrination he invokes by name the "immediate" land of his mystic longing, which then, in its landmarks of nature and architecture, cannot but point to symbols that reach out past the limits of the symbolic circle of the *nasīb* to the poem's closure:

> 35. When the fret of pain grips my heart, yet
> The sweet scent of grass from the Ḥijāz shall be my cure,
>
> 40. Its mountain clefts shall be my Paradise;
> Its domes, my shield; my soul's serenity,
> its Mount Ṣafā.[42] [82]

Specified thematically, not merely "formally," this yearning for the Ḥijāz of the pilgrimage sites might seem almost too explicit and too concrete in its toponymic referentiality—to the point where the archaic symbolic undercurrent would recede before a new, more precise repertory of symbols with an independent claim to poetic efficacy. Such is not the case, however, for it is only through the mystic specificity (itself a paradox) imbedded in the broader Bedouinity of the poem that the dialectic between the new symbolic intent and the old symbolic reference acquires its dynamic. In terms dictated by the poem, this dialectic is proclaimed by the poet's reminder that the source of all his yearning is after all Najd—that pagan, in symbolic terms never "converted," antagonist of the Ḥijāz. His is thus the archaic yearning for that forever Bedouin Najd that sends its zephyrlike breezes into the new, mystical, and yet paradoxically precise toponymy of the Ḥijāz, beginning with al-Zawrāʾ, otherwise known as Medina:

1. At night from al-Zawrāʾ
 came zephyr's redolence.
 At dawn it brought to life
 the dead among the live.
2. As offering it gave us
 the fragrant breaths of Najd:
 The air became a perfumed ambergris
 throughout![43] [83]

The symbolic crystallization of Najd has run its full course in a poem by Abū al-ʿAbbās Aḥmad Ibn Shuʿayb (d. 750/1349–50), the native of another outpost on the western periphery of Arabic poetry, Fez. To this contemporary, and poetic favorite, of Ibn Khaldūn, Najd belongs wholly to the symbolic domain of the "round abode" (*dār*) of the *nasīb:*

Passion's abode is Najd,
 and he who dwells there
Is the soul's utmost claim:

At morning, did spring's first rain
 fall on its yards?
And did it tarry over its bare plains?

Or did the languid breeze
 there linger through the night
To find a cure in the sweet bay and the willow,

Retelling tales of those who are
 my journey's aim,
Though they have turned and strayed,

Of days whose deep shadows
 were my dwelling,
Whose blue waters were my fount,

When piercing glances from a fawn
Dark eyed, lithe-limbed,

Gazed at me from chastising eyes:
Of these, a lover, knowingly I die![44] [84]

Having taken notice of the outpourings of Arabic poetic nostalgia over Najd, we cannot escape the intimation that in that very Arabian poetic Najd we are equally in contact with a cultural-historical archetype which transcends the self-containment of autochthony. The Arab poets who dwell upon Najd-nostaliga become to us very much like the poets of Greco-Roman antiquity, in whose own symbolic localization of yearning "myth and reality coalesce and affect each other," and where "that which is ***named*** [emphasis mine] is not both existing and signficant but is solely significant. Art becomes allegory, a domain of symbols. Beside the ordinary comes to stand a world of art."[45] Such to the classicist Bruno Snell is the foreshortening of the time-sequential panorama of the transformation of nostalgic time and space from their Homeric and Hesiodic origins to Vergil's Arcadia—a foreshortening that, in its own ripe time of perspectival vision, then found in Jacopo Sannazaro's *Arcadia* a continuation and a consciously post-Vergilian projection that did not fail to reveal the identity of its original "nostalgic time" and "nostalgic space." What thus crystallized was the entirely poetic vision of a region called Arcadia as the landscapoe of the soul.[46]

Both from the point of view of an anthropology of nostalgia and from a comparativist sensitivity to significant literary motifs, we ought to be ready to experience here that very lyrical and at the same time critically controllable sensation of recognition: that one who longs to be in Arcadia (*utinam ex vobis unus vestrique fuissem;* Vergil, *Eclogue* 10:35) is close to sharing al-Ṣimmah al-Qushayrī's or Ibn Khafājah's longing for Najd; and that, being in poetry's Najd, one is also very close to poetry's Arcadia. So, too, Goethe, who introduced his *Italian Journey* with the motto "*Auch ich in Arkadien,*" might have been tempted to give to his *West-östlicher Divan* the motto "I, too, in Najd." And if one corrects Goethe's idyllic "misprision" of the originally elegaic "*Et in Arcadia ego,*" as did Erwin Panofsky, one comes even closer to the equally originally elegaic poetic sense of Najd as a form of "being in Arcadia."[47]

Claiming such transcultural affinity in the symbolic sense ought to make us assume that certain objectivizing circumstances shared by both Arcadia and Najd might have prepared the ground for the occurrence of the symbolic "coincidence." The parallelism of geographical features, for instance, has to be explored for suggestive clues, so too that of demography, or rather of ethnicity with its legendary and ideological overtones. Thus the most obvious characteristic of Najd[48] is that it is the centrally located high plateau of the Arabian Peninsula. It is flanked by mountain ranges on the west and east and by inclement deserts on the north and south. There are only seasonal streams in Najd, as well as several springs that form oasislike ponds surrounded by vegetation, but even these are not stable in their water levels. Throughout the historical periods that concern us it was an arid, mostly camel-herding area of very limited resources. As purveyor of burden- and riding-camels for commerce and warfare, it nevertheless appears to have enjoyed a demographic stability of sorts, even through the first decades of the Islamic caliphate and well into the Umayyad period. Economic, social, and political oblivion, however, were already setting in during the rule of the Umayyads, while the consummation of decline and the final reduction to the status of irredeemable "periphery" in all those respects had only to wait for the arrival of the anti-Najdi Abbasid dynasty.

For reasons probably as much geopolitical as mythopoetic, this high plateau in the heart of the Arabian Peninsula has historically and legendarily enjoyed an undisputed claim to autochthony as regards purity of lineage and correctness of the Arabic language. This privileged status of Najd seems to be reflected politically already in the pre-Islamic Arabian kingdom of the Kindah dynasty, whose kings, beginning with Ḥujr and his son ʿAmr, legitimized their claim to the rule over Arabia by their control over Najd.[49]

As a strictly literary phenomenon, however, Najd enters its mythopoetic stage rather suddenly during the Umayyad period. What takes place at that point is Najd's explicit idealization not as a region but as a state of mind—all this accompanying, it is important to note, the birth of the idea of an Arab-Islamic dynastic state, which under the Umayyads still defines itself by its peninsular autochthony. An ideological paradox during this period is nevertheless provided by the fact that Najd as the old hub of Arab identity and legitimization, together with its adjacent, ideologically no less important (although in a new, Islamic, sense) region, the Ḥijaz, had to yield before the "outlying" Damascus, which had assumed its position as the hub of the newly emerged imperial authority. A state of tension between periphery claiming centrality and centrality reduced to periphery is the result of this displacement of positions and inversion of roles. In the realm of archetypal yearning, however, Najd withstood not only the primacy of Damascus but also that of Baghdad, and even the ultimate centrifugality of al-Andalus.

With this relationship of Najd to the Arabian Peninsula in mind, we must now view Arcadia in the same relative way, for a comparison of Najd with Arcadia is necessarily a comparison of relationships. In this respect, Arcadia, like Najd, forms physically the interior of its own peninsula, the Peloponnesus, and lacks access to the sea. For the most part it is a high plateau made inaccessible by the mountains that surround it. Its rivers, too, have the unusual characteristic of vanishing into the ground only to reappear after a subterranean run. The myth of the Arcadian Styx, whose waters no vessel could contain, probably derives from this peculiarity—the soil itself being here the vessel.[50] Arcadia's totally closed-in valleys change into inhospitable swamps, and its high regions are known for their harsh climate.

Since the most remote antiquity its economy was pastoral. Indeed, the shepherd-god Pan was himself a native of Arcadia. In order to supplement their meager livelihood, or merely in order to step outside their own constricting space, the Arcadian shepherds frequently served as mercenaries in the armies of other Greek polities. Their own statehood, or rather system of polities, was invariably precarious, however. In spite of this economic exiguity and political fragility, the Arcadians considered themselves to be the aboriginal stock of the Peloponnesus and referred to themselves as "the autochthonous peoples of sacred Arcadia," and Herodotus, too, acknowledged their autochthony (8.73).[51] To the state-building Athenians, Arcadia was equivalent to a political utopia, for "to dominate Arcadia Athens would have to have carried off a total victory over the Peloponnesians," which seems to hearken back to an oracle obtained by the Lacedemonians on the possession of Arcadia. "To ask for Arcadia" (Herodotus 1.66) becomes "the proverbial equivalent of 'asking for the impossible.'"[52]

Of the Arcadians themselves we possess an idealized and understandably partisan characterization by the historian Polybius, himself an Arcadian. They are said to have "a very high reputation for virtue among the Greeks, due not only to their humane and *hospitable* [emphasis mine] character and usages, but especially to their piety to the gods."[53] Polybius's emphasis on the virtue of hospitality among the Arcadians strikes a very familiar chord, making us think of the profession of a similar Najdi virtue and recognize in both these claims, or attitudes, quite pronouncedly the idealization of the compensating pose of the indigent. Furthermore, Polybius's view of the Arcadians as especially devoted to their gods seems at odds with their custom of flogging their favorite god, Pan, whenever their expectations of him were not fulfilled. Ironically, this is noted by Theocritus in his seventh *Idyll:*

> This do, sweet Pan, and never, when slices be too few,
> May the leeks o' the lads of Arcady beat thee black and
> blue.[54]

This view of the Arcadians would fall closer to the proverbial recalcitrance of the Najdians in matters religious.

Polybius registers further that the Arcadians, although growing up in austere circumstances that had impressed upon them a certain harshness of character, had nevertheless succeeded in mellowing and tempering that harshness by exercising themselves in the art of music, indeed by "incorporating music in their whole public life to such an extent that not only boys, but young men up to the age of thirty were compelled to study it constantly."[55] If any crudeness yet remained in such a people, this could only be in the exceptional cases of neglect of the discipline of music.

This unhindered idealization of the Arcadian hymn-singing and flute-playing shepherds, however, comes about only with the consummation of the political decline of classical Greece, when all of Hellas sees itself reduced to the status of a province of the vast empire of Rome. At this point Arcadia's "reality" recedes almost entirely into mythopoesis. It thus took this total provincialization within what was itself a province to crown Arcadia's destiny. Only now was it ripe to become a wholly symbolic landscape, peopled in its physical desolation with wholly spiritualized shepherds. In a stupendous literary-historical coincidence, Vergil, the scholiast-poet of the birth of the empire, was waiting in the wings.

Our Najdi-Arcadian chain of poetic, or poetically translatable, analogies that brought together seemingly extratemporal as well as extraterritorial points of subtle contact on levels that are mostly semiotic, designed to tap essences to the exclusion of circumstances, leads us finally to the most intriguing link—namely, to the presence in those privileged regions, and by extension in all the regions of Greco-Roman and Arab-Najdi *amoenitas,* of two singularly endowed and graced breezes, the zephyr and *al-ṣabā*. The Arabian breeze called *al-ṣabā* originates in Najd and blows westward, whereas the one that lingers over the Peloponnesian heartland and then extends itself over the rest of Greece blows *from* the west and is known as the zephyr. As is to be expected, the Arabic *al-ṣabā* has an almost exclusively lyrical poetic attestation and presence—it does not figure in the Qurʾān—while the Greek zephyr oscillates between poetry and myth, but in its Hellenistic, Latin, and Renaissance phases ends up being equally characteristic of the lyrical domain.

Iconographically and as a poetic motif, the Greek zephyr/Zephyros blows from the sea or comes down from the mountains. Since Homer and Hesiod it has been known in both its "primary" embodiment in myth and in its literary application. It is the wind that impregnates mares that graze by the seaside. According to Homer (*Iliad* 16.150), it fathered the horses of Achilles.[56] But with the messenger-goddess Iris, Zephyros, personified as a golden-haired youth, also fathered Eros;[57] and each spring this god-wind's breath, falling caressingly upon Chloris-Flora, fills meadows with new flowers. In his rivalry with Apollo over the handsome Hyakinthos, however, the jealous Zephyros shows his other face. During one of Apollo's discus-throwing exercises he blows down from Taÿgetos, the mountain range that separates Arcadia from Sparta, fatally changing the direction of Apollo's discus toward the forehead of the heedless Hyakinthos.

In the most archaic sense, however, the zephyr's main characteristic is its fecundating quality. This is expressed mythopoetically through its association with the equine mare, which is a symbol of fertility in its own right. It is in this quality, too, that the symbolism of the zephyr/Zephyros has an intriguing connection with Arcadia, where, according to Theocritus (*Idyll* 2.46–48), the zephyr's power of erotic arousal in mares is extended to the conspicuous property of an Arcadian plant:

> Horse-madness is a herb that grows in Arcady,
> And makes every filly, every flying mare
> Run a-raving in the hills.[58]

In the Renaissance Arcadia of Jacopo Sannazaro, Theocritus's herb of "horse-madness" reappears as the "herbs from all Arcadia" that, together with Arcadian priestly incantations, have the power to induce the desire of love in a manner "not otherwise than the frenzied mares on the cliffs of the farthest west are wont to await the generative breezes of Zephyrus."[59] As a motif, the zephyr is equally enduring in the manner in which it appears represented already on fifth-century B.C. Greek pottery: as a winged youth with flowers in the folds of his mantle. In a bucolic epigram of Bakchylides, also of the fifth century, the zephyr is the "kind breeze amongst the harsh gales."[60] In a like manner, in the ahistorical time of the idyll, in Sannazaro's hour of perfect repose, "No breath of Zephyrus sounds, his drowsiness makes mild the watery plains, the stars are winking in the slumbering sky,"[61] and it is his breathing that "tempers the heavy heat."[62] But above all it is the zephyr of the earliest and most archetypally privileged space of repose, the Elysian Fields of Menelaus in the *Odyssey,*

> where all existence is a dream of ease.
> Snowfall is never known there, nor long
> frost of winter, nor torrential rain,
> but only mild and lulling Ocean
> bringing refreshment for the soul of men—
> the Zephyr always blowing.[63]

And, again in the *Odyssey,* it is the edenic fructifier of the garden of Alcinous:

> Fruit never failed upon these trees: winter
> and summer time they bore, for through the year
> the breathing Zephyr ripened all in turn.[64]

Of the Arabian East Wind, associated poetically so closely with Najd, the encyclopedist al-Nuwayrī (d. 733/1332) reports the tradition that "never has God sent a prophet without sending with him the East Wind—*al-ṣabā*."[65] The Prophet Muḥammad, too, was supported by the East Wind.[66] Then there is the no less illuminating anecdote (*khabar*) that is clearly part of the beatific hagiography that developed around the latter days of the poet Labīd, who, it is important to note, comes from Upper Najd (ʿĀliyat Najd). The anecdote tells of the poet's vow to dispense benefits to the needy each time the East Wind blew.

> Once, already in the time of Islam, while he was in Kufa, destitute and barely able to sustain his own, it blew. Al-Walīd Ibn ʿUqbah, then the town's governor under ʿUthmān Ibn ʿAffān . . . , knew of it and thus addressed the people in sermon: "You know of the vow of Abū ʿAqīl [Labīd] and what he has bound himself to, so come to your brother's aid." Then he stepped down and sent to him one hundred she-camels.[67]

On the other hand, the legend-clad proto-Arabian people of ʿĀd were annihilated for their iniquity by *al-dabūr,* the baneful wind that blows from the west or the southwest toward the rising sun and against the point on the horizon from which *al-ṣabā* issues. In this binary antipodality, *al-dabūr* is "the worst of winds." It does not fecundate trees or raise clouds, and it is altogether a wind of ill omen.[68] *Al-ṣabā* opposes it with its softness, the ability to seed rain-laden clouds, and thus with fecundity. As a bearer of perfume-drenched messages from the beloved, *al-ṣabā* is also the wind of love's promise—or remembrance—and of good tidings.

This characterization of *al-ṣabā,* however, is not unreservedly applicable to the pre-Islamic layers of Arabic poetry, for there, if only in a few instances, it may also occur as a wind that is harsh and unrelenting—in all respects as harsh and unrelenting as the biblical Hebrew east wind, *qadīm* or *rūaḥ qadīm,* in its various, deliberately connotative contexts.[69] Such is then the appearance of *al-ṣabā* in Imru᾿ al-Qays's vignette of the ostrich that searches for its nest:

> It moved on from land to distant land,
> Wherever it knew of cracked shells around eggs,
>
> From horizon to horizon roaming, always westward,
> Flung far by the East Wind.[70] [85]

In the elegiac opening motif of ʿAbīd Ibn al-Abraṣ's ode, too, *al-ṣabā* is not yet the wind that will revive life in the ruinous abodes:

> Whose is the abode lying waste beside the yard,
> But for trenches and leavings, writing-like
>
> The East Wind altered it, and a South Wind's drive,
> And a North that winnows the fine dust.[71] [86]

Similarly in al-Ḥārith Ibn ʿAbbād's evocation of the abode's destruction, the milder jolt dealt by *al-ṣabā* is like a presage of the harshness of *al-dabūr:*

> The East Wind tussled it and moved on to the plain,
> Then, worn to naught, the West Wind rose against it.[72] [87]

In a poem attributed to ʿAdī Ibn Zayd, the courtier-poet of al-Ḥīrah, the older Bedouin elegiac accommodation of *al-ṣabā* within the motif of the ruinous encampment is fitted smoothly into the likewise generically elegiac mood of *ubi sunt,* with its dependence upon references to the transitoriness of royal pomp and power and to power's visible symbols, the palaces of Khawarnaq and Sadīr:

> Then, after prosperity, kingdom, and grace,
> They went there to their graves.
>
> Like a leaf that dried they became
> Awhirl in the winds, East and West.[73] [88]

It is, however, the mellow, the erotic, the rain-bringing and fertilizing *al-ṣabā* that not only enjoys a broad sway over significant motif-areas of pre-Islamic lyricism but that subsequently, as a mood signal, is destined to become one of Arabic lyricism's most enduring and potentially most intensely charged words. Much of this is already present in Imru' al-Qays's usage, as when he describes the "beloved" by likening the jewels of her necklace to glowing embers when the wind blows upon them and fans them into flames of hospitable campfires:

> On sundry mounds to mark the roads the wind blew on it,
> East and North, where home-bound travelers alight.[74] [89]

Compare his highly erotic *Muʿallaqah,* when he reminisces upon the charms of two of his past loves:

> When they rose, musk diffused itself about them
> Like the East Wind's soft breath of clover redolence.[75] [90]

So, too, by merely adding to his poetic diction the appropriate coloration, Imru' al-Qays engages *al-ṣabā* in a pastoral metaphor as a heavenly herdsman that calls in his herd—the rain cloud—to be milked:

> Then, as it hung over Ṭamīyah's peaks
> Gently the East Wind called it in,
> and milklike flowed its flow.[76] [91]

To another pre-Islamic poet, al-Ḥādirah, the East Wind and the rainfall it brings evoke the moist lips of a beautiful woman in a manner that, were it not so familiar a metaphorization in early Arabic poetry, would seem remote and highly excursive in its referentiality:

> With a night-traveling cloud, its yield morning-fresh,
> drawn by the East Wind,
> A water rain-roiled, well-collected in a pond.[77] [92]

Even when *al-ṣabā* is used in a genre that is one of blame or vituperation (*hijā'*), as we find it in a poem by Ṭarafah, such a "displacement" provides us with a very early example of irony—specifically, of the ironic use of *al-ṣabā*—precisely because it forces into a context of distortion that which is semantically familiar:

> To the close kin you're a cold northern blast
> That comes from Shām, face-writhing, damp.
>
> Yet to the alien, remote, you are
> an Eastern Breeze without a chill,
> Once richly muddying the ground,
> then filling rushing streams.[78] [93]

The decisive period of the fixation of the semantic and contextual range of *al-ṣabā,* however, is the Umayyad. There it can no longer be connotationally neutral. Its physical effect must now necessarily be translatable into a metaphor or symbol of poetically decisive significance that issues closely from the theme and mood structure of ***nasīb*** lyricism. What is of specific importance to the proper grasping of the full poetic identity of ***al-ṣabā*** is that, beginning with the Umayyad period, it will necessarily—explicitly or implicitly—be understood as having arisen in or come from Najd, as that region, too, acquires its full poetic identity only at that time.

We are already familiar with Majnūn's (or perhaps the historical Ibn al-Dumaynah's) passionate sigh, "O East Wind of the highlands, when did you stir from Najd?"[79] However, a clear reference to ***al-ṣabā*** as characteristically from Najd can also be made by way of an epithet such as ***ʿulwīyu al-rīḥi*** (the wind of the heights), in which case, albeit indirectly, the very heart and autochthony of the poetic Najd is evoked, namely Najd al-ʿUlyā or ʿĀliyat Najd (Upper Najd). Thus in an anonymous poem from the *Ḥamāsah:*

> When from the heights the wind blows, I feel
> As though by kinship to the High Wind bound.[80] [94]

Or in another sentimentally revered attribution to Majnūn:

> And of the winds from the heights when they bear
> Lavender's redolence, do they blow o'er Najd?[81] [95]

Within this new connotative semanticity of ***al-ṣabā*** it is nevertheless necessary to turn to an example of those among its occurrences that still mix contexts. Thus the Umayyad poet al-ʿUjayr al-Salūlī refers to ***al-ṣabā*** not in a ***nasīb*** or a ***ghazal*** but in an elegy (***rithā***ʾ). There its specific function is to heighten the pathos of the fateful night on which the person mourned met his death. His enemies then were as numerous as had once been those seeking his hospitality as supplicants:

> Paragon of hospitality, we left him
> on the night of the East Wind,
> At Marr, challenged by every dauntless foe.[82] [96]

ʿUmar Ibn Abī Rabīʿah, a practitioner of the most playful and least sentimental Umayyad ***ghazal*** verse, nevertheless makes a show of a broad and noticeably "evolving" repertory of motif placements of the breeze called ***al-ṣabā***. On the one hand, he does not shy away from using it in a manner that is consciously archaizing, immersed in the melancholy conceit of the abandoned encampment:

Whose are these abodes as though they were lines,
Tracks by the East Wind woven, warp and woof?[83] [97]

But then, even when he wants to remind us of the "cruder" age when *al-ṣabā* was still capable of scorching a desert-traveler's face, we must nevertheless be forewarned, for this poet-lover's enduring of the noon-time heat is in reality a scrupulously encoded metaphor of the fire of passion. With *al-ṣabā* as part of the lyrical-erotic code, even the pretense of *raḥīl* severity becomes *nasīb*-subservient:

And we remained at al-ʿAslāʾ, scorched
by the East Wind;
So, too, our mounts stood without shelter.[84] [98]

And at a time in Arabic love-poetry when meadows cease to be open pasture grounds, turning instead into privileged millefleurs, *al-ṣabā* becomes in ʿUmar Ibn Abī Rabīʿah's diction the soft breeze that nurtures such meadows-turned-gardens, so that they may bloom and turn into visions of the beloved's half-opened lips:

Her smile bares the likes of meadow-daisies
Lustered by the East Wind and the first
downpour of rain.[85] [99]

Barely into the Abbasid era, we find Muslim Ibn al-Walīd (d. 208/823) boldly, but still within the bounds of connotative accordance, using *al-ṣabā* to describe the potency of wine:

While water tries to temper it, it's yet a flame
That the East Wind makes flare up in live coals.[86] [100]

The sophisticated lyricist of courtly Baghdad, ʿAlī Ibn al-Jahm, allows *al-ṣabā* to retain its meaning of the fertility-bringing breeze. He contrasts it at first with his own despondency as lover but is ultimately unable to resist a lighter ironic gracefulness:

O night-traveling cloud that quenches
the earth's thirst
and gives it of its bounty,
With it I filled my wakeful eyes!

It came to us with the East Wind,
Quite as a maiden
by an old procuress pressed.[87] [101]

But in al-Buḥturī's elegy for Caliph al-Mutawakkil, *al-ṣabā,* no less infused with quintessential *nasīb* sensibility, passes over the ruinous abode that is al-Mutawakkil's grave as though in fulfillment of some sacred vow:

> As though the East Wind fulfilled some solemn vows
> When its drifts of sand trailed over [the halting place]
> at eve and morn.[88] [102]

To al-Ṣanawbarī (d. 334/945), the flower-growing librarian at Sayf al-Dawlah's court, *al-ṣabā* is the breeze that is at home in the interdicted garden of his symbolizing imagination, where cypresses sway gently like playful maidens and where the river ripples with delight:

> Swayed by the East Wind's breath,
> deep in the night,
> Each one a supple maiden
> in maidens' playful court.
>
> Across the river the breeze's sighs
> send ripples of delight
> And trail their mantle's frills.[89] [103]

Through the further honing of the Arabic lyrical sensibility that took place in the poetry of al-Andalus, this eastern breeze enters with increased subtlety into the domain of the love elegy and the idyll. Ibn Zaydūn's (d. 463/1071) use of *al-ṣabā,* however, may still seem almost timid. In his *Nūnīyah* of deserved elegiac fame, it remains the topically familiar messenger entrusted with a rejected lover's plea:

> And you, O gentle East Wind,
> my greetings bear
> To one who'd give me life
> even with greetings from afar![90] [104]

There is, however, no holding back the lyrical abandon of the Valencian Ibn Khafājah (d. 533/1137), as that poet allows *al-ṣabā* to enter with the greatest intimacy into his elegiac musings and imagist verse-vignettes. He associates its redolent quality with the prime of youth:

> Stirred to passion by narcissus' fragrance
> As it met the coolness of the Eastern Breeze, I said:
>
> Friends, Ḥimyarites, speak to this graying fellow
> Of the nights of youth![91] [105]

In an even more passionate way, that Najdi breeze makes the poet call out for his homeland, al-Andalus:

But when the wind blows from the East,
I shout:
How I yearn for you, O Andalus![92] [106]

And there is something quite exquisite about the haikulike imagist objectivity with which the poet introduces *al-ṣabā* into his personal garden of melancholy:

Then the East Wind teased
at the stem of the hillock,
And it swayed and bent over the rump-curve
of the dune.[93] [107]

A different kind of ambiguity comes to the surface in the complex correlation of mood and motif in Ibn Khafājah's understanding of the *nasīb*. *Al-ṣabā* works in two dimensions of connotative intent—that of the *nasīb* and the *raḥīl*—a distinction the poem tries to obliterate:

And here I am, facing each night
with one more night
Of grief, where flowing tears are stars.

I ride o'er hills' rumps
as though on camel-journeys,
I breathe in gulps of the East Wind,
aspire messages.

Of every rose I sip the spray of dew—
Not from the pearl-white teeth,
not from the lips' deep hue.[94] [108]

Also, in one of his characteristically highly condensed poems/vignettes, the East Wind, the horse, and the sea come together in a mythopoetic obbligato that is symbolically associative (Zephyros) even more than it is imagist:

A sea so deep, in fear or in love's ardor,
Its throbbing recesses unflagging,

A foaming restlessness by the East Wind stirred.
There I stood and gazed,

And I saw myself, on its littoral,
A horseman and before him
a piebald steed.[95] [109]

If in later periods the diverse metaphoric possibilities of *al-ṣabā* become a domain too readily accessible to assorted minor poets, and even if its symbolic vein appears to be reaching exhaustion, it is nevertheless, in the manner in which only the richest symbolic substances survive, lyrically indestructible. Forty years after Ibn Khafājah, another Valencian, Ibn Saʿd al-Khayr al-Balansī (d. 571/1175?), whose lyricism of archaizing places and objects paves the way for the articulations of the great mystic nostalgia of Ibn al-Fāriḍ (d. 632/1235), includes *al-ṣabā* in his diction with undiminished effectiveness. His imaginary questioner of passing riders—those riders that are soon to become mystical pilgrims—asks them of places such as Laʿlaʿ, which are shimmering mirage apparitions, whether dew has fallen on them ("a lā sā'ila al-rukbāni hal ṭulla laʿlaʿu"), pressing further and further:

> And the tamarisks of the winding valley,
> has their shade come round,
> And has the East Wind there
> followed its course?[96] [110]

Ultimately, still capable of filling spaces in the soul, *al-ṣabā* reaches the Egyptian poet Aḥmad Shawqī (d. 1932) in his Spanish exile, bringing back to him his, and a whole literary culture's, stubborn illusion of "youth and grace":

> Like the playful East Wind,
> they came in a gust
> and went by,
> A slumber sweet, a furtive charm.[97] [111]

While exploring the mythical-symbolic and the functional-poetic characteristics of both the Greek *zephyros* and the Arabian *al-ṣabā,* we realize that, despite the obvious, factually discommodious discontinuances of time and space, there is an arresting similarity. Beyond this there is the more insidious, and eventually more concrete, plane of similarity that is etymology. An intriguing philological riddle lies behind the compass-polarity of zephyr/*al-ṣabā* as indicated by their phonetic, and thus potentially etymological, closeness. Zephyr as Zephyros, the son of Aurora and Astraios and the grandson of Hyperion (who also fathered Helios, the sun) is commonly accepted to be etymologically related to the Greek word for darkness, *zophos,* which also came to designate the dark side of the horizon, that is, the west. The Zephyr is thus the wind that comes from where the western horizon darkens: ultimately the gentle, crepuscular breeze that carries the cooling moisture of the sea over the Peloponnesus. Paradoxically, however, in the realm of symbolic imagination this etymological offspring of "darkness" becomes the mythological scion of "light."

As for the Najdi breeze *al-ṣabā*, it does not seem to have a primary Arabic etymological basis—at least not in its apparent root *ṣ-b-w*—nor does it have a credible Semitic surface-etymology. On the other hand, prompted by considerations that are both phonetic and semantic-mythopoetic, it is plausible to suggest that the breeze *al-ṣabā* is none other than the *zophos*-derived zephyr. If this be so, then we should have in the case of *al-ṣabā*/zepyhr a truly paradigmatic case of mythopoeic "disease of language" à la Max Müller:[98] a breeze that started blowing from the sea's dark western horizon (although Aurora, "dawn," was its mother, and Astraios, "the progenitor of astral light," its father) had veered about over Najd and had become the Eastern Breeze that bears blessings instead of whirling sands from inhospitable highlands. We may then suggest further, mythopoeically, that the zephyr acquired its extraordinary restorative qualities when it passed over Arcadia, becoming "goodly" where it was once "dark"; and that *al-ṣabā*, too, "stirring from Najd," as the poets put it, gained associations and connotations that took it ever farther from the alienated *zophos* toward the charismatic purity of an Arabian *ṣafāʾ* and toward the always Najdi "childlike" longing (*ṣabā ilā*). In other words, when in the manner of Max Müller's disease of language the dark *zophos* was forgotten, the "diaphanous" qualities of *ṣafāʾ* (purity) and those of the poetically strongly associative *ṣibā* of "childhood," "youth," and "passion" came to mind.

Nevertheless, there exists another, equally plausible and mythopoeically not at all disruptive, etymology for both zephyr and *al-ṣabā*, which would set aside the zephyr/*zophos* direct etymological connection, reducing it to only a mythopoeic one. In that case the actual etymology of zephyr would be an onomatopoeic one, related to the Arabic *zafīr* (sigh, deep sigh) with the easy change of *z* into *ṣ*: *ṣafīr* (whistling). *Zafīr* itself is only a form of the more basically onomatopoeic *zafīf* (a gentle puff: of wind). This connection is further substantiated by the Arabic onomatopoeia of *musafsifah* (wind raising dust), derived from "dryness" (*saffa*/*saffan*), skimming along the ground like a bird (*saffa*/*safīfan*), and "to raise fine dust: wind" (*sāfiyāʾ*, derived from *safā*). This concentrated Arabic onomatopoeia that denotes the gentle, or swift, blowing of the wind and the birdlike skimming of the ground in flight, together with the whistling and crackling sibilants of volatile, powdered dryness, ought to contribute strongly to the onomatopoeic perception of the zephyr as much as to that of *al-ṣabā* and, furthermore, give back to the latter those elements of its more archaic poetic usage and realistic palpability—dryness and dust—that pure mythopoesis had taken such good care to conceal.[99] No matter which etymology one chooses, however, or which etymology prevails, the zephyr and *al-ṣabā* remain poetically unscathed and symbolically inseparable.

FOUR

Meadows in the Sky

1. Of Pastors and Their Dreams: A Digression into Common Grounds

BEFORE PURSUING FURTHER the symbolic theme permutations and crystallizations that ultimately define the meaning, or meanings, of the *nasīb,* we shall once more stop by the roadside and briefly digress into the common ground of an ancient genre. In dealing with thematic archetypes, one must never hesitate to face the consequences. Thus we shall keep in mind the late eighteenth-century Orientalist translators Sir William Jones and Joseph Dacre Carlyle. As is the case with translations with the power to survive, those of Jones and Carlyle are to be viewed today as robust period pieces. A scholarly minded reader will undoubtedly find in them some obvious fallacies: like the transformation of the wild, untamed landscape of Labīd's *Muʿallaqah* into the bucolic countryside of Claude Lorrain. "Nor towers, nor tents, nor cottages are there, / But scattered ruins and a silent plain."[1] And yet, by the same token, both Jones and Carlyle have given us something more than what we are capable of today: they have left us an authentic eighteenth-century view of Arabian poetry, a truly uninhibited version of it according to their own aesthetic vision. Theirs, therefore, are versions in the fullest sense, not translations; and together with a fair glimpse of the original texture of form and theme, they communicate a clear, unabashed notion of an epoch of taste that is sophisticated in its own context, although, in some points, amusingly naïve in its claim to being a reflection of the original sensibility.

A more lasting and important aspect of this eighteenth-century view of pre-Islamic Arabic poetry, however, is its clear recognition of major genre-characteristics. There may be something of the neoclassicist demand for classification, definition, and terminological nomenclature in the unqualified references to Arabic generic forms as "purely pastoral"[2] and as providing a "simple delineation of pastoral manners," however, which is an essentially valid critical discovery. As artificial as an analogy between the Arabian desert scene and the European neoclassical pastoral may appear, it ought to be taken seriously. If our contemporary critical attitudes toward Arabic poetry seem to reject such artificiality as the eighteenth-century pastoral, our change of taste is not so much the discovery of an entirely new dimension in the aesthetic object, nor is it necessarily a profounder understanding of already familiar data. What happens to us today is that we are simply at a loss for a better term than that of the pastoral;[4] or rather, that we fail to recognize the continuity in the changing allegories which have constituted our modes of vision of nature—and of society. And yet the whole universal phenomenon of literature seems to be tied in with that somewhat confectioned perception that man entertains of himself as a pastoral persona; and his social and political symbols of authority and hierarchy, too, emerge as a development of pastoral metaphors. Himself a "pastor," the poet also becomes a "stargazer." He then extends the metaphor to the order of the universe and, like Ovid and Marlowe, calls upon the "horses of the night" to run slowly across the sky[5] or, like the pre-Islamic poet al-Nābighah, as we shall see, despairs that the morning star, "he who herds the stars, will not return."[6] To Fray Luis de León, a lyrical poet of the Spanish Renaissance, Solomon's Song of Songs is a pastoral eclogue with two lovers answering each other as in Vergil; while he himself turned Horace's bucolic "*beatus ille*" (*Epode* 2) into the motto of, and perhaps the most popular line in, Spanish Renaissance poetry.[7] "No other single illusion has charmed humanity for so long and with such an ever-fresh splendor as the illusion of the pining shepherd's pipe," observes Huizinga, and "Pan is still the most alive of the Greek gods."[8]

More than an illusion, however, the pastoral is an ideal. Its stuff is the stuff of the original dream of perfect happiness. It is engendered in elusiveness and its ultimate goal is elusiveness. It tries to do the impossible, the self-contradictory. The typological history of the pastoral has been a history of finding for itself a time and a place, and ultimately its diminute *hortus conclusus,* and the "rose." In the end, however, the *hortus conclusus* itself must remain an elegiac place tainted with unanswered questions about expulsion and the impossibility of beatific repose.

The times and places which led to the pastoral, or which were produced by the pastoral as its necessary circumstance, were the temporally, geographically, and culturally widely scattered *loci amoeni,* Elysian Fields, the land of the Hyperboreans, Arcady, Fortunate Islands, Terrestrial Paradise, Eternal Paradise, Promised Land, El Dorado, and, always and everywhere, the Garden; and they were in the time of all times, in the Golden Age, in the age before the Fall, before civilization, or in the future of Utopia, Salvation, the Proletarian Revolution—always too far to reach, always in somebody else's time to be experienced, always short of the possible.

The literature which arises out of such an atmosphere of archetypal yearning is then either one of wish fulfillment and the febrile irreality of reverie, at its most real spun around myth, or of the melancholy sorrow and nostalgia produced by lost objects of love and goodness, by one's own youth spent but still recoverable somewhere along the vanishing perspective of the tunnel of the mind where all the *temps perdues* nest and dream.

Hesiod's Golden Age, still in contact with cosmic forces, is rivaled only by the biblical Earthly Paradise in influence upon the development and the ultimate consequence of the pastoral. In both, man, in unison with nature, lives a life which is pure existence. Bliss is an unconscious condition. To be converted into a conscious one, it has to end.[9] The pastoral aspect of Hesiod's Golden Age or of Homer's Elysian Fields is as yet only implied. The explicit pastoral vision of a happy life could not have been clearly stated in a heroic (itself "archaic") era. At that stage the myth still rises above the human averageness of nostalgia. Only the promise of an existence in a "dream of ease"[10] seems to mediate between archaic myth and the most general form of proto-pastoral nostalgia.

It is with Theocritus's Sicilian idylls that the pastor becomes the true inhabitant of the ideal landscape hitherto inseparable from the chronology of the Golden Age and the original bliss of the species. Subsequently, the bucolic poetry of Vergil, with appreciable help from Horace, provides the definitive classical formulation of the pastoral theme. Vergil's Arcady, the native ground of Pan, ignores entirely the harsh reality of the true landscape and becomes the point of convergence of all the previous idealizations of environment. The inhabitants of Arcady are Golden Age pastors, but outside the scheme of the conceit they are more like personifications in an "interlude" in which the urban dream of escape is enacted, its true theme being the redemptive reversal of civilization. Upon closer analysis, the bucolic dream may even appear surprisingly petty—and familiar. *Beatus ille* . . . , a happy man is one who cultivates his inherited fields and is free from usury's ties. He is tired of being a soldier, stirred by the trumpet's wild cry, weary of the intrigues of the Forum and of waiting at the proud doorways of influential men. The Vergilian-Horacian pastoral is the pseudorustic ideal of a culture which is reaching the height of its self-realization and which, standing at the threshold of empire, begins to feel the strain of sustained historical effort. Moreover, this ideal had been crystallizing in Roman consciousness at least since the fifth century B.C., when the rustic reclusion of Cincinnatus started a legend which was to shape popular poetic imagination. Cincinnatian "puritan" rusticity proved to be both an ideological resource and a fertile ground for less austere, idyllically pastoral sentiments.

It was Vergil's merit to have introduced into the pastoral landscape of an unreal Arcady the element of poetic melancholy, which had not been clearly present in the earlier pastoral vision of the Golden Age. "In Vergil's Arcady," observes Erwin Panofsky, "human suffering and superhumanly perfect surroundings create a dissonance. This dissonance, once felt, had to be resolved, and it was resolved in that vespertinal mixture of sadness and tranquility which is perhaps Vergil's most personal contribution to poetry. With only slight exaggeration one might say that he 'discovered' the evening."[11]

In confluence with the myths of the Golden Age and the Fortunate Islands we find the development of another "compound" archetype, even more basically archaic and perhaps for that reason even more symbolically fertile. This archetype is that of the Garden, and it, too, in a varied and complex way, combines connotations both of a time and of a place. The time is that of creation and eternal life, an unresolved leap between past and future, and the place is the Earthly Paradise, the Garden of Eden, the Paradise of Eternal Life, the garden of precious stones visited by Gilgamesh.[12]

This archetypal garden symbolism conveys the idea of original bliss so far present mostly in the form of unspoiled goodness in the concept of the Golden Age. On another level we also obtain the interplay of the individual in his Garden and in his own state of original bliss with the species or collective entity enjoying a "golden" order of empathy which permits bliss. The symbolic abstraction of the Garden is all the more compact and quintessential because both sides of the symbolic order, the individual and the communal, lead in equally direct lines to the pastoral conclusion. The pastoral ideal that the animal world, too, as part of the empathetic order, should submit to man's rule is already implied in the tradition of the harmonious existence of the animal world in the Garden of Eden;[13] and even after the Fall, Abel, the first pastor, is also the first truly "pastoral" figure, who, for reasons which symbolic imagination took upon itself to explain, was nearer to divine grace.

The symbolism of Earthly Paradise and original bliss becomes more concentrated as it finds embodiment in the new dimensionality of the *hortus conclusus,* the Avestan *pairidaeza* (royal park, enclosure), then the Greek *paradeisos* and the rarer Hebrew *pardeṣ*. In the Song of Songs, its paraphrastic Hebrew rendering brings the full etymology back:

> A garden locked is my sister, my bride,
> a garden locked, a fountain sealed.[14]

Only so much later, in the complex idiom of allegory, in the sublimation of the erotic image of the *Roman de la Rose,* does poetry recover access to such gardens. In the meantime, late classical antiquity was producing by means of the pastoral idyll a syncretion, as it were, of the various visions of original bliss. Descriptive *paradeisoi* become standard motifs in Greek romances. Longus's *Daphnis and Chloe* and Achilles Tatius's *Leucippe and Cleitophon* have retained an enduring presence.[15] Perhaps an even more sustained influence, however, was exercised by such courtly epithalamic poets as the Neapolitan Statius (d. A.D. 96) and the Latinized Alexandrian Claudian (d. ca. A.D. 404). At this late stage of the classical pastoral tradition, the Arcadian pastoral landscape undergoes a process of further decorative stylization as the "bower of Venus" and then a full fusion with the Christian vision of Earthly Paradise. In both cases the characteristic symbolism of circumscription or enclosure tends to predominant over the openness of more purely bucolic Arcadian landscapes. The symbolic character of the landscape and its inhabitants increases in explicitness as the original, broad metaphorization is replaced by a precise repertory of allegories. It is this allegorization which permits a neutralized, abstracted bucolic setting to be transposed into medieval—and then Renaissance—Christian versions of the old symbols.[16] It was easy for the garden from which Adam and Eve were banned, and whose tree of life was guarded by a flaming sword, to develop its rich symbolism of loss, remote promise, yearning, and intimation of return. This symbolism could be sacred as well as worldly, erotic as well as mystic. Indeed, the Song of Songs, at its various levels of reception, had already prepared the ground for such symbolic fullness.

In its late classical stage, however, the *hortus conclusus,* the "bower of Venus," is as yet the old royal enclosure meant to contain pagan pleasures. The Alexandrian Claudian, who may even have been a Christian, introduces in his *Epithalamium* (A.D. 398) a bower of Venus protected by a golden hedge. Here, amidst luscious vegetation, among traditionally pastoral nymphs and cupids, there are hosts of other allegorical figures which are to reappear later in so many medieval love gardens: "License bound by no fetters, easily moved Anger, Wakes dripping with wine, inexperienced Fears, Pallor that lovers ever prize, Boldness trembling at his first thefts, happy Fears, unstable Pleasure, and lovers' Oaths, the sport of every lightest breeze. Amid them all wanton Youth with haughty neck shuts out Age from the grove."[17]

The serenity of the Elysian and Golden Age tradition is replaced in Claudian by the games of love and the dallyings of allegorizations of passions which, in themselves, are products of a rapidly progressing allegorization of Ovid. In various disguises, these allegorical figures will then enter the gardens of medieval and Renaissance literature, "though there they struggle about haunted by Christianity."[18] Attempts may even be made not to allow them through what now becomes a high, battlement-crowned wall. Thus, on the wall encircling the garden of the Rose, the richest of all the medieval gardens, there are "portrayed and chiseled" allegories of "qualities which will never enter."[19]

The one who enters the enclosed garden is the Dreamer, the wandering knight, or the poet. To the allegorical beings which used to populate Claudian's enclosure of Venus, the garden of the Rose remains closed. Whether it is the new Christian ethos which excludes pagan allegories of pleasure, indolence, and intemperance from entering the garden that once used to welcome them, or whether the garden itself no longer belongs to Venus and her dissolute retinue but to the Rose of new, recondite splendor and spiritual solitude, the medieval poet at first does not say, but as his Dreamer enters the garden, he exclaims:

> Once entered, I was joyous and glad
> And believe me that I thought I was
> Looking at the earthly paradise,[20]

in a tone which, although as yet quite antithetically explicit, nevertheless brushes the portals of feeling which will later be found in mystic recollections of a similar "garden."[21] To the Dreamer in the garden of the Rose, the enclosure is the localization of ancient happiness, the yearning for which may then so easily be transferred into the future, to the ultimate garden of delight, the heavenly Paradise.

Within the *Roman de la Rose* itself, those two intimations are present. Guillaume de Lorris, in the first part of the poem, suggests the earthly Paradise, while Jean de Meung, in the continuation, substitutes this earthly vision with that of the Good Pasture, which is not entered through a poetic dream but through a life of merit. Otherwise, however, both gardens are very similar: the wall surrounding the latter has carvings, too, and inside, the atmosphere of joy, delight, and eternal springtime is indistinguishable from that found in the earlier, earthly garden; and yet, Jean de Meung's garden is "real" in the Platonic sense, whereas Guillaume's is only a shadow. Thus in the *Roman de la Rose* the medieval Platonic theological view clashes with the medieval Platonic poetic view as point and counterpoint of a poem and its sequel, or as a dialectic of the two faces of love and beauty, and ultimate happiness.[22]

In the "false paradises" of the Renaissance, as A. Bartlett Giamatti calls them, the return to the poetic dream of Paradise takes place again, but the allegorization is by now entirely disembodied—if a paradox can be carried so far. The poet's vision now is neither an enraptured reverie nor a sedate, Platonic contemplation of the ideal: it is a convention and a highly developed medium for his display of allegorized conceptualization and aesthetic refinement. Now the poet thinks of himself and of his peers when he calls his paradise "closed to many" and his garden "opened for but few." Indeed, such is the title of one of the most characteristic Spanish garden allegories by Pedro Soto de Rojas (1585?–1658), a poet from Granada.[23] The garden-paradise is now metamorphosed into the favorite Baroque setting of a "literary republic," as in Michael Drayton's *The Muses' Elizium* (1630):

> The poets paradice this is,
> To which but few can come
> The muses onely bower of blisse
> Their deare Elizium.[24]

Having lost most of the poetic enchantment of the daydream and even more so the Platonic "realness" of the ideal, these late literary garden allegories are nonetheless firmly enough anchored in the essential theme of tension between loss and hope. But the application of the archetype had to adapt itself to contemporary concerns.[25] Renaissance worldly playfulness and aestheticism are thus hardly less serious—if more self-conscious—than the straight myth reconstructions of the classics or the naïve sublimations of the Middle Ages. After all, the rare encounter which does not add to the painful list of disenchantments in Don Quijote's quest is the one with the pseudo-Arcadian shepherds.[26] Thus in the *Quijote,* nostalgic idealization of the Golden Age remains intact even when the long-time companion ideal of chivalry falls. The irony of reality which defeats the realization of ideals in the social realm does not affect the poetic dream of flight from society. The pseudo-Arcady of Cervantes remains an effective poetic *locus amoenus*. In imitation of the creator of poetic Arcady, Vergil, poets continue to address their imaginary pastoral companions, invoking his "utinam ex vobis unus . . . fuissem" (Would that I were one . . . of you!);[27] and in the plastic arts the medieval *hortus conclusus* loses its walls and battlements and becomes the Arcady of Poussin,[28] not visibly enclosed, except for the static harmonies of composition.

Paradise, the Golden Age, the Garden, live on as works of art, which alone seems to be capable of perpetuating the symbol. Even the "concrete" garden itself, the ancient royal park/paradise, in its reduction to ornamental rather than environmental function, retains its symbolic meaning precisely as a work of art. By developing into flat surfaces in need of being decoratively filled, it not only becomes stylized, but its symbolic meaning as garden has to be retained within such a visually representational conception. The blocked-in, compartmentalized design of the *parterre* then comes to represent enclosure. The enclosure of all enclosures in abstract design, however, is the symbol of the labyrinth.[29] This motif, as it appears in the Italian Renaissance garden and evolves further into the French eighteenth-century clipped *parterre,* coincides with the fullest development of European literary garden symbolism. As one of the most ancient symbolic-decorative abstractions, the labyrinth is equally present in the mystic dimension of the arabesque. In effect, one could call an arabesque a *hortus conclusus* transported to a wall.[30]

2. *Toward a Cosmic Pastoral Space*

If Najd has led us to Arcadia and the breeze *al-ṣabā* to the zephyr, allowing these discrete figments of lyricism to intermingle and form common pools of the elegiac and the idyllic, there is a further inference that thrusts itself upon our self-conscious, form-searching sense of Arabic lyricism. It is the inference of the existence of the themes and moods, as well as, ultimately, the form, of the pastoral in Arabic poetry. For there, too, the dimension of a peculiarly stylized, rarefied—what we may call pastoral—human presence develops in the atmosphere of melancholy and the idyll. To say that those who inhabit such privileged realms as Najd must be poets is to be immediate and to the point. To say that they must be pastors is to reach further back, to speak of things archaic, of man dwelling upon himself and, out of his own substance, trying to order his world; but also—and always—it means to speak of a life of loneliness and a yearning to create links of empathies and harmonies.

If at first glance it appears that Arabic poetry lacks a developed pastoral genre, this only confirms a preliminary critical notion regarding Arabic poetry as a whole. Indeed, we ought to be warned not to look too single-mindedly for such separate, extracontextually familiar genre-notions in Arabic poetry. Arabic poetry is simply not like that. We must therefore ask other critical questions: Does Arabic poetry speak of things pastoral? Does the pastoral mood shape that poetry to any appreciable extent? Does the pastoral element in that poetry have any symbolic meaning or function?

As far as the pre-Islamic poetic landscape of the early odes is concerned, it undoubtedly has certain broad pastoral affinities. We have only to remember the encroachment of elegiac untamed, and yet pristinely "pastoral," nature upon abandoned human habitation in odes such as the *Muʿallaqah* of Labīd. The framework of that landscape is set by the melancholy mood of the *nasīb,* a mood which lingers on and carries over even into all further nature description in other formal vestiges of the ode, such as the Najdi nostalgic elegies and idylls. Our experience with the Arabic *qaṣīdah* has taught us, however, not to expect full elaboration of themes, or even explicitness in stating them. Beyond the pre-Islamic elegiac-idyllic landscapes of the *nasīb,* our interest in that which is recognizably pastoral in Arabic poetry ought to lead us once again to the period of the Umayyad lyrical flowering, when Najd was discovered as the closest thing to a poetic *locus amoenus* and *al-ṣabā* was given its full symbolic accolade.

Thus some of the episodes connected with the Majnūn romance as it was acquiring its quasi textuality through the blending of verse fragments and anecdotal commentary display strong pastoral genre-characteristics that echo equally genre-defining traits of Longus's *Daphnis and Chloe.* "Majnūn loved Laylā," goes the Arabic story/commentary in *Al-Aghānī,* "and they were youngsters then. They had become attached to each other while pasturing the herds of their clan. And so they remained till they grew up. Then she was veiled from him, . . . and it is to this that his verses point:"

I fell in love with Laylā,
still ringlets in her hair,
The contours of her breasts still
unheeded by her peers.

Two children were we,
pasturing our lambs,
Oh, had we not, nor had the lambs,
yet grown![31] [112]

Forcefully interpretive in spite of its indirectness is then the anecdote, also in *Al-Aghānī,* in which not even a ***mu'adhdhin***'s ministering could remain unaffected by the pastoral charm of these lines, for in the midst of his ministration his thoughts wandered off with the overhead verses, making him call out "Come to the lambs!" instead of "Come to prayer!"[32]

Having recognized the pastoral stream-of-mood that is thus set in motion by the above two "opening" lines of Majnūn's elegiac predicament and that, as a narratively construable sequence of stylized mood pieces, makes up that poet's "Dīwān, we soon arrive at verses that are no less pastoral:

> If only we were two gazelles, grazing
> On meadows of Ḥawzān, in desolate land!
>
> Oh, were we two doves amidst a wide waste,
> We'd fly and fly, and at evening time seek the sheltered nest!
>
> Oh, were we two fishes swimming in the sea,
> Daring ever farther into waters deep!
>
> Oh, were we one now,
> and would that
> When death comes
> one grave were our bed![33] [113]

As long as we remain in the fold of Umayyad "desert" lyricism, this pastoral-elegiac stance is in its topicality at times almost interchangeable between poet and poet. Thus, for instance, Ibn al-Dumaynah gives us what amounts to a motif-by-motif paraphrase (or perhaps a model?) of the above poem, which, of course, was to begin with only an archetypally triggered attribution to the already rigorously archetypal construct of the poetic persona called Majnūn:

> If only we were two antelope in the wild,
> together by night,
> On rugged ridges grazing,
> hid in far-cast plains,
>
> And would that dusky sand-grouse there
> soared on high with us,
> That under wing we dwelt, close to the sky,
>
> That on a mountain's crown, lofty and unapproached,
> we were as one—[34]

"If only" and again "If only,"
all to no avail,
The soul always longing,
wishes ever unfulfilled.[35] [114]

Moreover, Ibn al-Dumaynah seems to have been quite enamored of this pastoral motif, for we encounter it once again in his *Dīwān*, inserted almost without change into another of his elegiac *nasīb*-poems, giving it an unmistakable pastoral imprint.[36]

Stemming originally from the pre-Islamic *nasīb* but ultimately, in its ʿUdhrī phase, oscillating between stylized pastoral elegy and mannered, self-consciously Bedouinizing idyll—both newly sentimental rather than archaically pathetic—is the motif that weighs the proverbially intense yearning of the she-camel for her native pasture grounds against the Bedouin poet's passion and yearning for the places and landscapes of his home and youth, usually in Najd, or for the ground walked upon by his beloved. Once again from the poetry of Majnūn comes the finest wrought, and soon to become paradigmatic, Umayyad phrasing of this sensibility-determining motif:

No passion of a Bedouin maiden
tossed about unforewarned
By the caprice of distant places
is as strong.

When she recalls Najd, the fragrance of its earth,
The coolness of its pebbles, she sobs and moans!

No passion is more ardent, none deeper than mine,
For the hills at Liwā
when the shadows have spread.

She craved milk brought from the pastures
and for a tent in Najd,
But what she wished fate did not grant.[37] [115]

Here, in the still recognizable mode of the *nasīb*, under the cloak of a *ghazal* that is soon to become customary, the poet speaks of his own soul as a Bedouin maiden—forlorn, unsteady, driven by adversities, with the great yearning of Najd before her. But the image and its diction are strongly bivalent and evocative of the poetically more archaic image of the "yearning she-camel." It is significant that Ibn Khafājah, the poet from al-Andalus who understood the idiom of the *nasīb* so well, should have included verses 1 and 4 of this poem/fragment in a gentle, melancholy prose vignette, where, however, no archaic she-camel is suggested. Instead, the one that yearns is the poet's soul. The desire is one of repose in pastoral simplicity, and the place is Najd, the ever-haunting Arcadian dream.[38]

Besides these prima facie recognizable pastoral motif elements in Arabic poetry, another, quite specific motif, or rather mode of vision, which defines the pastoral dimension of Arabic lyricism most of all, claims our attention. But precisely because of the genre-quality of this motif there also emerges the critical precaution to stress the profound difference that exists—as far as the specificity of pastoral vision is concerned—between the Greek and Latin pastoral (with its European genre-adherence which has proven to be nothing short of archetypally self-sustaining) and that Arabic manifestation of the pastoral, in its own way quite strikingly explicit, that takes as its theater not the earth but the sky. Nevertheless, because of an inversion of perspective between the poet and his pastoral landscape, which the proper recognition of this motif presupposes, Arabic, including Orientalist, literary criticism has found itself unable, or otherwise unprepared, to explore it significantly.

Quite literally, this motif speaks of the Bedouin poet as *the pastor of the stars,* and its ubiquitousness in the pre-Islamic elegiac *nasīb* and in the earliest formal elegy and then, increasingly, in the Umayyad and subsequent Arabic lyrical stances ought to have alerted literary criticism and scholarship to the existence of an Arabic pastoral mode that is different in a critically challenging way. It is certainly not a formally definable genre (and nothing short of the obviousness of the "genre" was what scholarship and criticism seemed to need in order to become alerted to it), but it is nonetheless equally certainly a vision whose very specificity holds the key to its literary significance.

It was undeniably quite in keeping with Ignaz Goldziher's discernment and familiarity with Arabic poetic texts to have called attention in 1902 to the motif of the "pastor of the stars" in the oldest Arabic poetry. To him it qualified as reflective of "the circumstances of Arab Bedouinity," for the "watching of the stars" is perceived as watching herds on a meadow and "is connected with the fact that the ancient Arabs had viewed the stars from their perspective as herdsmen."[39] And yet, even though Goldziher then proceeds to identify the main range of meaning in Arabic poetry of this poetic image, he lacks the incentive to overstep the bounds of philology, reducing his hermeneutic perspicacity to a mere corrective footnote to the reading of medieval Hebrew poetry.[40]

The Egyptian critic Luṭfī ʿAbd al-Badīʿ, too, comes close to an interpretively productive awareness of the inverted perspective of an Arabic pastoral. He speaks of the early Arabs as having represented astral groupings through familiar animal images and of having given them corresponding names, "as though they had transferred the earth to the sky. Thus came into being a pageant both animal and luminous, to which the eyes reach out. The poets addressed it in their intimacy, and so did their rational and irrational poetic figurations."[41] What we are left with here, however, is not so much a reference to the pastoral poetic vision of a "transfer of the earth to the sky" as rather the abstracted and certainly quite universal rudiments of animistic astronomy.

Another contemporary Arabic critic misses the point completely when he speaks almost resentfully of his failed search for an Arabic pastoral self-view: "I should have spoken of man as pastor in the pre-Islamic poetic image, only that I found out that pre-Islamic poetry is well-nigh devoid of the image of the pastor."[42] Such a confession is especially disappointing, since it comes almost three quarters of a century after Goldziher.

It is nevertheless true that conventional pastoral images in Arabic poetry do not command broader contexts that necessarily lead to a notion of genre, and that those images that are not conventional, namely those of the "pasturing of the stars," are as a rule meant to unfold in complete disengagement from the familiar Arabian landscape, even from the most stylized landscape of the idyll. Within these confines, however, the Arabic poet indeed sees himself as a pastor; and this he expresses so many times, especially in so many elegiac openings of poems. He constantly uses the word "to herd," "to pasture," when he speaks of himself. So he is a pastor. His herds and pastures, however, must not be real—and here Arabic poetry once again proves how true to itself it is. Like the campsite ruins and abandoned abodes, like so many place-names in the *nasīb*, like the poet's yearning itself, everything must be a filtration of many experiences, a symbol and an archetype.

Escaping the obviousness of things pastoral, and escaping the "genre" in the Western sense, the Arabic poet's self-view becomes instead a projection onto a personified firmament. The nightly sky of his loneliness is his pasture, the scattered constellations his herds. He will remain the restless, watchful herdsman, or he will delegate this role to the companions of his journey, to his beloved, or to the planets in the firmament, who will then share his loneliness. This cosmic pastoral projection is frequent in Arabic poetry of all periods. We may insist that it constitutes a traditional motif with a metaphoric applicability;

but then, particularly in the ***nasīb,*** every motif is meant to have metaphoric applicability. Such is the protean dimensionality of the form itself. The ultimate extent of the cosmic metaphor in the ***nasīb,*** like the ultimate extent of the motif of the abandoned abodes, depends on its starting point: man's yearning for his first abode of happiness and man's vision of himself as reflected in the order of things. The Arab poet did not develop, or rather, did not insist on, the explicit pastoral metaphor of idyllic Arcady. But, whereas Vergil had literally to discover melancholy in the distilled idyll of his Arcady, the poet of the ***nasīb*** was given every sadness generously and freely by the endless repository of that substance, the nightly sky.

Thus the pre-Islamic poet al-Nābighah al-Dhubyānī despairs of the morning star, as pastor, ever bringing in his herds:

Leave me, O Umaymah, to wearisome care
And to a night of slow-wheeling
stars that I bear—

A night that stretched on till I said:
It will not end,
And he who herds the stars will not return.[43] [116]

So, too, the two most famous early elegists, the "archaic" Muhalhil Ibn Rabīʿah and the already transitional (***mukhaḍramah***) poetess al-Khansāʾ resort to that pastoral motif as expressive of their heightened states of disconsolation. Muhalhil opens his elegy for his brother Kulayb still more as a stargazer than a "pastor":

Memories in the still of night
nettled my eyes,
And tears had to flow.

The night engulfed us all as though
There were no daylight after night.

And through it I watched the Gemini
Till their firstlings had nearly set—

Sending my gaze after a folk
Whom land after land carried off,
and they were no more.

I wept as the stars surged and surged,
As though no ocean could contain
and hide them.[44] [117]

The pastoral quality of the image in an elegy by al-Khansāʾ comes through more clearly, and her choice of diction is more explicit: she uses the verb *raʿā* (to pasture) instead of Muhalhil's intentional synonym *raqaba* (to watch):

In restless wakefulness I spend the night.
My eyes seem smeared with pus not with collyrium.

I tend the stars, although not tasked to tend them,
Throwing at times about me the flaps of my rags.[45] [118]

Inasmuch as the motif of pasturing the stars in a genre-specific elegy falls where it might otherwise belong in any paradigmatically structured *qaṣīdah*—thus in the above case of al-Nābighah al-Dhubyānī—it ought to be associated in its mood-effect, as well as structurally, with the motif of the ruinous abodes (*aṭlāl*). In another of al-Khansā's elegies, however, this pastoral motif's belated figuring as verse 23[46] necessarily interferes with its affective association with the *aṭlāl*—and thus with the *nasīb*. In such a position the motif is absorbed more explicitly into the overall context of the dirge with its overruling mood and rhetorical requirements. Even then, however, it retains enough of its original modal quality to be "functional" as a pastorally evocative *lyrical* break in the dramatic directness and intensity of the dirge-diction that preceded it. It allows passion a respite but also makes it possible for the dirge to resume its drama with renewed intensity thereafter. Furthermore it is necessary to notice that in this poem the stargazing/starpasturing motif emerges from the context set by verse 22:

22. A trusted man confirmed to me the death
of a brave man's son,
When before there had been rumor of his doom.
23. And through the night, wakeful with the star,
I kept watch,
Till shrouds fell, and there was no star.[47] [119]

The verb *turajjamu* in verse 22 alerts us to the centrality of the semiotics of the semantic field of *najm* (star) in the following line, for *rajjama* as "to guess," "have uncertainty about something," but also "to try to know the unknown," points toward *najjama*, "to read (interpret) the stars," "to practice astrology"; and moreover, *rajjama* as "to throw stones at the dangerous, evil, or ominous unknown" is also, as it were, a way of throwing pebbles at the stars. And still within the established, etymologically associative circle, the meaning of *rujum* is that of "shooting stars." The context thus formed by verses 22 and 23 of this elegy is, and is not, that of the more generally familiar "pasturing of the stars," for that motif is here a very flexible metaphor for other things as well. Thus the star which the poetess watches, or pastures, through the night must also be seen as the projection of the impending confirmation of the rumor that her brother has fallen in battle, ultimately because it—the star—*is* her brother himself. Pastoral melancholy is thus no more. The imprint of the ***nasīb*** is no more. Their place has been taken over by the stronger dynamism of tragedy.

At times the pre-Islamic poet will see his camel herds, or caravans, projected onto the nightly firmament. Thus ʿAdī Ibn Zayd:

> And as though stars, when they rose above my head,
> Were she-camels driven by their driver's chant.[48] [120]

The longevous Ḥassān Ibn Thābit, who in the latter half of his life became the Prophet's most loyal bard, left us from his earlier poetic phase one of the finest and best articulated visions of the pastoral firmament. The ***nasīb*** of this ode begins in an apparently objectivized manner. It seems as if the only thing that interests him poetically is to develop to its fullest extent an attractive metaphor. But then, in the fifth verse, the poet's personal feeling, his melancholy, which had been there all the time, interferes and breaks through in almost a cry of panic:

> At Khammān the night had length to spare.
> The firstlings of the stars
> did not intend to lead the flock to set.
>
> Tending it, as if entrusted, I shunned sleep,
> Lest first they come to set and rest.
>
> Star upon star went down. The night had run its course,
> But always one last star remained to hold
> my scanning eye.
>
> An endless train over the firmament,
> of road-worn camels, you would say,
> And in their trail, as morning breaks,
> you wander on.
>
> I fear the sudden jolt of separation, that our roads
> May each one go its way,
> scatter us, cast us apart.[49] [121]

In a poem by the pre-Islamic brigand-poet Ta'abbaṭa Sharran, the poet's brooding thoughts are set on blood vengeance but are misconstrued by his carefree travel companion, who asks him whether it is love for which he pines and pastures the stars:

Is it for want of Suʿād that pasturing of stars
is on your mind, or are you
lost and moonstruck?[50] [122]

It is thus melancholy, the self-distancing sense of loneliness of the star-crossed lover, that makes even the earliest textually documented Arab poets lyrically apprehend and multifariously develop the contemplative potential of the star-studded firmament—until that firmament becomes their great pastoral metaphor. The Arabic pastoral mood is therefore preeminently elegiac and for the most part directly tied to the emotive matrix of the *nasīb*. Only in the rarest of instances and, as it were, working in a studied way against the "canon" does the pre-Islamic warrior-poet ʿAntarah opt for a *ghazal*-like alternative in the employment of this motif: not to speak of a "night of solitude" but of a "night of love." Even then, however, we realize that the motif continues to function structurally within the *nasīb* proper, not in the customary elegiac opening but instead in verses 20 and 21, firmly in the *nasīb*'s "development," where that which was elegiacly "real" forgets itself momentarily in reverie:

With the night's veils lowered,
I sported with her
Till dawn burst in light's splendor—

Tending the nightly stars,
Flasks with quicksilver aquiver.[51] [123]

On the other hand, while still preserving its mood-fidelity, the Arabic cosmic pastoral vision is also capable of breaking out of the tender strictures of *nasīb* melancholy into modal and thematic ranges such as those of the dirge and the poem of vengeance. Then we do not fail to register in them echoes of cosmically present tragedy. Such is the pre-Islamic warrior-poet Bishr Ibn Abī Khāzim's watching, or pasturing, of the celestial bier carriers, the Bier's Daughters,[52] in the closure, or recapitulation, of a *nasīb* that is built upon a transference of the departure of the maidens of the tribe (*ẓaʿāʾin*)—and with them of the poet's beloved—onto the nightly firmament of his loneliness:

Awake I spent the night
As if with wine leaching through my joints,

Keeping watch in the sky
over the Bier's Daughters
That turned the way
the antelope herd veers about—

Only the Pleiades yet persisting,
after the still of night,
And Capella, their neighbor.[53] [124]

In the poetry of the Umayyad period, however, the celestial pastoral metaphor appears to be more restricted or more unidirectional in its lyrical diapason. It rarely extends beyond mere affective believability in the newly sprung *ghazal* genre. Above all, Umayyad lyricism and Umayyad sensibility appear to have had little use for the archaic pathos of the Jāhilīyah and for the drama that could change elegy into dirge or into an ode of blood vengeance.[54] A less articulated lyricism thus prevailed.

Quite appropriately, the representative of this new *ghazal*, ʿUmar Ibn Abī Rabīʿah, is also one of the most adept Umayyad poets at cultivating the astral pastoral metaphor of old. In one poem, he combines it skillfully with another motif of great ascendance in his day and genre, that of the dream vision (*ṭayf al-khayāl*):

A dream vision alighted and my passion rose
The night we spent by the dunes.

When the riders rested it settled near me:
Memories' inveterate malady, my care.

And I spent the night on my elbow pillowed,
pasturing the stars, love-struck—
For toil is the lover's lot.[55] [125]

Then, too, with equal skill, he allows the motif to have its own mood-quality and imagist skyscape familiarity:

And so I remain a pastor of the night,
And I wait
for Spica to sink,
for Aquila to fall.[56] [126]

And then quite in the old mold:

The carefree one slept, while I spent the night
        not on a pillow,
But pasturing stars, bleary-eyed.[57] [127]

From the Umayyad poets' unimpaired ability to register poetically the Bedouin experience, critically important instances of objectivization of the cosmic pastoral vision have come to us. More intently than their Jāhilī forerunners, the Umayyad herder-hunters draw precise contours upon the sky. Their imaginative indebtedness to concrete pastoral surroundings then emerges stronger than the impact of the cosmic spectacle. Thus we read in Dhū al-Rummah (d. 117/735–36):

When I came, the stars were trailing
        Arcturus and Spica,
Turning their rumps like
        wild cows and gazelles.[58] [128]

The precision of the language in the visual apprehension of wild cows and gazelles as they turn away in flight adds a special liveliness and earthbound reality to the poet's vision of the firmament. It brings it down. It also validates and interprets critically much of the Arabic pastoral conceit as what it may also be: a visual shortcut, an allusion.

With the transition from the Umayyad to the Abbasid period, the Arabic poet's pastoral vision of the nightly sky becomes more varied and imaginatively engaged, while at the same time his terminological familiarity with astronomy comes into stronger evidence. Abū al-Hindī,[59] the wine-loving precursor of Abū Nuwās, is an early representative of this revitalization of the old pastoral metaphor, only that now (albeit not without indebtedness to the still centrally Umayyad Dhū al-Rummah[60]) the poet himself is not necessarily the pastor of the flocks of the starry meadow/firmament. The pastoral image may now also possess its own referentiality of aesthetic objectivity, and the poet may be no more than the aesthetically alert spectator:

When I heard the cock announce the dawn
And when the two Vultures [Vega and Aquila]
        centered in Scorpio's fold,

And throngs of stars followed each other
Like dust-colored antelope on lookout peaks,

And Canopus appeared in the sky as though
A bull had faced a herd of full-breeds,

Then I roused my companion and said:
O son of nobles, partake, with the morning,
of this red wine![61] [129]

Ibn Shuhayd (d. 426/1035) was a poet who was still a pastor of the stars in the archaic elegiac manner of the *nasīb,* but his aesthetic sensibility also reflects a prolonged courtly honing, the effects of which manifested themselves so brilliantly and abundantly in eleventh-century al-Andalus. Quite knowingly, he develops his starry pastoral metaphor from within the formal givens of the *nasīb;* then he allows it to grow into its own poem-within-a-poem, where he, as the observing and speaking persona, is first the traditional melancholy pastor-lover, then the aesthetically enraptured observer. He allows the enchanted nocturnal sky to turn into beds of flowers only to see the brilliance of flowers turn into flashes of swords—but still playful, courtly—and the cosmic grandeur of overspreading darkness to be garlanded with bubbles, and the stars to turn once again into flowers: narcissus that overgrow the banks of the Milky Way. But he makes other stars and constellations act out the semiotics of their own names, their own allegory and mythopoesis: the Gemini, the Throne, Aldebaran, the Pleiades. These then turn into doves that gather to drink of the waters of the full moon, itself turned into a pool. And in the end, this "digressive" pastoral metaphor returns to where it began: the reverie is reabsorbed into the elegiac whole of the *nasīb,* stars turn into the poet's tears, and the night ends, but slowly:

Sleepless I spent the night, pasturing the stars
in flocks large and small—
Stars that rise but do not set
for those who tend them.

Every flower held its mouth agape there
For the milk-rich udder of the cloud,

And armies of rain clouds bouyantly passed
Like hosts of Negroes brandishing gilded blades,

And the meteor-studded firmament soared—
A fathomless depth, bubble-crowned.

Bright constellations there you deemed narcissus
On a wadi's strand, flowing toward the Milky Way,

And in the Gemini, as they set, you beheld
A tottering, leaning, tumbling Throne.

Aldebaran you thought a Falcon fallen
On Pleiades' nest, on her red-cropped brood,

And the full moon in the dark a pool circled
With stars like flights of doves that set to slake their thirst . . .

As though night's darkness were my care,
    its stars my tears
That over the fated fortunes of the vile
    stream down in woe.

But for a few, the stars on high have fallen.
They took in their decline
    what men of sense attain![62] [130]

In another poem Ibn Shuhayd again succumbs to melancholy as he witnesses the cosmic motions of the nightly sky, again in the metaphorical pastoral manner; but the serene grandeur of the cosmic spectacle prevails over what started merely as an inward-turned musing:

And I wept over a time
  whose journey-stations were behind me
And over youth whose bloom I brought to seed,

And heaven's countenance was to my tending eye
    as though a thicket green,
And from its ponds the full moon shone.

In its midst the scattered stars
    seemed sheep,
And Gemini their shepherd,

Like jewels were the Pleiades
Strewn by Taurus's pawing,

And like a prim beauty of the tribe, Sirius,
    her children left behind,
Came down with Aquila's highest star.[63] [131]

In between such varieties of images and metaphorizing perspectives, a more "traditional" cultivation of the celestial pastoral continued to rule without losing the charm of its indwelling lyricism. Thus Abū Tammām, whose innovative poetics had otherwise assaulted traditional Arabic sensibility, is here both new and old:

O Rāmah, had you but savored longer
    old intimacy's ties,

You'd have been the concourse
 of every white antelope.

Many a night I spent keeping watch
 as if mortally wounded,
Or sleepless over one by viper stung.

Of its stars I pastured
 white, free-grazing camels,
That do not return to him
 who in the pasture frees them.

But had you asked the dark of night about me,
 I swear,
Of a great passion it would have brought you news![64] [132]

Within the same heightened sensibility with a strong traditional imprint, we find also the Damascene al-Wa'wā' (d. 390/999):

O night that I donned, like the night of bereft mothers,
Its eastern confines not leading to the west,

The green hue of its air
 as if a tower of chrysolite,
With pearls strewn
 from a full-bosomed maiden's neck—

As though recondite constellations
 in darkness overspread
Were flashes of succor in my anxious heart,

And on clouds' meadows there grazed
 a flock of nightly stars,
Their pastor the full moon.[65] [133]

With an unabashedly literalist observance of the traditional phrasing, the Valencian Ibn Khafājah nonetheless superimposes upon that Bedouin vision of the nightly sky the strikingly inventive (precisely because it is itself as old as the myth of Atlas) conceit of making a sorrow-burdened mountain, apparently the cliff of Gibraltar, pronounce the archaic Bedouin pastoral complaint:

How long shall I pasture stars
 through sleepless nights,
For, when all nights have ended,
 they still will set and rise?[66] [134]

But it is the Cordovan Ibn Ḥazm (d. 456/1063) who gives us the most polyfaceted and "conceptualized" version of this motif. In a didactic guise, that is, well in accordance with the general stylistic conceit of his detailed essay on love, *The Dove's Neck-Ring*, he briefly introduces the particular manner in which the lovelorn, star-gazing poets are given to musing away their sorrows. His own verses then illustrate the conceit and thus include him, too, among the "pastors of the stars":

> I pasture the stars as though entrusted
> To tend all fixed constellations
> and planets that incline to set.
>
> For, when the night's ablaze
> with passion's flames, they seem
> To have ignited out of the darkness of my mind,
>
> And I become like a green meadow's keeper,
> Its grasses cross-garlanded with narcissus.
>
> Were Ptolemy alive, he'd vouch
> that of all men
> I am the ablest one to chart
> the movement of the stars![67] [135]

What the poet has done in this pastoral vignette (in spite of his minimalistic claim to merely having successfully structured into one poetic line multiple comparables[68]) is that in a series of allusions and mixed metaphors he has drawn what might be the ultimate perimeter of this motif within the Arabic lyrical-elegiac mode, or genre, that remains indebted to the *nasīb*. He opened his first verse with a fully intentional, strong allusion to al-Khansā', mainly, but also to her contemporary Ḥassān Ibn Thābit, as both these poets were to him not only a manageable source but also a legitimate literary-historical moment of "classicism." Through them he, the Cordovan, could seize and hold his own sense of closeness to the origins of the Arabic cosmic pastoral. His "ar'ā al-nujūma ka'annanī kulliftu" (I pasture the stars as though entrusted) is thus only a "version" of al-Khansā''s "ar'ā al-nujūma wa mā kulliftu" (I pasture the stars, although not entrusted)[69] and a paraphrase of Ḥassān Ibn Thābit's "urā'īhā ka'annī muwakkalun" (I tend them as though entrusted).[70] But he also closes the verse by obliquely evoking al-Khansā''s epithetic name ("the camous-nosed antelope-cow") through the panoply of meanings of the astral epithet *al-khunnas*, "the planets," or "the movable stars," "the stars that incline to set and hide (but that always 'return')."[71]

While still mindful of the effect of the transference of his Bedouin meadows and flocks to the starry firmament, the poet transforms those stars/flocks in his second verse into his own consuming passion's fires. Such fires, however, do not ignite the "pathetic" commonplace of the heart, as the customary courtly poetic stance might have dictated, but instead they burn in, and out of, the darkness of the poet's mind. Is the poet making here another archaizing allusion, this time to the anthropologically more than poetically ancient seat of the "mind" whose ability to "know" is still as much passionate as it is plastically mimetic? Has he returned to the archaic *qalb* (heart), which had long since ceased "thinking" and "knowing" and given itself to "feeling" only as the sentimental *qalb/fu'ād?* The poet's state of mind is unmistakable in its effect: the luminosities and projections of the cosmic pastoral have found their place in the paradoxically expansive microcosmos that is the poet's mind. In it is ignited the universe of his thoughts/sorrows.

The third verse then effects a further important change in the complex cosmic/pastoral landscape. The poet sees himself as "the keeper of a green meadow." In the referential context of the Arabic *nasīb* and, from there, of Arabic garden-poetry, what the image is and what it tells us is quite clear. The archaic Arabic poetic meadow (*rawḍah*) must now be understood as "a garden"; and a garden with its poetic "keeper" (*ḥāris*) must be seen as having undergone the subtle metamorphosis into a privileged space, a *hortus conclusus,* of which the poet, by being capable of "vision," is the keeper. The stars, too, have changed and have become cross-garlanded beds of narcissus on which, we must assume, as the Arab poets did, "no reprobate shall tread."[72]

Finally, verse 4 rounds off this stratified metaphor with, it seems, scientific sobriety: "Were Ptolemy alive . . . ! ," or, "If only Ptolemy were alive . . . !" Certainly that father of scientific astronomy would vouch that Ibn Ḥazm of Cordova was truly the foremost watcher of the course of the stars. But has all this "scientific sobriety" really done away with the pastoral metaphor or with the pastoral vision? To demand of this Arab poet, or of any poet, explicitness of things pastoral beyond the conceit is almost to miss the whole point—at least on levels of poetic meaning; and explicitness of vision would fare even worse. Implicit identification of meaning and vision should be the poet's legitimate entitlement. For such an identification we must look into the "language" of this verse. Thus, beginning with the sidereal term *al-khunnas,* "the stars, or planets, of erratic course," we cannot but become aware of the virtual transparency of its etymology—for it is an epithet whose original meaning was, and still is in an active poetic sense, "gazelles repairing to their covert." Immediately, too, come to mind the *kunnas* of the poem's closure as *jawārī al-kunnas,* "the runners" among such gazelles, which are also "the movable stars" of the poet-turned-astronomer, as well as "the celestial maids in attendance," and "the angels." All these, we have to remember, had their origin in the pastoral root-etymology *k-n-s/kh-n-s* and in the pastoral vision of things celestial.

Still, the archaic Bedouin poet from whom such language stems was not only a pastor but also a hunter. His "astronomer's watching" (*raṣd*)—in the fourth verse—was not only pastoral herding but also "lying in wait" for antelope and other grazing animals as his quarry. Being a "chivalrous" hunter, he had to chase such quarry on his "strong steed." He was thus a *muqwī,* "a rider on a powerful steed," and himself "most able" (*aqwā*). Even the meaning of *al-warā* ("men, mankind") in this context is further enriched, albeit through a false etymology, for it, too, suggests "being behind, or in pursuit," of that herd or quarry. Ultimately, therefore, the poet sees himself as that astronomer who understands the many meanings of the night and of its stars; and if his watching the stars and charting their course fills him with a very Bedouin *fakhr*-like pride, enough to secure him Ptolemy's *shahādah* (testimony, entitlement), such "astronomy" only underscores the fact that he is inextricably caught up in and torn between a hopeless "chase of love"—no matter how gallant—and his melancholy pastoral contemplation.[73]

With the "run of the gazelles repairing to their covert" (*jary al-kunnas*) in mind once again, we must then return to the celestial gazelles, or rather antelope, that, especially as *al-kunnas,* have become the distinctly feminine personifications of "movable" planets. Furthermore, while evoking the name of the poetess al-Khansā', they also tell us that, etymologically, they are indistinguishable from the antelope-stars *al-khunnas.* We thus know firmly that there is a pastoral continuum in this short poem's condensation of individual motifs and that the explicitly pastoral *arʿā* does not stand alone but is supported by an intentionally cohesive poetic diction. So, too, in verse 2, the poet's thought, or mind, which has become the very darkness of the night (*fikratī min ḥindisi*) or, as it were, his "dark night of the soul," is announcing the disturbing ambiguity of the *rawḍah khaḍrā'* (green meadow) of the verse that follows; for, as green as the grass of a meadow may be—especially if the meadow has become a *hortus conclusus*—the word *khaḍrā'* in archaizing poetic Arabic points to the tone, or color, of darkness, of the steely blackness of the nightly firmament.[74]

The gloom of the poet's thoughts is thus not dispelled by his being a pastor/guardian of a "green meadow." This preserves the pastoral melancholy mood of the poem even as the poet luxuriates in visions of "the garden," or is it that only then is he tempted to luxuriate in them?

As a second underlying grid, a further element is to be accounted for in both the motival construct and the diction of Ibn Ḥazm's pastoral vignette. That element is a discreet, but not opaque, echoing of verses 15 and 19 of the qur'ānic Sūrah of The Darkening, or The Setting (*al-takwīr*), where not only all three of Ibn Ḥazm's pastoral/celestial key terms—*al-khunnas, al-jawārī, al-kunnas*—appear but where, furthermore, the qur'ānic speaker's oath by the celestial/pastoral bodies is meant to confirm the validity of the prophetic Messenger (v. 19). A hermeneutically cogent compounded reading of Ibn Ḥazm thus emerges: the divine guarantor, now Ptolemy, validating with respective *shahādah*s once the Messenger, then the poet. Poetically, the equation works so well—and indeed must have been irresistably tantalizing to Ibn Ḥazm—because the archaic pre-Islamic resonance of the pastoral vision is itself clearly perceptible in the qur'ānic choice of phrase as well.

Outside the pale of this Arabic poetic conceptism in full bloom, Ibn Ḥazm's appeal to the authority of astronomy may be seen as supplemented by Ibn Khafājah's reading of the stars, in which the latter forswears astrology:

> I tend the nightly stars for full-moon's love,
> And may no one so lightly deem me an astrologer.[75] [136]

The Arab poetic view of the cosmos may indeed not be thought of as a derivative of astrology. It is, however, a form of astronomy. It is, after all, an image of the sky which the poet sees and understands initially on an objectivized level, even if it be on the level of a receding pastoral experience. The otherwise evasive and infinitely distancing vision-scape of the sky becomes knowable to the poet as the spread-out pasture with all the grazing animals in projection. In so simple and poetically convincing a way, the Arab poet faces the problem of giving form to vision: he speaks of the sky in as clear a language as he has at his disposal. In this, within his own confines, he is being objective. The objectivity of the Arabic poetic retina, however, must not be carried beyond the limits of the once apprehended image. What happens to the pastoral image of the sky when it enters into the designs of the *nasīb* is what really determines it as poetry; and it is once again through the prism of the *nasīb* that we perceive the decisive transformations which take place in themes and motifs. We realize that the pastoral Bedouin poet rarely speaks of true pastures and meadows when he is constructing metaphors and deriving abstractions adrift in the mood of loneliness and loss. His idyllic landscapes and evocations all have about them the rarefied halo of the pastoral, but this halo hardly ever materializes. In the poetic Najd we have very strong intimations as to where we are, but the poet refuses us the repose of final explicitness. Instead, he transposes to the nightly sky what would have been the true pastoral landscape and thus seemingly irrevocably splits his sorrow and yearning: all the ***diyār,*** the Ḥijāz and Najd, remain as symbolic references tied to the ground, while at the same time their meadows and grazing herds are lifted into the dark nightly firmament, where they, too, can subsist only as images of something else and as abstracted symbols. Thus his yearning for things lost retains him below, while his sense of loneliness carries him upward. And yet by this method of dissociation of images in the physical sense—if we may presume that there survives in metaphors and symbols the tight logic of physical interdependence of objects—the ***nasīb*** as the supreme container of mood only combines what formerly were opposites into a unity of perception within which one becomes the reflection of the other. The Bedouin poet seems more ready to develop his resulting imagist reductionism of the pastoral theme in the abstracted landscape of the cosmic projection. As a symbolist faithful to his formal tradition, the Arab poet thus chooses the more direct road to the ultimate symbol of his pastoral condition. If he then refuses to develop the symbol further, past its archetypal condensation, this, once again, is entirely true to the nature of Arabic poetry and to the archetypal theme-abstraction which in so special a way takes place in the ***nasīb***.

To round off our Arabian pastoral argument, it is hermeneutically convenient—and textually felicitous—to be able to furnish from within the Arabic interpretive tradition an instance of a narratively construed, deliberate lapse in the identification of the cosmic projection of the pastoral state of mind by turning it into a pastoral tableau that is explicitly earth-bound. Quite significantly, such a hermeneutically relevant instance comes once again from the "anonymous"—and thus collectively validating—verse of Majnūn, as that verse blends with the prose narrative of its commentary or fable (***akhbār***).

Thus there is in Majnūn's ***Dīwān*** a short poem of eight verses (nine in the Cairo edition), in which the motif of "pasturing the stars" appears in the opening verse as well as in the closure, providing an almost rondeau-like tension between finality and openness:

O herders of the nightly flock,
what has the morning done,
And what its spritely heralds?

And those who hold captive my heart,
what do they care
Whether they alight or once again set out?

And unrelenting stars, suspended
from a lover's heart,
What do they care?

The night they said: "Come morning,
or come evening,
Laylā ʿĀmirīyah will have left,"

My heart was like a sand-grouse
gulled into a snare.
She tugged at it all night,
the wing already trapped.

She left two chicks on a bare plain,
Their nest rent by the wind.

The night brought her no hope,
No respite gave the morn.

O herders of the nightly flock,
mind me no more,
My fated love has slain me well![76] [137]

Without its storied commentary, the poem's herders are the poet's companions, other sympathetic lovers and travellers in the poetic desert who, together, spend their nights in melancholy contemplation of the starlit sky. But in the story accompanying this poem we actually obtain a "realistic" pastoral scenario: after receiving the news of his father's death and after ritually slaughtering a she-camel on his father's grave (a scene which in itself gives room to a two-line epigram), "he then rose and walked off; and as he roamed about, there he saw a fire at the foot of a hill. He approached it only to find a party of herdsmen bent over the flames. He joined them, and they recognized him."[77]

It is at this point that Majnūn intones his pastoral elegy, but his "herders of the night" are now no longer cosmic pastors. It would be interpretively incorrect, however, to assume that all the lyrical effectiveness and the "pastoral empathy" that inhere in the genre's Arabic idiosyncrasy have thereby become lost either to the verses or to the narrative, for something poetically quintessentially "pastoral" is perceived here, too. Moreover, we are closer to the genre's familiar and more easily verified specificity.[78]

Finally, as intrinsically Arabic as this cosmic projection of the pastoral vision may be, the literary universality and archetypal primacy of the principle of such transference of experience must not be left out of sight, for it will provide both a contextualization and a further interpretive vantage point. We may begin from within the Arabic cosmological tradition as it is reflected in the Qur'ān, where God's raising of the dome of the sky "does not require visible pillars" (*bi ghayri ʿamadin tarawnahā*)[79] and stands as metaphor in reference to the raising of other domes that rest on pillars, especially Bedouin tents, which with terminological explicitness are also raised on *ʿamad*. The Bedouin referentiality, however, is here not the only one, for such tents, canopies, or domes, as the full context of verse 2 of the Sūrah of the Thunder suggests, are ultimately the canopies and domes of sovereignty. In the *Muʿallaqah* of Labīd, verse 83, we read:

> And he built for us a house,
> high its roof,
> And there ascended [in pageant]
> their grown men and their youths.[80] [138]

Such a "Bedouin" high roof, too, is a potential metaphor of the cosmic canopy with its capacity to bestow power and authority. Both the Qur'ān's and Labīd's mutually complementary uses of the cosmic canopy, however, are inseparable from the universal, and especially Middle Eastern, ancient mythic visualization of the dome of the sky as a roof, or rather as a tent, that is supported by the world-pillar or world-tree, or, as in Isaiah 40:22, where "the heavens spread like a curtain and extend like a tent to live in." Of crucial importance to the archetypal pastoral visualization of the "tent of heaven" is that, as such, it was "the pastoral tent of the world" (*das Hirtenzelt der Welt*) of the Babylonians,[81] or "house of the pastoral tent of the world" (*Haus des Hirtenzeltes der Welt*).[82] Within their archaic mythopoesis, the Romans, too, viewed the world (*mundus*) as the reflection of the nightly firmament—or as reflected in it—for the Latin word *mundus* has, among its perplexing array of actually etymologically and merely mythopoetically relatable meanings not only that of the world as "the earth" (and/or its inhabitants, "humankind") but also that of "the sky" (or "heaven"), "decked with stars"; and even when placed in the Underworld of the ancestral spirits as archaic Rome's hub, *mundus* was "shaped like the vault of heaven."[83] Ovid's lover's call in *Amores*, "Lente currite, noctis equi"[84] (Run slowly, O horses of the night) thus resounds across familiar mirrored spaces.

Nevertheless, the pastoral imagination transferred to the nightly sky remains a distinctly rare disposition in Western poetry, and when it occurs it has to be formally constructed and developed in each instance, even if it does not go beyond the confines of mere "image" toward the broader functionality of a motif or theme. This, of course, has then the possible advantage of imaginative and expressive freshness. Despite the disparity of frequency of occurrence, there is a strong genre-characteristic that links the "rare" Western cosmic pastoral to the "frequent" cosmic pastoral of Arabic poetry. It is by no means a minor fact that in both genre-ranges of lyricism such a pastoral vision is linked to the mood, and the genre, of what in poetry is either a formal elegy or is otherwise in a genre-determining way enveloped in the elegiac mood, as is the case in the classical Arabic *nasīb*.

Thus in the overall idyllic mood-range of Jacopo Sannazaro's *Arcadia,* we come across intimations of a cosmic pastoral projection only in Eclogue 5, which comes introduced to us through "some ten cowherds that were dancing in a round about the venerable tomb of the shepherd Androgeo," readying themselves for "performing the melancholy rite,"[85] which consisted of pouring milk, blood, and wine upon the flower-strewn tomb.[86] Then the shepherd Ergasto sings his song/eclogue of the venerated Androgeo, who, from his star among the translucent spirits, treads with holy footprints the wandering stars and among pure fountains and sacred myrtles pastures the heavenly flocks and governs his beloved shepherds. These are "other mountains, other plains, other woods and rills."[87]

The effect of this early Renaissance essay in the cosmic pastoral is felt in Friedrich Spee, a poet pastoralist of the German Baroque. This poet is also more explicit and elaborate in his treatment of the motif of the nightly sky. In his lyrical collection *Trutznachtigall* (Untoward Nightingale), he devotes to this theme two eclogues (nos. 30 and 39). The time in both eclogues is the night. In both the starry firmament is the meadow, the stars are the herds of golden-fleeced sheep, and the moon is the shepherd. The first eclogue is an unadulterated idyll. In it two genre-familiar shepherds, Halton and Damon, watch the nightly firmament in lyrical rapture and address their cosmic peer, Shepherd Moon, calling upon him to praise the Creator for the felicitousness of his cosmic design. In the second eclogue, however, the air of pastoral idyll turns to elegiac sorrow and tragic pathos. While the moon is still the shepherd and the stars are the flock, the counterpoint to the cosmic pastoral is now the night of Christ's agony in the Garden of Gethsemane. Nevertheless, in a genre-conscious manner, Christ is given here the "pastoral" name of Daphnis and the emblem of the shepherd's staff. He is the supreme pastor, upon whose agony Shepherd Moon, in tears, looks down with prescient sadness and ultimately with tragic despair.[88]

In both eclogues we thus have, refracted rather than mirrored, pairs of parallel pastorals: one a projection into the nightly sky and the other a Baroque variation in style on the Renaissance "genre." Only in the second eclogue (no. 39), however, do we fully obtain what Gerhard H. Lemke calls a "heightened stylization and cosmic pathos."[89] In that eclogue, too, Friedrich Spee combines the late-medieval tradition of "Jesus-Minne" with some of the most topical Renaissance genre-characteristics of the pastoral, as well as with motifs of German folklore, such as *Sternenschäflein* (star-lambs).[90] Altogether, because of its elegiac character, Friedrich Spee's second astral pastoral is not alien to the Arabic sense of the cosmic pastoral space and mood—even if the deep green color of the Arabic nightly cosmic meadow becomes pronouncedly blue in the German pastoral.[91] Also the eclogue's closing turn, where "grazing" changes to "separation" ("Ja nit weidet / sondern scheidet"),[92] strikes the kindred elegiac chord of the Arabic *bayn* of separation.

More image than story, and thus closer to the Arabic poetic method, if not sensibility, is the evidence (equally curtailed) of the cosmic pastoral projection in the poetry of the Spanish Baroque, where Luis de Góngora introduces his *First Solitude* with an evocation of springtime in its lunar-solar month of April, when Taurus, "the feigned abductor of Europa . . . grazes upon stars in fields of sapphire."[93]

Different in tone, different in diction, disturbingly direct in its elegiac grip on sensibility, and above all compellingly close to both the pathos and the fragility of the Arabic elegiac stargazing is an example, once again isolated, from Walt Whitman's *Leaves of Grass:* his elegy for Abraham Lincoln, "When lilacs last in the dooryard bloom'd."

There is no actual "pasturing" in the imagery of that elegy, however, and, formally, in it we are dealing more with elegy than with pastoral. And yet, somewhere between stanza 8, which touches so closely upon Arabic star-fixed sensibility, and stanza 11, which echoes both the Song of Songs and Vergil's vespertinal bucolic eclogues, we also realize that the separation of those two genres is neither easy nor necessary, especially where stars are concerned.[94] It suffices that in stanza 8, with great imaginative cosmos-absorption, there are reflected the poet's manifold relationships to the starry heavens and to the intrinsic nature of his loss and that these then become one and, quite necessarily, evoke in an Arabic-nurtured sensibility similar instances, now explicitly pastoral, from al-Khansāʾ, Ḥassān Ibn Thābit, and Ibn Shuhayd, indeed from a whole familiar mode of feeling:

> O western orb sailing the heaven,
> Now I know what you must have meant as a month
> since I walk'd,
> As I walk'd in silence the transparent shadowy night,
> As I saw you had something to tell as you bent
> to me night after night,
> As you droop'd from the sky low down as if to my
> side, (while the other stars all look'd on,)
> As we wander'd together the solemn night, (for
> something I know not what kept me from sleep,)
> As the night advanced, and I saw on the rim of
> the west how full you were of woe,
> As I stood on the rising ground in the breeze
> in the cool transparent night,
> As I watch'd where you pass'd and was lost in
> the netherward black of the night,
> As my soul in its trouble dissatisfied sank,
> as where you sad orb,
> Concluded, dropt in the night, and was gone.[95]

An explicitly cosmic pastoral metaphor—of a Baroque-like complexity that is almost the equal of Friedrich Spee's—is developed by Unamuno, the "aquiline-leonine" Spanish poet of the "landscapes of the soul." In his poem entitled *In a Cemetery Somewhere in Castille,* he, too, chooses the crepuscular time of Vergil's Eclogue 10, the most pastoral of times. But Unamuno is a poet of high drama and of a distinctly "conceptist" propensity: the cross over the cemetery, where there reigns the Unamunian tragic paradox of "immortal silence" ("el silencio immortal de tu cercado"), is likened to a faithful dog that "remains like a guardian that never sleeps," watching the flock of the dead, who, like sheep, or indeed as sheep, herd together, penned against he sky.

> And from night's heaven, Christ,
> the pastor sovereign,
> with countless shimmering eyes
> recounts the herd's sheep![96]

The cosmic projection of the pastoral metaphor is inverted in this case, or rather, it becomes a counterpointed metaphor of shiftings from one *rebaño acorralado* to another, between heaven and earth.

Thus the cross, as it enters the "pastoral" sphere, becomes a shepherd's dog, and Christ's watchful eyes take over the shepherd's function. But the very same stars must also be seen in the other projection—of the flock in the cosmic "immortal silence."

It was entirely to be expected of a strong genre such as the pastoral that it participate in the poetic assimilation of the newly gained visual familiarity with the actual landscapes of the cosmos. Such is the poetic purpose of Diane Ackerman already in the title of her collection of poems *The Planets: A Cosmic Pastoral,* which promises to adhere to the "genre." This promise is indeed fulfilled if no more than in the collection's prevailing gentle, painterly objectivity of vision. The poetical result, however, is that of the idyll, not of elegy. In the poem *Mars* we read:

> So this is where Elysium lies,
> just north of Atlantis,
> on the far side of Barsoom:
> a velvet landfall, where volcanoes
> dome gently like saucers.[97]

Such poetry has not yet come in touch with the tragic sense of the cosmos, for it is being unveiled rather than conquered; there seems to be no room for elegy, nor is the pastor present in it yet.

FIVE

In Search of the Garden

1. On the Periphery of Autochthony

PROVOKED BY THE REALIZATION of how much the theme of Paradise and of its topical ramifications in Arabic literature demands the muse, Gustave E. von Grunebaum gives to Muḥammad and the Qur'ān what he takes away from the rest of Arabic literature. To him, "the full extent of his [Muḥammad's] achievement in introducing those novel themes into convention-bound Arabic literature will be understood through the failure of the next generations to resume the eminently poetical subjects of Paradise and Hell, Last Day and Judgment, in their verse."[1]

Leaving aside the contextually related subjects of Hell, Last Day, and Judgment, it would indeed appear that, taken strictly as an outgrowth of the qur'ānic topical treatment of Paradise, this "eminently poetic subject" is, as a rule, of limited scope and elaborateness in post-qur'ānic Arabic poetry. What is more, precisely when it is a "poetic" rephrasing of the qur'ānic topical model, it may not even qualify as a "theme," remaining merely an integrated motif, engaged to consolidate aspects of more primary textual intent of larger compositional units which indeed are fully articulated themes and which determine not only the content but also the structural design of poems. More properly, only these units deserve to be called "poetic subjects" in the sense demanded by von Grunebaum. In Umayyad and early Abbasid verse the subject of Paradise of qur'ānic provenance, if viewed in purely formalist literary terms, differs minimally from its appearance and formal integration in the "primary" qur'ānic contexts, inasmuch as in these, too, Paradise is *not* a full-fledged, self-referential "subject" (i.e., a theme) but, in this formalist sense, merely a motif. It is important to keep this terminological distinction in mind for the sake of a better compositional and functional understanding of the form-semiotics of both types of text—the poetic as well as the qur'ānic. We are thus faced with the provocative proposition that what von Grunebaum recognizes as the eminently poetic subject of Paradise in the Qur'ān may not have had the necessary "power" to engender truly *theme-centered* poetic developments, for the theme in literary-textual terms had not been there as a model to begin with. It would thus be wrong methodologically to accuse Arabic post-qur'ānic poetry of this particular flaw. On the level of a formal critical debate there was no ex post facto flaw.

For instance, we may want to compare one of the most extensive and seductive qur'ānic treatments of the subject of Paradise, in the Sūrah of Man (Al-Insān), verses 12–21, with the way it is reflected in a reportedly impromptu banquet scene attributed to Abū Nuwās. There the irreverently demythologizing Abbasid courtly poet, who is familiar with all the conceits of travesty,[2] invades his qur'ānic source with the aim of exploiting the shock effect of the literal quote that, nevertheless, fits smoothly into a traditional prosodic meter (*rajaz*). What we are dealing with in such a case is basically the transfer into a new context and into a different medium of the literal phrasing of a *motif* (Al-Insān, v. 14: "and near over them shall be its shades, its fruit clusters ready to be plucked") that in its source, as part of an overall rhetorical intent of exhortation, had functioned "earnestly." In its new place, as verse 2 of Abū Nuwās's extant two-liner, this motif, now part of a formal travesty, is meant to be both lyrical and diffusedly ironic:

> Such gallant, youthful company,
> by dull fret not beset,
> their countenances fragrant
> with sweet basil.
>
> Trees shad them closely overhead,
> ripe fruits hang ready
> to be plucked.[3] [139]

The intentionality of Abū Nuwās's literal quotation from the Qur'ān in his own banquet scene and the brevity of the poetic text relative to the ten-verse length of the qur'ānic source, however, do not alter certain essential literary-critical points: ultimately it is the original, qur'ānic usage that arrests the "subject" of Paradise within the terminological specificity of a motif without allowing it to assert itself as theme—at least not in this and other instances of qur'ānic textuality. In the Qur'ān the subject of Paradise is throughout "functional" and in a consistent way rhetorically subordinated to the clear, overriding purposes of *waʿd/waʿīd* (promise/threat) and *raghbah/rahbah* (desire/awe). It is only those "purposes" phrased rhetorically in the Qur'ān that may be identified as themes. Other elements, no matter how attractive and replete with extratextual potential, are in their immediate contexts secondary and rely on the principal rhetorical validation.

This narrowly circumscribed functionality of the qur'ānic Paradise, however, also leads to the motif's multiple rhetorically desirable and efficacious recurrences in the Qur'ān's larger rhetorical strategies. Only in a cumulative sense and only when speaking of all the instances of the subject of Paradise in the Qur'ān, may we also speak of the "theme" of Paradise in the qur'ānic text.

On the other hand, if the subject of Paradise as "theme" is not easily apparent in Arabic poetry, this is due more to quantitative formal reasons than to qualitative ones, for, as is the case with the two-liner of Abū Nuwās, the subject of Paradise is comprehensive. The banquet scene as such is a scene that symbolically and iconically may not be separated from the subject of Paradise as "theme." Irrespective of their size, all other *banquet scenes* in archaic Bedouin and in later classical Arabic poetry are equally thematic icons of Paradise, whether qur'ānically influenced or not. Indeed, the symbolic depth perception should here be reversed.

If not entirely a "failure" in von Grunebaum's critically condemning sense, the question of Paradise as "subject" in Arabic poetry may yet, on the surface of things, strike a Dante-bred critic unaware of any further symbolic encodings that take place in Arabic poetry as being a somewhat short-winded recourse to the qur'ānically reformulated archetype. If nothing else, however, one might then view such commerce in archetypal sources as a conceit aiming at reclaiming for the garden of earthly reverie what the Qur'ān had transported to the garden of celestial promise. Aside from that, and indeed aside from the varying levels of earnestness and poetic diction involved, the difference between qur'ānic and qur'ānically inspired uses of Paradise in the Arabic poetic tradition does not justify the verdict of "failure." Ultimately, there is no verdict, only a complex literary fact, for, on other planes, with less ease, perhaps, but with more textually inward-looking urgency, a closer, interpretive look at Arabic literature should reveal an almost diametrically opposed picture of palimpsest-like hidden lines and symbols—*kamā ḍamina al-wuḥīya silāmuhā* (as stone slabs preserve what is inscribed on them)[4]—all pointing toward unending reservoirs of memories of a happiness which may not have belonged to anybody in particular or which all the poets are losing in all their poems again and again. What remained for poetry of such memories of never-experienced happiness, it seems, was only the yearning. "The great music of Europe," Malraux once said, "is the song of Paradise Lost."[5] By the same token one could say that underneath the clichés, the material palpability and sensuality, the great poetry of the Arabs is the song of Paradise Lost—but not there where we seem to be searching for such tender figments.

Poetic references to the qur'ānic concreteness of the Garden of Paradise and to the opulence of eternal delights available to the blessed are scanty. In its surface idiom Arabic poetry always encodes itself. It appears to be so much of this world and to speak only of familiar landscapes and of a happiness that remains within the reach of experience. Even in its consciousness of the qur'ānic model it touches upon perceptions of religious absolutes with great economy. Such absolutes—and the afterlife is one of them—are at first expressed with metaphors of quite direct equivalence, as when a poet symbolizes life's transitoriness by the door and life's arrival by the abode. Thus, in a dialogue between an anonymous questioner and the thoughtful moralist Ṣāliḥ Ibn ʿAbd al-Quddūs, executed by the caliph Hārūn al-Rashīd for what seems to have been the poet's otherwise irreverent familiarity with the Qur'ān, we read:

> Death is a door, with mankind rushing through it.
> Would I but knew, after the door, which the abode?
>
> Why? The abode is Eden's Garden,
> if your deeds please the Lord.
> Be you remiss, then—Fire!
>
> Such are the options—man has none other.
> Look out then, yours is the choice![6] [140]

Even in verses of such simplicity, however, we must remember that the word "abode" (or "house") in Arabic poetry does not generate simple, unstratified metaphors, and that its symbolic burden can be heavier than almost any purely qur'ānic designation of the afterlife. Thus, even though man's *dār* is here clearly understood to be either Paradise or Hell, this is still only the surface meaning, and the poetically important factor is the recognition of the Bedouin symbol of the archetypal opening of the *qaṣīdah*. Only then does a fully poetic statement come into existence.

A reference to a real, potential, or cumulative great theme, even if it resonates on more than one symbolic level, is still no more than a hesitancy between theme and motif—a poetic incident. We have many poetic incidents around the qur'ānically based "subject" of the Garden. A thematically developed and self-contained poem that is not subordinated to extrapoetic purposes and that by being "qur'ānic" risks being "un-qur'ānic" is nevertheless a rarity. We shall therefore quote in full one such poem by Ibn al-Rūmī (d. 283/896), a poet who, so far, has not figured in our discussions of the *nasīb* and its *diyār* nostalgia. It is, however, precisely because Ibn al-Rūmī is *not* a poet of archaic Bedouin sentiment that he can comfortably dwell upon the vision of a garden of reverie and fulfillment, of a garden "gained," not "lost." Such a garden, then, being poetically one of *ghazal,* is referentially also that of the Qur'ān. In its thematic articulation as a poem in the now only "classicist" Arabic sense, it does not have to deprive itself of diction and motifs that are part of the reverie "development" of the *nasīb* nor, of course, of those elements that had become part of pure *ghazal* sentiment. Such vestiges of an extra-qur'ānic texture do not clash with the ultimately identifiable qur'ānic organizing conception of the whole when it is perceived cumulatively as a theme:

Chide the restive heart,
Check the cupid eye,

Your fancy turn to one from Paradise,
All play, abandon, mirth!

Her radiant cheek so tender, a minute insect's
Minute wing would make it bleed.

If her bright face should show
          through curtain flaps,
You'd say: A lightning-flash
          through clouds on high.

And for the fullest moon to rise,
          knowing her presence,
Would be to bear contempt and scorn—not light.

An ancient wine in bowl and chalice
Her hands to yours entrust,

The fingers thin, the glow
Of gliding rosary upon translucent tips.

Each time she pleases you, her word is:
Be bless'd with more and more!

My love, my whole desire's realm,
In you life grows so ever sweet,
so ever fair!—

Like this the two in Eden's Garden dwell,
Where eyes on far horizons feast,

Where birds from end to end
Sing songs to cheer the heart,

Where zephyr brings to them
Breezes from fragrant fields.

How well deserved their bliss
After so many tears so richly shed!

Take, then, this verse as pearls well strung,
It now will end as it begun![7] [141]

The poem begins with an appeal to self-control and abstinence. Shall we then obtain an ascetic, moralizing sermon? This thought crossed the poet's own mind and brushed his imagination briefly—but only as a conceit, only in order to lead it toward something else, to thoughts of reward quite hasty yet, not quite earned. After only the evocation of an *ʿadnīyah,* or maiden from Eden's Garden, the poet is ripe for reverie, which is perhaps its own reward. What follows are lines of pure erotic description, traditional and of the finest, but the thematic context has now changed. We are now in the imagery of quite earthy Arabic love lyric.[8] The ancient wine is not yet that of Ibn al-Fāriḍ. The glow of gliding rosary upon translucent finger tips is purely sensual. In verse 8, the qur'ānic reference reappears, but by now the sensual image is too entrenched. The paradisiac maiden is now clearly a woman. And this is the true Garden of Eden, which above all is a garden. As Bartlett Giamatti says, "in a garden we are at the heart of a poem";[9] yet Ibn al-Rūmī has kept us at the heart of the poem all along. His was the garden of the poets all the time, perhaps a reflection of the other garden, perhaps vice versa. Even when considered as a reward for tears shed, the garden is still the garden of the lovers; and the tears, weren't they lovers' tears as well? The final verse is of a twofold interest. As a thematic conceit it is supposed to take us back to the first, austere statement of the poem, even though now with a perceptibly lightened touch; as a formal element it constitutes a clean closure of a structure. Closures of this kind are quite rare in the Arabic poem at this time, however. Ibn al-Rūmī's closure foreshadows the favorite, and structurally characteristic, closure of the

Andalusian *muwashshaḥah*. It has the same lightness and the same definitiveness.

For us to return to the mainstream of Arabic poetry and set a more precise locus for the symbolic object of paradise/garden with its projection of archetypal preoccupations, we may do well, however, to reach across formal limits to Arabic prose first. The many allegories of happiness which one can discern behind the smooth narrative surface of the Arabian Nights alone are all variants of the same myth. The Fifth Voyage of Sindbad, for instance, allows us a glimpse of a garden of delights which, however, becomes immediately clouded by the appearance of a grotesque, parasitic spoiler, the Old Man of the Sea. The Sixth Voyage takes Sindbad to the island of Serendib (Ceylon),[10] which figures preeminently in medieval Arabic legend and literature as one of the paradisiac *loci amoeni*. The climate on the island is pleasing; the days and nights are of equal length. The island's happy and good-natured inhabitants live a Golden Age existence at the foot of a centrally located mountain, which is the highest mountain in the world, upon whose summit Adam stepped first when he was banished from Paradise.[11] When Sindbad ascends to the summit, he finds there rare and beautiful vegetation, but also familiar palm and cedar trees;[12] there are also the inevitable rubies and other precious stones. But to reach this delightful place, Sindbad had to let himself float down a mysterious, totally dark subterranean stream that began in a diamond-studded cave at the point on the shore to which all ships are drawn for certain destruction.

Because of its transparency, it is quite unnecessary to analyze and explain all the mythic-symbolic content of the Sixth Voyage beyond the archetypal scheme.[13] The popular oral character of the narrative in this Voyage, as well as in the other Voyages or in the Arabian Nights as a whole, facilitates an almost massive, but charmingly simple, compilation of myths, legends, and symbolic references of all sources and ages, among which the loci of bliss are one of the most lavishly scattered motifs.

Thus quite an unsuspected Paradise motif surfaces in the story of Abū Muḥammad the Lazy (Night 480), where we hear of golden trees with leaves of emeralds and fruits of rubies and pearls. These are trees which seem to have come down directly from the bejeweled garden visited by Gilgamesh,[14] trees which are obviously the work of the genii, but which Abū Muḥammad the Lazy brings as gifts for the caliph well-crated, as if shipped from afar.

In another episode, the touchingly romantic story of Ḥasan al-Baṣrī (Night 395ff.), we find an accumulation of symbolically related places that are unmistakable versions of the theme of the Fortunate Islands/Garden of Delights. Thus a garden as an "individualized" idea of bliss appears to Ḥasan al-Baṣrī when he opens the forbidden door in the Castle in the Sky. With the delightful vision of the garden, however, comes also the sorrow of unobtainable love. In this way the symbol of the forbidden door clashes with the myth of supreme delight. On the level of "communal" symbols of blissful time and space, the latter part of Ḥasan's story takes us to such remote places as the Islands of the Amazons and the Land of Wāq al-Wāq,[15] to the mythic, idealized, invariably interdicted, rarely violated locations of all the desirable—or simply curious—figments of bliss-configurations, which bear many resemblances to the earliest myths of pristine forms of "Golden Age" life.

It is interesting to see the Island of Wāq al-Wāq reappear as a *locus amoenus* in Ibn Ṭufayl's (twelfth century A.D.) delightful philosophical novelette of self-generation and spiritual discovery, entitled *Ḥayy Ibn Yaqẓān*.[16] In it the suggestion is made that perhaps it was here, on this island mentioned by as famous an authority in oddities as al-Masʿūdī,[17] where there are trees which bear women for fruit,[18] or maybe only women's heads, which then issue the enigmatic word *wāq-wāq,* that it might have been here that, given ideal conditions of climate and a peculiar, bubbling viscosity of soil, a live cell might have generated itself spontaneously, and out of that cell a whole, physically and spiritually (potentially) perfect human being might then have developed. Furthermore, next to this propitious place there happens to be another island where a people of "golden Age" righteousness and simplicity dwell.[19]

Outside the sphere of *mirabilia* (*ʿajāʾib*),[20] the mythologically articulated, archetypal allegories of bliss are quite rare in Arabic literature. But here, too, we must distinguish between extended allegorical stories or episodes like the ones we have discussed so far and another type of allusion, which is locked in the metaphor or in the individual, self-contained symbol—like the symbol of the garden, for instance. Mainly, however, we have to consider the interference, on the symbolic level, of what to the medieval mind were quite "concrete" images of ultimate bliss, the detailed, precise (or at least extremely insistent and repetitive) qurʾānic messages of otherworldly reward. Furthermore, those much-delineated places of delight become part of a believer's future concern. They are not his spiritual past. In other words, they are not his mythology but rather exclusively his eschatology, and thus much less manageable as literary-symbolic material. Literature prefers to deal with more "data" in the past and with all the vagueness in the future. The Qur'ān, it seems, has taken out of the Arabic literary imagination much of the creative vagueness concerning the future stages of felicity or *loci amoeni,* while neglecting at the same time to furnish that imagination with a narratively construed, or construable, repertory of mythogenic, imaginative data about original bliss and the causes of its loss. The Qur'ān only rarely uses symbols of the garden outside a strict, almost mechanically repetitive, eschatological context; and yet it could be through truly archetypal metaphors like the one about the righteous, "who are as a garden on a hill, on which heavy rain falls, and it yields its fruit twofold; and even if heavy rain falls not on it, yet there is dew,"[21] that some symbolic pollen might conceivably have fallen upon Arabic worldly literature, from one garden to another.

In the "normal" qur'ānic visualization, Paradise appears like a desert in its fleeting moment of bloom, an oasis of sweet waters, pavilions of pleasure, eternally pleasing wine, eternally enjoyable, idealized female companionship, and the service of mysterious, youthful cupbearers of courtly comportment. It is the sublimation of what is recognized in the Qur'ān itself as comprising man's "appetites" in this world.[22] In the Qur'ān this is a beautiful promise, but it is a very concrete, explicit one, too. It is excessively insisted upon, and in its "cumulative" rhetorical intent, it works too single-mindedly. It should perhaps not be surprising to find Arabic secular literature shunning such explicit, rhetorically unidirectional representation of eternal happiness. A refuge into ironic allegory on the one hand and into vague archetypal symbolism on the other might almost be expected.

And indeed, the two major medieval Arabic literary works which nevertheless insist on raising the celestial curtain from the already overexposed stage of the qur'ānically delineated afterworld both prove to be ironic conceits in structure and content. They are epistles by name but close in form to the mixed genre of the Menippean satire. They are the *Risālat al-Ghufrān* (Epistle of Forgiveness) by the Syrian Abū al-ʿAlā' al-Maʿarrī (d. 449/1057)[23] and the *Risālat al-Tawābiʿ wa al-Zawābiʿ* (Epistle of Familiar Spirits and Demons) by the Cordovan Abū ʿĀmir Ibn Shuhayd (d. 426/1035).[24]

Both works appear in the early part of the eleventh century, and Ibn Shuhayd's now substantially shrunk *Risālah* seems to have been written only a few years before that of al-Maʿarrī. If both works try to pierce through the sublunar barrier to allow us a more leisurely glance at what lies ahead, or beyond, they do it with highly curtailed weapons nonetheless, or we should say, rather, that their conceit was purposefully limited. We should not expect to find here the full sweep and complexity of Dante's moral and eschatological scheme or of the Miltonian grandeur of rebellion and collision of wills. Rather, the Arabic works are concerned largely, as in al-Maʿarrī's case, or entirely, as in that of Ibn Shuhayd, with scenes from the Parnassus or from an allegorical "literary republic." At their best, both epistles are works of refined wit and exquisite irony.

The image of the afterworld which emerges in Ibn Shuhayd is of less relevance to our present discussion, because he does not introduce us directly into those heavenly spheres which are destined as permanent abodes for humans. His allegorical outline of a Parnassian world of the genii only represents the true locale and the true protagonists. A Platonizing projection,[25] or inversion, becomes obvious here. Even the irony of a heavenly animal world is thus allegorically neutralized.

In al-Maʿarrī's *Epistle of Forgiveness,* on the other hand, all heavenly imagery is directly based upon qur'ānic models, allowing for the intentional distortions of very close parody. Thus, for the righteous in the Garden of Paradise there are trees, each one of which spreads its shadow from horizon to horizon. So what are the absurd Bedouin dreams of a bush like *dhāt anwāṭ* by comparison? Under such trees, brooks and rivers flow with water that gives eternal life, with milk that never sours, and with wine that is always of good effect.[26] And fish swim in these sweet streams, even if they come from the salty waters of the sea. And such fish—even the poet al-Mutanabbī had never seen the likes![27]

Poets and men of letters inhabit this Paradise. For one verse that can be interpreted favorably, some pre-Islamic poets easily merit entry among the blessed. But there is no room for half-wits in Paradise.[28] And would the heedless intruder into Paradise dare to mount there a spirited steed? It is possible that he would be thrown on rocks of emerald, breaking an arm or a leg, only to become a laughingstock to the blessed! But no, the intruder may rest assured. No such petty things happen on these grounds.[29] When in one of these lovely gardens a flight of geese alights, they are "geese of Paradise"; it is natural for them to be endowed with speech, and they have been "inspired" to alight precisely there, for the pleasure of an ongoing drinking party. As they shake off their feathers, full-breasted maidens are revealed, certainly to nobody's surprise except that of the intruder. And their voices, and their knowledge of music! The truly bothersome question, however, is: How did they shake off the stupidity characteristic of geese? But he is told that even now he is standing only on the shore of the sea of miracles![30]

When the patriarch poet Labīd, each one of whose reverential verses is now a splendid palace in Paradise, decides to invite all the worthy and the not-so-worthy poets among the blessed to a feast, the occasion has to be truly Bedouin. First a mill is built on the most bountiful of the streams of Paradise, Kawthar, with millstones of diamonds, pearls, and assorted jewels; but there are also hand-mills operated by dark-eyed maidens and other, larger mills turned by heavenly camels, mules, cows, and donkeys. The wheat is of the best. No poet ever sang of the likes of it. Then birds and cattle are brought in to be slaughtered, all of which at the sight of the butcher's knife raise such a deafening noise that one might think that there is fear and pain in Paradise. It is not so, however. The earnestness of it all is more like jest.[31]

And the supreme morsel of delight, isn't it the promised company of dark-eyed houris? The visitor in Paradise finally gains a solitary moment with two such ravishing creatures. But how the thoughts of that devilish lover Imru' al-Qays yet crowd his mind: thoughts of Umm al-Ḥuwayrith and her neighbor Umm al-Rabāb. Still, what a comparison! He rushes into the arms of pleasure, first one, then the other; he sips saliva from their lips. But there is always Imru' al-Qays, poor Imru' al-Qays! There he burns in hell-fire, yet his verses, how they cling to the back of one's mind—here in Paradise!

Curiosity, however, can spoil things even in Paradise. The visitor wants to know who his lovely mates are. Have they been created especially for the gratification of the righteous as was so beautifully promised, and are they to be likened to rubies and pearls only? But one says she is actually from Aleppo. Her father was a miller who had given her in marriage to a junk dealer, and even he could not stand her bad breath, thus divorcing her. This made her take a good look at herself and realize that she was the ugliest woman in Aleppo. The road to piety and to salvation—and to her present metamorphosis—had thus been paved. As for the other nymph, she once was the black servant who used to shuffle about dusty scrolls in Baghdad's library. Who doesn't remember her?

Decidedly there must be more to beauty in Paradise. An angel who just passes by is willing to enlighten the visitor. Indeed there are those houris who do not come from this world but are unmitigated miracles of God. To behold them, one has to enter very intimate enclosures of Paradise, where there are strange, fruit-bearing trees. They are called "the trees of the houris."[32] The visitor takes a fruit—perhaps it is a quince or a pomegranate, or perhaps an apple—and splits it open; and indeed a maiden appears from within, so perfectly beautiful as to dazzle even her own peers. She asks the redeemer of her beauty who he might be, and upon hearing his name solemnly informs him that she has been burning with desire to meet him since four thousand years before God had created the mortal world. In the face of so much glory the visitor dares only to quote the appropriate reference from the Ḥadīth and to fall down in humble prostration. But as he lies there, he can't avoid a stealthy glance at the maiden, and somehow, in all her beauty, she yet appears on the thin, almost emaciated side, not quite the Bedouin paragon. After due prostration, however, as he raises his head, he beholds a miracle that literally seems to have no end. The buttocks of the heavenly maiden, which only a moment ago had seemed to him so modest, are now like all the most sinuous dunes all the poets of the desert had ever dared to sing about: horizons of undulating delight. Nonetheless, what a relief it is to find out that in Paradise there is a back-and-forth dimension between concupiscent will and limit-conscious mind, whereby a monster easily done may just as easily be undone.[33]

Arabic imaginative prose, whether ramblingly narrative or speculative, operating with strict parsimony of expressive means or even hermetically aestheticist and crisply, almost naturalistically, ironic, has had sufficient access to the archetypal symbology of the time and place of original, as well as ultimate, bliss. The easy transparency and inordinate accumulation of these symbols in the stories of the Arabian Nights is due to a naïve popular eclecticism which is based on the principle of associative attraction rather than on that of conscious selection. In such a system a generic series of symbols, once started, propagates itself by way of free chain-formation. The entire corpus of native and neighboring, contemporary folkloric as well as ancient legendary sources flows freely into seemingly simple stories of marvel, adventure, and boundless riches. Medieval Arabic so-called popular prose literature, quite contrary to poetry, has as its milieu the mercantile urban centers. Stories originate in marketplaces and ports, in Baghdad or Basra, but once under way, as volatile imaginative figments, they become transformed into pure adventure, moving daringly along the main overland and oversea trading routes, reaching out for the supreme treasure beyond the seven mountains and the seven seas. But then the return is once again along the same trading route, and the ultimate success of the adventure is crowned by a surprisingly homely happy ending which is anticlimactic after the intensity of boldly incurred adventure. True success, thus, is measured by standards which are "real" in the sense that they conform to the social realities of the normal milieu of this literature—which is artisan and merchant. Gardens in the sky and Fortunate Islands inhabited by erotic dream-symbioses of flora and fauna retain their true imaginative magic when "remembered" and told from the perspective of a "real" happy ending which is socially framable. This way there is no confusion of goal with dream. One stops; the other goes on. Sindbad probably never ceased dreaming of an Eighth Voyage—but the door of the seventh chamber opens upon itself alone.

The highly refined, consciously hermetic, literate character of a work like the *Risālat al-Ghufrān,* on the other hand, has a very controlled imaginative sphere. Its author, in a veritable tour de force of sustained ironic exercise, is always bound by the "straight" thematic prototype around which he spins the fine web of his ironic wit. The "straight" model, it is true, is complex enough, but it is not ultimately the way it is in popular imaginative narrative. What the *Risālat al-Ghufrān* is thus able to give us of symbols and images is only a wittily distorted, albeit devastatingly lucid, mirror image of the qur'ānic archetype of the place and mode of bliss. At the end of the ironic process it leaves us drained of all archetypal yearning and of every symbolic dream.[34] Here, then, the ironic familiarity with the symbol produces a demythologizing effect. The cold laughter of the mind is a new pleasure to the medieval man. It may have caught Arabic literature quite unprepared.

2. *Spaces of Delight: Perceived, Lost, Remembered*[35]

"In its countless alveoli space contains compressed time. That is what space is for." If an insight needs a paradox, Gaston Bachelard has an inexhaustible reserve of both, but his poetics of space which grows out of and develops around the phenomenology and, using his own term, the "topoanalysis"[36] of the house brings him particularly close to the paradox that meanders through the alveoli of the *manāzil* (dwellings) and the *diyār* (abodes) of the Arabic *nasīb:* the poet of the *nasīb* uses his space, especially the many versions of the abodes, as a resting place for his memories, which have become motionless and have turned into images, into "the spaces of our intimacy."[37] They have become the abodes of the hearts, and as such they will remain inhabited forever, as al-Mutanabbī (d. 354/965) knew so well:

> O abodes, in our hearts you abide.
> You stand deserted,
> While they with you abound.[38] [142]

In their very stillness, those abodes of the heart, of motionless memories, have become places toward which it is possible to turn for refuge and protection. They are therefore not mere temporal points. They now possess the spaciousness of a material dimension. In the last chapter of his "topological" analysis of the house, Bachelard hints at the shape of this special space which is the house, or rather, he speaks of the "roundness of life," of the "roundness of the inner space," and even of the roundness of the tree, "slowly giving itself the form that eliminates hazards of wind."[39] And elsewhere he quotes the poet Jean Cayrol:

> May no one wound the Fruit
> It is the past of joy which is
> becoming round.[40]

Thus we know that our house as motionless memory is waiting for us in that very special realm of the past which has nothing to do with finite, historical time and which has a certain protective quality and shape. This is the realm where flowers become "silent gardens of Paradise."[41]

No poetry speaks more insistently of the inner space which is all memory and yearning than does Arabic poetry. As poetic image, this space may appear under many names and manifestations, but the suggestive force of Arabic etymology makes poet and reader experience an intimation of the prevailing shape of roundness. ***Dār*** and ***diyār*** are etymologically round forms (***d-w-r*** = roundness), and conceptually this fundamental etymology extends by association to all the abandoned campsites, wasted halting places, ruins, and courtyards of the ***nasīb***. In all of them there lies dormant the archetype of that abode which has the imaginative tendency toward roundness, the roundness of our inner space.[42] When the entire earth becomes our inner space of consciousness, it too becomes our circumference. The circumference of the abodes in the Arabic ***nasīb*** is also, and above all, one of intimacy and of memory. Whether an abode will be a beloved's seasonal encampment, the poet's own birthplace, or his ***awṭān*** (native grounds), the purely material fact of the space has ceased to have poetic importance. Everything has become part of the warm, intimate roundness of remembrance. If the echoes of remembrance reverberate deep enough, however, and this in poetry is a necessity as much as it is for a tree to grow anchoring roots, we obtain contact with the archetypal, with the bedrock of the image as remembrance. It is on this level that the symbolism of all the abodes, of all the spaces of intimacy, and of all the images of those spaces acquires the ultimate desirability of something first possessed, something by cultural habit referred to as Paradise.

Here the circumscription of intimacy may also be transferred to another space of archetypal remembrance, which is the garden. The containment or enclosure of a garden, its roundness, so to speak, may not always be explicit. In Arabic poetry the garden receives its form mostly as the inner space of intimacy. When it becomes a "garden in the heart," it has claimed its birthright, which is the same as that of the symbolic "abodes of the heart" of the *nasīb*. Without this vessel of intimacy, a garden might appear open and sprawling—an impressionistic reverie of pure images. When it is in the heart, however, and the heart is in the Ḥijāz, and the yearning is for past happiness and memories of home, then such a garden acquires its contours of inner space as does the garden of Abū al-Ḥasan al-Tihāmī (d. 416/1025):

I entrust to God a fawn in the land of the Ḥijāz:
May the garden of the heart be its retreat
    and pasture plentiful.

My God, be gentler to my heart, O yearning!
What you so do to me, I cannot bear.

And you, O lovers' union, alight
    at separation's camping place!
Perhaps you'll yet join once more
    what went such sundry ways.

And let there rain with blessings
    a night-traveling cloud,
For now there's only waste,
    erased all former sign.

Would that those bygone nights,
    those memories of home,
Returned and here remained
    never to bid farewell![43] [143]

At the other extreme of perceiving the garden poetically will be the whole idyllic landscape, spread out from horizon to horizon, of garden paradise as impressed on the retina of Ḥāzim al-Qarṭājannī (d. 684/1285). We would be tempted to see it as merely idealized, touched-up scenery, were it not for the poet's ultimate resistance to hiding from us the fact that this landscape, too, is only a memory arrested as image and as a daydream from which the heart is unwilling to awake:

I roam enraptured in this paradise on earth,
My heart unwilling to awake.

O Murcia of the rivers,
O land of intimacies, home of my joys!

Many a lover of ease and glee has anchor cast
In your sweet basil, in your wine!

How I remember your river, its waters tumbling down
There by the bank, with the Waḍḍāḥ dam above!

All the world's beauty seemed to rest
Between two bridges—of Ṭabīrah and of Sabbāḥ.

Full seventy miles we'd wander there,
Past river dams, beneath majestic trees.[44] [144]

Commonly we observe in Arabic garden poetry a certain tension between the objective and the subjective as well as between the symbolic and the realistic vision. As soon as the theme of the garden appears to free itself from the symbolic context of the *nasīb*—that means as soon as the garden in the poem does not participate closely in the mood of sorrow and loss, where it would inevitably develop symbolic affinities with the abodes and the ruins—a clear lessening of symbolic intensity seems to set in. This does not mean that a poem's lyrical intensity lessens too. Indeed, the resulting concreteness and objectivity, and the unmitigated coming face to face with the image or thing, may in instances of fulfillment produce a poetry approaching modern definitions of "imagism" or rather of "pure poetry" as understood by George Moore: a poetry "born of admiration of the only permanent world, a world of things."[45]

In one of his most directly descriptive lingerings over the natural landscape, which nonetheless retains the place of the *nasīb* within the *qaṣīdah,* Abū Tammām (d. 231/845) reaches this poetically revealing but collected and objective conclusion:

A place of sustenance is the world to man.
Then spring's veil lifts,
and all is vision.[46] [145]

The renewal of the object as image has set in. Its poetic essence is perceived as it were for the first time, and it is with this apprehended newness that it will survive from here on.

But the symbol of the ultimate garden does not have to be banned from the gardens which actually show themselves to the eye and where delight seems only a poetic moment. Indeed, even separated from the compelling symbolism contained in the *nasīb,* Arabic garden poetry resounds with its own archetypal echoes. The garden and its inhabitants, the flowers, are privileged poetic entities, capable of radiating their own symbolic halo. Thus, if at first a garden reverie like the one by the poet from Aleppo Abū Bakr al-Ṣanawbarī (d. 334/945) may seem to aim only at the seizing of one image and of one instant in the poet's awareness of pleasure, at the end of the reverie we yet detect a new desire in the poet: this seized image/moment must remain inviolate and pure. Somehow it does change substance and intimates other spaces which must not be defiled:

Rise, O gazelle! Look up, don't tarry!
The hills are in wondrous reverie.

Veiled was their face's fairness,
Which now the spring unveiled.

Roses their cheeks, daffodils
Eyes which the beloved see,

Anemones their gowns of silk:
Purple engrossed with black.

The blooming bean like
Piebald doves' flared tails,

And fields of grain like soldiery in battle-line:
Notched arrows readied on the bow.

And wondrous starwort flowers seem
The heads of peacocks as they turn their necks.

The cypresses the eye would deem coy maidens,
Their skirts above their shanks, tucked up.

Swayed by the East Wind's breath,
deep in the night,
Each one a supple maiden
in maidenly playful court,

As over the river the breeze's sighs
send ripples of delight
And trail their mantles' frills.

Were the garden's guardianship
ever in my hands,
No base foot ever would tread that ground![47] [146]

Furthermore, a broadening of the thematic reach of al-Ṣanawbarī's poem tells us that its motif of closure must also be its first thematic impulse and determinant—to the extent to which it was the seed that preceded the poem as influence and lingered on as its intertextual residue. This becomes quite clear when we compare al-Ṣanawbarī's poem with its much older precursor out of Abū Tammām's *Ḥamāsah,* where it is attributed to an obscure poet by the name of Abū Qamqām al-Asadī:

To Washal, the mountain-spring,
  my greetings take and say:
"Since leaving you, I find
  all water foul.

Morning and evening
  be your shadows fresh,
Your water cool
  when other waters simmer.

Were it in my domain
  your water to deny,
Never would a base lip
  drink from your rocky bowl."[48] [147]

In observance of the lyrical integrity of the poem, al-Ṣanawbarī's garden must not appear "enclosed" from its first visual, imagist appearance, however. It must not be a thematic abstraction. Like the flower-decked landscape of Abū Tammām,[49] it is at first a radiant, open space of idyllic hills (*al-rubā*), transfigured by the coming of spring. In its luminosity it seems to exclude the idea of boundaries. Only gradually the garden becomes the poet's inner space, and as such it is then no longer an open landscape but an enclosed garden which has to be protected from all that would disturb its inner perfection. Slowly arriving but yet suddenly dawning, "Earthly Paradise" is on the Arab poet's mind. The Arab poet's enclosed garden is nevertheless unlike the bower of Venus in Claudianus's *Epithalamium* or the *hortus conclusus* of the *Roman de la Rose*. There are no allegorical beings dallying inside or drawn on the wall and excluded from entering. Neither is the Arab poet's garden like that of Michael Drayton or Pedro Soto de Rojas, a realm for the muses and the select ones among the poets.[50] Even while reverberating with the echoes of places of ultimate delight and secluded perfection, the garden of Aleppo remains an enclosure for flowers. It is a localization of the ultimate dream which nevertheless will be experienced through the senses. As such, however, it is perhaps even better able to generate its aura of sacrality quite kindred to very archaic sanctuaries which, as *ḥimās*, once crowned the wooded hills of the eastern Mediterranean and whose network of symbolic efficacy extended toward the *diyār* of Arabia. Thus W. Robertson Smith reminds us of how Iamblicus still speaks of Mount Carmel as "sacred above all mountains and *forbidden of access to the vulgar*" (my italics);[51] and we read of the "new Jerusalem" in Revelation 21:27 that "nothing unclean shall enter it, nor any one who practices abomination or falsehood." No less significantly, Bramante's *giardino segreto* of the Belvedere gardens of the Vatican, designed to be the first museum of the Renaissance and appropriately conceived as a secret grove, has an inscription over its entrance that warns all visitors with the Sibyl's words to Aeneas: "procul este prophani" (let the profane keep their distance).[52]

As motif, the enclosed garden in Arabic poetry delights above all in the guise of metaphor. It can be explicitly subordinate and implicitly central—once as metaphor and again as symbol, making a concrete contact with its object only to abduct it into a deconcretized realm. It is a snatcher and ultimate keeper of reality. The beloved of the pre-Islamic bard ʿAntarah is reached through the mediation of a still quite pastoral meadow,[53] but thereafter, once the vision, or image, of such a "place" has been dwelled upon not just metaphorically but symbolically, the realm of reality changes. The pastoral meadow as *rawḍatun unufun* turns into an interdicted, privileged space[54] of an interdicted and privileged reality and begins its transformation into the garden. Thus the early Islamic Shabīb Ibn al-Barṣāʾ al-Murrī knows his beloved to be a more specifically Edenic garden: fenced around or otherwise protected from entry (*jannatun ḥīla dūnahā*).[55] He reduces the distance, as well as the tension, between metaphor and symbol. The sense of calm joy and of protective intimacy, which a pond in the garden may produce, will make the already fully courtly poet of the late Abbasid period al-Sarī al-Raffāʾ (d. after 360/970) think of a garden within a garden. It will lead him to the inner core of seclusion. This poet from the Aleppo of Sayf al-Dawlah finds his heightened metaphor of enclosure and safety in the placidity of a pond as it lies mirrorlike, rimmed by the real garden:

How secure it is, its herd
  by predators not frightened,
No bird of prey bloodies its talons there!

A garden whose flowers' redolence
  the thickets never breathed,
And over which a rain cloud need not
  drain its tears,

As among groves it spreads, you'd deem it
An emperor's carpet over playgrounds cast.[56] [148]

In this compounded metaphor, so characteristic of Arabic garden poetry as it reaches its highest degree of courtly refinement, three symbolic components intertwine: water with its placidity, goodness, and import of deeper safety; the ideal of pastoral harmony; and the garden of the senses—all partaking as it were of the courtly apotheosis of privileged delight symbolized by the carpet of an emperor.[57]

But the joy of the garden does not last. Its heightened beauty evokes in the poet disquieting feelings. Beauty is jealous of its own child, of the joy it produces, so it sows sadness in the heart. Flowers become the many mirrors of this sadness:

A narcissus, its pupils agaze,
Never knowing slumber's delight,

Bending under raindrops, pale,
it only sees
The sky's hand upon the earth.[58] [149]

The verses are by al-Wa'wā' al-Dimashqī (d. 390/999), one more poet of filigree-like refinement to gather at the court of Sayf al-Dawlah. In lines like his, which take hold of the imagination in spite of the louder tones of the surrounding mood of courtly celebration, the delicate, insinuating melancholy appears like a brocaded thread of especially pale silver on the rich damask of Arabic garden and flower poetry. The theme of sorrow in a blooming garden, however, is always more than an element of antithetic composition. Sorrow in a garden echoes the loss of something which is in the nature of the garden itself, and poetic melancholy is the middle ground between the disbelief in such loss and its acceptance.

In Arabic poetry we may not obtain full certainty of this ulterior meaning of the sad garden until we encounter it as part of the symbolic idiom of the traditional *nasīb*. It is only when the abandoned abodes, tribal enclosures, and nightly phantoms turn before our eyes into a melancholy garden, awakening in the morning as it were from an ancient dream, and when, as if remembering something of that dream, the narcissus sheds its dewy tears of sadness, which is the same sadness that awakens in the poet's heart—it is only then that an equation between archaic abode and garden sets in and the metaphor of the poetic instant blends into the symbol of the archetype. Ibn Khafājah is always ready with an example:

1. Suffice it of grief that abodes be far
 And the only visitor a phantom;

2. That for messengers but winds at nightfall blow
 In charge and flight between us, south and north.

3. To the North Wind greetings I entrust,
 And questions from the South Wind I inhale.

7. Should all I forget, I shall not forget
  a night over Ḥimā,
 Aquiver with moonlight, in beauty dissolved,

8. When in the dark the moon had visited a star
 To spend the night in union,
  quite as the Dioscuri.

11. Rain clouds were generous there
  both morning and eve,
 Tossed about on strong winds till exhaustion.

12. One nightly cloud darkness led astray,
 But a refulgent lightning lit for it a wick.

13. And in the early morning, my God, how sadly
  the dove cooed there,
 And how dew-laden were the shadows
  of the *arāk*-tree!

14. Then the easterly breeze teased
  at the stem on the hillock,
 And it swayed and bent over the rump-curve
  of the dune.

15. The chill of morning stirred
  narcissus' lid.
 A tear of dew first gleamed on it
  and then rolled down.[59] [150]

Thus the "romantic," melancholy garden, in which there is nothing sadder than the cooing of its doves, and whose shadows are the freshest, where the narcissus is the frailest in the tearfulness of the morning dew, becomes the place where the memory of ancient abodes may be recaptured. To the Arab poet who can thus revert to the symbolic idiom of the *nasīb,* this is not at all a hermetic way of speaking of the garden as Paradise, nor is it when, within the same fold of the *nasīb,* he expresses his yearning for that garden which has been his native land and which was lost and then remembered as fragrance, color, purity, joy, and passion, all sensations and things of beauty which conjure the intermediate metaphor of the woman as a garden. Such is Paradise, because such must have been the Valencia of Ibn Khafājah:

A garden in al-Andalus
Is a bride's beauty first unveiled,
a perfumed breath.

Its morning splendor is a dazzling,
smiling mouth,
The darkness of its night,
the deepest hue of lips.

And when the wind blows from the east,
I shout out: How I yearn for you,
O Andalus![60] [151]

In the poetry of nostalgia or of lost *manāzil,* it is characteristic for poets to use images and expressions which in themselves connote ancient loss. Thus the effectiveness of the proverbial expression *tafarraqū aydiya Sabā* (they scattered in all directions) relies on the vague reverberation of the name of Sabā, the old Yemeni kingdom which was destroyed by the breaking of the dam of Ma'rib and the dispersal of its people. Particularly in the revival of antiquarian nostalgia in the Abbasid period, this expression is much echoed. Abū Nuwās, for instance, even while giving to the old, Bedouin feeling of desolation the contemporary, Islamic setting of a place of prayer (*muṣallā*), nevertheless turns to such a legend-laden evocation to convey the fullness of his loss:

1. Muṣallā is no more, desolate
the dunes which saw me once . . . ,
3. Those places where once a prosperous life I led,
Till youth's down left and gray hair came,
4. In the midst of gallant lads like blades aquiver,
In the bloom of youth and courtly grace.
5. Then at the hand of fretful time they broke apart
like ancient Sabā's might,
And in the land each took a separate way.[61] [152]

The Sassanids, too, became a favorite antiquarian topic. Already the pre-Islamic poet al-Munakhkhal al-Yashkurī had introduced into his verse their fabled palaces of Khawarnaq and Sadīr—but for obvious reasons not yet as a motif of elegiac "ruinous perfection."[62] In al-Munakhkhal the motif (for the reference to these palaces clearly becomes a "reusable" motif) occurs not in an elegiacally tone-setting *nasīb* of a *qaṣīdah* but rather toward the end of a thematically quite circular structure that ends in a tone that strictly paradigmatically might have been the poem's *nasīb* opening. Somehow, if only by attraction, the fact that the Khawarnaq-and-Sadīr motif is used in such a circular closure will subsequently facilitate its chronologically plausible, truly ruinous, and more perceptibly elegiac reemergence within the *nasīb* proper.[63]

Thus, as we recall from another context,[64] it was Abū al-ʿAtāhiyah, the courtly Abbasid poet not otherwise remembered for symbolist leanings within the structured *qaṣīdah* form, who precisely in one such *qaṣīdah* drew the correct thematic and structural conclusion by giving these Sassanid relics the enriched symbolic hue of *loci amoeni*.[65] In a primary way, he filled the idyllic, antiquarian landscape around Khawarnaq and Sadīr with reveries which were reminiscent of qurʾānic visions of bliss. There, however, his sense of loss, which emanated not from the Qurʾān but from the "obligatory" sequence of moods in the *qaṣīdah,* was mellowed to the extent to which the pathos-laden Bedouin abodes and desolate campsites were replaced by structures whose ruinous state had acquired the characteristic aptness to convey graceful melancholy instead. The ensuing transition from elegy to idyll, however, remained intentionally incomplete precisely because the symbolic framework of the *nasīb* continued sending out deeper reverberations of the poet's, or the poem's, melancholy rather than joy and, ultimately, because everything had only been conjured out of time past, which is the only time of the *nasīb*. Kindred but far more explicit in tone and in the use of the Sassanid backdrop is al-Buḥturī's (d. 284/897) elegy on the great arched palace of Ctesiphon, the Īwān Kisrā.[66] It figures among that poet's most loved and quoted works. Al-Sharīf al-Murtaḍā (d. 436/1044), too, composes a melancholy ode to the ancient Īwān of Ctesiphon. Even more than his precursor al-Buḥturī, he maintains throughout the poem the mood of loss and remembrance:

> Behold what the sovereign Sassanids built,
> How time battered it, tore it down, effaced it.
>
> Courtyards, once the canopy of heaven,
> Then by adversities brought down to earth,
>
> And a soil so rich, it sprouted sweet delight,
> While the dust of other lands issued
> but acid weeds and grass.[67] [153]

Then the poet speaks of the great arch of Ctesiphon itself, which still bears signs of royal pomp and luster. It is its desolate state that is illusory, however, and that can be dispelled by memories (v. 12):

> [To disbelieving eyes] it looms worn
> and desolate.
> Then, transported by memories,
> it flourishes anew.[68] [154]

This antiquarianism of allusions has its natural mood and place in the *nasīb,* where it easily blends with the Islamic references. Quite characteristic in this respect is the early Umayyad poet ʿUbayd Allāh Ibn Qays al-Ruqayyāt (d. ca. 75/694):

> I stopped at the abode, but what I found
> Was only recollection,
> the figment of a dream.
>
> All was decay, all desolation, where once
> reigned cheer and fellowship,
> And empty stood the lofty halls
> of nations past.[69] [155]

The magnitude of the poet's sorrow over the desolation of the abode shall be measured only by that ancient scene of desolation which has engraved itself upon Arabia's historic consciousness in a most characteristically archetypal manner. The "lofty halls," in their qurʾānic context, are those built for King Solomon by the *jinn.*[70] But still more important is the fact that within its qurʾānic chapter this verse is only an introduction to the story of the destruction of the city of Sabā and the dispersal of its people. The "lofty halls" thus become the fateful, tragic city, immortalized by legend and by its homiletic use in the Qurʾān. Furthermore, the etymology of "lofty halls" (*maḥārīb*), which may also point to the elevated choirs or apses in Mithraeums, prompts an immediate and poetically necessary association of meaning with the holiest spot in the mosque, the niche of prayer (*miḥrāb*), which points in the direction of Mecca; and finally, *maḥārīb* are also referred to as *ghuraf,* a word which, ever so gently, turns the symbolic meaning toward the pavilions and "upper chambers" of Paradise. Such is then the loss of the poet.

Associations and reverberations grow in poetic efficacy when historical, or qurʾānic, references become part of the language of a poet's *nasīb* without altering the symbolically vigorous Bedouinity of the mood. We have seen this happen in the verses of Ibn Qays al-Ruqayyāt.

The great adept in metaphoric shifts of meaning and in abstraction, Abū Tammām, blends references to religious objects or rites into the language and the purpose of the *nasīb* to the extent that such things begin to function as abstractions, having in an abiding manner expanded their semantic and symbolic connotations. In his *nasīb,* Abū Tammām is able to erase the confining semantic concreteness which words possess in the course of normal usage and turn them into symbiotic expressions of poetic purpose. In the emerging idiom, the abode, the garden, the rich soil, the rain, and the mosque become one, as do the question and the prayer, the search and the song:

> O abode, may perpetual dew surround you,
> And may the flowers of your garden quiver
> and be lulled in rich soil!
>
> A ruinous abode, by it I stopped
> in supplication,
> And its site almost became my mosque.
>
> In song I called it up,
> searched for its folk,
> With grief for company both in my quest
> and in my song.[71] [156]

Here the "abode" may not be abandoned at all. The poet wishes it well as if still from a distance, remembering. And it is not a desert but a garden. Is it then a "ruin" still? If so, then it is one of memories. The poet's traditional "questioning" of the mute ruins is also of a different kind. It is rather a call to elicit an echo and a supplication—and thus a prayer; and with his prayer the poet no longer stands before an abode or a ruin but before a mosque, and his prayer is now his quest, which is also his song. All concreteness has left the *nasīb*. As Abū Tammām himself said, intoning another *nasīb,*

> You are not you, and these abodes
> are not abodes:
> Passion was blown away and purposes
> turned about.[72] [157]

But something remained and crystallized further: the sense of loss and sadness, that which weighed upon the hearts of all the other poets too.

Among the Arab poets who weave their own experience of loss and sadness most tightly and cohesively into the thematic-emotive fabric of what was once the Bedouin *nasīb* is the Cordovan Ibn Zaydūn. With quite clearly a heightened consciousness of the symbolic acumen of the old mold, he reaches out for the essentials of the *nasīb*. There he finds, above all, the enfolding, almost cocooning quality of mood. He gives in to it. But this is as far as his surrender to the form will go. After that the poet remains explicitly himself, and the broad, archetypal symbolism of the *nasīb* is put to the service of his precise circumstance and state of mind. What is important to us is that by means of the turned-inward, creative way in which Ibn Zaydūn faces his own self vis-à-vis the poetic tradition, the meaning abeyant in the archetype of the *nasīb* becomes more explicit.

Follies and misfortunes had made Ibn Zaydūn taste the bitterness of unrequited love, imprisonment, and exile. In addition to the personal sense of loss born out of such vicissitudes, the poet saw crumble at much too close a distance the glory that was the house of the Andalusian Umayyads and the grandeur that was Cordova. Indeed, his scornful beloved, Wallādah, was herself the daughter of al-Mustakfī, a pathetic descendant of the great ʿAbd al-Raḥmān III.

When the poet was eight years old, the palace city of al-Zahrāʾ was plundered and put to the torch. His memories of youth and love, one should imagine, are closely connected with the elegiac withering of that golden dream of the caliphs of Cordova. Divested of its imperial functions, al-Zahrāʾ was now turning into a sprawling, almost contrivedly poetic landscape of desolation. Much of the architectural splendor was still there, however, perhaps only dramatized by the violence done to it. The parks and gardens must still have been luxuriantly inviting and harboring:

> And the garden smiled silvery streams,
> Like necklaces loosened over breasts.[73] [158]

During the day there may have been some movement among the ruins. Here and there richly carved marble slabs and capitals and fusts of columns were carted off to be sold and reused. But away from the melancholy business of ravage there could always be found more secluded halls, corners, and niches visited only by lovers, poets, and fugitives.[74] And then there were the nights.

Such was al-Zahrāʾ when Ibn Zaydūn roamed in it, dreamed in it, and hid in it as poet, lover, and fugitive. And yet in his poetic evocations all ruins become abodes of beauty and happiness, and indeed of perfection. They would best be imagined as an idea of Paradise even without the poet's explicitness. If there are ruins, they lie in the poet's heart—and then only in that part of the heart which remains exiled from Cordova, from al-Zahrāʾ, and from Wallādah. The remembering heart seems to know no ruins. It is the wholeness of happiness, for it is the vision of reverie captured in the poem. Whereas other poets, faithful to the conventions of the archaic theme sequence of formal odes, had entertained such dreams of the wholeness of happiness only within the recondite folds of the ancient symbolic mold of the opening of the Bedouin *qaṣīdah* with its abandoned campsites and abodes, Ibn Zaydūn tells us unequivocally which are his abodes, which his ruins, and where his ultimate model of happiness lies:

12. To al-Zahrāʾ, the fair,
    is an exile ever to return,
  His eyes with no more tears to weep?

15. A place of mirth it was, its redolence
    a presage of Eternity,
  Where a gallant youth rose above thirst
    and scorching sun,

16. Where dewy shadows framed deep,
    azure waters,
  Where I knew time ready to oblige.

17. Yet there I exchanged the chant
    of artful maidens
  For the desert's fearful echoes and panting snorts
    which took away my sleep,

18. And instead of the cup, whose bearer is spared,
  I bore the spear and rushed blindly
    into horrors.[75] [159]

Ibn Zaydūn's al-Zahrāʾ is an intimation of eternity, but of an eternity which is a garden of delights very much the way it is described in the Qurʾān.[76] The perfection of the poetically recollected, indeed recaptured, moment of happiness in this al-Zahrāʾ-turned-Paradise excludes the earthly details of the true al-Zahrāʾ of the melancholy face. And thus when loss occurs it is only in the recesses of the poet's heart. The ideal image in the remembering heart does not suffer. But the realization that Paradise, that al-Zahrāʾ as dream and symbol, is lost even at the inception of the metaphor becomes all the more painful. Here the explicitness of the qurʾānic allusions in the poem is helpful perhaps not so much because it brings al-Zahrāʾ closer to Paradise as because it draws Paradise closer to al-Zahrāʾ and to the poet. There are forebodings even in those qurʾānic allusions to Paradise. The wording of verse 15 alerts us to the fact that the poet's thoughts of Paradise are of a happiness which will be lost. In vain is God's promise to Adam of a garden where he will know neither thirst nor scorching sun. Satan already whispers to him of the tree of life and power. This is what Sūrah 20, which is behind Ibn Zaydūn's lines, tells us.[77] Verses 17 and 18 in the poem are only too explicit about whose call the poet himself had followed. But that explicitness is no longer tied to qur'ānic allusions as much as it stems from equally magisterial Arabic poetic sources. Even so, however, there is still heard the seemingly distant qur'ānic echo of the oathlike invocation of Sūrah 100:1, "Wa al-ʿādiyāti ḍabḥan," with its snorting steeds rushing into battle.[78]

In another poem that also draws on the poet's Cordovan memories, the metaphor of the garden and the symbol of Paradise reappear with equal directness. This poem is the *Nūnīyah* (poem rhyming in the letter *nūn*), praised by critical tradition as Ibn Zaydūn's best achieved work and celebrated by centuries of Arabic poetry lovers as the haunting song of the exile and of the scorned lover, a song capable of casting the spell of the poet's own fate on those who commit its verses to memory.[79] In this poem, too, however, direct references to the qur'ānic Paradise occur only in order to stress the loss of happiness. The garden itself is at first no more than a conjured vision of earthly delight (v. 32):

> O garden, wherein long since our eyes
> plucked roses,
> Which youth displayed so fresh,
> and sweet eglantines.[80] [160]

In the succeeding verses the poet develops further the theme of remembered happiness, abstracted from whatever the present may contain. Here qur'ānic echoes are still only scattered. Perhaps the delight (*naʿīm*) the poet enjoyed in that garden had the taste of supreme delight (v. 33). Perhaps the beloved had appeared to the poet as a unique, unshared being (v. 35). But then (v. 36) comes the outcry of loss. The reverie is broken. There is not even room for melancholy. Such a realization of loss is dramatic:

> O Garden Eternal, for your lote-tree
> and sweet Kawthar-stream
> We received in trade Hell's fruit of bile
> and gush of purulence.[81] [161]

And so for the first time in the poem, the poet tells us clearly where he had experienced his happiness, and by inference he also tells us about the quality of that happiness, enjoyed at the waters of the Kawthar, under the heavenly lote-tree. The poet has been in heaven. He has tasted it and lost it. This is the substance of his experience.

But the drama and the pain subside, and again all becomes the volatile gossamer of reminiscence. Melancholy begins to set in. Perhaps the lyrical mood of remembrance seems as yet hesitant, as if there were someone to be reproached (v. 38):

> As if we had never passed a night
> when the third of us was union,
> When the star of good fortune made
> talebearers look aside.[82] [162]

This is the voice of a poet whose love has already become nostalgia—but not an entirely untroubled nostalgia, not yet one fully transported into the calm world of reverie. Why does the poet think of "union" as an intervening third? There is something ambiguous and self-conscious about such a personification of the union of love, about its being like a conspiring, extraneous part in an act of intimacy. One almost wishes one were free to think of Cupid or of amorettes. But what comes to mind is the association of such a "third one" with the snake of the Garden of Eden and with the Ḥadīth-like saying that "man and woman are never alone without Satan being the third one present."[83] And indeed, hasn't the poet told us before that the union took place in a garden? And when that garden was lost, didn't it become clear that the poet had lost none other than Paradise itself? It is as if a garden could be recognized as Paradise—recognized symbolically, that is—only after it had been lost. The eighteenth-century French writer Chamfort spoke perhaps for all poets and for all lovers when he said that he "would willingly write over the gate of paradise the line that Dante inscribed over the gate of hell: Lasciate ogni speranza, voi ch'entrate."[84]

As the poet's voice of sorrow mellows, it acquires a tone of resignation. In his poetic idiom this is reflected in a growing balance between the recourse to qur'ānic allusions to loss or to fate—a recourse to quick, handy ideas one could almost say—and the tendency to look for ultimate poetic validation in the more ancient yet symbolically elusive Bedouin frame of reference of the *nasīb*.

Thus the poet's return to memories brings him to "the day of departure" (v. 41):

> On the day of departure we read
> from the book of grief
> Sūrahs of our fate, and memorized
> lessons of endurance.[85] [163]

On that day of departure, which is an archaic, Bedouin day of the *nasīb*, the voice of impending grief is, however, no longer the foreboding call of the crow. In the poet's more immediate consciousness it becomes the reading of the book of fate, of the "sūrahs" of resignation. Once again, to stress the presence of his sorrow, the poet reaches for a language which is more explicit. Such language to him has qur'ānic associations. It is then set into the mood framework of melancholy and lyrical reverie which in turn will use language and allusions that are archaic, Bedouin. We thus notice that, whenever a greater immediacy of sorrow or loss or a dramatic quickening of the pulse is the purpose, the poet will have at hand language of qur'ānic provenance, direct in its reference and, as it were, more contemporary. When, however, he wants to convert this drama and this feeling of the instant into symbol and into lyricism, when he wants to lose himself in the vague poetic plasma of reverie, he turns to the archaic, Bedouin chain of *nasīb* motifs, which will give a sense of depth and intimately felt authenticity to the poetic atmosphere he has achieved through such complex means, and which, in the end, will make him touch the meaning of his experience.

Not all of Ibn Zaydūn's mood pieces around Wallādah and Cordova, be they *nasīb*s or *nasīb*-poems, are as closely interwoven with qur'ānic allusions as the poems seen above; and yet the poet's purpose, which is the conveying of loss and sorrow, is achieved there too. The poet well understands the mood quality of traditional *nasīb* motifs, and he is a consummate artist when it comes to structuring them into extensive poems where they blend effortlessly into sustained outpourings of feeling.

Thus in a poem of twenty stanzas of five half-lines each (*mukhammas*), which Ibn Zaydūn directs out of the Cordovan jail to the Cordova of his happy days, he lets the once compacted thematic core of the *nasīb* unfold into a wide repertory of contributing motifs. The determining and organizing feature of mood, so important when the *nasīb* is only a structural part of an ode, becomes even more essential to this diffused and independently articulated poem. Unwaveringly, the substance in which everything is suspended is the melancholy air of lost happiness. Through this volatile substance, which in the *nasīb* tradition develops so strong a structural function, the poet is able to integrate into the poem even motifs and thematic elements which otherwise might belong to a context of praise (*madīḥ*) or self-praise (*fakhr*); except that the object of praise in this poem is the poet's native city, which he is losing, which is rejecting him; and his self-praise, too, is only an elegiac reminiscence of a self which belongs to another time. Everything is now transposed into the past; everything is ended, lost. This, however, is the realm of the *nasīb* in its oldest form. And so, when Ibn Zaydūn sings of his Cordova and of the happy time spent in al-Zahrā', his nights are the nights of the poets of old, of al-Nābighah and of al-Khansā':

> I waste my days on sham illusions
> And hang my hopes on nights under
> slow-moving stars;
> But the slowest night-traveler is a star
> with eyes upon it.[86] [164]

Only that by now the poem is in the closure of its third stanza. The poet's complaint did not begin with this opening motif of kindred ancient odes. There is no surprise, however, and there is no sense of breach of traditional patterns, since the preceding stanzas, too, were of the repertory of opening ***nasīb*** motifs. The sad and soul-searching third stanza only establishes the definitive elegiac tone. Its use of a more archaic motif is a unconscious poetic achievement—but then poetic unconsciousness does work in mysterious ways.

After this ***nasīb*** within a ***nasīb,*** before giving entirely free rein to his song in praise of Cordova, the poet establishes his personal bond with the city. "Wasn't I first created out of your dust," the poet asks, "and wasn't I safely cradled in your fold?"[87] His claim to Cordova is thus not different from Adam's claim to Paradise. Nor will his fate be different. Indeed, by what sinuous yet quite unequivocal means the poet chooses to convey his praise of Cordova underneath the polished mirror of memory and reverie! Now having forced down the lump of sadness which had formed in his throat, the poet virtually bursts out in a true ode to his native gardens and fields and to those echoing, familiar places of pleasure or just of pure delight in living—places like al-ʿUqāb, al-Ruṣāfah, al-Jaʿfarīyah, the unfailingly evocative, ubiquitous al-ʿAqīq, then ʿAyn Shuhdah, al-Jawsaq al-Naṣrī, etc., but above all al-Zahrā', to describe which the poet can only turn to a comparison with the Garden of Eden:

> Let be all beauty in desert and in town,
> And Eden's Garden as it beckons,
> and Kawthar sweet,
> When you behold such vision
> of life-giving glee.[88] [165]

In a familiar manner, Ibn Zaydūn stresses the moment of highest exultation in the poem by reaching for images out of the Qur'ān, specifically images of Paradise; and here, too, we know that the poet's comparisons between the gardens of al-Zahrā and the Garden of Eden issue out of lyrically filtered memories and idealizations, that his reverie is a meeting place for one garden which is a personal myth and another garden which is an archetypal myth.

But Ibn Zaydūn's second, almost parallel elegiac idyll, composed also in the ***mukhammas*** style, which is even more truly and simply the poet's song to lost youth and to Cordova, does not rely on references to qurʾānic concepts and motifs.[89] More than any other of his poems in this vein—possibly with only a qualified exception of the *Nūnīyah*—it invites the designation of a thematically expanded ***nasīb***. Its balmlike flow of a sustained elegiac mood issues directly out of that poetically communal, ancient well. There are no dramatic high points, no consciously intruding non-***nasīb*** imagery or diction. Flowers and gardens could not be felt as alien to the ***nasīb***. Their capacity for beauty is only surpassed by their capacity for sadness.

The first stanza of this poem of ten five-liners opens on a landscape of ruins and beloved enclosures seized in a lyrical timelessness, and with it opens the book of the poet's memories:

I. Let lavish rain drench the ruins
  of loved ones at Ḥimā,
Let it weave over them a mantle
  of striped embroidery,
Let it bring out galaxies of flowers!
Oh how virgins once walked there
  in stately pomp, so statuelike,
When life was lissome and time
  in its prime.[90] [166]

The last stanza bids time and those memories farewell and softly closes the book:

X. So say to time whose bliss has turned
  and gone,
Whose imprints, with the nights,
  grew slight—
And yet how tender was
  its evening breeze,
How the night farer was guided
  by its stars—
Say to it: "One who loves and yearns
  salutes you!"[91] [167]

Against this melancholy framework there runs through the other stanzas in this poem the counterpoint of erotic images, which, although entirely stylized and indebted to the lighter strains of ***nasīb*** motifs, are now cast into the present:

II. Enthralled by a tyrannous heart,
      where I submit she reigns,
Her sleeves in a whiff of musk.
When I come to her with passion's woe,
      she listens not,
Yet no more do I long for love's delight,
Nor for sleep to visit my eyes.[92] [168]

If left to their own devices, these motifs would effortlessly have invited a transition to pure ***ghazal*** verse. Indeed, the third stanza does surrender playfully to such an invitation. But the intertwined harmony of mood and countermood is only bittersweet. In succeeding stanzas the poem becomes a song of Cordova, of beloved places out of a beautiful past. The idyll remains an elegy. At the end the salute of the poet who loves and yearns when everything else has become memory is only an assuaging, lyrical paradox, a gesture which tries not to appear desperate. The play between the moods of happiness in the past and of sadness in the present is not allowed to assume the character of dramatic antiposition. Rather, as the poet makes the memory of joy linger in suspension over the awareness of loss, a softening, lyrical light envelops everything.[93]

Allowing our discussion of the above poem to lead us back to what interests us most in Ibn Zaydūn, we take notice of the fact that in it the poet does not have to step outside the connotative sphere of traditional Arabic poetic diction and imagery to obtain the clear effect of meaning which elsewhere he had been obtaining through symbolically more explicit qur'ānic reference. In other poems, Ibn Zaydūn has come close to taking the seventh veil off the Bedouin ***nasīb*** symbolism. In this poem, he still hesitates. As he speaks of the loss of his youth, of love, and above all of the places which once saw his happiness, he allows the diffused, concealing rather than revealing, translucency of traditional ***nasīb*** diction to wrap his memories in one last gauzy mantle of ancient discretion.

It is true that the central ***nasīb*** symbolism was becoming ever clearer to all the poets and that along the historical path of Arabic poetry individual poets have had at times a very intimate access to the symbolic recesses of the ***nasīb***. Through such poets some major changes had taken place in form and meaning, but also, one by one, the symbolic veils were falling off the archetype, as if setting it free. During this development, however, it was not total clarity of the archetype but as yet only the tempting intimation of it that was providing for the *nasīb*'s ever increasing symbolic expansion and adaptability. It is in Ibn Zaydūn's lyricism of loss that the possibility arises that there may be a more explicit alternative to the archaic *nasīb* with its Bedouin symbolic language.

To pursue this alternative, however, would have meant to expose the symbolism of the *nasīb* to the danger of conceptual clarity. Such a danger was nevertheless dissipated even by Ibn Zaydūn himself, and, for better or for worse, in the end the weight and import of the old symbolic language and of the entire formal tradition of the poem remained both Arabic poetry's glory and its limitation. The Arabic poetic muse, like her sister in Keats's sonnet, remained "Fetter'd, in spite of pained loveliness, . . . bound with garlands of her own."[94]

In a poetic tradition as firmly anchored upon its own bedrock as the Arabic, the ultimate symbolic substance imbedded in the archetypal thematic nuclei—particularly in the *nasīb*—retained its elemental, never entirely yielding, force. It resisted being analytically apprehended and projected into the externality of concepts. And, speaking almost in behalf of that tradition, one ventures to say that perhaps the archaic symbolic dimension of Arabic poetry had to remain without being consciously laid bare. If it had become entirely clear to the poets at any time, it would have been by that very fact exposed, exhausted, and turned poetically inoperative.[95]

As things were, however, the Arab poet's soul retained access to its symbol by always thirsting for it and never fully daring to know it. Through those apparently obsolete, elusive words, names, and places of the *nasīb*, through its never-ending farewells, departures, and melancholy salutes, that stubbornly naïve poetic soul, which on the surface was burdened with so much artifice, could yet go on remembering and dreaming of things as they were, as they always are, in the beginning.

APPENDIX

[1]

كَلَّفْتُمُونا حُدُودَ مَنْطِقِكُمْ   في الشِّعْرِ يُلْغَى عَنْ صِدْقِهِ كَذِبُهْ

[2]

فإمّا هلكْتُ ولم آتِهِمْ   فأَبْلِغْ أماثِلَ سَهْمٍ رَسُولاَ

[3]

أَلاَ أَبْلِغِ الأَحلافَ عَنّي رسالَةً   وذُبيانَ هَلْ أَقْسَمْتُمُ كُلَّ مُقْسَمِ

[4]

أَبْلِغَا حَسّانَ عَنّي آيَةً   فَقَرِيضُ الشِّعْرِ يَشْفِي ذا ٱلْغُلَلْ

[5]

فيا راكبًا إمّا عرضْتَ فَبَلِّغَنْ   بَنِي مالِكٍ والرَّيْثِ أَلاَّ تَلاَقِيَا

وَبَلِّغْ أَخِي عمرانَ بُردِي وَمِئْزَرِي   وَبَلِّغْ عَجُوزِي اليومَ أَلاَّ تَدانِيَا

[6]

أَلاَ مَنْ مُبْلِغٌ أُمَّ الصَّرِيخِ رسالةً   يُبَلِّغُهَا عَنّي وإنْ كُنْتُ نائِيَا

[7]

ما بالُ دَفِّكَ بِالفِراشِ مَذِيلاَ   أَقَذًى بِعَيْنِكَ أم أَرَدْتَ رَحِيلاَ

لَمّا رأَتْ أَرَقِي وَطُولَ تَقَلُّبِي   ذاتَ العِشاءِ ولَيْلِيَ المَوْصُولاَ

قالتْ خُلَيْدَةُ ما عَراكَ ولَمْ تكُنْ   قَبْلَ الرُّقادِ عَنِ الشُّؤونِ سَؤُولاَ

أَخُلَيْدَ إنَّ أَباكِ ضافَ وِسادَهُ   هَمّانِ باتَا جَنْبَةً وَدَخِيلاَ

طَرَقا فَتِلْكَ هَمَاهِمِي أَقْرِيهِمَا   قُلُصًا لَواقِحَ كَٱلْقِسِيِّ وَحُولاَ

[8]

تَقُولُ ابْنَتِي حِينَ جَدَّ الرَّحِيلُ   أَرانا سَواءً وَمَنْ قَدْ يَتِمْ

[9]

أَبْلِغْ أَمِيرَ المُؤْمِنِينَ رسالةً   شَكْوَى إِلَيْكَ مُطِلَّةً وَعَوِيلاَ
مِنْ نازِحٍ كَثُرَتْ إِلَيْكَ هُمُومُهُ   لَوْ يَسْتَطِيعُ إلى اللِّقاءِ سَبِيلاَ

[10]

وَلَيْلٍ كَمَوْجِ البَحْرِ أَرْخَى سُدُولَهُ   عَلَيَّ بِأَنْواعِ الهُمُومِ لِيَبْتَلِي
فَقُلْتُ لَهُ لَمَّا تَمَطَّى بِصُلْبِهِ   وأَرْدَفَ أَعْجازًا وَناءَ بِكَلْكَلِ
أَلا أَيُّها اللَّيْلُ الطَّوِيلُ أَلا ٱنْجَلِي   بِصُبْحٍ وما الإصباحُ فِيكَ بِأَمْثَلِ
فَيا لَكَ من لَيْلٍ كَأَنَّ نُجُومَهُ   بِكُلِّ مُغارِ الفَتْلِ شُدَّتْ بِيَذْبُلِ
كَأَنَّ الثُّرَيّا عُلِّقَتْ في مَصامِها   بِأَمْراسِ كَتّانٍ إلى صُمِّ جَنْدَلِ

[11]

عَلَوْنَ رَباوةً وَهَبَطْنَ غَيْباً   فَلَمْ يَرْجِعْنَ قائِلَةً لِحِينِ
فَقُلْتُ لِبَعْضِهِنَّ وَشُدَّ رَحْلِي   لِهاجِرةٍ نَصَبْتُ لها جَبِينِي
لَعَلَّكِ إنْ صَرَمْتِ الحَبْلَ مِنِّي   أَكُونُ كَذاكَ مُصْحِبَتِي قَرُونِي
فَسَلِّ الهَمَّ عَنْكَ بِذاتِ لَوْثٍ   عُذافِرةٍ كَمِطْرَقَةِ القُيُونِ

[12]

فَظِلْتُ أُتْبِعُهُمْ عَيناً على طَرَبٍ   إنسانُها غَرِقٌ في مائِها مَغِطُ
وَكُلُّ مُجْتَمِعٍ لا بُدَّ مُفْتَرِقٌ   وَكُلُّ ذِي عُمُرٍ يَوْمًا سَيُحْتَنَطُ

[13]

فَبِتُّ مُسَهَّدًا أَرِقًا كَأَنِّي   تَمَشَّتْ في مَفاصِلِيَ العُقارُ
أُراقِبُ في السَّماءِ بَناتِ نَعْشٍ   وقَدْ دارَتْ كما عَطَفَ الصِّوارُ
وعانَدَتِ الثُّرَيّا بعد هَدْءٍ   مُعانَدةً لها العَيُّوقُ جارُ

فَقَدْ كانتْ لنا ولَهُنّ حتّى   زَوتْنا الحَرْبُ أيّامٌ قِصارُ

[14]

نَظَرْتُ كأَنّي من وراءِ زُجاجةٍ   إلى الدار من ماء الصُّبابة أَنْظُرُ
فَعَيْناي طَوْرًا تَغْرَقان منَ الْبُكا   فَأَعْشَى وَحِينًا تَحْسُران فَأُبْصِرُ

[15]

اَلْعِيسُ والهَمُّ والليلُ التَمامُ مَعًا   ثلاثةٌ أَبَدًا يُقْرَنّ في قَرَنِ

[16]

أَحْمَتْ رِماحُ بني سَعْدٍ لِقَوْمِهِمُ   مَراعِيَ الحُمْرِ والظِّلْمانِ والعِينِ

[17]

ولَنَا دارٌ وَرِثْنا عِزَّها الْ   أَقْدَمَ القُدْمُوسَ عن عَمٍّ وَخالِ

[18]

فَبَنَى لنا بَيْتًا رَفيعًا سَمْكُهُ   فَسَما إليه كَهْلُها وغُلامُها

[19]

وإنْ يَلْتَقِ الحَيُّ الجَميعُ تُلاقِنِي   إلى ذِرْوَةِ البَيْتِ الكَريمِ الْمُصَمَّدِ
نَداماي بِيضٌ كالنُّجومِ وقَيْنةٌ   تَروحُ إلينا بين بُرْدٍ وَمُجْسَدِ

[20]

وَباتَ عليه سَرْجُهُ ولِجامُهُ   وباتَ بعَيْنِي قائِمًا غيرَ مُرْسَلِ

[21]

وقَدْ أَقودُ أمام الحَيِّ سَلْهَبَةً   يَهْدِي بها نَسَبٌ في الحَيِّ مَعْلومُ

[22]

لِمَنِ الدّيارُ بِقُنّةِ الحِجْرِ   أَقْوَيْنَ من حِجَجٍ ومن دَهْرِ

[23]

ولَقَدْ حَمَيْتُ الحَيَّ تَحْمِلُ شِكَّتِي   فُرُطٌ وِشاحِي إذْ غَدَوْتُ لِجامُها

[24]

فإنْ يَهْلِكْ أبو قابوسَ يَهْلِكْ   رَبيعُ الناسِ والشَّهْرُ الحَرامُ
وَنُمْسِكُ بَعْدَهُ بِذِنابِ عَيْشٍ   أَجَبَّ الظَّهْرِ ليس له سَنامُ

[25]

طابَ فيه المَديحُ وٱلتَذَّ حتّى   فاقَ وَصْفَ الدّيارِ والتَّشْبيبَا

[26]

ما أنت أوّلُ من تَناءَتْ دارُهُ   فَعَلامَ قَلْبُكَ ليس تَخْبُو نارُهُ

[27]

خَفّفِ الوَطْءَ ما أَظُنُّ أديمَ الْ   أرْضِ إلا من هذه الأَجْسادِ

[28]

١. أَناةً أَيُّها الفَلَكُ المُدارُ   أَنَهْبٌ ما تُطَرّقُ أَمْ جُبارُ

٤. وَما أَهْلُ المَنازِلِ غيرُ رَكْبٍ   مَناياهُمْ رَواحٌ وٱبْتِكارُ

٥. لَنا في الدّهْرِ آمالٌ طِوالٌ   نُرَجّيها وأَعْمارٌ قِصارُ

[29]

عُوجا علي الطّلَلِ المُحيلِ لَأنّنا   نَبْكِي الدّيارَ كما بَكَى ٱبْنُ خِذامِ

[30]

أُزْجُرِ العَيْنَ أَنْ تُبَكّي الطُلولاَ   إنّ في الصّدْرِ من كُلَيْبٍ غليلاَ

إنّ في الصّدْرِ حاجةً لَنْ تُقَضّى   ما دامَ في الغُصونِ داعٍ هَديلاَ

كيف يَبْكِي الطُلولَ من هو رَهْنٌ   بِطِعانِ الأَنامِ جيلاً فَجيلاَ

[31]

جَرَى ناصحٌ بالوُدّ بَيْنِي وبَيْنَها   فَقَرّبَنِي يَوْمَ الحِصابِ إلى قَتْلِي

فَطارَتْ بِحَدٍّ من فُؤادي ونازَعَتْ   قَرِيبَتُها حَبْلَ الصّفاءِ إلى حَبْلِي

فَما أَنْسَ مِلْأَشْياءِ لا أَنْسَ مَوقِفِي   وَمَوْقِفَها وَهْنًا بِقارِعَةِ النّخْلِ

فَلمّا تَواقَفْنا عَرَفْتُ الّذي بها   كَمِثْلِ الّذي بي حَذْوَكَ النّعْلَ بالنّعْلِ

[32]

١٨. فَقُمْنَ وقَدْ أَفْهَمْنَ ذا اللُبّ أَنّما   فَعَلْنَ الّذي يَفْعَلْنَ في ذاك من أَجْلِي

[33]

صِفَةُ الطُلولِ بَلاغَةُ الفَدْمِ   فَٱجْعَلْ صِفاتِكَ لِٱبْنَةِ كَرْمِ

[34]

وَدارٍ نَدامَى عَطَّلوها وأَدلَجُوا   بها أَثَرٌ مِنْهُمْ جَديدٌ وَدارِسُ
مَساحِبُ من جَرِّ الزِّقاقِ على الثَّرَى   وأَضْغاثُ رَيْحانٍ جَنِيٌّ وَيابِسُ
حَبَسْتُ بها صَحْبِي فَجَدَّدْتُ عَهْدَهُمْ   وَإِنِّي على أَمْثالِ تلك لَحابِسُ
ولَمْ أدْرِ من هم غيرَ ما شَهِدَتْ به   بِشَرْقِيِّ ساباطَ الدِّيارُ البَسابِسُ

[35]

فَدَعِ الدِّيارَ وَذِكْرَ كُلِّ خَرِيدةٍ   بَيْضاءَ آنِسةِ الحَديثِ كَعابِ
وَاشْكُ الهُمُومَ إلى الإِلهِ وما تَرَى   من مَعْشَرٍ مُتَأَلِّبِينَ غِضابِ

[36]

ألاَ يا لَقَوْمٍ هل لِما حُمَّ دافِعُ   وَهَل ما مَضَى من صالحِ العَيْشِ راجِعُ
تَذَكَّرْتُ عَصْرًا قَدْ مَضَى فَتَهافَتَتْ   بَناتُ الحَشا وَانْهَلَّ مِنِّي المَدامِعُ
صَبابةُ وَجْدٍ ذَكَّرَتْنِي أَحِبَّةً   وَقَتْلَى مَضَوا فِيهِمْ نُفَيْعٌ وَرافِعُ
وَسَعْدٌ فَأَضْحَوا في الجِنانِ وَأَوْحَشَتْ   مَنازِلُهُمْ وَالأَرْضُ مِنْهُمْ بَلاقِعُ

[37]

بِطَيْبَةَ رَسْمٌ لِلرَّسولِ وَمَعْهَدُ   مُنيرٌ وَقَدْ تَعْفُو الرُّسومُ وَتَهْمَدُ
ولا تَنْمَحِي الآياتُ من دارِ حُرْمَةٍ   بها مِنْبَرُ الهادِي الّذي كان يَصْعَدُ
وَواضِحُ آياتٍ وَباقِي مَعالِمٍ   وَرَبْعٌ له فيه مُصَلًّى وَمَسْجِدُ
بها حُجُراتٌ كان يَنْزِلُ وَسْطَها   مِنَ اللّه نُورٌ يُسْتَضاءُ وَيُوقَدُ
مَعالِمُ لم تُطْمَسْ على العَهْدِ آيُها   أَتاها البِلَى فَالآيُ منها تَجَدَّدُ
عَرَفْتُ بها رَسْمَ الرَّسولِ وَعَهْدَهُ   وَقَبْرًا به واراهُ في التُّرْبِ مُلْحِدُ

[38]

وأَمْسَتْ بِلادُ الحَرْمِ وَحْشًا بِقاعُها   لِغَيْبَةِ ما كانتْ مِنَ الوَحْيِ تَعْهَدُ
قِفارًا سِوَى مَعْمورَةِ اللَّحْدِ ضافَها   فَقِيدٌ يُبَكِّيهِ بَلاطٌ وَغَرْقَدُ

وَمَسْجِدُهُ فَالمُوحِشاتُ لِفَقْدِهِ   خَلاءٌ لَه فيه مَقامٌ وَمَقْعَدُ
وَبِالجَمْرَةِ الكُبْرَى له ثَمَّ أَوْحَشَتْ   دِيارٌ وَعَرْصاتٌ وَرَبْعٌ وَمَوْلِدُ

[39]

عَفا المُصَلَّى وأَقْوَتِ الكُثُبُ   مِنّيَ فَالمِرْبَدانِ فَاللَّبَبُ
فَالمَسْجِدُ الجامِعُ المُرُوءَةِ والـ   ـدّينِ عَفا فَالصِّحانُ فَالرَّحَبُ

[40]

نَداماي بِيضٌ كالنُّجومِ وقَيْنَةٌ   تَروحُ إلينا بَيْنَ بُرْدٍ وَمُجْسَدِ

[41]

رُبَّ لَهْوٍ شَهِدْتُهُ أُمَّ عَمْرٍو   بَيْنَ بِيضٍ نَواعِمٍ في الرِّياطِ
مع نَدامَى بِيضِ الوُجوهِ كِرامٍ   نُبِّهوا بَعْدَ خَفْقَةِ الأَشْراطِ

[42]

يا رُبَّما راقَنِي بِساحَتِها   طِيبُ هَواها وَلَهْوُ سامِرِهَا
أَيّامَ لا خَوْفَ من شَتاتِ نَوًى   تُخْشَى ولا رَوْعَ من تَطايُرِهَا
كُنّا بِها حِقْبَةً فَأَزْعَجَنا   خَطْبٌ نَفَى الخَفْضَ عن مُجاوِرِهَا

[43]

لَهْفِي علي الزَّمَنِ القَصِيرِ   بَيْنَ الخَوَرْنَقِ والسَّدِيرِ
إذْ نحن في غُرَفِ الجِنا   نِ نَعُومُ في بَحْرِ السُّرورِ
في فِتْيَةٍ مَلَكُوا عِنا   نَ الدَّهْرِ أَمْثالِ الصُّقُورِ
ما مِنْهُمُ إلا الجَسُو   رُ على الهَوَى غيرُ الحَصُورِ
يَتَعاوَرُونَ مُدامَةً   صَهْباءَ من حَلَبِ العَصِيرِ
عَذْراءَ رَبّاها شُعا   عُ الشَّمْسِ في حَرِّ الهَجِيرِ
لم تُدْنَ من نارٍ ولم   يَعْلَقْ بِها وَضَرُ القُدُورِ
وَمُقَرْطَقٍ يَمْشِي أَما   مَ القَوْمِ كالرَّشَأِ الغَرِيرِ

بِزُجاجَةٍ تَسْتَخْرِجُ الـ   ـسِّرَّ الدَّقيقَ مِنَ الضَّميرِ
زَهْراءَ مِثْلِ الكَوْكَبِ الـ   ـدُّرِّيِّ في كَفِّ المُديرِ
تَدَعُ الكَريمَ وليس يَدْ   ري ما قَبيلٌ من دَبيرِ
وَمُخَصَّراتٍ زُرْنَنا   بَعْدَ الهُدوءِ مِنَ الخُدورِ
رَيّا رَوادِفُهُنَّ يَلْـ   ـبَسْنَ الخَواتِمَ في الخُصورِ
غُرِّ الوُجوهِ مُحَجَّبا   تٍ قاصِراتِ الطَّرْفِ حُورِ
مُتَنَعِّماتٍ في النَّعيـ   ـمِ مُضَمَّخاتٍ بِالعَبيرِ
يَرْفُلْنَ في حُلَلِ المَحا   سِنِ وَالمَجاسِدِ وَالحَريرِ
ما إنْ يَرَيْنَ الشَّمْسَ إ   لاَّ الفَرْطَ من خِلَلِ السُّتورِ
وَإلي أَمينِ اللّهِ مَهْـ   ـرَبُنا مِنَ الدَّهْرِ العَثورِ
وَإليه أَتْعَبْنا المَطا   يا بِالرَّواحِ وَبِالبُكورِ
صُعْرَ الخُدودِ كَأَنَّما   جُنِّحْنَ أَجْنِحَةَ النُّسورِ
مُتَسَرْبِلاتٍ بِالظَّلا   مِ على السُّهولَةِ وَالوُعورِ
حَتّى وَصَلْنَ بنا إلي   رَبِّ المَدائِنِ وَالقُصورِ
ما زال قَبْلَ فِطامِهِ   في سِنِّ مُكْتَهِلِ كَبيرِ

[44]

أُحِبُّ المَكانَ القَفْرَ من أَجْلِ أَنَّني   به أَتَغَنّى بِٱسْمِها غيرَ مُعْجِمِ

[45]

وَلَقَدْ مَرَرْتُ على دِيارِهِمُ   وَطُلولُها بِيَدِ البِلَى نَهْبُ
فَوَقَفْتُ حَتّى ضَجَّ من لَغَبٍ   نِضْوي وَلَجَّ بِعَذْلِيَ الرَّكْبُ
وَتَلَفَّتَتْ عَيْني فَمُذْ خَفِيَتْ   عَنْها الطُّلولُ تَلَفَّتَ القَلْبُ

[46]

وما أنسَ مَنْ وَدّعْتُ بِالشّطّ سُحْرَةً   وَقَدْ غَرّدَ الحادُونَ وَٱسْتَعْجَلَ الرَّكْبُ
أَلِيفانِ هذا سائِرٌ نَحْوَ غُرْبَةٍ   وهذا مُقيمٌ سارَ عن جِسْمِهِ القَلْبُ

[47]

يا ظَبْيَةَ البانِ تَرْعَى في خَمائِلِهِ   لِيَهْنِكِ اليَوْمَ أنّ القَلْبَ مَرْعاكِ
الماءُ عِنْدَكِ مَبْذولٌ لِشارِبِهِ   وليس يُرْوِيكِ إلا مَدْمَعِي الباكِي

[48]

أنْتِ النّعيمُ لِقَلْبِي وَالعَذابُ له   فما أَمَرّكِ من قَلْبِي وَأَحْلاكِ

[49]

فَقَضَى حُكْمُ الهَوَى أَنْ تُصْبِحِي   لِلْمُحِبّينَ مُناخًا وَمُقامَا

[50]

وَحَنّتْ رِكابِي والهَوَى يَبْعَثُ الهَوَى   فَلَمْ أَرَ في تَيْماءَ إلا مُتَيَّمَا

[51]

أُقَلّبُ طَرْفِي في السّماءِ لَعَلّنِي   أَشِيمُ سَنا بَرْقٍ هُناك تَطَلّعَا

[52]

قِفْ بِالدّيارِ وَحَيِّ الأَرْبُعَ الدُّرُسَا   . . . .

[53]

يا جَنّةً فارَقَتْها النّفْسُ مُكْرَهَةً   لو لا التّأَسّي بِدارِ الخُلْدِ مُتُّ أَسَى

[54]

كما قَدْ أَعَرْنا لِلْغُصونِ مَلابِسًا   وَلِلرَّوْضِ أَخْلاقًا وَلِلْبَرْقِ مَبْسِمَا

[55]

أَبَرْقٌ بَدا من جانِبِ الغَوْرِ لامِعُ   أَمِ ٱرْتَفَعَتْ عن وَجْهِ لَيْلَى البَراقِعُ
أَنارُ الغَضا ضاءَتْ وَسَلْمَى بِذِي الغَضا   أَمِ ٱبْتَسَمَتْ عَمّا حَكَتْهُ المَدامِعُ
أَنَشْرُ خُزامَى فاحَ أَمْ عَرْفُ حاجِرٍ   بِأُمّ القُرَى أَمْ عِطْرُ عَزّةَ ضائِعُ
أَلا لَيْتَ شِعْرِي هل سُلَيْمَى مُقيمَةٌ   بِوادِي الحِمَى حَيْثُ المُتَيَّمُ والِعُ

وَهَلْ لَعْلَعَ الرَّعْدُ الهَتونُ بِلَعْلَعٍ   وهل جادَها صَوْبٌ من المُزْنِ هامِعُ
وَهَلْ أَرِدَنْ ماءَ العُذَيْبِ وَحاجِرٍ   جِهارًا وَسِرُّ اللَّيْلِ بِالصُّبْحِ شائِعُ
وَهَلْ قاعَةُ الوَعْساءِ مُخْضَرَّةُ الرُّبَى   وهل ما مَضَى فيها من العَيْشِ راجِعُ
وَهَلْ بِرُبَى نَجْدٍ فَتُوضِحَ مُسْنِدٌ   أُهَيْلَ النَّقا عَمّا حَوَتْهُ الأَضالِعُ
وَهَلْ بِلِوَى سَلْعٍ يُسَلْ عن مُتَيَّمٍ   بِكاظِمَةٍ ماذا به الشَّوْقُ صانِعُ
وَهَلْ عَذَباتُ الرَّنْدِ يُقْطَفُ نَوْرُها   وهل سَلَماتٌ بِالحِجازِ أَيانِعُ
وَهَلْ أَثَلاتُ الجِزْعِ مُثْمِرَةٌ وهل   عُيونُ عَوادِي الدَّهْرِ عنها هَواجِعُ
وَهَلْ قاصِراتُ الطَّرْفِ عِينٌ بِعالِجٍ   على عَهْدِيَ المَعْهودِ أَمْ هوَ ضائِعُ
وَهَلْ ظَبَياتُ الرَّقْمَتَيْنِ بُعَيْدَنا   أَقَمْنَ بها أَمْ دونَ ذلك مانِعُ
وَهَلْ فَتَياتٌ بِالغُوَيْرِ يُرِينَنِي   مَرابِعَ نُعْمٍ نِعْمَ تلك المَرابِعُ
وَهَلْ ظِلُّ ذاك الضّالِ شَرْقِيَّ ضارِجٍ   ظَليلٌ فَقَدْ رَوَّتْهُ مِنّي المَدامِعُ
وَهَلْ عامِرٌ من بَعْدِنا شِعْبُ عامِرٍ   وهل هو يَوْمًا لِلْمُحِبّينَ جامِعُ
وَهَلْ أُمَّ بَيْتَ اللّٰهِ يا أُمَّ مالِكٍ   عُرَيْبٌ لَهُمْ عندي جَميعًا صَنائِعُ
وَهَلْ نَزَلَ الرَّكْبُ العِراقي مُعَرِّفًا   وهل شُرِعَتْ نَحْوَ الخِيامِ شَرائِعُ
وَهَلْ رَقَصَتْ بِالمأْزِمَيْنِ قَلائِصٌ   وهل لِلْقِبابِ البِيضِ فيها تَدافُعُ
وَهَلْ لي بِجَمْعِ الشَّمْلِ في جَمْعَ مُسْعِدٌ   وهل لِلَيالِي الخَيْفِ بِالعُمْرِ بائِعُ
وَهَلْ سَلَّمَتْ سَلْمَى على الحَجَرِ الّذي   به العَهْدُ وَٱلْتَفَّتْ عليه الأَصابِعُ
وَهَلْ رَضَعَتْ من ثَدْيِ زَمْزَمَ رَضْعَةً   فلا حُرِّمَتْ يَوْمًا عليها المَراضِعُ
لَعَلَّ أُصَيْحابِي بِمَكَّةَ يُبْرِدُوا   بِذِكْرِ سُلَيْمَى ما تُجِنُّ الأَضالِعُ
وَعَلَّ اللُّيَيْلاتِ الّتي قد تَصَرَّمَتْ   تَعُودُ لنا يَوْمًا فَيَظْفَرَ طامِعُ

وَيَفْرَحَ مَحْزُونٌ وَيَحْيا مُتَيَّمٌ   وَيَأْنَسَ مُشْتاقٌ وَيَلْتَذَّ سامِعُ

[56]

أَسَرَى لِخالِدَةَ الخَيالُ ولا أَرَى   طَلَلاً أَحَبَّ مِنَ الخَيالِ الطّارِقِ

[57]

خَيالٌ مُلِمٌّ أَمْ حَبِيبٌ مُسَلِّمُ   وَبَرْقٌ تَجَلَّى أَمْ حَرِيقٌ مُضَرَّمُ

[58]

بِثَمْدِينَ لاحَتْ نارُ لَيْلَى وَصُحْبَتِي   بِذاتِ الغَضَى تُزْجِي المَطِيَّ النَّواحِيَا
فَقالَ بَصِيرُ القَوْمِ أَلْمَحْتُ كَوْكَبًا   بَدا في سَوادِ اللَّيْلِ فَرْدًا يَمانِيَا
فَقُلْتُ له بَلْ نارُ لَيْلَى تَوَقَّدَتْ   بِعَلْيَا تَسامَى ضَوْؤُها فَبَدا لِيَا

[59]

أَلا سائِلَ الرُّكْبانِ هل طَلَّ لَعْلَعٌ   كما كان مَطْلولَ الأَصائِلِ سَجْسَجَا
وَهَلْ وَرَدُوا ماءَ العُذَيْبِ مَناهِلاً   إذا صافَحَتْ كَفُّ النَّسِيمِ تَأَرَّجَا

[60]

١. بِاللّٰهِ قُلْ لِلنِّيلِ عَنِّي إِنَّنِي   لم أَشْفِ من ماءِ الفُراتِ غَلِيلاَ
٢. يا قَلْبُ كَمْ خَلَّفْتَ ثَمَّ بُثَيْنَةً   وَأُعِيذُ صَبْرَكَ أَنْ يَكُونَ جَمِيلاَ

[61]

ليس في الأَرْضِ ما يَفُوقُ سِوَى الشّـ   ـامِ وَدَعْني مِن سائِرِ الآفاقِ
يا رِياحَ الشَّآمِ أَنْتِ رَسُولٌ   يَتَعَنَّى في حاجَةِ العُشّاقِ
وَإِذا زُرْتِ غُلَّتِي بِنَسِيمٍ   قامَ بَيْنَ الحَشا مَقامَ العِناقِ
لَكِ من أَدْمُعِي مَيادِينُ شَوْقٍ   فَارْكُضِي فيه مِثْلَ رَكْضِ العِتاقِ
ذَخِرَتْ مُقْلَتِي كُنُوزَ دُمُوعٍ   فَاجْهَدِي يا هُمُومُ في الإِنْفاقِ
فَكَأَنَّ الأَنْداءَ نَفْثَةُ راقٍ   وَكَأَنَّ الحَفِيفَ صَوْتُ الرّاقِي
وَسَلامٌ على اللَّيالِي الخَوالِي   من مُعَنًّى من اللَّيالِي البَواقِي

عَلِّلُونِي عَنِ الشَّآمِ بِذِكْرٍ   إِنَّ قَلْبِي إليه بِالأَشْوَاقِ
مَثَّلَتْهُ الذِّكْرَى لِعَيْنِي كَأَنِّي   أَتَمَشَّى هُنَاكَ بِالأَحْدَاقِ
لا أَغَبَّ الغَمَامُ عنه تَحَايَا   تُلْبِسُ الغُصْنَ سُنْدُسَ الأَوْرَاقِ
عَذَّبَ اللّٰهُ بِالتَّنَائِي التَّنَائِي   وَأَذَاقَ الفِرَاقَ طَعْمَ الفِرَاقِ

[62]

ماذا بِبَغْدَادَ من طِيبِ الأَفَانِينِ   ومن عَجَائِبَ لِلدُّنْيَا وَلِلدِّينِ
ما بين قُطْرُبُلٍ فَالكَرْخِ نَرْجِسَةٌ   تَنْدَى وَمَنْبَتُ خِيرِيٍّ وَنِسْرِينِ
تَحْيَا النُّفُوسُ إذا أَرْوَاحُهَا نَفَحَتْ   وَخَرَّشَتْ بين أَوْرَاقِ الرَّيَاحِينِ
سَقْيًا لِتِلْكَ القُصُورِ الشَّاهِقَاتِ وما   بها مِنَ البَقَرِ الإِنْسِيَّةِ العِينِ
تَسْتَنُّ دِجْلَةَ فيما بينها فَتَرَى   دُهْمَ السَّفِينِ تَعَالَى كَالبَرَاذِينِ
مَنَاظِرٌ ذاتُ أَبْوَابٍ مُفَتَّحَةٍ   أَنِيقَةٍ بِزَخَارِيفٍ وَتَزْيِينِ
فيها القُصُورُ الَّتي تَهْوِي بِأَجْنِحَةٍ   بِالزَّائِرِينَ الى القَوْمِ المَزُورِينِ
من كُلِّ حَرَّاقَةٍ يَعْلُو فَقَارَتَهَا   قَصْرٌ مِنَ السَّاجِ عالٍ ذو أَسَاطِينِ

[63]

وَمَنَازِلٍ لَكَ بِالحِمَى   وَبِهَا الخَلِيطُ نُزُولُ
وأَيَّامُهُنَّ قَصِيرَةٌ   وَسُرُورُهُنَّ طَوِيلُ
وَسُعُودُهُنَّ طَوَالِعٌ   وَنُحُوسُهُنَّ أُفُولُ
وَالمَالِكِيَّةُ وَالشَّبَا   بُ وَقَيْنَةٌ وَشَمُولُ

[64]

أَلا أيُّها القَلْبُ المُصَرَّحُ بِالوَجْدِ   أما لَكَ من بادِي الصَّبَابَةِ من بُدّ
وَهَلْ من سُلُوٍّ يُرْتَجَى لِمُتَيَّمٍ   له لَوْعَةُ الصادِي وَرَوْعَةُ ذِي الصَّدّ
يَحِنُّ إلى نَجْدٍ وَهَيْهَاتِ حَرَّمَتْ   صُرُوفُ اللَّيَالِي أَنْ يَعُودَ إلى نَجْدِ

فَيا جَبَلَ الرَّيّانِ لا رِيَّ بَعْدَما   عَدَتْ غِيَرُ الأَيّامِ عن ذلك الوِرْدِ

وَيا أَهْلَ وُدّي وَالحَوادِثُ تَقتَضي   خُلُوّيَ عن أَهْلٍ يُضافُ إلى الوُدّ

ألا مُتْعَةٌ يَوْمًا بِعارِيَةِ المُنَى   فَإِنّا نَراها كُلَّ حِينٍ إلى الرَّدّ

أمِن بَعْدِ رُزْءٍ في بَلَنْسيَةٍ ثَوَى   بِأحْنائِنا كالنّارِ مُضْمَرَةُ الوَقْدِ

يُرَجّي أُناسٌ جُنّةً من مَصائِبٍ   تُطاعِنُ فيهِمْ بِالمُثَقَّفَةِ المُلْدِ

ألا لَيْتَ شِعْري هَلْ لَها من مَطالِعٌ   مَعادٌ إلى ما كان فيها مِنَ السَّعْدِ

وَهَلْ أذْنَبَ الأَبْناءُ ذَنْبَ أبِيهِمُ   فَصارُوا إلى الإخْراجِ من جَنّةِ الخُلْدِ

[65]

عُيُونُ المَها بَيْنَ الرُّصافَةِ وَالجِسْرِ   جَلَبْنَ الهَوَى من حَيْثُ أدْرِي ولا أدْرِي

أعَدْنَ لِيَ الشَّوْقَ القَدِيمَ وَلَمْ أكُنْ   سَلَوْتُ ولٰكِنْ زِدْنَ جَمْرًا على جَمْرِ

[66]

قِفا نَبْكِ من ذِكْرَى حَبِيبٍ وَمَنْزِلِ   بِسِقْطِ اللِّوَى بَيْنَ الدَّخُولِ فَحَوْمَلِ

فَتُوضِحَ فَالمِقْراةِ لَمْ يَعْفُ رَسْمُها   لِما نَسَجَتْها من جَنُوبٍ وَشَمْأَلِ

[67]

فَأَتْبَعْتُهُمْ طَرْفِي وَقَدْ حالَ دُونَهُمْ   غَوارِبُ رَمْلٍ ذِي أَلاءٍ وَشِبْرِقِ

على إثْرِ حَيٍّ عامِدِينَ لِنِيَّةٍ   فَحَلُّوا العَقِيقَ أوْ ثَنِيَّةَ مُطْرِقِ

[68]

بِعَيْنَيْكَ أوْقَدَتْ هِنْدٌ النّا   رَ أخِيرًا تُلْوِي بِها العَلْياءُ

أوْقَدَتْها بَيْنَ العَقِيقِ فَشَخْصَيْـ   ـنِ بِعُودٍ كَما يَلُوحُ الضِّياءُ

[69]

لِمَنْ طَلَلٌ بِذاتِ الخَمْسِ أمْسِ   عَفا بَيْنَ العَقِيقِ فَبَطْنِ ضَرْسِ

[70]

أُناشِدُ الغَيْثَ كَيْ تَهْمِي غَوادِيهِ   عَلَى العَقِيقِ وَإنْ أقْوَتْ مَغانِيهِ

على مَحَلٍّ أرَى الأيّامَ تَضْحَكُ عن   أيّامِهِ واللّيالِي عن لَيالِيهِ

[71]

هذا العَقيقُ فَعَدِّ أيْـ   ـدِي العِيسِ عن غُلَوائِهَا

[72]

مَرَرْنا بأكْنافِ العَقيقِ فأعْشَبَتْ   أباطِحُ من أجْفانِنا وَمَسايِلُ

[73]

وَكَمْ مَشْهَدٍ عِنْدَ العَقيقِ وجِسْرِهِ
قَعَدْنا على حُمْرِ النَّباتِ وصُفْرِهِ
وظَبْيٍ يُسَقّينا سُلافَةَ خَمْرِهِ

[74]

وقُلْتُ وقَدْ شاقَنِي مُلْتَقَى   شَمِيمِ العَرارِ وبَرْدِ الصَّبَا
خَلِيلَيَّ من حِمْيَرٍ حَدِّثا   أخا شَيْبَةٍ عن لَيالِي الصِّبَى

[75]

أحِنُّ إلى نَجْدٍ وإنّي لَآيِسٌ   طِوالَ اللّيالِي من قُفولٍ إلى نَجْدِ
وإنْ يَكُ لا لَيْلَى ولا نَجْدَ فاعْتَرِفْ   بِهَجْرٍ إلى يَوْمِ القِيامَةِ والوَعْدِ

[76]

ألا يا صَبا نَجْدٍ مَتَى هِجْتَ من نَجْدِ   فَقَدْ زادَنِي مَسْراكِ وَجْدًا على وَجْدِ

[77]

أحِنُّ إلى أرْضِ الحِجازِ وَحاجَتِي   خِيامٌ بِنَجْدٍ دونَها الطَّرْفُ يَقْصُرُ
وما نَظَرِي من نَحْوِ نَجْدٍ بِنافِعِي   أجَلْ لا ولَكِنّي على ذاكَ أنْظُرُ

[78]

قِفا وَدِّعا نَجْدًا وَمَنْ حَلَّ بِالحِمَى   وقَلَّ لِنَجْدٍ عِنْدَنا أنْ يُوَدَّعا
بِنَفْسِي تلك الأرْضُ ما أطْيَبَ الرُّبَى   وما أحْسَنَ المُصْطافَ والمُتَرَبَّعا
ولَيْسَتْ عَشِيّاتُ الحِمَى بِرَواجِعٍ   عَلَيْكَ ولَكِنْ خَلِّ عَيْنَيْكَ تَدْمَعا

[79]

أقولُ لِصاحِبِي والعِيسُ تهْوِي   بنا بَيْنَ المُنيفَةِ فالضِمارِ

تَمَتَّعْ من شَمِيمِ عَرارِ نَجْدٍ   فما بَعْدَ العَشِيَّةِ من عَرارِ

ألا يا حَبَّذا نَفَحاتُ نَجْدٍ   ورَيّا رَوْضِهِ غِبَّ القِطارِ

وأهْلُكَ إذْ يَحُلُّ الحَيُّ نَجْدًا   وأنْتَ على زَمانِكَ غيرُ زارِ

شُهورٌ يَنْقَضِينَ وَما شَعَرْنا   بِأنْصافٍ لَهُنَّ ولا سَرارِ

[80]

أعارِضَ مُزْنٍ أوْرَدَ البَحْرَ ذَوْدَهُ   فلَمّا تَرَوَّتْ سارَ شَوْقًا إلى نَجْدِ

سَما نَحْوَهُ مَلْكُ الرِّياحِ بِجُنْدِهِ   فَمَزَّقَهُ دُونَ الإرادَةِ والوُدّ

[81]

فَيا خَيْمَ نَجْدٍ دُونَ نَجْدٍ تِهامَةٌ   وَنَجْدٌ وَوَخْدٌ لِلسُّرَى وَذَمِيلُ

[82]

٣٥. إذا أذَى ألَمٍ ألَمَّ بِمُهْجَتِي   فَشَذا أُعَيْشابِ الحِجازِ دَوائِي

٤٠. وَشِعابُهُ لِيَ جَنَّةٌ وقِبابُهُ   لِيَ جُنَّةٌ وعلى صَفاهُ صَفائِي

[83]

أرَجُ النَّسيمِ سَرَى مِنَ الزَّوْراءِ   سَحَرًا فَأحْيا مَيِّتَ الأحْياءِ

أهْدَى لَنا أرْواحَ نَجْدٍ عَرْفُهُ   فالجَوُّ مِنْهُ مُعَنْبَرُ الأرْجاءِ

[84]

دارُ الهَوَى نَجْدٌ وَساكِنُها   أقْصَى أمانِي النَّفْسِ من نَجْدِ

هَلْ باكَرَ الوَسْمِيُّ ساحَتَها   واسْتَنَّ في قِيعانِها الجُرْدِ

أوْ باتَ مُعْتَلُّ النَّسيمِ بها   مُسْتَشْفِيًا بِالبانِ والرَّنْدِ

يَتْلُو أحادِيثَ الَّذينَ هُمُ   قَصْدِي وإنْ جارُوا عنِ القَصْدِ

أيّامَ سُمْرُ ظِلالِها وَطَنِي   مِنْها وَزُرْقُ مِياهِها وِرْدِي

مَطارِحُ النَّظَراتِ في رَشَاٍ   أَحْوَى المَدامِعِ أهْيَفِ القَدِّ
يَرْنُو إلَيْكَ بِعَيْنِ جازِيَةٍ   قُتِلَ المُحِبُّ بها على عَمْدِ

[85]

تَرَوَّحَ من أرْضٍ لأرْضٍ نَطِيَّةٍ   لِذِكْرَةِ قَيْضٍ حَوْلَ بَيْضٍ مُفَلَّقِ
يَجُولُ بآفاقِ البِلادِ مُغَرِّبًا   وتَسْحَقُهُ رِيحُ الصَّبا كُلَّ مَسْحَقِ

[86]

لِمَنِ الدّارُ أقْفَرَتْ بالجَنابِ   غيرَ نُؤْيٍ وَدِمْنَةٍ كالكِتابِ
غَيَّرَتْها الصَّبا وَنَفْحُ جَنوبٍ   وَشَمالٍ تَذْرُو دُقاقَ التُّرابِ

[87]

زَعْزَعَتْهُ الصَّبا فَأَدْرَجَ سَهْلاً   ثُمَّ هاجَتْ له الدَّبورُ نَحيلاً

[88]

ثُمَّ بَعْدَ الفَلاحِ والمُلْكِ والنِّعْـ   ـمَةِ وارَتْهُمْ هُناكَ قُبورُ
ثُمَّ صارُوا كأنَّهُمْ وَرَقٌ جَفْـ   ـفَ فألْوَتْ به الصَّبا والدَّبورُ

[89]

وَهَبَّتْ له رِيحٌ بِمُخْتَلَفِ الصُّوَى   صَبًا وَشَمالٌ في مَنازِلِ قُفَّالِ

[90]

إذا قامَتا تَضَوَّعَ المِسْكُ مِنْهُما   نَسيمَ الصَّبا جاءَتْ بِرَيّا القَرَنْفُلِ

[91]

فَلَمّا تَدَلَّى من أعالِي طَمِيَّةٍ   أبَسَّتْ به رِيحُ الصَّبا فَتَحَلَّبا

[92]

بِغَرِيضِ سارِيَةٍ أدَرَّتْهُ الصَّبا   من ماءِ أسْجَرَ طَيِّبِ المُسْتَنْقَعِ

[93]

فَأَنْتَ على الأَدْنَى شَمالٌ عَرِيَّةٌ   شَآمِيَّةٌ تَزْوِي الوُجُوهَ بَليلُ
وأنْتَ على الأَقْصَى صَبًا غَيْرُ قَرَّةٍ   تَذاءَبُ مِنْها مُرْزِغٌ وَمُسِيلُ

[94]

إذا هَبَّ عُلْوِيُّ الرِّياحِ وَجَدْتُني   كَأنِّي لِعُلْوِيِّ الرِياحِ نَسيبُ

[95]

وَعَنْ عَلَوِيّاتِ الرِّياحِ إذا جَرَتْ   بِريحِ الخُزامَى هل تَهُبُّ على نَجْدِ

[96]

تَرَكْنا أَبا الأَضْيافِ في لَيْلَةِ الصَّبا   بِمَرٍّ وَمِرْدَى كُلِّ خَصْمٍ يُجادِلُهْ

[97]

لِمَنِ الدِّيارُ كَأَنَّهُنَّ سُطورُ   تُسْدِي مَعالِمَها الصَّبا وتُنِيرُ

[98]

فَظِلْنا لَدَى العَصْلاءِ تَلْفَحُنا الصَّبا   وَظَلَّتْ مَطايانا بِغَيْرِ مُعَصَّرِ

[99]

وتَفْتَرُّ عن كالأُقْحُوانِ بِرَوْضَةٍ   جَلَتْهُ الصَّبا والمُسْتَهَلُّ مِنَ الوَبْلِ

[100]

وَكَأَنَّها والماءُ يَطْلُبُ حِلْمَها   لَهَبٌ تُلاطِمُهُ الصَّبا في مَقْبَسِ

[101]

وَسارِيَةٍ تَرْتادُ أَرْضًا تَجودُها   شَغَلْتُ بها عَيْنًا قَليلاً هُجودُها

أَتَتْنا بها ريحُ الصَّبا وَكَأَنَّها   فَتاةٌ تُزَجِّيها عَجوزٌ تَقودُها

[102]

كَأَنَّ الصَّبا تُوفِي نُذورًا إذا ٱنْبَرَتْ   تُراوِحُهُ أَذْيالُها وتُبارِكُهْ

[103]

وَكَأَنَّ إحْداهُنَّ من نَفْحِ الصَّبا   خَوْدٌ تُلاعِبُ مَوْهِنًا أَتْرابَهَا

والنَّهْرُ قد هَزَّتْهُ أَرْواحُ الصَّبا   طَرَبًا وَجَرَّتْ فَوْقَهُ أَهْدابَهَا

[104]

وَيا نَسيمَ الصَّبا بَلِّغْ تَحِيَّتَنا   مَنْ لو على البُعْدِ حَيٌّ كان يُحْيِينَا

[105]

وَقُلْتُ وقد شاقَني مُلْتَقَى   شَميمِ العَرارِ وَبَرْدِ الصَّبَا

خَليلَيَّ مِنْ حِمْيَرٍ حَدِّثا   أخا شَيْبَةٍ عن لَيالِي الصِّبَى

[106]

فَإذا ما هَبَّتِ الرِّيحُ صَبًا   صِحْتُ وَاشَوقِي إلى الأَنْدَلُسِ

[107]

وقد جاذَبَتْ ريحُ الصَّبا غُصْنَ النَّقَى   فَمادَ على رِدْفِ الكَثيبِ وَمالاَ

[108]

فَها أنا أَلْقَى كُلَّ لَيْلٍ بِلَيْلَةٍ   مِنَ الهَمِّ تَستَجْرِي مِنَ الدَّمْعِ أَنْجُما

وَأَرْكَبُ أَرْدافَ الرُّبَى مُتَسَنِّمَا   وَأَنْشَقُ أَنْفاسَ الصَّبا مُتَنَسِّمَا

وَأَرْشُفُ نَشْرَ الطَّلِّ من كُلِّ وَرْدَةٍ   مَكانَ بَياضِ الثَّغْرِ مِنْ حُوَّةِ اللَّمَى

[109]

وَلُجَّةٍ تَفْرَقُ أَوْ تَعْشَقُ   فما تَنِي أَحْشاؤُها تَخْفِقُ

شارَفْتُها وَهْيَ بما هاجَها   مِنَ الصَّبا مُزْبِدَةٌ تَقْلَقُ

فَخِلْتُها في شَطِّها فارِساً   قُرِّبَ مِنْهُ فَرَسٌ أَبْلَقُ

[110]

وَعَنْ أَثَلاتِ الجِزْعِ هل حالَ ظِلُّها   وَهَلْ تَخِذَتْ ريحُ الصَّبا فيه مَدْرَجَا

[111]

عَصَفَتْ كالصَّبا اللَّعُوبِ وَمَرَّتْ   سِنَةً حُلْوَةً وَلَذَّةَ خَلْسِ

[112]

تَعَلَّقْتُ لَيْلَى وَهْيَ ذاتُ ذُؤابَةٍ   وَلَمْ يَبْدُ لِلأَتْرابِ من ثَدْيِها حَجْمُ

صَغيرَيْنِ نَرْعَى البَهْمَ يا لَيْتَ أَنَّنا   إلى اليَوْمِ لم نَكْبَرْ ولم تَكْبَرِ البَهْمُ

[113]

أَلا لَيْتَنا كُنَّا غَزالَيْنِ نَرْتَعِي   رِياضًا مِنَ الحَوْزانِ في بَلَدٍ قَفْرِ

أَلا لَيْتَنا كُنَّا حَمامَيْ مَفازَةٍ   نَطيرُ وَنَأْوِي بِالعَشِيِّ إلى وَكْرِ

أَلا لَيْتَنا حُوتانِ في البَحْرِ نَرْتَمِي   إذا نَحْنُ أَمْسَيْنا نُلَجِّجُ في البَحْرِ

أَلا لَيْتَنا نَحيا جَميعاً ولَيْتَنا   نَصيرُ إذا مِتْنا ضَجيعَيْنِ في قَبْرِ

[114]

يا لَيْتَنا فَرْدا وَحْشٍ نَبيتُ مَعًا   نَرْعَى المِتانَ وَنَخْفَى في فَيافِيهَا

وَلَيْتَ كُدْرَ القَطا حَلَّقْنَ بي وَبِها   دونَ السَّماءِ فَعِشْنا في خَوافِيهَا

وَلَيْتَ أَنّي وَإِيّاها على جَبَلٍ   في رَأْسِ شاهِقَةٍ صَعْبٍ مَراقِيهَا

أَكْثَرْتُ مِنْ لَيْتَنِي لو كان يَنْفَعُني   وَمِنْ مُنَى النَّفْسِ لو تُعْطَى أَمانِيهَا

[115]

فَما وَجْدُ أَعْرابِيَّةٍ قَذَفَتْ بها   صُروفُ النَّوى من حَيْثُ لَمْ تَكُ ظَنَّتِ

إذا ذَكَرَتْ نَجْدًا وَطيبَ تُرابِهِ   وَخَيْمَةَ نَجْدٍ أَعْوَلَتْ وَأَرَنَّتِ

بِأَكْثَرَ مِنّي حُرْقَةً وَصَبابَةً   إلى هَضَباتٍ بِاللِّوَى قَدْ أَظَلَّتِ

تَمَنَّتْ أَحاليبَ الرِّعاءِ وَخَيْمَةً   بِنَجْدٍ فَلَمْ يُقْدَرْ لها ما تَمَنَّتِ

[116]

كِليني لِهَمٍّ يا أُمَيْمَةَ ناصِبِ   وَلَيْلٍ أُقاسيهِ بَطِيءِ الكَواكِبِ

تَطاوَلَ حتّى قُلْتُ ليس بِمُنْقَضٍ   وليس الّذي يَرْعَى النُّجومَ بِآئِبِ

[117]

أَهاجَ قَذاءَ عَيْنِي الإذِّكارُ   هُدُوًّا فَالدُّموعُ لها انْحِدارُ

وَصارَ اللَّيْلُ مُشْتَمِلاً عَلَيْنا   كَأَنَّ اللَّيْلَ ليس له نَهارُ

وَبِتُّ أُراقِبُ الجَوْزاءَ حتّى   تَقارَبَ مِن أَوائِلِها انْحِدارُ

أُصَرِّفُ مُقْلَتِي في إثْرِ قَوْمٍ   تَبايَنَتِ البِلادُ بِهِمْ فَغارُوا

وَأَبْكي وَالنُّجومُ مُطَلِّعاتٌ   كَأَنْ لَمْ تَحْوِها عَنّي البِحارُ

[118]

إنّي أَرِقْتُ فَبِتُّ اللَّيْلَ ساهِرَةً   كَأَنَّما كُحِلَتْ عَيْني بِعُوّارِ

أَرْعَى النُّجومَ وَما كُلِّفْتُ رِعْيَتَها   وَتارَةً أَتَغَشَّى فَضْلَ أَطْماري

[119]

لَقَدْ نَعَى آبْنَ نَهِيكٍ لِي أَخو ثِقَةٍ   كانَتْ تُرَجِّمُ عنه قَبْلُ أَخْبارُ

فَبِتُّ ساهِرَةً لِلنَّجْمِ أَرْقُبُهُ   حتّى أَتَى دُونَ غَوْرِ النَّجْمِ أَسْتارُ

[120]

وَكَأَنَّ النُّجومَ لَمّا آسْتَقَلَّتْ   فَوْقَ رأْسِي نُوقٌ حَداهُنَّ حادِي

[121]

تَطاوَلَ بِالخَمّانِ لَيْلِي فَلَمْ تَكُنْ   تَهُمُّ هَوادِي نَجْمِهِ أَنْ تَصَوَّبا

أَبِيتُ أُراعِيها كَأَنّي مُوَكَّلٌ   بها لا أُرِيدُ النَّوْمَ حتّى تَغَيَّبا

إذا غارَ منها كَوْكَبٌ بَعْدَ كَوكَبٍ   تُراقِبُ عَيْنِي آخِرَ اللَّيْلِ كَوْكَبا

غَوائِرُ تَتْرَى من نُجومٍ تَخالُها   مع الصُّبْحِ تَتْلُوها زَواحِفَ لُغَّبا

أَخافُ مُفاجاةَ الفِراقِ بِبَغْتَةٍ   وَصَرْفَ النَّوَى من أَنْ تُشِتَّ وَتَشْعَبا

[122]

أَطِبٌّ من سُعادَ عَناكَ منه   مُراعاةُ النُّجومِ أَمَ آنْتَ هِيمُ

[123]

لَهَوْتُ بها وَاللَّيْلُ أَرْخَى سُدولَهُ   إلى أَنْ بَدا ضَوْءُ الصَّباحِ المُبَلَّجُ

أُراعِي نُجومَ اللَّيْلِ وَهْيَ كأَنَّها   قَوارِيرُ فيها زِئْبَقٌ يَتَرَجْرَجُ

[124]

فَبِتُّ مُسَهَّدًا أَرِقًا كَأَنّي   تَمَشَّتْ في مَفاصِلِيَ العُقارُ

أُراقِبُ في السَّماءِ بَناتِ نَعْشٍ   وَقَدْ دارَتْ كما عَطَفَ الصِّوارُ

وَعانَدَتِ الثُّرَيّا بَعْدَ هَدْءٍ   مُعانَدَةً لها العَيُّوقُ جارُ

[125]

أَلَمَّ طَيْفٌ فَهاجَ لي طَرَبِي   لَيْلَةَ بِتْنا بِجانِبِ الكُثُبِ

أَلَمَّ بي وَالرِّكابُ ساكِنَةٌ   لَيْلاً وَهَمّي بِذُكْرِتِي وَصَبِي

فَبِتُّ أَرْعَى النُّجومَ مُرْتَفِقًا   من حُبِّها وَالمُحِبُّ في تَعَبِ

[126]

أَبِيتُ أَرْعَى اللَّيْلَ مُرْتَقِبًا مَجْرَى السِّماكِ وَمَسْقَطَ النَّسْرِ

[127]

نامَ الخَلِيُّ وَبِتُّ غيرَ مُوَسَّدِ أَرْعَى النُّجومَ بها كَفِعلِ الأَرْمَدِ

[128]

وَرَدْتُ وَأَرْدافُ النُّجومِ كَأَنَّها وَراءَ السِّماكَيْنِ المَها وَاليَعافِرُ

[129]

وَلَمَّا سَمِعْتُ الدِّيكَ صاحَ بِسُحْرَةٍ وَتَوَسَّطَ النَّسْرانِ بَطْنَ العَقْرَبِ

وَتَتابَعَتْ عُصَبُ النُّجومِ كأَنَّها عُفْرُ الظِّباءِ على فُروعِ المُرْتَقَبِ

وَبَدا سُهَيْلٌ في السَّماءِ كأَنَّهُ ثَوْرٌ وَعارَضَهُ هِجانُ الرَّبْرَبِ

وَتَبَّهْتُ نَدْمانِي فَقُلْتُ له ٱصْطَبِحْ يا ٱبْنَ الكِرامِ مِنَ الشَّرابِ الأَصْهَبِ

[130]

سَهِرْتُ بها أَرْعَى النُّجومَ وَأَنْجُمًا طَوالِعَ لِلرّاعِينَ غيرَ أَوافِلِ

وَقَدْ فَغَرَتْ فاها بها كُلُّ زَهْرَةٍ إلى كُلِّ ضَرْعٍ لِلغَمامَةِ حافِلِ

وَمَرَّتْ جُيوشُ المُزْنِ رَهْوًا كَأَنَّها عَساكِرُ زَنْجٍ مُذْهَباتُ المَناصِلِ

وَحَلَّقَتِ الخَضْراءُ في غُرِّ شُهْبِها كَلُجَّةِ بَحْرٍ كُلِّلَتْ بِاليَعالِلِ

تَخالُ بها زُهْرَ الكَواكِبِ نَرْجِسًا على شَطِّ وادٍ لِلمَجَرَّةِ سائِلِ

وَتَلْمَحُ من جَوْزائِها في غُروبِها تَساقُطَ عَرْشٍ واهِنِ الدَّعْمِ مائِلِ

وَتَحْسَبُ صَقْرًا واقِعًا دَبَرانَها بِعُشِّ الثُّرَيّا فَوْقَ حُمْرِ الحَواصِلِ

وَبَدْرَ الدُّجَى فيها غَدِيرًا وَحَوْلَهُ نُجومٌ كَطَلْعاتِ الحَمامِ النَّواهِلِ

كأَنَّ الدُّجَى هَمِّي وَدَمْعِي نُجومُهُ تَحَدَّرَ إشْفاقًا لِدَهْرِ الأَراذِلِ

هَوَتْ أَنْجُمُ العَلْياءِ إلاّ أَقَلَّها وَغِبْنَ بما يَحْظَى به كُلُّ عاقِلِ

[131]

فَبَكَيْتُ من زَمَنٍ قَطَعْتُ مَراحِلاً   وَشَبيبَةٍ أَخْلَقْتُ من رَيْعانِهَا
وَرَعَيْتُ من وَجْهِ السَّماءِ خَميلَةً   خَضْراءَ لاحَ البَدْرُ من غُدْرانِهَا
وَكَأَنَّ نَثْرَ النَّجْمِ ضَأْنٌ وَسْطَهَا   وَكَأَنَّما الجَوْزاءُ راعِي ضانِهَا
وَكَأَنَّما فيه الثُّرَيّا جَوْهَرٌ   نَثَرَتْ فَرائِدَهُ يَدا دَبَرانِهَا
وَكَأَنَّما الشِّعْرَى عَقيلَةُ مَعْشَرٍ   نَزَلَتْ بِأَعْلَى النَّسْرِ من وِلْدانِهَا

[132]

١. أَرامَةُ كُنْتِ مَأْلَفَ كُلِّ رِيمِ   لَوِ ٱسْتَمْتَعْتِ بِالأُنْسِ القَديمِ
٦. وَلَيْلٍ بِتُّ أَكْلَؤُهُ كَأَنّي   سَليمٌ أَو سَهِرْتُ على سَليمِ
٧. أُراعِي من كَواكِبِهِ هِجانًا   سَوامًا ما تَريعُ إلى المُسيمِ
٨. فَأُقْسِمُ لَوْ سَأَلْتِ دُجاهُ عَنّي   لَقَدْ أَنْباكِ عن وَجْدٍ عَظيمِ

[133]

وَلَيْلٍ كَلَيْلِ الشّاكِلاتِ لَبِسْتُهُ   مَشارِقُهُ لا تَهْتَدِي لِلمَغارِبِ
كَأَنَّ ٱخْضِرارَ الجَوِّ صَرْحُ زَبَرْجَدٍ   تَناثَرَ فيه الدُّرُّ من جِيدِ كاعِبِ
كَأَنَّ خَفِيّاتِ الكَواكِبِ في الدُّجَى   بَياضُ وَلاءٍ لاحَ في قَلْبِ ناصِبِي
كَأَنَّ نُجومَ اللَّيْلِ سِرْبٌ رَواتِعٌ   لها البَدْرُ راعٍ في رِياضِ السَّحائِبِ

[134]

وَحتّى متى أَرْعَى الكَواكِبَ ساهِرًا   فَمِنْ طالِعٍ أُخْرَى اللَّيالِي وَغارِبِ

[135]

أَرْعَى النُّجومَ كَأَنَّنِي كُلِّفْتُ أَنْ   أَرْعَى جَميعَ ثُبوتِها وَالخُنَّسِ
فَكَأَنَّها وَاللَّيْلُ نِيرانُ الجَوَى   قد أُضْرِمَتْ في فِكْرَتِي من حِنْدِسِ
وَكَأَنَّنِي أَمْسَيْتُ حارِسَ رَوْضَةٍ   خَضْراءَ وُشِّحَ نَبْتُها بِالنَّرْجِسِ
لو عاشَ بَطْلَيموسُ أَيْقَنَ أَنَّنِي   أَقْوَى الوَرَى في رَصْدِ جَرْيِ الكُنَّسِ

[136]

أُراعِي نُجومَ اللّيْلِ حُبًّا لِبَدْرِهِ   ولَسْتُ كما ظَنّ الخَلِيُّ مُنَجِّمَا

[137]

رُعاةَ اللّيْلِ ما فَعَلَ الصّباحُ   وما فَعَلَتْ أَوائِلُهُ المِلاحُ
وما بالُ الّذينَ سَبَوْا فُؤادِي   أَقامُوا أَمْ أَجَدّ بِهِمْ رَواحُ
وما بالُ النُّجومِ مُعَلّقاتٍ   بِقَلْبِ الصّبّ ليس لها بَراحُ
كأَنّ القَلْبَ لَيْلَةَ قِيلَ يُغْدَى   بِلَيْلَى العامِرِيّةِ أَوْ يُراحُ
قَطاةٌ عَزّها شَرَكٌ فَباتَتْ   تُجاذِبُهُ وقد عَلِقَ الجَناحُ
لها فَرْخانِ قد تُرِكا بِقَفْرٍ   وَعُشُّهُما تُصَفِّقُهُ الرِّياحُ
فلا بِاللّيْلِ نالَتْ ما تُرَجّي   ولا في الصُّبْحِ كانَ لها بَراحُ
رُعاةَ اللّيْلِ كونُوا كَيْفَ شِئْتُمْ   فقد أَوْدَى بِيَ الحُبُّ المُتاحُ

[138]

فَبَنَى لنا بَيْتاً رَفيعاً سَمْكُهُ   فَسَما إليه كَهْلُها وَغُلامُهَا

[139]

وفِتْيَةٍ في مَجْلِسٍ وُجوهُهُمْ   رَيْحانُهُمْ قد عَدِمُوا الثّقيلاَ
دانِيَةً عَلَيْهِمُ ظِلالُها   وَذُلِّلَتْ قُطوفُها تَذْليلاَ

[140]

المَوْتُ بابٌ وكُلُّ النّاسِ داخِلُهُ   فَلَيْتَ شِعْرِي بَعْدَ البابِ ما الدّارُ
الدّارُ جَنّةُ عَدْنٍ إنْ عَمِلْتَ بما   يُرْضِي ٱلإلٰهَ وإنْ فَرّطْتَ فَالنّارُ
هُما مَحَلّانِ ما لِلنّاسِ غيرُهُما   فَٱنْظُرْ لِنَفْسِكَ ماذا أَنْتَ مُخْتارُ

[141]

أُزْجُرِ القَلْبَ إذا القَلْبُ جَمَحْ   وَٱرْدَعِ الطّرْفَ إذا الطّرْفُ طَمَحْ
وَٱصْرِفِ النّفْسَ إلى عَدَنِيّةٍ   ذاتِ غُنْجٍ وَدَلالٍ وَمَرَحْ

زانَها اللّٰهُ بِخَدٍّ مُشْرِقٍ   لَوْ مَشَى الذَّرُّ عليه لَجُرِحْ
لَوْ بَدَتْ غُرَّتُها من خِدْرِها   قُلْتَ بَرْقٌ في ذُرا المُزْنِ لَمَحْ
أَوْ رَآها البَدْرُ في مَطْلَعِهِ   لَاكْتَسَى ذُلًّا وَهُونًا وٱفْتَضَحْ
فازَ مَنْ عاطَتْ يَداها يَدَهُ   عاتِقَ الرّاحِ بكَأْسٍ وقَدَحْ
بِبَنانٍ كَالمَدارِي بَضَّةٍ   طُرِّقَتْ بِالنُّورِ في مَجْرَى السُّبَحْ
كُلَّما سُرَّ بِها قالَتْ لَهُ   زادَكَ اللّٰهُ سُرورًا وَفَرَحْ
يا حَبيبِي وَمَدَى أُمْنِيَّتِي   بِكَ زادَ العَيْشُ طِيبًا وَصَلَحْ
وَهُما في رَوْضَةٍ عَدْنِيَّةٍ   يَفْسَحُ الطَّرْفُ مَداها ما ٱنْفَسَحْ
تَتَغَنَّى الطَّيْرُ في حافاتِها   بِلُحونٍ تَدَعُ القَلْبَ فَرِحْ
وَنَسيمُ الرِّيحِ يَهْدِي لَهُما   نَفَحاتِ الوَرْدِ من تلك الفُسَحْ
عُوِّضَتْ عَيْناهُما قُرَّتَها   ثَمَرَ الدَّمْعِ الّذي كان سُفِحْ
هاكَها دُرِّيَّةً مَنْظُومَةً   شاكَلَ الخاتِمُ مِنْها المُفْتَتَحْ

[142]
لَكِ يا مَنازِلُ في القُلوبِ مَنازِلُ   أَقْفَرْتِ أَنْتِ وهُنَّ مِنْكِ أَواهِلُ

[143]
أَسْتَوْدِعُ اللّهَ في أَرْضِ الحِجازِ رَشًا   في رَوْضَةِ القَلْبِ مَأْواهُ وَمَرْتَعُهُ
بِاللّٰهِ يا شَوْقُ رِفْقًا بِالفُؤادِ فما   أُطيقُ أَكْثَرَ مِمّا أَنْتَ تَصْنَعُهُ
وَأَنْتَ يا وَصْلُ عُجْ في رَبْعِ فُرْقَتِنا   عَساكَ تَجْمَعُ شَمْلًا عَزَّ مَجْمَعُهُ
وَسَقِّهِ من حَيا التَقْرِيبِ سارِيَةً   فَإِنَّهُ داثِرٌ قد مُحَّ مَوْضِعُهُ
عَسَى اللَّيالِي بِأَوْطانِي الّتي سَلَفَتْ   تَرْجِعْنَ فيه رُجوعًا لا نُوَدِّعُهُ

[144]
بِجَنَّةِ الأَرْضِ هِمْتُ يا صاحِ   فَلَيس عنها الفُؤادُ بِالصّاحِ

تلك مَحَلُّ النُّهورِ مُرْسِيَةٌ   مَوْطِنُ أُنْسِي وَدارُ أَفْراحِي
مَرْسيَ كم ناعِمٍ وَكَمْ جَذِلٍ   بين الرّياحِينِ فيكِ وَالرّاحِ
هابِطَةُ النَّهْرِ منكِ أذْكُرُها   من شَطِّ آعْلاهُ جِسْرُ وَضّاحِ
فَكُلُّ حُسْنٍ ما بين قَنْطَرَتَيْ   طَبيرَةٍ منهُما وَسَبّاحِ
سَبْعونَ مِيلاً كُنّا نَجولُ بها   بين جُسورٍ وَبين أَدْواحِ

[145]

دُنْيا مَعاشٌ لِلوَرَى حتّى إذا   جُلِيَ الرّبيعُ فَإنّما هي مَنْظَرُ

[146]

يا رِيمُ قُومِي الآنَ وَيْحَكِ فآنْظُرِي   ما لِلرُّبَى قد أَظْهَرَتْ إعْجابَهَا
كانتْ مَحاسِنُ وَجْهِها مَحْجوبَةً   فَالآنَ قد كَشَفَ الرّبيعُ حِجابَهَا
وَرْدٌ بَدا يَحكِي الخُدودَ وَنَرْجِسٌ   يَحكِي العُيونَ إذْ رأَتْ أَحْبابَهَا
وَشَقائِقٌ مِثْلُ المَطارِفِ قد بَدَتْ   حُمْرًا وقد جُعِلَ السّوادُ كِتابَهَا
وَنَباتُ باقِلاّءَ يُشْبِهُ نَوْرُهُ   بُلْقَ الحَمامِ مُشيلَةً أَذْنابَهَا
وَالزَرْعُ شِبْهُ عَساكِرٍ مُصْطَفّةٍ   قد فَوّقَتْ عن قَسِيِّها نُشّابَهَا
وَكَأَنّ خُرّمَةَ البَديعَ وقد بَدا   رُوسُ الطّواوِسِ إذْ تُديرُ رِقابَهَا
وَالسّرْوُ تَحْسَبُهُ العُيونُ غَوانِيًا   قد شَمّرَتْ عن سُوقِها أَثْوابَهَا
وَكَأَنّ إحْداهُنّ من نَفْحِ الصّبا   خَوْدٌ تُلاعِبُ مَوْهِنًا أَتْرابَهَا
وَالنّهْرُ قد هَزّتْهُ أَرْواحُ الصّبا   طَرَبًا وَجَرّتْ فَوْقَهُ أَهْدابَهَا
لو كُنْتُ أَمْلِكُ لِلرّياضِ صِيانَةً   يَوْمًا لما وَطِئَ اللِّئامُ تُرابَهَا

[147]

اِقْرَأْ على الوَشَلِ السّلامَ وَقُلْ له   كُلُّ المَشارِبِ مُذْ هُجِرْتَ ذَميمُ
سَقْيًا لِظِلِّكَ بِالعَشِيِّ وَبِالضُّحَى   وَلِبَرْدِ مائِكَ وَالمِيَاهُ حَميمُ

لو كُنْتُ أَمْلِكُ مَنْعَ مائِكَ لم يَذُقْ   ما في قِلاتِكَ ما حَيِيتُ لَئِيمُ

[148]

وَآمِنَةٍ لا الوَحْشُ تَذْعَرُ سِرْبَها   ولا الطَّيْرُ منها دامِياتُ المَخالِبِ

هي الرَّوْضُ لم تَنْشَ الخَمائِلُ زَهْرَةً   ولا آخْضَلَّ عن دَمْعٍ مِنَ المُزْنِ ساكِبِ

إذا آنْبَعَثَتْ بين الخَمائِلِ خِلْتَها   زَرابِيَّ كِسْرَى بَثَّها في المَلاعِبِ

[149]

نَرْجِسَةٌ لم تَزَلْ مُحَدِّقَةً   لم تَكْتَحِلْ قَطُّ لَذَّةَ الغُمْضِ

أَمالَها القَطْرُ فَهْيَ باهِتَةٌ   تَنْظُرُ فِعْلَ السَّماءِ بِالأَرْضِ

[150]

كَفَى حَزَنًا أَنَّ الدِّيارَ قَصِيَّةٌ   فلا زَوْرَ إلاّ أَنْ يَكونَ خَيالاَ

ولا رُسْلَ إلاّ لِلرِّياحِ عَشِيَّةً   تَكُرُّ جَنوبًا بيننا وَشَمالاَ

فأَسْتَوْدِعُ الرِّيحَ الشَّمالَ تَحِيَّةً   وأَسْتَنْشِقُ الرِّيحَ الجَنوبَ سُؤالاَ

فما أَنْسَهُ لا أَنْسَ لَيْلاً على الحِمَى   وقد راقَ أَوْضاحًا وَرَقَّ جَمالاَ

وَزارَ به نَجْمَ السُّهَى قَمَرُ الدُّجَى   فَباتا بِحالِ الفَرْقَدَيْنِ وِصالاَ

فَجادَ الحِمَى غادٍ مِنَ المُزْنِ رائِحٌ   تَهاداهُ أَعْناقُ الرِّياحِ كَلالاَ

وَسارِيَةٌ دَهْماءُ حارَ بها الدُّجَى   فَشَبَّ لها البَرْقُ المُنيرُ ذُبالاَ

فَلِلّٰهِ ما أَشْجَى الحَمامَةَ غُدْوَةً   هُناك وما أَنْدَى الأَراكَ ظِلالاَ

وقد جاذَبَتْ رِيحُ الصَّبا غُصْنَ النَّقَى   فَمادَ على رِدْفِ الكَثِيبِ وَمالاَ

وَأَيْقَظَ بَرْدُ الصُّبْحِ جَفْنَ عَرارَةٍ   تَرَقْرَقَ دَمْعُ الطَّلِّ فيه فَسالاَ

[151]

إنَّ لِلجَنَّةِ بِالأَنْدَلُسِ   مُجْتَلَى حُسْنٍ وَرَيَّا نَفَسِ

فَسَنَا صُبْحَتِها من شَنَبٍ   ودُجَى لَيْلَتِها من لَعَسِ

فَإذا ما هَبَّتِ الرِّيحُ صَبًا   صِحْتُ واشَوْقِي إلى الأَنْدَلُسِ

[152]

١. عَفا المُصَلّى وأَقْوَتِ الكُثُبُ   . . . .

٣. مَنازِلٌ قد عَمَرْتُها يَفَعًا   حتّى بَدا في عِذارِيَ الشَّهَبُ

٤. في فِتْيَةٍ كَالسُّيوفِ هَزَّهُمُ   شَرْخُ شَبابٍ وَزانَهُمْ أَدَبُ

٥. ثُمَّ أَرابَ الزَّمانُ فَٱقْتَسَمُوا   أَيْدِي سَبا في البِلادِ فَٱنْشَعَبُوا

[153]

وتَلَفَّتْ فيما بَنَى آلُ ساسانَ   عَفاهُ الزَّمانُ ثَلْمًا وَنَقْضَا

عَرَصاتٌ أَصْبَحْنَ وَهْيَ سَماءٌ   ثُمَّ أَمْسَيْنَ بِالحَوادِثِ أَرْضَا

وتَرَى يُنْبِتُ النَّعيمَ إذا أَنْ   بَتَ تُرْبُ البِلادِ عُشْبًا وَحَمْضَا

[154]

فَهْيَ تَغْشاهُ بِالتَّنَكُّرِ وَحْشًا   خَلَقًا ثُمَّ بِالتَّذَكُّرِ غَضَّا

[155]

وقَفْتُ بِالدّارِ ما أُبَيِّنُها   إلاّ ٱدِّكارًا تَوَهُّمَ الحُلُمِ

بادَتْ وأَقْوَتْ مِنَ الأَنيسِ كما   أَقْوَتْ مَحاريبُ دارِسِ الأُمَمِ

[156]

يا دارُ دارَ عليكِ إرْهامُ النَّدَى   وٱهْتَزَّ رَوْضُكِ في الثَّرَى فَتَرَأَّدا

طَلَلٌ عَكَفْتُ عليه أَسْأَلُهُ إلى   أَنْ كادَ يُصْبِحُ رَبْعُهُ لِيَ مَسْجِدا

وَظَلِلْتُ أُنْشِدُهُ وأَنْشُدُ أَهْلَهُ   والحُزْنُ خِدْنِي ناشِدًا أَوْ مُنْشِدا

[157]

لا أَنْتِ أَنْتِ ولا الدِّيارُ دِيارُ   خَفَّ الهَوَى وتَوَلَّتِ الأَوْطارُ

[158]

والرَّوْضُ عن مائِهِ الفِضِّيِّ مُبْتَسِمٌ   كما شَقَقْتَ عَنِ اللَّبّاتِ أَطْواقَا

[159]

أَلا هل إلى الزَّهْراءِ أَوْبَةُ نازِحٍ   تَقَضَّى تَنائِيها مَدامِعَهُ نَزْحَا

مَحَلُّ ٱرتِيَاحٍ يُذَكِّرُ الخُلْدَ طِيبُهُ   إذا عَزَّ أَنْ يَصْدَى الفَتَى فيه أَوْيَضْحَى
هُنَاك الجِمامُ الزُّرْقُ تُنْدِي حِفافَها   ظِلالٌ عَهِدْتُ الدَّهْرَ فيها فَتًى سَمْحَا
تَعَوَّضْتُ من شَدْوِ القِيانِ خِلالَها   صَدَى فَلَواتٍ قد أَطارَ الكَرَى ضَبْحَا
ومن حَمْلِيَ الكَأْسَ المُفَدَّى مُدِيرُها   تَقَحُّمَ أَهْوالٍ حَمَلْتُ لها الرُّمْحَا

[160]
يا رَوْضَةً طالَما أَجْنَتْ لَواحِظَنا   وَرْدًا جَلاهُ الصِّبا غَضًّا وَنِسْرِينَا

[161]
يا جَنَّةَ الخُلْدِ أُبْدِلْنا بِسِدْرَتِها   وَالكَوْثَرِ العَذْبِ زَقُّومًا وَغِسلِينَا

[162]
كأَنَّنا لم نَبِتْ وَالوَصْلُ ثالِثُنا   وَالسَّعْدُ قد غَضَّ من أَجْفانِ واشِينَا

[163]
إنَّا قَرَأْنا الأَسَى يَوْمَ النَّوَى سُوَرًا   مَكْتوبَةً وأَخَذْنا الصَّبْرَ تَلْقِينَا

[164]
أُقَضِّي نَهارِي بِالأَمانِي الكَواذِبِ
وآوِي إلى لَيْلٍ بَطِيءِ الكَواكِبِ   وأَبْطَأُ سارٍ كَوْكَبٌ باتَ يُكْلأُ

[165]
وَناهِيكَ من مَبْدًا جَمالٍ وَمَحْضَرِ
وَجَنَّةِ عَدْنٍ تَطَّبِيكَ وَكَوْثَرِ   بِمَرْأًى يَزِيدُ العُمْرَ طِيبًا وَيَنْسَأُ

[166]
سَقَى الغَيْثُ أَطْلالَ الأَحِبَّةِ بِالحِمَى
وَحاكَ عليها ثَوْبَ وَشْيٍ مُنَمْنَمَا
وأَطْلَعَ فيها لِلأَزاهِيرِ أَنْجُمَا
فَكَمْ رَفَلَتْ فيها الخَرائِدُ كَالدُّمَى   إذِ العَيْشُ غَضٌّ وَالزَّمانُ غُلامُ

[167]

فَقُلْ لِزَمانٍ قد تَوَلّى نَعيمُهُ
وَرَثّتْ على مَرّ اللّيالي رُسومُهُ
وَكم رَقّ فيه بِالعَشِيّ نَسيمُهُ
ولاحَتْ لِساري اللّيْلِ فيه نُجومُهُ   عليكَ من الصّبّ المَشوقِ سَلامُ

[168]

أهيمُ بِجَبّارٍ يَعِزُّ وأَخْضَعُ
شَذا المِسْكِ من أرْدانِهِ يَتَضَوّعُ
إذا جِئْتُ أَشْكُوهُ الجَوَى ليس يَسْمَعُ
فَما أنا في شَيْءٍ مِنَ الوَصْلِ أَطْمَعُ   ولا أَنْ يَزُورَ المُقْلَتَيْنِ مَنامُ

[169]

أَبْلِغْ هَدِيّتِي الفَرَزْدَقَ إنّها   ثِقَلٌ يُزادُ على حَسيرٍ مُثْقَلِ

[170]

كأَنّ بَناتِ نَعْشٍ في دُجاها   خَرائِدُ سافِراتٌ في حِدادِ

[171]

إنّنِي آمْرُؤٌ من بَنِي ذُبْيانَ قد عَلِمُوا   أَحْمِي شَرِيعَةَ مَجْدٍ غيرِ مَوْرودِ

[172]

وَكأَنّ كُلّ سَحابَةٍ وَقَفَتْ بها   تَبْكِي بِعَيْنَيْ عُرْوَةَ بنِ حِزامِ

[173]

طَرِبْتُ وما شَوْقًا إلى البِيضِ أَطْرَبُ   ولا لَعِبًا مِنّي وَذُو الشّوْقِ يَلْعَبُ
ولم تُلْهِنِي دارٌ ولا رَسْمُ مَنْزِلٍ   ولم يَتَطَرّبْنِي بَنانٌ مُخَضّبُ

[174]

وأَخْرُجُ من بَيْنِ البُيوتِ لَعَلّنِي   أُحَدّثُ عنكِ النّفْسَ بِاللّيْلِ خالِيَا

[175]

فَقُلْتُ له إنّ الشّجا يَبْعَثُ الشّجا   فَدَعْنِي فهذا كُلُّهُ قَبْرُ مالِكِ

[176]

وَحَنّتْ قَلوصِي فَٱسْتَمَعْتُ لِسَجْرِها   بِرَمْلَةِ لُدٍّ وَهْيَ مَثْنِيّةٌ تَحْبُو

[177]

قِفا غيرَ مَأْمورَيْنِ ولْتَصْدَيَا بها   على ثِقَةٍ لِلغَيْثِ فَٱسْتَقِيَا القَطْرا

بِجِسْرِ مَعانٍ وَٱلرُّصافَةِ إنّهُ   على القَطْرِ أنْ يَسْقِي الرُّصافَةَ وَٱلجِسْرا

[178]

خَليلَيّ إنْ حانَتْ بِمِصْرَ مَنِيّتِي   وَأَزْمَعْتُما أَنْ تَحْفِرا لي بها قَبْرا

فلا تَنْسَيَا أَنْ تَقْرَآ لي على الغَضَى   وَنَجْدٍ سَلامًا لا قَليلاً ولا نَزْرا

[179]

وما وَجْدُ أَظْآرٍ ثَلٰثٍ رَوائِمٍ   أَصَبْنَ مَجَرًّا من حُوارٍ وَمَصْرَعَا

يُذَكّرْنَ ذا البَثّ الحَزِينَ بِبَثّهِ   إذا حَنّتِ الأُولَى سَجَعْنَ لها مَعَا

إذا شارِفٌ مِنْهُنّ قامَتْ فَرَجّعَتْ   حَنينًا فَأَبْكَى شَجْوُها البَرْكَ أَجْمَعَا

بِأَوْجَدَ مِنّي يَوْمَ قامَ بِمالِكٍ   مُنادٍ بَصيرٌ بِالفِراقِ فَأَسْمَعَا

[180]

ليس من ماتَ فَٱسْتَراحَ بِمَيْتٍ   إنّما المَيْتُ مَيّتُ الأَحْياءِ

إنّما المَيْتُ من يَعيشُ كَئيبًا   كاسِفًا بالُهُ قَليلَ الرّجاءِ

[181]

مَغانِي الشّعْبِ طِيبًا في المَغانِي   بِمَنْزِلَةِ الرّبيعِ مِنَ الزّمانِ

طَبَتْ فُرْسانَنا وَٱلخَيْلَ حتّى   خَشِيتُ وَإنْ كَرُمْنَ مِنَ الحِرانِ

يَقولُ بِشِعْبِ بَوّانٍ حِصانِي   أَعَنْ هذا يُسارُ إلى الطّعانِ

أَبوكُمْ آدَمٌ سَنّ المَعاصِي   وَعَلّمَكُمْ مُفارَقَةَ الجِنانِ

[182]

تَقولُ إذا دَرَأْتُ لها وَضِينِي   أهذا دِينُهُ أبَدًا وَدِينِي

أكُلُّ الدَّهْرِ حَلٌّ وَٱرْتِحالٌ   أما يُبْقِي عَلَيَّ وما يَقِينِي

[183]

إثْلِثْ فإنَّا أيُّها الطَّلَلُ   نَبْكِي وتُرْزِمُ تَحْتَنا الإبِلُ

NOTES

Chapter One

1. From the Arabic genre-critical vantage point, it is fascinating to see C. S. Lewis extract out of the European medieval "primary epic" and the heroic-courtly literary tradition a theory of thematic range which comes very close to that of the classical Arabic *qaṣīdah,* which is also a form developed within an aristocratic (*khāṣṣah*) social ethos, and which is either directly "courtly" or in a broader, tribal sense ceremonial and ritual (which in turn brings it close to what we understand as courtly). Thus, Lewis writes: "In lines 2105 and following [of *Beowulf*] we have a performance given by Hrothgar himself. We learn that he sometimes (*hwilum*) produces a *gidd* or lay which was *sop* and *sarlic* (true and tragic), sometimes a tale of wonders (*sellic* spell), and sometimes, with the fetters of age heavy upon him, he began to recall his youth, the strength that once was his in battle; his heart swelled within him as he remembered the vanished winters. Professor Tolkien has suggested to me that this is an account of the complete range of courtly poetry, in which the three kinds of poem can be distinguished—the lament for mutability . . . , the tale of strange adventures, and the "true and tragic" lay . . . , which alone is true epic" (*A Preface to Paradise Lost* [New York: Oxford University Press, 1969], pp. 15–16). It is of no passing interest that what Lewis and Tolkien identify as "the complete range of courtly poetry" is precisely the *complete range* of the Arabic *qaṣīdah.* Furthermore, the *qaṣīdah,* too, presents certain "genre-tensions" between the lyrical and the epic-dramatic. The three main sections of the *qaṣīdah* (the *nasīb,* the *raḥīl,* and the *fakhr* or *madīḥ*) are at the same time the main courtly poetic subjects. In the Arabic case, however, the *qaṣīdah* combines all three elements: it is complete, but it has the inevitable triadic tension.

2. Al-Jāḥiẓ, *Kitāb al-Ḥayawān* (Cairo: Dār al-Maʿārif, 1938), vol. 3, p. 131. Wolfhart Heinrichs remarks correctly that in ʿAbd al-Qāhir al-Jurjānī, who also quotes al-Jāḥiẓ, the term *taṣwīr* already means "forming" ("*Gestaltung*"). See his *Arabische Dichtung und griechische Poetik: Ḥāzim al-Qarṭāgannīs Grundlegung der Poetik mit Hilfe aristotelischer Begriffe* (Wiesbaden: F. Steiner, 1969), p. 71. But then, too, the grouping of these terms seems to have become commonplace by the time of ʿAbd al-Qāhir al-Jurjānī; see his *Dalāʾil al-Iʿjāz,* ed. Maḥmūd Muḥammad Shākir (Cairo: Maktabat al-Khānjī, 1404/1984), p. 34. Otherwise, already to the late Sophist Hermogenes (*On ideas*), ideas (precisely the Arabic *al-maʿānī*) are general qualities found in composition and are not characteristic of an individual author. See George A. Kennedy, *Greek Rhetoric under Christian Emperors* (Princeton: Princeton University Press, 1983), p. 97. Even more precisely, *al-maʿānī* should be identified with the *topoi* (topics) of classical rhetoric, where the "science of *topoi*" corresponds to the Arabic *ʿilm al-maʿānī.* "Originally, then," observes Ernst Robert Curtius, "topoi are helps

toward composing orations. They are, as Quintilian (V, 10, 20) says, 'storehouses of trains of thought' ('argumentorum sedes'), and thus can serve a practical purpose." See his *European Literature and the Latin Middle Ages,* trans. Willard R. Trask (New York: Harper and Row, 1963), p. 70.

3. Abū al-Faraj Qudāmah Ibn Jaʿfar, *Naqd al-Shiʿr,* 3d ed., ed. Kamāl Muṣṭafā (Cairo: Maktabat al-Khānjī, 1979), p. 19.

4. Abū Hilāl al-ʿAskarī, *Kitāb al-Ṣināʿatayn* (Istanbul: Maṭbaʿat Maḥmūd Bey, 1320/1902), p. 51.

5. Muḥammad Ibn Aḥmad Ibn Ṭabāṭabā al-ʿAlawī, *ʿIyār al-Shiʿr,* ed. Ṭāhā al-Ḥājirī and Muḥammad Zaghlūl Sallām (Cairo: Al-Maktabah al-Tijārīyah al-Kubrā, 1955), p. 5.

6. For my discussion of some pertinent aspects of Samuel Johnson's neoclassical theory vis-à-vis analogously neoclassical Arabic critical attitudes and actual textual formulations, see "Arabic Poetry and Assorted Poetics," in Malcolm H. Kerr, ed., *Islamic Studies: A Tradition and Its Problems* (Malibu, Calif.: Undena Publications, 1980), pp. 109–10.

7. Ibn Rashīq al-Qayrawānī, *Al-ʿUmdah fī Maḥāsin al-Shiʿr wa Ādābih wa Naqdih,* 3d ed. (Cairo: Al-Maktabah al-Tijārīyah al-Kubrā, 1963), vol. 1, p. 128. Consider, for instance, his "hearing words is like seeing images" in the context of Simonides of Ceos's calling "painting inarticulate poetry and poetry articulate painting," an expression much quoted and of enormous proverbial appeal over the centuries (Plutarch, *Moralia* 346, Loeb Classical Library, vol. 4, pp. 500–501).

8. Al-Jurjānī, *Dalāʾil al-Iʿjāz,* pp. 63–64. Nevertheless, his discussion of "meaning" (*al-maʿnā*) as not merely something that remains isolated in the specific instances of the lexicon (*alfāẓ*) but as determined by syntactic as well as stylistic context, which he calls *naẓm,* indicates that his understanding of the production of meaning transcended that of his contemporaries (ibid., pp. 80ff.). Muḥammad Mandūr, already during his pre–World War II studies in France, had turned his attention to the theoretical possibilities of *naẓm* in ʿAbd al-Qāhir al-Jurjānī (*Fī al-Mīzān al-Jadīd,* 3d ed. [Cairo/al-Fajjālah: Maktabat Nahḍat Miṣr wa Maṭbaʿatuhā, (1963)], pp. 188–89, 190–201). See also Iḥsān ʿAbbās, *Tārīkh al-Naqd al-Adabī ʿind al-ʿArab: Naqd al-Shiʿr min al-Qarn al-Thānī ḥattā al-Qarn al-Thāmin al-Hijrī* (*sic*), 2d ed. (Beirut: Dār al-Thaqāfah, 1398/1978), pp. 420, 421, 424. These and other current studies on, and references to, the theory of *naẓm* have been reworked by Kamal Abu-Deeb in his *Al-Jurjānī's Theory of Poetic Imagery* (Warminster, England: Aris and Phillips, 1979), pp. 24–38 esp.

9. See J. Christoph Bürgel's detailed monograph on the problem of truth in Arabic poetry: "Die beste Dichtung ist die lügenreichste: Wesen und Bedeutung eines literarischen Streites des arabischen Mittelalters im Lichte komparatistischer Betrachtung," *Oriens* 23 (1974): 7–102. The discussion of "sincerity in poetry" should be differentiated from the discussion of "truth in poetry," even though the difference may seem to be only one of point of view or aspect. The topic of truth tends to lead us into historically and metaphysically oriented

investigations, while that of "sincerity" will appear more literary, dealing with practical criticism and with psychology before metaphysics, implying in the end what is now termed poetic experience. Sincerity in Western literature is discussed by Henry Peyre, *Literature and Sincerity* (New Haven: Yale University Press, 1969).

10. Abū ʿUbādah al-Walīd Ibn ʿUbayd al-Buḥturī al-Ṭāʾī, *Dīwān*, ed. Ḥusayn Kāmil al-Ṣīrafī (Cairo: Dār al-Maʿārif, 1963), vol. 1, p. 209. Helmut Ritter understands the verse more literally, perhaps, when he translates the second hemistich "aber in der Dichtung schwatzt man statt Wahrheit eitle Lügen." More than anything, however, he is following the sense intended by ʿAbd al-Qāhir al-Jurjānī's interpretation, which accounts only for the topos as applied to a very straightfoward satire (ʿAbd al-Qāhir Ibn ʿAbd al-Raḥmān al-Jurjānī, *Die Geheimnisse der Wortkunst* [*Asrār al-Balāghah*] *des ʿAbdalqāhir al-Curcānī*, trans. Helmut Ritter [Wiesbaden: Franz Steiner Verlag 1959], p. 291). In another reading known to me, whose source, however, I no longer have at hand, the verb *yulghā* shifts, apparently intentionally, to become *yughnī* (to make dispensable), thus quite clearly reverting al-Buḥturī's verse back to the established topos.

11. William Shakespeare, *As You Like It*, act 3, scene 3.

12. Giovanni Battista Vico, *La scienza nuova*, ed. Fausto Nicolini (Bari: Gius. Laterza and Figli, 1928), vol. 1, p. 146 (367), and p. 150 (383): "che la di lei propia materia e l'impossibile credibile."

13. See, for example, a review of the definitions of Arabic poetry revolving around this concept by Bint al-Shāṭiʾ in her *Al-Ḥayāh al-Insānīyah ʿind al-ʿArab* (Cairo: Al-Maʿārif, 1944), pp. 32–33.

14. Horace, *Satires, Epistles and Ars poetica*, Loeb Classical Library, pp. 452–53. The whole argument presented in the first sixty-odd verses of *Ars poetica* is adequately discussed by William K. Wimsatt, Jr., and Cleanth Brooks in *Literary Criticism: A Short History* (New York: Knopf, 1965), pp. 81–82.

15. See al-Jāḥiẓ quoted in Ibn Rashīq, *Al-ʿUmdah*, vol. 1, p. 257.

16. See this chapter, section 1.

17. Abū ʿAlī Muḥammad Ibn al-Ḥasan al-Ḥātimī, *Ḥilyat al-Muḥāḍarah fī Ṣināʿat al-Shiʿr*, ed. Jaʿfar al-Kattānī (Baghdad: Dār al-Rashīd li al-Nashr [Silsilat Kutub al-Turāth], 1979), vol. 1, p. 215. For a discussion of al-Ḥātimī integrated into the broad spectrum of Arabic *qaṣīdah* criticism, see G. J. H. van Gelder, *Beyond the Line: Classical Arabic Literary Critics on the Coherence and Unity of the Poem* (Leiden: E. J. Brill, 1982), pp. 82–89.

18. Albin Lesky, *A History of Greek Literature*, trans. James Willis and Cornelis de Heer (New York: Crowell, 1966), p. 137.

19. This section was presented under the title of "Beyond Ibn Qutaybah: The Epistolary Structure of the Classical Arabic *Qaṣīdah*" at the meeting of the American Oriental Society in New Haven, Conn., Mar. 1986. Its full text appeared in Arabic translation as "Ibn Qutaybah wa mā baʿdah: al-Qaṣīdah al-ʿArabīyah al-Kilāsīkīyah," in *Fuṣūl* 6, no. 2 (1986): 71–78.

20. Ibn Qutaybah, *Al-Shiʿr wa al-Shuʿarāʾ,* ed. Aḥmad Muḥammad Shākir (Cairo: Dār al-Maʿārif bi Miṣr, 1966), vol. 1, pp. 74–75. The following is the still indispensable full quotation of the pertinent passage from Ibn Qutaybah:

> I heard a discriminating man of letters [*baʿḍa ahli al-adabi*] comment that the composer of odes began by mentioning the abandoned abodes, the decay, the ruins. Then he wept, complained, and apostrophized the vernal camping grounds and bade his companion to halt, so as to turn this into an occasion for recollection of those who have lived there and then departed; for in their abiding and departing those dwelling under tent posts differ from sedentary villagers because of their migration from water source to water source in search of fresh pasture, following rainfall wherever it be.
>
> To this he linked the *nasīb* [here to be understood more specifically as the evocation of the beloved]. Thus he wept over the vehemence of passion, the pain of separation, the excess of love's ardor and longing so as to dispose favorably, attract attention, and exact a hearing—because rhapsodizing a beloved touches souls and clings onto the hearts. . . .
>
> Then, assured of being heard and listened to, he followed up, impressing his entitlements. Thus in his poetry he undertook journeys, complained of exertion, of sleepless vigils, of traversing the darkness of night and the heat of noontime, and of emaciating mount and camel.
>
> At that point, knowing that he had thus duly obligated his patron to fulfill his claim and expectation and impressed upon him the adversities which he had borne on his journey, he commenced with the panegyric [*madīḥ*].

Other early Arabic definitions of the *qaṣīdah* structure are either too loosely formulated or else addressed to the largely post-Mutanabbian binary structure of the courtly *qaṣīdah,* which no longer gives a structural role to the *raḥīl,* except, perhaps, as a vaguely phrased or insinuated motif of transition from the *nasīb* to the *madīḥ*. A comprehensive survey of such critical references and formulations is provided by van Gelder (*Beyond the Line,* esp. pp. 36–37, 43, 82, and 115; this last occurrence being none other than Ibn Rashīq's rephrasing of Ibn Qutaybah's formulation). Furthermore, even when Arabic philosophy in its golden age turns to Aristotelian poetics, where it has to face the problematics of the tripartite structure of the tragedy (prologue, episode, exode), the analogy with the *qaṣīdah* that results from this encounter no longer takes into consideration the *raḥīl* section, the second part of the *qaṣīdah* now being the panegyric, and the third a *khātimah* (closure/peroration), which on a deeper level of structure should not be separated from the second section, thus ending up in a basic binary form (van Gelder, ibid., pp. 166ff.). Al-Qarṭājannī (d. 684/1285), the most faithful Aristotelian of that school, is, however, also the one most conditioned by the post-Mutanabbian *qaṣīdah,* and thus by the binary notion of structure, even if van Gelder detects in his phrasing "fī ʿaṭfi aʿinnati al-kalāmi ilā al-madīḥi" (in "turning the reins" of speech toward panegyric) the awareness that here the use of *aʿinnah* goes beyond being a mere metaphor of a lost *raḥīl*. Of one thing we may be certain, however, and that is al-Qarṭājannī's perception that whatever there is left of the *raḥīl* is part and parcel of the rhetorical function or intent of the *nasīb*. To al-Qarṭājannī the overall structure of the *qaṣīdah* thus remains binary, with only a remote vestigial remembrance of a more classical form. See Abū al-Ḥasan Ḥāzim al-Qarṭājannī, *Manāhij al-Bulaghā' wa Sirāj al-Udabā'*, ed. Muḥammad al-Ḥabīb Ibn al-Khūjah (Tunis: Dār al-Kutub al-Sharqīyah, 1966), pp. 304–5; and van Gelder, *Beyond the Line*, pp. 183–85.

21. Ibn Qutaybah, *Al-Shi'r wa al-Shu'arā'*, vol. 1, p. 75.

22. The source of some misconceptions regarding Ibn Qutaybah seems to lie in his critics' inability to differentiate between *philological* and *rhetorical* correctness in defining terminology. Thus Gustav Richter thinks that Ibn Qutaybah was guided by "philological" considerations in his linking of the term *qaṣīd* (from the root *q-ṣ-d*, "to direct oneself to," "to intend something") with the structural and thematic makeup of the Arabic ode: "One notices how our *philologist* [my italics] attempts to deduce the intent of the poem from the term *qaṣīdah*" ("Zur Entstehungsgeschichte der altarabischen Qaṣīde," *Zeitschrift der Deutschen morgenländischen Gesellschaft* 92, n.s. 17 [1938]: 554–55). It is important to keep in mind, however, that in this case Ibn Qutaybah is a *rhetorician* before being a philologist ("*unser Philologe*," as Richter somewhat condescendingly calls him); and as a rhetorician he "interprets" correctly there where he might have erred as a philologist. Seeger A. Bonebakker, too, in summing up other basically kindred views (Goldziher, Gibb), could not go beyond the accepted view that Ibn Qutaybah's discussion of the *qaṣīdah* is an aspect of his philology. See his "Poets and Critics in the Third Century A.H.," in Gustave E. von Grunebaum, ed., *Logic in Classical Islamic Culture* (Wiesbaden: Otto Harrassovitz, 1970), pp. 85–111. Alfred Bloch was thus much closer to the truth of the matter when he linked the term *qaṣīdah* to the specifically rhetorical intent of the formal variant of the separately definable missive poem (*Botschaftsgesätz*). He sums up his argument with great self-assurance, and for his own reasons joins in the indictment of the Arabic philologists: "Qaṣīda bedeutet also von Hause aus gar nicht speciell das, was die arabischen Philologen später so bezeichneten, nämlich das 'vollständige,' mit dem Nasīb beginnende Langgedicht" (Alfred Bloch, "Qaṣīda," *Asiatische Studien: Zeitschrift der Schweizerischen Gesellschaft für Asienkunde* 2 [1948]: 117, and 122).

23. Ibn Ṭabāṭabā, *'Iyār al-Shi'r*, pp. 78, 126. I follow van Gelder in the assumption that Ibn Ṭabāṭabā is the earliest source for the *qaṣīdah-risālah* comparison. Van Gelder also suggests that this comparison issued from the fact that in the eighth and ninth centuries the art of letter writing had developed in directions showing formal analogy with the *qaṣīdah* (*Beyond the Line*, pp. 56–57).

24. If not explicitly establishing an analogy between *qaṣīdah* and *khuṭbah*, al-Jāḥiẓ may have implied it when he explained the ascendancy of the status of the orator as being due to the (vulgarized?) proliferation of poets—this obviously with reference to the epideictic function of both literary kinds. See his

Al-Bayān wa al-Tabyīn, 3d ed., ed. ʿAbd al-Salām Muḥammad Hārūn (Cairo: Maktabat al-Khānjī, 1388/1968), vol. 4, p. 83.

25. Kennedy, *Greek Rhetoric under Christian Emperors,* p. 147.

26. Ibid., p. 28.

27. We may expand the image and connect the reciting poet's bow with the Prophet Muḥammad's *ʿanazah,* which was the name for the short spear that, beginning in the second year of the Hijrah, the Prophet's devoted "adjutant," Bilāl, used to carry before him, planting it into the ground during prayers. The tradition of the *ʿanazah* as *Vortragslanze* was then ritualized and tied in with other attributes of "pastoral" authority, among which was the Friday preacher's ascension of the pulpit with the *ʿanazah*-staff in hand. Such developments, which are regressions into the symbol itself, only stress the *ʿanazah*'s archaizing of ritualized authority, where the pastoral-patriarchal leads to the priestly-spiritual and ultimately to the forensic, in which it symbolizes both the right to dispense justice and the privilege to plead for it. See Franz Altheim and Ruth Stiehl, *Die Araber in der Alten Welt,* vol. 1, *Bis zum Beginn der Kaiserzeit* (Berlin: Walter de Gruyter and Co., 1964), esp. pp. 584ff.; also *The Encyclopaedia of Islam,* new ed. (Leiden: E. J. Brill, 1960), vol. 1, p. 482. In the archaic Achaean world of the *Iliad* the equivalent of the *ʿanazah* as *Vortragslanze* is the staff which Achilles holds in his hand during his impassioned, solemn, and obviously forensically ritualized confrontation with Agamemnon when the latter transgresses the bounds of the heroic ethos regulating the division of spoils by taking the beautiful Briseis away from Achilles. In a manner very close to the digressive motif-expansion characteristic of pre-Islamic Arabic poetic styles, Achilles delivers his angry—but at the same time descriptively far-flung—outburst against Agamemnon:

> verily by this staff, that shall no more
> put forth leaves or shoots since
> at the first it left its stump among
> the mountains, neither shall it again
> grow green, for that the bronze hath
> stripped it of leaves and bark,
> and now the sons of the Achaeans
> that give judgment bear it in their
> hands, even they that guard
> the dooms by ordinance of Zeus;
> and this shall be for thee a mighty
> oath. . . .
> So spake the son of Peleus, and
> down to the earth he dashed the staff
> studded with golden nails, and himself
> sate him down (Homer, *The Iliad,* Loeb Classical Library, pp. 20–21, vv. 234ff.)

In the literary sense amply illustrative of the purposes and semiotics of the staff (*al-ʿaṣā*) that concerns us here is Usāmah Ibn Munqidh's *Kitāb al-ʿAṣā* (ed.

Ḥasan ʿAbbās [Alexandria: Al-Hay'ah al-Miṣrīyah al-ʿĀmmah li al-Kitāb, 1978]). See esp. pp. 264 (*al-ʿaṣā* and the pulpit), 266 (*al-ʿaṣā* and the seal of the Prophet), 282–84 (*al-ʿaṣā* and the orators and the orator-poet's lance as his *al-ʿaṣā*).

28. James J. Murphy, *Rhetoric in the Middle Ages: A History of Rhetorical Theory from St. Augustine to the Renaissance* (Berkeley and Los Angeles: University of California Press, 1981), p. 205. Apparently independent of the Arabic publication of the present section (1986), is Julie Scott Meisami's brief but cogent treatment of the place of Ibn Qutaybah's *qaṣīdah* theory within the Ciceronian concept of rhetorical structure. Its should be noted, however, that the phrasing of the term *captatio benevolentiae* is actually post-Ciceronian (Cicero, *De inventione* 1.15.20, Loeb Classical Library, pp. 42–43). Her overall discussion of the two-part (*nasīb-madīḥ*) *qaṣīdah* is also noteworthy (*Medieval Persian Court Poetry* [Princeton: Princeton University Press, 1987], pp. 53–54.).

29. Murphy, *Rhetoric in the Middle Ages*, p. 206.

30. The *nasīb,* too, ultimately fell victim to the formally reductionist trend in the evolution of the epideictic courtly *qaṣīdah,* but again only after the poet's own voice had become part of the new Abbasid poem of praise sanctioned by al-Mutanabbī (d. 354/965). In the compositional practice of many poets, the *nasīb* then ceases to exist formally, becoming instead stylistically pervasive in the structurally dominant *madīḥ*. In this manner, the poet's voice diffuses itself throughout the new epideictic poem, thus making the separate rhetorical device of an "exordium" unnecessary.

31. Ilfat Kamāl al-Rūbī, *Naẓarīyat al-Shiʿr ʿind al-Falāsifah al-Muslimīn* (*min al-Kindī ḥattā Ibn Rushd*) (Beirut: Dār al-Nashr li al-Ṭibāʿah wa al-Nashr, 1983), p. 193.

32. Bloch, "Qaṣīda," pp. 117–22.

33. Alfred Bloch stops to compare (ibid., p. 122) the development of the term *qaṣīdah* with that of *qāfiyah* in the latter's elucidation by Ignaz Goldziher (*Abhandlungen zur arabischen Philologie* [Leiden: E. J. Brill, 1896], vol. 1, p. 105). I may add to Ignaz Goldziher's proven terminological and semantic precision that the word *qāfiyah* in modern idiomatic usage has retained much of its archaic invective connotation: thus in the expression *bi lā qāfiyah* (No offense! Don't get me wrong! No pun intended.).

34. Abū al-ʿAbbās al-Mufaḍḍal Ibn Muḥammad al-Ḍabbī, *Dīwān al-Mufaḍḍalīyāt,* commentary by Abū Muḥammad al-Qāsim Ibn Muḥammad Ibn Bashshār al-Anbārī, ed. Charles James Lyall (Beirut: Maṭbaʿat al-Ābā' al-Yasūʿīyīn, 1920), vol. 1, p. 88 (poem no. 10, v. 29); idem, *Al-Mufaḍḍalīyāt,* 5th ed., ed. Aḥmad Muḥammad Shākir and ʿAbd al-Salām Muḥammad Hārūn (Cairo: Dār al-Maʿārif bi Miṣr, 1976), p. 59. Henceforth both editions will be referred to, respectively, as *Al-Mufaḍḍalīyāt* (Lyall) or (Shākir).

35. Abū Bakr Muḥammad Ibn al-Qāsim al-Anbārī, *Sharḥ al-Qaṣā'id al-Sabʿ al-Ṭiwāl al-Jāhilīyāt,* 2d ed., ed. ʿAbd al-Salām Muḥammad Hārūn (Cairo: Dār

al-Maʿārif bi Miṣr, 1969), p. 265, v. 26. Examples with *abligh risālatan* are, for instance, Imru' al-Qays: "abligh subayʿan in ʿaraḍta risālatan" (*Dīwān,* 3d ed., ed. Muḥammad Abū al-Faḍl Ibrāhīm [Cairo: Dār al-Maʿārif bi Miṣr, 1969], p. 117, v. 15); Ṭarafah Ibn al-ʿAbd: "alā ablighā ʿabda al-ḍalāli risālatan" (*Dīwān* [Damascus: Majmaʿ al-Lughah al-ʿArabīyah, 1975], p. 82, v. 6); then also the *mukhaḍram* Kaʿb Ibn Zuhayr: "alā ablighā ʿannī Bujayran risālatan" (*Sharḥ Dīwān Kaʿib Ibn Zuhayr,* ed. Abū Saʿīd al-Ḥasan Ibn al-Ḥusayn Ibn ʿAbd Allāh al-Sukkarī [Cairo: Al-Dār al-Qawmīyah li al-Ṭibāʿah wa al-Nashr, 1385/1965] [photo-offset of Dār al-Kutub ed., 1369/1950], p. 3, v. 1); or the Umayyad al-Rāʿī al-Numayrī: "ablighā amīra al-mu'minīna risālatan" (*Dīwān,* ed. Reinhard Weipert [Beirut and Wiesbaden: Franz Steiner Verlag, 1980], p. 226, v. 32).

36. Yaḥyā al-Jabūrī, ed., *Shiʿr ʿAbd Allāh al-Zabaʿrī* [or *al-Zibaʿrā*] (Beirut: Mu'assasat al-Risālah, 1401/1981), p. 41. Regarding *āyah* as synonym of *risālah,* see E. W. Lane, *Arabic-English Lexicon,* vol. 1, p. 135. Here, however, it is clear that the poet has chosen the term *āyah* in order to underscore the superior quality of his own verse as the vehicle of the message. Such a meaning of *āyah* already points in the direction of the qur'ānic usage, especially since the poet has been witness to the Meccan debate over qur'ānic revelation. In al-Nābighah al-Dhubyānī's usage (*Dīwān,* ed. Karam al-Bustānī [Beirut: Dār Ṣādir, n.d.], p. 76), we must not yet look for such an enhancing connotation in the synonymity of *āyah* and *risālah.*

37. Al-Nābighah al-Dhubyānī, *Dīwān,* pp. 58, 76.

38. Kaʿb Ibn Zuhayr, *Dīwān,* pp. 112–13. The term *mukhaḍram* designates someone "straddling two historical or generational periods." It is used primarily with reference to those poets who, having been poetically productive in the pre-Islamic period, had reached the age of Islam.

39. Abū Zayd Muḥammad Ibn Abī al-Khaṭṭāb al-Qurashī, *Jamharat Ashʿār al-ʿArab fī al-Jāhilīyah wa al-Islām,* ed. ʿAlī Muḥammad al-Bijāwī (Cairo: Dār Nahḍat Miṣr li al-Ṭibāʿah wa al-Nashr, 1387/1956), vol. 2, p. 767. For another version of the formulaic v. 54, see W. Wright, *A Grammar of the Arabic Language,* 3d ed. (Cambridge: Cambridge University Press, 1971), vol. 2, p. 86.

40. Al-Qurashī, *Jamharat Ashʿār al-ʿArab,* vol. 2, p. 768.

41. To be added here is the frequent occurrence of the verb *ahdā* (to present as a gift; to bring [the bride] to [the bridegroom]; to offer as sacrifice [animal]). Thus in the closing line of one of Jarīr's *naqā'iḍ* the *hadīyah* as "missive" is closer to *anathema/ḥarām/iḥrām* than it is to the "positive" meaning of offering-as-gift:

Convey to al-Farazdaq my *missive-offering.*
It is a burden overloading
  an already burdened, jaded beast. [169]

See Anthony Ashley Bevan, ed., *The Naḳā'iḍ of Jarīr and al-Farazdaḳ* (Leiden: E. J. Brill, 1905), vol. 1, p. 231, poem 40. Alfred Bloch's careful attention to this contextually determined meaning of *ahdā* has special merit. With only a rhetorical hesitation, he also correctly identifies ***hadīyah*** as being denominative of that specific meaning of ***ahdā*** ("Qaṣīda," p. 21). As an analogy to this semantic development of ***ahdā,*** one can cite the word ***anathema,*** which within the Greek ritual context means "votive offering" (Walter Burkert, *Greek Religion* [Cambridge: Harvard University Press, 1985], pp. 93 and 384, n. 96), but which by way of the Hebrew context and semantic range of ***ḥ-r-m*** develops into the now familiar meaning of "excommunication," thus "accursedness." Here the Arabic synonymity of ***ihdā'*** and ***iḥrām*** is particularly instructive.

42. Imru' al-Qays, *Dīwān,* pp. 114–18, poem 15.

43. *Al-Mufaḍḍalīyāt* (Lyall), pp. 79–90, poem 10, of which the pertinent "signal" verse has already been quoted); and 826–30, poem 122. In poem 10 the structural subdivision is ***nasīb*** (vv. 1–9), ***raḥīl*** (vv. 10–27), missive/***fakhr*** (vv. 28–37); in poem no. 122 the structure is ***nasīb*** (vv. 1–6), ***raḥīl*** (vv. 7–12), missive (vv. 13–17). Note, however, that in poem 122 the ***raḥīl*** falls short of being entirely paradigmatic, since the poet's mount is not a she-camel (***nāqah***) but a horse, associated by way of the customary simile procedure to the topical characterization of a she-camel and an ostrich. The matter of the structural and functional distribution of riding animals in the classical Arabic ***qaṣīdah*** is discussed in my article "Name and Epithet: The Philology and Semiotics of Animal Nomenclature in Early Arabic Poetry," *Journal of Near Eastern Studies* 45, no. 2 (Apr. 1986): 103–4, 112ff.

44. Al-Nābighah al-Dhubyānī, *Dīwān,* pp. 30–37. Another famous poem of "personally delivered" apology coupled with panegyric, which in most respects is strikingly paradigmatically constructed as well, is the *Burdah Ode* by Ka'b Ibn Zuhayr. In this poem, however, the identity of the signal is complicated by the fact that the she-camel is meant to carry the poet to where his self-willed beloved has gone or, in a sense only implied by subsequent contexts, to other equally inaccessible and hazardous objectives—that is, to where the poet will ultimately deliver his plea and panegyric before the Prophet Muḥammad. Thus, here the eliciting, in vv. 13 and 14, of ***lā yuballighuhā*** (there will not reach it) and ***wa lan yuballighahā*** (and there shall not reach it) is only an enhanced echo of the paradigmatic signal as employed by al-Nābighah al-Dhubyānī. For a study of Ka'b Ibn Zuhayr's full ***qaṣīdah*** in this regard, see Suzanne Pinckney Stetkevych, "Pre-Islamic Panegyric and the Poetics of Redemption: *Mufaḍḍaliyyah* 119 of 'Alqamah ibn 'Abadah and *Bānat Su'ād* of Ka'b ibn Zuhayr," in idem, ed., *Reorientations/Arabic and Persian Poetry* (Bloomington: Indiana University Press, 1993).

45. Besides al-Rā'ī al-Numayrī's *Dīwān,* pp. 213–92, the *Malḥamah* figures prominently in al-Qurashī's *Jamharat Ash'ar al-'Arab,* vol. 2, pp. 912–30. Fuat Sezgin cites the year 90/709 as only a "hypothetical" date for al-Rā'ī al-Numayrī's death: "sein Todesjahr ist unbekannt" (*Geschichte des arabischen Schrifttums,* vol. 2, *Poesie: bis ca. 430 H.* [Leiden: E. J. Brill, 1975], p. 388).

46. Thus in the *Jamharat Ash'ār al-'Arab;* whereas Reinhard Weipert's count reaches ninety-two lines with obvious lacunae in between the final lines.

47. Al-A'shā, *Dīwān* (Beirut: Dār Ṣādir, 1966), p. 200.

48. Ḥātim al-Ṭā'ī, *Dīwān Shi'r Ḥātim Ibn 'Abd Allāh al-Ṭā'ī wa Akhbāruh*, ed. 'Ādil Sulaymān Jamāl (Cairo: Maṭba'at al-Madanī, 1395/1975), see esp. poems 32 (p. 200) and 45 (p. 229), but also 36 (p. 209), where the *'ādhilah* theme determines implicitly the tone of voice in the *nasīb;* in poem 47 (pp. 233–41) the *'ādhilah* figures as a closing "development" (vv. 12–31) of a more "standard" *nasīb* opening. A number of shorter, isolated *'ādhilah* fragments (pp. 260, 280, 305, 309) do not allow us to form an opinion as to their structural position in their respective hypothetical *qaṣīdahs*.

Another pre-Islamic poet, 'Abīd Ibn al-Abraṣ, also begins one *qaṣīdah* with a quasi *nasīb* that implicitly hearkens back to the *'ādhilah* ('Abīd Ibn al-Abraṣ, *Dīwān,* ed. Karam al-Bustānī [Beirut: Dār Ṣādir/Dār Bayrūt, 1384/1964], pp. 52–54 [rhyming in *ḥī*]). Even his other poem with the same rhyme (ibid., pp. 49–51) should be interpreted as owing its opening motif to the *'ādhilah,* however. Also, see the *Aṣma'īyah* 12 by Sahm Ibn Ḥanẓalah al-Ghanawī (Abū Sa'īd 'Abd al-Malik Ibn Qurayb Ibn 'Abd al-Malik al-Aṣma'ī, *Al-Aṣma'īyāt,* 2d ed., ed. Aḥmad Muḥammad Shākir and 'Abd al-Salām Hārūn [Cairo: Dār al-Ma'ārif bi Miṣr, 1964], pp. 53–56).

49. Meïr M. Bravmann calls attention to the ambiguities, and priorities, in the meaning of *hamm* (pl. *humūm*). See his "Heroic Motives in Early Arabic Literature," *Der Islam: Zeitschrift für Geschichte und Kultur des islamischen Orients* 33 (1958): 274ff. For additional discussion of *hamm/humūm,* see below, n. 69.

50. So far, the only major published study on this important topic is Ḥasan al-Bannā 'Izz al-Dīn, *Al-Ṭayf wa al-Khayāl fī al-Shi'r al-'Arabī al-Qadīm* (Cairo: Dār al-Nadīm li al-Nashr wa al-Tawzī' wa al-Ṣiḥāfah, 1988). Another interesting and imaginative study is John Seybold's "The Earliest Demon Lover: The *Ṭayf al-Khayāl* in *al-Mufaḍḍalīyāt,*" in S. Stetkevych, ed., *Reorientations.*

51. In the *Jamharat Ash'ār al-'Arab* the direct address begins with v. 44 ("a khalīfata al-raḥmāni," O vicar of the Merciful), whereas in the Weipert edition of the *Dīwān* the turn occurs already in v. 41 ("a walīya amri Allāhi," O executor of God's authority), only to be reiterated in v. 47.

52. Some of the ideas presented in this section were previously presented in my "The Arabic Qaṣīdah," in I. Ševčenko, ed., *Eucharisterion: Essays Presented to Omeljan Pritsak,* Harvard Ukrainian Studies, vol. 3/4, pt. 2 (1979–80), pp. 774–80. See my discussion of Goethe's poem *Lied und Gebilde* in "Arabic Poetry and Assorted Poetics," pp. 103–5.

53. We shall thus not approach the formal questions of the Arabic poem with the kind of mimesis in mind that is prone to be reduced to an unfairly undifferentiated Aristotelianism first and then offered as an almost irresistible bait to literary criticism through Horace's lapidary formulation. Once this mimetic misunderstanding is resolved, *ut musica poesis*—always wary of the Herderian sentimental entrapment—ought to come quite close even to Aristotle's "mimesis of means," which, according to Jean H. Hagstrum, "seems to deny the validity of associating painting and poetry in any special way." Hagstrum concludes that painting and poetry "are not sisters but cousins; and the sisters

of poetry, when one considers the *means*—but only the *means*—of imitation employed, are music and dancing (the arts of temporal movement) and not the visual or graphic arts (the arts of spatial stasis)." He stresses further, this time hearkening back to Werner Jaeger, that in Greek culture "poetry and music, 'blest pair of Sirens,' were inseparable sisters." See Jean H. Hagstrum, *The Sister Arts: The Tradition of Literary Pictorialism and English Poetry from Dryden to Gray* (Chicago: University of Chicago Press, 1987), pp. 6, 9; also see Werner Jaeger, *Paideia,* trans. Gilbert Highet (New York: Oxford University Press, 1943), vol. 2, pp. 224, 228. It is quite likely thanks to Simonides, however, who saw poetry as image in movement and painting (i.e., "image") as poetry in a state of repose, that a depolarized view of painting and poetry reaches Horace as a "positive" comparison. Theoretically at least, the original Greek positive comparison was between the two art forms that were of the domain of hearing—music and poetry—and Aristotle's siding with "hearing" opposite "sight" is a recognition not only of poetry's temporality but also of its orality even in the post-Platonic age of Greek literacy. Eric A. Havelock (*The Muse Learns to Write: Reflections on Orality and Literacy from Antiquity to the Present* [New Haven: Yale University Press, 1986]) discusses at considerable length the Greek dialectic of orality and literacy, specifically with Plato as pivot. He talks of the Greek replacement of the "oral state of mind" (p. 8); of Euripides' *Hippolytus* (428 B.C.), where an inscribed tablet "shouts" as "a song speaking loud" (pp. 21–22); and also of Plato's reassertion of the "primacy of speaking and hearing in personal oral response even as he wrote" (p. iii). The Platonic dialogued style itself he considers to be an aspect of a surviving orality.

54. Thus, to Adrian Stokes, the complex pattern of the symphony is a "shape, handy as a coin"—no more, no less (Richard Wollheim, ed., *The Image in Form: Selected Writings of Adrian Stokes* [New York: Harper and Row, Icon Editions, 1972], p. 117; the quotation is from the chapter "Art and the Body," originally in *Reflections on the Nude* [1967]. Any such unselfconscious form-acceptance would, however, be rejected by Philip Barford as no more than an impressionistic affect that hides behind mechanistic formalism and refuses to see the "sonata-principle" behind the "sonata-form." To Barford, it "is a highly thought-provoking fact that the rise and establishment of the sonata-principle corresponded in the most intimate way with the gradual emergence and full flowering of a comprehensive metaphysical system which, in so many respects, is the ultimate rationale of the logic of the sonata-principle. Ideally, one has a wordless insight into this profound and subtle matter; in words one can do little more than employ the language of analogy. The Hegelian system, at its finest, is a superb justification of the sonata-principle. Similarly, the classical sonata, at its finest, is a sensuous embodiment of the dialectical relationship of opposed terms. In the collective consciousness of late eighteenth-century man, some vital force was at work which found expression in music, literature and philosophy—in Haydn, Mozart and Beethoven, in Goethe, in Hegel. It was the same force. It found diverse expressions. . . . When, therefore, we approach the sonatas of Emanuel Bach, we are considering manifestations of the creative consciousness which were intimately bound up with a wave of mental and

spiritual activity which rippled through the entire field of art and philosophy" (*The Keyboard Music of C. P. E. Bach: Considered in Relation to His Musical Aesthetic and the Rise of the Sonata Principle* [London: Barrie and Rockliff, 1965], p. 83).

55. In its full complexity, the sonata form is perhaps best discussed by Charles Rosen in his valuable theoretical study *The Classical Style: Haydn, Mozart, Beethoven* (New York and London: W. W. Norton and Co., 1972), pp. 99–108, and in his *Sonata Forms,* rev. ed. (New York and London: W. W. Norton and Co., 1988), esp. pp. 1–7 and 16ff.. Rosen would, however, shun terming structural accretions upon the ternary model as being mechanical or ancillary, preferring such attested formal distinctions as "minuet sonata form" and "finale sonata form." On the whole, his approach to the sonata form is strongly revisionist and at first more pugnacious sounding than is warranted by his insightful and ultimately well balanced discussion of structure. Furthermore, his identification of a multiplicity of sonata forms beyond the "scholastically" normative intent and stricture of a structural monolith called *the* sonata form also helps accommodate form-significant departures from the rigidity of the "model" in Arabic *qaṣīdah* criticism. Both the sonata form and the *qaṣīdah* with its form-specific *nasīb* section, however, ought ultimately to be able to retain the imprint of their common denominators.

56. Romain Rolland, *Beethoven the Creator: The Great Creative Epochs, From the Eroica to the Appassionata* (New York: Dover Publications, 1964), pp. 91–92.

57. Ibn Qutaybah, *Al-Shiʿr wa al-Shuʿarāʾ,* vol. 1, pp. 75–76.

58. Whereas from the Arabic side the analogy and near-identity between sonata/sonata form and *qaṣīdah/nasīb* derives from an entire literary culture's sense of form, Western literature has known the sonata/sonata form in its mood and structure only through incidental imitations or transpositions. For the most part, these imitations and transpositions were not formally co-essential, however, but rather melodic and harmonic gropings for consonances or impressionistic imitations of the sequence of moods in specific musical works or else studied experiments in form-transplantation that only rarely retained their own integral literary form-consciousness capable of carrying coherent formal ideas safely across the limits separating medium from medium. René Wellek and Austin Warren represent the minimalistic critical position when they try to muster their apologia for a kind of formal neutrality by timidly throwing in that "it is hard to see why repetitive motifs or a certain contrasting and balancing of moods, though by avowed intention imitative of musical composition, are not essentially the familiar literary devices of recurrence, contrast, and the like which are common to all the arts" (*Theory of Literature,* 3d ed. [New York: Harcourt, Brace and World, 1956], p. 127). Following the first insights of Baudelaire, the confusion of the senses produces an ever farther reaching terminological blending of the critical differentiation and apprehension of the arts. In poetry there appear titles like Théophile Gautier's *Symphonie en blanc majeur* (*Poésies compètes,* ed. René Jasinski [Paris: A. G. Nizet, 1970], vol. 3 pp. 22–24) and its fin de siècle sequel, the *Sinfonía en gris mayor,* by the great

Nicaraguan poet Rubén Darío, which, however, reveals the appropriate ternary structure of *a-b-a* (*Poesias completas* [Madrid: Aguilar, 1967], vol. 1, pp. 591–92). Beyond that, among the best-achieved formal approximations to a musical composition by a literary work that is not a poem, there ought to figure Tolstoy's *Kreutzer Sonata.* In that novella the formal analogies are developed out of the identification of the two instruments, the piano and the violin, with two of the story's protagonists. One indeed seems to hear Beethoven's two interweaving instrumental voices as one allows the voices and moods of the novella to take their own shape and weave their course. It is then to Tolstoy's *Kreutzer Sonata* rather than to T. S. Eliot's *Four Quartets* that Lloyd Frankenberg's method of reading structure into the different instrumental voices applies (Lloyd Frankenberg, *Pleasure Dome: On Reading Modern Poetry* [Boston: Houghton Mifflin, 1949], pp. 97–117). It is interesting to observe further that whereas Tolstoy derives his sense of form from Beethoven, a more recent composer, Leos Janacek, bases his string quartet, also entitled *Kreutzer Sonata* (1923), in a conspicuously circular way on Tolstoy's novella, thus ending up in the original medium without much dissipation of the sense of form. As for Ramón del Valle-Inclán's four "Sonatas"—of spring, summer, autumn, and winter (*Sonatas: memorias del Marqués de Bradomín* [Madrid: Espasa-Calpe, 1969])—they are, in spite of their Art Nouveau stylization of line and mood, formally closer to the Baroque genre of the musical panels (which could also be pictorial panels) of the four seasons. It is in T. S. Eliot's *Four Quartets* that we are made aware with some clarity of the internally articulated, as well as actually *framing,* structure of the sonata form (see, e.g., among an increasing number of structure-conscious analyses, D. Bosley Brotman, "T. S. Eliot: 'The Music of Ideas,'" *University of Toronto Quarterly* 8, no. 1 [Oct. 1948]: pp. 20–29; S. Marshall Cohen, "Music and Structure in Eliot's Quartets," *Dartmouth Quarterly* 5 [1950]: esp. 3–4; Grover Smith, *T. S. Eliot's Poetry and Plays: A Study in Sources and Meaning* [Chicago: University of Chicago Press, 1967], esp. pp. 252–53; and Philip Wheelwright, *The Burning Fountain: A Study in the Language of Symbolism,* rev. ed. [Bloomington: Indiana University Press, 1968], pp. 242ff., who falls back significantly on Cohen's essay). Thus Cohen's specific: "The *Quartets* are written in the 'cyclic' style of the Cesar Franck sonata or the C♯ minor quartet of Beethoven. The first movements generally follow the bare essentials of sonata form: exposition, development, recapitulation" ("Music and Structure," p. 3). So, too, is Keith Alldritt (*Eliot's "Four Quartets": Poetry as Chamber Music* [London: Woburn Press, 1978]) aware of the problem of structure in Eliot's *Quartets,* which to him illustrate the "sonata-principle," albeit only as a binary vehicle for "the expression and the reconciliation of opposites in experience and feeling" (p. 28). One must add here, however, that both Cohen and Smith end up being less than fully convincing in their identification of specific Beethovenian models for T. S. Eliot's *Quartets.* Thus there are substantial discrepancies in structure as far as the number of "movements" is concerned between Eliot's sustained five-movement structure and Beethoven's changeability of movements—from four to seven—precisely in the suggested model quartets (Opp. 127, 130–32, and 135). Furthermore, the especially singled out B flat major and C sharp minor quartets themselves should in all rigor not even be considered as being in sonata form (see J. W. N. Sullivan, *Beethoven: His Spiritual Development* [New York: Alfred A. Knopf, 1964], p. 230).

59. In his *Histoire de la littérature arabe des origines à la fin du XV*[e] *siècle de J.-C.* (Paris: Librairie d'Amérique et d'Orient, 1964), vol. 2, p. 378, Régis Blachère, for instance, speaks of the pre-Islamic (sixth century A.D.) *qaṣīdah* as representing "une 'suite' ou plutôt un 'mouvement,'" saying farther on: "Dans ce 'mouvement poétique' qu'est la *'qaṣīda,'* le poète n'est point entièrement dominé par les servitudes de la tradition." His musical terminology and reference to musical structures would indeed be of critical interest if they were not so hastily applied. Thus, if it is debatable whether or not a sixth-century A.D. Arabic *qaṣīdah* in some instances has the characteristic, formally forced eclectic fluency of a suite, it is entirely awkward to speak of a whole structured *qaṣīdah* as a "movement" when, in fact, it is a structure consisting of clearly differentiated "movements."

60. The fast tempo (movement) does not always retain its primary structural position in the "classical" symphony/sonata, however. Thus Haydn's *Farewell Symphony* must not necessarily be indebted to a surviving structural pull of the *sonata da chiesa* but should owe its ordering of moods, and tempi, to elegiac formal dictates, priorities, and tensions. On the other end of the spectrum of formal "classicism" lies Beethoven's *Moonlight Sonata,* following nonetheless similar dictates.

61. Al-Anbārī, *Sharḥ al-Qaṣā'id al-Sab'*, pp. 517–29.

62. Ibid., pp. 132–35.

63. Ibid., pp. 529–31.

64. Ibid., pp. 135–38.

65. Ibid., pp. 139–46.

66. Ibid., pp. 307–15.

67. Ibid., pp. 32–73. In his article "Towards a Structural Analysis of Pre-Islamic Poetry (II): The Eros Vision," *Edebiyât* 1, no. 1 (1976): 3–69, Kamal Abu-Deeb, although appropriately calling Labīd's *Mu'allaqah* the Key Poem and that of Imru' al-Qays the Eros Poem, nevertheless imposes on those poems a theory of structure that is much too rigid and monotonous. To him structure exhausts itself in the concept of binary opposition. "The Key Poem moves essentially within the oppositions of death/life, dryness/freshness, barrenness/fertility, transience/permanence, severance/continuity." "By contrast, the Eros Poem moves essentially within the oppositions fragility/solidness, subject to time/timeless, lack of vitality/vitality, relativity/absoluteness, stillness/motion, flatness (lack of intensity)/intensity, meditative/emotional" (p. 66). To my mind, such an approach does not facilitate a discrete idea of structure—certainly not of a structure such as the *qaṣīdah,* which, being ternary, is inherently too dynamic for absolute binarism.

68. On the plane of our musical analogues, we have only to think of Beethoven's idiosyncratically conceived first movements in the *Hammerklavier Sonata* or in the *Eroica.*

69. Meïr M. Bravmann, "Heroic Motives in Early Arabic Literature," pp. 274ff. If Bravmann's stress falls somewhat excessively on the determination and endeavor aspect of the root *h-m-m,* such a preference may be due in part to the general framework within which this topic is discussed—that of "heroic motifs." Certainly, sentiment, and even sentimentality, were not perceived as unheroic in the medieval "chivalrous" context, which, quite decisively, must include the Bedouin poet of the classical Arabic *qaṣīdah*. As the ethos and even basic "anthropology" of knighthood abundantly prove, sorrow, tears, pathos, and sentimentality were not considered unworthy of knightly-heroic comportment. Thus Perceval may fall into a sentimental, contemplative trance at the sight of three drops of blood upon fresh snow, for they will remind him of his beloved's fresh complexion. To his companion, Gawain, such behavior will appear "full of sweet courtesy." See John Stevens, *Medieval Romance: Themes and Approaches* (New York: Norton Library, 1974), pp. 96–97.

Also, Martin Heidegger's discussion (following Karl Burdach) of the "twofold structure," or "twofold meaning," of "care" (*cura/Sorge*) as not only "apprehensive endeavor" but also as "care" and "devotion" is a strikingly pertinent hermeneutical addition to our understanding of the Arabic *humūm/himmah* of the closure of the *nasīb*. Heidegger begins his argument with the Latin story of "*Cura,*" an allegorical fable from Hyginus (Karl Burdach, "Faust und die Sorge," *Deutsche Vierteljahrsschrift für Literaturwissenschaft und Geistesgeschichte* 1 [1923]: 1ff.). In this allegory, "Cura" shapes a "being" out of clay but asks Jupiter to give it a spirit, to which Jupiter gladly accedes. When Cura insists on giving that being her own name, however, Jupiter objects, claiming that right for himself. At this, Earth (Tellus) appears as the third claimant to the right of naming the being. Ultimately, Saturn, as the god of Time, is brought in to adjudicate. His decision is that Jupiter, having contributed the spirit, shall, after the being's death, obtain its spirit; Earth, the provider of the body, shall then claim the body; while Cura, who first shaped this being, shall possess it for the duration of its life. Also, Saturn decrees that the being's name shall be *homo,* for it was fashioned out of earth (*humus*). Heidegger stresses that this allegorical being fashioned by Cura "has the source of its being in care." It is a Herderian "child of care." See Martin Heidegger, *Sein und Zeit,* 10th ed. (Tübingen: Max Niemeyer Verlag, 1963), pp. 197–200.

70. Al-Anbārī, *Sharḥ al-Qaṣā'id al-Sab',* pp. 73–79.

71. Imru' al-Qays's seeing the stars as if they were tied to a mountain also suggests another image, which is that of sojourning riders' mounts held immobile through the night. This image is prompted by the two words *mughār* and *fatl* (for *fatal*), which each suggest meanings that are epithetic of horses or eventually of she-camels (*fatal*). Thus *mughār* also means "a strong horse: as though twisted tightly," "a horse strong in the joints," "a horse that runs swiftly"; while *fatl/fatal,* with reference to riding animals (she-camels primarily), denotes "wideness between the elbows," that is, their being sufficiently apart during the animal's run, thus facilitating running. So, while the first image that comes into being is that of stars staying fixed in the night sky as if

tied to a mountain, the further metaphorization is that of those stars appearing as if they were horses tied down to Mount Yadhbul. From here we are led to the representation of the darkness of the night that imprisons the horses of morning/night—very much like Ovid's, and Marlowe's, "o lente, lente / currite noctis equi." And when in v. 48 Imru' al-Qays reiterates the metaphor by placing the Pleiades *fī maṣāmihā*, which means "in a horse's standing place," or "in a stall," we are no longer allowed to entertain any doubts regarding this underlying metaphor of the "horses of the night." But this metaphor also makes us keep in mind that the tying down of the horses ultimately implies preventing the morning sun from rising, and that in pre-Islamic poetry any explicit, or implicit, reference to horses is, if not a reference to rain, necessarily a reference to the rising sun. In the above lines by Imru' al-Qays, we therefore have the oppressiveness of the night symbolized by the cosmic she-camel and the never-coming daybreak by the tying down of the horses (of the chariot of the sun?).

72. *Al-Mufaḍḍalīyāt* (Lyall), poem 76, esp. pp. 574–81. The verses of the recapitulation/closure of the *nasīb* (16–19) are 17–20 in the Shākir edition.

73. ʿAbīd Ibn al-Abraṣ, *Dīwān*, pp. 91–93.

74. The elegiac, indeed funerary, connotation of *banāt naʿsh* comes out with abundant clarity in later poetic usage, such as al-Mutanabbī's

As if Bier's Daughters, in the dark,
Were virgin pearls in mourning unveiled. [170]

See that poet's *dīwān*, *Al-ʿArf al-Ṭayyib fī Sharḥ Dīwān Abī al-Ṭayyib*, ed. Nāṣīf al-Yāzijī (Beirut: Dār Ṣādir/Dār Bayrūt, 1964), vol. 1, p. 208, and below, Chap. 4, n. 52.

75. Bishr Ibn Abī Khāzim al-Asadī, *Dīwān*, ed. ʿIzzat Ḥasan, 2d ed. (Damascus: Wizārat al-Thaqāfah, 1392/1972), pp. 65–66.

76. Such a re-membering/re-collecting is also the lyrically genre-determining etymological understanding of *Erinnerung* in Emil Staiger, to whom "what is present, what is past, and what is future can in lyrical poetry be *erinnert*," and to whom lyrical poetry is by definition *Erinnerung* (*Grundbegriffe der Poetik* [Zurich: Atlantis Verlag, 1946], p. 67). Thus enriched by a distinctly Heideggerian etymological procedure, Staiger's *Erinnerung* also comes strikingly close to defining the Arabic lyrical mode and within it the lyrical specificity of the *nasīb*.

77. This has been expressed clearly by Sir Hamilton Gibb (*Arabic Literature: An Introduction*, 2d rev. ed. [Oxford: Clarendon Press, 1963], p. 16). More recently Ḥusayn ʿAṭwān, too, stressed that the love theme was originally part of the "desolate encampment scene." See his *Muqaddimat al-Qaṣīdah al-ʿArabīyah fī al-Shiʿr al-Jāhilī* (Cairo: Dār al-Maʿārif bi Miṣr, 1970), pp. 95–96, 104–7. The source of both of these critical observations is al-Tibrīzī, and it is always *dulce et decorum* to remind ourselves of the importance of an explicit and correct referral to classical Arabic critical literature as the basis of our commerce with the Arabic literary past. This should be especially valid in the

instances where classical Arabic literary criticism transcends its customary rhetorical confines. See Abū Zakarīyā Yaḥyā Ibn ʿAlī al-Tibrīzī, ***Sharḥ Dīwān Ashʿār al-Ḥamāsah*** (Cairo: Būlāq, 1296/1879), vol. 3, p. 112. See also Suzanne Pinckney Stetkevych and her due reference to al-Tibrīzī in ***Abū Tammām and the Poetics of the ʿAbbāsid Age*** (Leiden: E. J. Brill, 1991), p. 321–22.

78. What is habitually referred to as ʿUdhrī *ghazal* may therefore not even be properly subsumed under this separate *ghazal* genre, for in its motif components and, more important, in its mood and poetic time it never quite cuts the umbilical cord that links it with the *nasīb*. On this subject see my article "Sīnīyat Aḥmad Shawqī wa ʿIyār al-Shiʿr al-ʿArabī al-Kilāsīkī," written for the Cairo conference on Aḥmad Shawqī (1983) and published in *Fuṣūl* 7, nos. 1/2 (Oct. 1986/Mar. 1987): 16; see also the highly relevant article by Renate Jacobi, "Time and Reality in *Nasīb* and *Ghazal*," *Journal of Arabic Literature* 16 (1985): 1–17. On the term "Udhrī," see chap. 3, section 2. On *ghazal*, see chap. 2, section 1.

79. Prosser Hall Frye, *Romance and Tragedy: A Study of Classical and Romantic Elements in the Great Tragedies of European Literature* (Lincoln: University of Nebraska Press, 1961), p. 5.

80. Concerning the obligatory gender polarization of camel and rider in the pre-Islamic *qaṣīdah*, see my article "Name and Epithet," pp. 95, 112ff.

81. Harry Slochower's (*Mythopoesis: Mythic Patterns in the Literary Classics* [Detroit: Wayne State University Press, 1970], p. 24) generalization about the "re-creation or homecoming" in the Oriental sense of myth vis-à-vis Western mythopoesis ought to be looked into more carefully, namely: What happens when that Oriental pattern of myth in its own turn makes allowance for mythopoesis? Here the classical Arabic *qaṣīdah* becomes the most striking example of the development of a strong structure-inherent sense of "re-creation or homecoming" that is not a return to the state before the journey/quest. It allows for a highly varied repertory of choices of "homecoming," among which is then also the option to "return" to the state before the "journey." But that latter option, being only the expression of a vague yearning, does not have a possible "home" to return to—except that of the dream itself. In the formal sense, this produces what I shall call the "circular *qaṣīdah*" as opposed to the predominant form, the "linear *qaṣīdah*," which leads to a resolution outside the poet's self-absorption. The concept of the "circular poem" is being theoretically considered in connection with Andalusian models, such as poems by Ibn Quzmān, by my colleague James Monroe (verbal communication).

82. Imru' al-Qays, *Dīwān*, p. 21 (v. 58). In al-Anbārī's *Sharḥ al-Qaṣā'id al-Sabʿ* (p. 99) the verse is no. 70. This pre-Islamic apotheotic representation of the horse calls to mind the equally symbolic and apotheotic horse statuary that is so characteristic of the Chinese T'ang dynasty, which overlaps chronologically with the Orthodox Caliphate, the entire Umayyad period, and the first century and a half of the Abbasid period (see, e.g., exemplars at the Chicago Art Institute [Russel Tyson Collection] and at the Metropolitan Museum in New York). For a further discussion of this emblematic quality of the horse

for Imru' al-Qays, see Suzanne Pinckney Setkevych, "Structuralist Interpretations of Pre-Islamic Poetry: Critique and New Directions," *Journal of Near Eastern Studies* 42, no. 2 (1983): 104, and idem, *The Mute Immortals Speak: Pre-Islamic Poetry and the Poetics of Ritual* (Ithaca: Cornell University Press, 1993), chap. 7.

83. See Philip Pettit, *The Concept of Structuralism: A Critical Analysis* (Dublin: Gill and Macmillan, 1975), p. 79. Pettit refers specifically to Claude Lévi-Strauss's *L'homme nu* (Paris: Plon, 1971), p. 583.

84. Viewed through Lévi-Strauss's conceptualization of "symmetry," Arabic poetry emerges as the poetry that is pronouncedly "structural," and Western poetry as "phenomenological"—except for the strong tendency in modern Arabic poetry toward the phenomenological. This should also be one of the reasons why the most recent Arabic poetry, having become thoroughly phenomenological, is at such a loss for a new sense of structure capable of giving it the comfort of its former (traditional) strong "sense of form."

85. [Ismā'īl Ibn al-Qāsim] Abū 'Alī al-Qālī, *Kitāb al-Amālī,* 3d ed. (Cairo: Al-Maktabah al-Tijārīyah al-Kubrā, 1373/1953), vol. 1, p. 206.

86. Joseph Campbell, *The Hero with a Thousand Faces* (Princeton: Princeton University Press, 1973), p. 168.

87. Despite the fact that in the literal sense *al-'īs* means amber-colored camels of both genders, such purely lexicographic ambiguity resolves itself in the classical Arabic *qaṣīdah* with ease if the term occurs in the *raḥīl* section, where, as we already know, there rules the law of gender polarization between rider and the camel that is his mount.

88. Abū Tammām, *Dīwān,* 3d ed., recension of al-Khaṭīb al-Tibrīzī, ed. Muḥammad 'Abduh 'Azzām (Cairo: Dār al-Ma'ārif bi Miṣr, 1970), vol. 3, p. 338.

89. Al-Ḥuṭay'ah, *Dīwān,* recension of Ibn al-Sikkīt, ed. Nu'mān Muḥammad Amīn Ṭāhā (Cairo: Maktabat al-Khānjī, 1987), p. 296.

90. In the qur'ānic narrative of the She-Camel of Ṣāliḥ there is ascertainable a reference to the *ḥimā* of the proto-Arabian people of Thamūd and to precisely one such votive/miraculous milch-camel, the *nāqat Ṣāliḥ,* whose slaughtering, and thus the violation of its *ḥimā,* brought destruction upon the entire people of Thamūd. Thus, as suggested by J. Chelhod, should be read v. 73 of the Sūrah of al-A'rāf (7) and v. 64 of the Sūrah of Hūd (11). See *The Encyclopaedia of Islam,* new ed., s.v. "*Ḥimā.*" Also see below, n. 134.

91. 'Abīd Ibn al-Abraṣ, *Dīwān,* p. 122.

92. See Labīd Ibn Rabī'ah al-'Āmirī, *Dīwān* (Beirut: Dār Ṣādir, n.d.), pp. 179–80; idem, *Sharḥ Dīwān Labīd Ibn Rabī'ah al-'Āmirī,* ed. Iḥsān 'Abbās (Kuwait: Al-Turāth al-'Arabī, 1962), pp. 320–21. In al-Anbārī (*Sharḥ al-Qaṣā'id al-Sab',* pp. 594–95) the present verse is no. 83, whereas the verse with the reference to *al-malīk* follows it as no. 84.

93. The act of ascension to such communal "high houses" or "halls" points in itself to an archetypal, not merely royal but ultimately celestial, symbolic provenance. Linked to and even generated by the setting of the high house,

then, are the scenes of the courtly banquet, in which the imbibing of wine is implicitly inseparable from ceremony. In her study of Sassanian iconography of the hunt and of the banquet, Dorothy G. Shepherd defines such ceremony as that of "apotheosis and heroization" and ultimately as representation of Paradise. See her "Banquet and Hunt in Medieval Islamic Iconography," in Ursula E. McCracken, Lilian M. C. Randall, and Richard A. Randall, Jr., eds., *Gatherings in Honor of Dorothy E. Miner* (Baltimore: Walters Art Gallery, 1974), pp. 70–92. As poetic motifs, and indeed as themes, these ceremonial scenes, regulated by a recognizably formalized diction, have the same essentially archaic ring in practically all the higher literary traditions. Thus nothing makes us think more of Ṭarafah's *Muʿallaqah* and of so much of the wine and boon-companion revelry in Abbasid verse as *Odyssey* 9.5–11:

> For I think there is no occasion accomplished that is more pleasing
> than when mirth holds sway among the *demos,*
> and the feasters up and down the house are sitting
> in order and listening to the singer,
> and beside them the tables are loaded
> with bread and meats, and from the mixing bowl the wine-steward
> draws the wine and carries it about and fills the cups.
> This seems to my own mind to be the best of occasions.

In the archaic heroic sphere, this is what Gregory Nagy calls "the earlier and ideal context of performance, namely, an evening's dinner-hour entertainment as described by Odysseus himself before he begins his own narration" (*The Best of the Achaeans: Concepts of the Hero in Archaic Greek Poetry* [Baltimore: Johns Hopkins University Press, 1979], pp. 18–19). And no less kindred should appear Dryden's *Ode on St. Cecilia's Day,* for there the pretense of the Royal Feast placed in a throne hall that is closest to Heaven continues to fascinate. As for the "courtly" character and quality of the total circumstance of such occasions, the Bedouin ones not excluded, see above, n. 1.

94. Al-Anbārī, *Sharḥ al-Qaṣā'id al-Sabʿ,* pp. 187–88, vv. 47 and 48 of Ṭarafah's *Muʿallaqah.*

95. Ḥassān Ibn Thābit, *Dīwān,* ed. Sayyid Ḥanafī Ḥasanayn and Ḥasan Kāmil al-Ṣīrafī (Cairo: Al-Hay'ah al-Miṣrīyah al-ʿĀmmah li al-Kitāb, 1974), p. 184.

96. Zuhayr Ibn Abī Sulmā, *Dīwan,* recension of Abū al-ʿAbbās Aḥmad Ibn Yaḥyā Ibn Zayd al-Shaybānī Thaʿlab (Cairo: Dār al-Kutub al-Miṣrīyah, 1363/1944), p. 276.

97. Al-Anbārī, *Sharḥ al-Qaṣā'id al-Sabʿ,* p. 99; but also pp. 82–99. The verse numbers added to those of al-Anbārī's redaction are from Imru' al-Qays, *Dīwān,* pp. 20–23. The verse cited as no. 70/58 represents, in al-Anbārī, the scene preceding the chivalrous hunt, while in the *Dīwān* it is the hunt's medallion-like conclusion.

98. Imru' al-Qays, *Dīwān,* pp. 19–23. A structurally significant treatment of the same theme—almost literally so—is also found in Imru' al-Qays's *qaṣī-*

dah rhyming in *bī*. There it comprises the entire concluding section (vv. 20–55) and thus that part of the poem that structurally equals the tribal *fakhr* or the *madīḥ* (*Diwān*, pp. 46–55).

99. *Al-Mufaḍḍalīyāt* (Lyall), p. 820, poem 120, v. 52.

100. Chrétien de Troyes, *The Knight with the Lion, or Yvain* (*Le Chevalier au Lion*), ed. and trans. William W. Kibler (New York and London: Garland Publishing, 1985); idem, *Erec und Enide,* 3d ed., ed. Wendelin Foerster (Halle/Saale: Max Niemeyer Verlag, 1934).

101. In my discussion of *Yvain* and *Erec,* I shall make frequent reference explicitly (through quotation marks) as well as implicitly to Jean Frappier's essay "Crétien de Troyes," in Roger Sherman Loomis, ed., *Arthurian Literature in the Middle Ages: A Collaborative History,* 2d ed. (Oxford: Clarendon Press, 1961), pp. 181–82 (on *Yvain*), pp. 164–68 (on *Erec*).

102. See van Gelder's survey of *takhalluṣ* in Arabic literary-critical literature (*Beyond the Line,* esp. pp. 33–34, 60–63, but also p. 227 [Index of Arabic Terms]).

103. Jean Frappier would go along with Roger Sherman Loomis in the interpretation of the meaning of "la Joie de la Cort" where *cort* (court) would be a substitution for the Celtic *cor* (horn), which becomes symbolically the "horn of plenty" (*Arthurian Literature in the Middle Ages,* p. 168).

104. Slochower, *Mythopoesis.* See above, n. 81.

105. Ibid., p. 22.

106. Ibid., p. 28.

107. Ibid., p. 41.

108. Al-Nābighah al-Dhubyānī, *Dīwān,* pp. 30–37.

109. Al-Anbārī, *Sharḥ al-Qaṣā'id al-Sab',* pp. 517–29.

110. Slochower, *Mythopoesis,* p. 37.

111. Arnold van Gennep, *The Rites of Passage,* trans. Monika B. Vizedom and Gabrielle L. Caffee (Chicago: University of Chicago Press, 1960), pp. 10ff.

112. Ibid., p. 34.

113. According to C. G. Jung, "the triadic numbers are connected with principles of intellectual and physical movement," whereas the number 2, with its "otherness" vis-à-vis the in-itself-unknowable "oneness," only achieves a fixed epistemological stasis. Marie-Louise von Franz expatiates on Jung's thought in this respect in her *Number and Time: Reflections Leading towards a Unification of Depth Psychology and Physics,* trans. Andrea Dykes (Evanston: Northwestern University Press, 1974), pp. 101 and 98.

114. Van Gennep, *The Rites of Passage,* p. xxv.

115. Even Froma I. Zeitlin's very felicitous literary application of the van Gennepian paradigm concerns itself primarily with the liminality part of the "true initiatory experience" of Aeschylus's Orestes, whose personal "passage" takes place inside a structurally not yet identified (or to the critic not explicitly relevant) containing "form." See Froma I. Zeitlin, "The Dynamics of Misogyny: Myth and Mythmaking in the Oresteia," *Arethusa* 11, nos. 1/2 (Spring

and Fall 1978): esp. 160–67. I thank my student Yaseen Noorani for bringing the above article to my attention. Treatment of the liminality aspect alone, without a further linkage with the paradigmatic van Gennepian structure, is also evident in A. C. Spearing's discussion of the *Gawain*-poet's *Purity*. Spearing, however, has a better justification for, theoretically, he falls back directly on Mary Douglas's liminality-centered *Purity and Danger,* of which he says: "I have certainly gained more help from *Purity and Danger* in understanding the way the *Gawain*-poet thinks, and especially in understanding *Purity,* than from any literary criticism or scholarship that I have so far encountered." See his *Readings in Medieval Poetry* (Cambridge: Cambridge University Press, 1989), pp. 173ff.

116. Suzanne Pinckney Stetkevych's conference paper of 1980 was published as "Structuralist Interpretations of Pre-Islamic Poetry: Critique and New Directions," *Journal of Near Eastern Studies* 42, no. 2 (1983): 85–107. See also her subsequent articles "The Ṣuʿlūk and His Poem: A Paradigm of Passage Manqué," *Journal of the American Oriental Society* 104, no. 4 (1984): 661–78; "Al-Qaṣīdah al-ʿArabīyah wa Ṭuqūs al-ʿUbūr: Dirāsah fī al-Bunyah al-Namūdhajīyah," *Majallat Majmaʿ al-Lughah al-ʿArabīyah bi Dimashq* 60, no. 1 (1985): 55–85; "Archetype and Attribution in Early Arabic Poetry: al-Shanfarā and the Lāmiyyat al-ʿArab," *International Journal of Middle East Studies* 18 (1986): 361–90; "Ritual and Sacrificial Elements in the Poetry of Blood-Vengeance: Two Poems by Durayd Ibn al-Ṣimmah and Muhalhil Ibn Rabīʿah," *Journal of Near Eastern Studies* 45, no. 1 (1986): 31–43; "The Rithā' of Ta'abbaṭa Sharran: A Study of Blood-Vengeance in Early Arabic Poetry," *Journal of Semitic Studies* 31, no. 1 (1986): 27–45. These findings are set in a fuller ritual and literary-critical framework in her *The Mute Immortals Speak*.

117. See mainly Victor Turner's *The Ritual Process: Structure and Antistructure* (Ithaca: Cornell University Press, 1977); but also idem, *Dramas, Fields, and Metaphors: Symbolic Action in Human Society* (Ithaca: Cornell University Press, 1975).

118. Mary Douglas, *Purity and Danger: An Analysis of Concepts of Pollution and Taboo* (London: Routledge and Kegan Paul, 1966).

119. Van Gennep, *The Rites of Passage*, p. 11.

120. See esp. S. Stetkevych, "The Ṣuʿlūk and His Poem," pp. 661–78; but also her "Archetype and Attribution," esp. pp. 371ff.; and *The Mute Immortals Speak,* chaps. 3 and 4.

121. In a general and comprehensive way there is to be mentioned once again Victor Turner's *The Ritual Process* and also his *Dramas, Fields, and Metaphors*. Equally relevant are Mary Douglas's *Purity and Danger* and her *Implicit Meanings: Essays in Anthropology* (London: Routledge and Kegan Paul, 1975). Also, as already observed by S. Stetkevych ("The Ṣuʿlūk and His Poem," p. 664; and *The Mute Immortals Speak,* chap. 3), of great interest is the French classicist and cultural anthropologist Vidal-Naquet's distinction between ephebe (liminal) and hoplite (reaggregated). See Pierre Vidal-Naquet, "The Black Hunter and the Origin of the Athenian *Ephebeia,*" in R. L. Gordon, ed., *Myth,*

Religion and Society (Cambridge: Cambridge University Press, 1981), pp. 147–62; idem, "Sophocles' *Philoctetes* and the Ephebeia," in Jean-Pierre Vernant and Pierre Vidal-Naquet, *Myth and Tragedy in Ancient Greece,* trans. Janet Lloyd (New York: Zone Books, 1988), pp. 161–79; also see his definition of the hoplite as specifically a warrior in his essay "Oedipus in Athens," in *Myth and Tragedy in Ancient Greece,* p. 320.

122. Zuhayr Ibn Abī Sulmā, *Dīwān,* p. 86. Ahlwardt, however, claims that this *qaṣīdah*'s short *nasīb* was forged by Khalaf al-Aḥmar. Renate Jacobi restates this claim in her *Studien zur Poetik der altarabischen Qaṣide* (Wiesbaden: Franz Steiner Verlag, 1971), pp. 17–18.

123. Al-Nābighah al-Dhubyānī, *Dīwān,* p. 31.

124. The formal effect and the semiotics of the polarization of gender in the *qaṣīdah* into poet/she-camel and *ẓaʿīnah*/male camel is dealt with in my article "Name and Epithet," pp. 112–20.

125. Imru' al-Qays, *Dīwān,* p. 170.

126. Here we should notice that it has to be the poet himself—the "passenger"—who, on his she-camel, arrives at the water hole only to find the water brackish—for example, the pre-Islamic poet ʿAlqamah Ibn ʿAbadah (*Al-Mufaḍḍalīyāt* [Lyall], p. 778, poem 119, v. 20; [Shākir], p. 394, v. 23); and the *mukhaḍram* ʿAbdah Ibn al-Ṭabīb (ibid. [Lyall], pp. 283–84, poem 26, vv. 45–46). This liminal property of brackish water comes into evidence even more as we move into the Umayyad period, especially with the great practitioner of the *raḥīl* Dhū al-Rummah. If the one arriving at the water hole is the wild ass as the protagonist of an extended simile characterized by exuberant earthiness, the water it encounters is always pure, in spite of the implicit association of danger with the finding of water. The pre-Islamic poet Labīd probably illustrates best the association of the wild ass with clear water. See his *Muʿallaqah,* vv. 34–35 (Al-Anbārī, *Sharḥ al-Qaṣā'id al-Sabʿ,* pp. 552–53).

127. See S. Stetkevych, "Archetype and Attribution," esp. p. 382: "these anti-humans the ṣuʿlūk calls his people (*ahl*)"; and p. 389, where she insists further on the metaphorical principle of "the feralization of the human and the personification (or socialization) of the feral"; see also idem, *The Mute Immortals Speak,* chap. 4.

Notice also that the companions of Aeneas during their escape from flaming Troy—a thoroughly liminal situation—are called wolves (*The Aeneid of Virgil,* ed. T. E. Page [New York: St. Martin's Press, 1967], vol. 1, p. 33 [bk. 2, vv. 355–58]), even as the companions of the *ṣuʿlūk* (brigand) poet al-Shanfarā (*Qaṣīdat Lāmīyat al-ʿArab, wa yalīhā ʿAjab al-ʿAjab fī Sharḥ Lāmīyat al-ʿArab* [Istanbul: Al-Jawā'ib, 1300 H.], vv.- 26–29) are wolves too. For "wolf" as the liminal banished individual in ancient Germanic lore and for *ulfur* (wolves) as the followers and fighting men of Odin, the god of Death, see Hans Peter Duerr, *Dreamtime: Concerning the Boundary between Wilderness and Civilization,* trans. Felicitas Goodman (Oxford: B. Blackwell, 1985), p. 61 (p. 79 in the German text: *Traumzeit,* 5th ed. [Frankfurt am Main: Syndikat, 1980]).

128. See al-Muraqqish the Elder's poem 47 of the *Al-Mufaḍḍalīyāt* (Lyall), p. 466, vv. 12–14; and (Shākir), p. 226, vv. 14–16).

129. We may note here that to Pierre Vidal-Naquet such a hunt is "an expression of the transition between nature and culture" (Jean-Pierre Vernant and Pierre Vidal-Naquet, *Myth and Tragedy in Ancient Greece,* p. 143).

130. *Al-Mufaḍḍalīyāt* (Lyall), pp. 268–93, poem 26. ʿAbdah Ibn al-Ṭabīb's "wa qad ghadawtu" (v. 66) is to be viewed within the formulaic-motival tradition of "wa qad aghtadī," with which Imru' al-Qays opens the theme of the chivalrous hunt in his *Muʿallaqah* (*Dīwān,* p. 19, v. 49; al-Anbārī, *Sharḥ al-Qaṣā'id al-Sabʿ,* p. 82, v. 53). As such it should be a clear indication of referential linkage between the hunt and the banquet. Or else, in its specific phrasing, it represents even more closely an echo of ʿAlqamah's *Mufaḍḍalīyah* (Lyall), p. 817, poem 120, v. 46, where, however, "wa qad ghadawtu ʿalā qirnī" introduces a knightly *fakhr:* "Oft I set out in the morning to face my peer [in combat]."

131. *Al-Mufaḍḍalīyāt* (Lyall), pp. 817–20, poem 120.

132. Zuhayr Ibn Abī Sulmā, *Dīwān,* pp. 128–30, vv. 9–11; and pp. 130–37, vv. 12–29.

133. Al-Anbārī, *Sharḥ al-Qaṣā'id al-Sabʿ,* p. 579.

134. In a verse by the *mukhaḍram* al-Shammākh Ibn Ḍirār al-Dhubyānī, Labīd's younger contemporary and, perhaps more than coincidentally, a strict coeval of al-Ḥuṭay'ah, the concept of *al-ḥimā* comes through with particularly convincing clarity, despite its "verbal" phrasing (*aḥmī,* "I protect"):

I am a man of Banū Dhubyān!
Well do they know that I protect
The unassailable pathway to glory. [171]

See his *Dīwān,* ed. Ṣalāḥ al-Dīn al-Hādī (Cairo: Dār al-Maʿārif bi Miṣr, 1968), p. 119. Here the poet protects—declares inviolable as much as *al-ḥimā* is held inviolable—the "path to water" (*sharīʿah*), which to him is still the original pastoral/heroic "pathway to glory" (*sharīʿatu majdin*); water is the tribe's most precious possession and may not be encroached upon. Ironically, however, precisely in that poet's own lifetime, that pathway to water/glory was being recast semantically and politically and was destined to become the technical term for a wholly new system of communal legality and ethos. Also see above, at nn. 89 and 90.

135. In some recensions of this verse in the *Muʿallaqah,* instead of *al-ḥayy* we find *al-khayl* (the horsemen), for example, in the recension of Abū Zakarīyā al-Tibrīzī (*Sharḥ al-Qaṣā'id al-ʿAshr,* ed. ʿAbd al-Sallām al-Ḥūfī [Beirut: Dār al-Kutub al-ʿIlmīyah, 1405/1985], p. 195). Not even such a variant reading, however, interferes with the semiotics of the *qaṣīdah* in the third stage of the "passage," since horse and horseman are in themselves reintegrative, postliminal entities, clearly delineated as such within the scope of the semiotics of the *qaṣīdah.*

136. For Pierre Vidal-Naquet's discussion of the nonliminal hoplite as opposed to the liminal ephebe and of their role in the hunt (as well as in war), see above, n. 121.

137. Al-Nābighah al-Dhubyānī, *Dīwān,* pp. 36–37. The Euphrates metaphor in al-Nābighah's ode, with its characteristic style of overstretched enjambment and syntactical stress between subject and predicate, comprises lines 45–48. Representative of the great and rapid currency of this metaphor/symbol (together with the peculiarity of its style) in the Arabic panegyric is al-Aʿshā, who follows the "master" al-Nābighah with near-literal approximation (*Dīwān,* pp. 198–99).

138. Kuthayyir ʿAzzah, *Dīwān,* ed. Iḥsān ʿAbbās (Beirut: Dār al-Thaqāfah, 1971), p. 281.

139. Al-Nābighah al-Dhubyānī, *Dīwān,* p. 110.

140. Sibṭ Ibn al-Taʿāwīdhī, *Dīwān* (Beirut: Dār Ṣādir, 1967) (photo-offset of Cairo ed., 1903), p. 238.

141. See above, at n. 88.

142. Abū Tammām, *Dīwān,* vol. 1, p. 161.

Chapter Two

1. But even al-Mutanabbī was capable of some of the most beautiful "Bedouin" *nasīb.* See above, p. 180.

2. Harry Joshua Leon's translation: "Other mountains, other plains, / Other woods and streams / You behold in heaven, and fresher flowers" (*The Pastoral Elegy: An Anthology,* ed., with introduction, commentary, and notes by Thomas Perrin Harrison, Jr. [Austin: University of Texas Press, 1939], p. 96).

3. Usāmah Ibn Munqidh, *Al-Manāzil wa al-Diyār,* ed. Muṣṭafā Ḥijāzī (Cairo: Al-Majlis al-Aʿlā li al-Shuʾūn al-Islāmīyah, 1968), pp. 3–4.

4. Ibid., p. 307.

5. Abū al-ʿAlāʾ al-Maʿarrī, *Shurūḥ Saqṭ al-Zand* (Cairo: Dār al-Kutub al-Miṣrīyah, 1947), bk. 2, vol. 3, p. 974. The above is the fifth verse of a long elegy (sixty-four verses) considered to be one of the finest elegiac poems in Arabic literature (for instance, by Ṭāhā Ḥusayn, *Tajdīd Dhikrā Abī al-ʿAlāʾ,* 5th ed. [Cairo: Dār al-Maʿārif bi Miṣr, 1958], pp. 213–14).

6. Only lines 4 and 5 are actually quoted by Usāmah Ibn Munqidh (*Al-Manāzil wa al-Diyār,* p. 8). For the opening line, and the entire poem, see al-Buḥturī, *Dīwān,* vol. 2, pp. 959–61. In this edition, however, instead of *manāyāhum* in line 4, we find *maṭāyāhum,* which is a comparatively rare reading.

7. Imruʾ al-Qays, *Dīwān,* p. 114.

8. Ibn Sallām al-Jumaḥī (*Ṭabaqāt Fuḥūl al-Shuʿarāʾ,* 2d ed., ed. Maḥmūd Muḥammad Shākir [Cairo: Maṭbaʿat al-Madanī, 1974], vol. 1, p. 39) is the first authority to quote and briefly comment on the above verse by Imruʾ al-Qays.

A comprehensive and detailed, but in the end not very fruitful, survey of the problem of Ibn Ḥidhām or Ḥadhām or Khidhām, etc., is given by Ḥusayn ʿAṭwān in his *Muqaddimat al-Qaṣīdah al-ʿArabīyah fī al-Shiʿr al-Jāhilī,* pp. 73–78. What is important, however, is the fact that, centuries after Imru' al-Qays, a poet like al-Mutanabbī will in one of his finest *nasīb*s link that nebulous predecessor of Imru' al-Qays to the memory of the ʿUdhrī "martyr of love," ʿUrwah Ibn Ḥizām, himself of faint authenticity, thus transforming both traditions into a composite, symbolically valid personification of poetic sorrow, whose tears are contained in all the rain clouds that pass (or shall ever pass) over purely inward-turned, abandoned encampments (Al-Mutanabbī, *Dīwān,* vol. 2, p. 269):

> And as though every cloud that stops there
> Weeps with the eyes of ʿUrwah Ibn Ḥizām. [172]

9. Abū al-Faraj al-Iṣfahānī, *Kitāb al-Aghānī* (Cairo: Al-Mu'assasah al-Miṣrīyah al-ʿĀmmah li al-Ta'līf wa al-Tarjamah wa al-Nashr, 1963) (photo-offset of Dār al-Kutub ed.), vol. 5, pp. 56–57.

10. Ibid., vol. 1, p. 116. There seems to be a specific innovative critical atmosphere developing in the Umayyad period, with al-Farazdaq as its spokesman. Thus his reported approval of the alternative to the *nasīb* offered by ʿUmar Ibn Abī Rabīʿah has a close parallel in his approval of the traditional *nasīb* being replaced by an expression of devotion to the house of Banū Hāshim as proposed by al-Kumayt in his Hāshimī ode that begins:

> I was moved, but not with longing for fair damsels
> Nor to wanton play, as one stirred to passion plays,
>
> Nor was I distracted by abode or trace of habitation
> Nor thrilled to tinted fingertips. [173]

On hearing this poem—at least its opening—al-Farazdaq is reported to have said to al-Kumayt: "You were moved by something that moved no one before you. As for us, like those before us, we are moved by things that no longer move you." He then extended to him the customary *shahādah* of being "the best [most poetic] of the poets past and present" (Muḥammad al-Khuḍarī, ed., *Muhadhdhab al-Aghānī* [Cairo: Maṭbaʿat Miṣr, 1925], vol. 5, pp. 207–8; see also Zakī Mubārak, *Al-Madā'iḥ al-Nabawīyah fī al-Adab al-ʿArabī* [Cairo: Dār al-Shaʿb, n.d.], p. 88).

11. The entire poem does not appear in the *Aghānī.* See ʿUmar Ibn Abī Rabīʿah, *Dīwān* (Beirut: Dār Ṣādir/Dār Bayrūt, 1385/1966), pp. 293–94.

12. A similarly elegant and lively handling of the dialogue may be observed in another Umayyad *ghazal* poet, Waḍḍāḥ al-Yaman. The chronological coincidence of the use of this device by both poets is significant. Two particularly effective dialogued *ghazal*s by Waḍḍāḥ al-Yaman are found in al-Iṣfahānī, *Al-Aghānī,* vol. 8, pp. 216–17. The clearest examples of the dialogued *ghazal* are by a poet who bridges the Umayyad and the Abbasid eras, Bashshār Ibn Burd. It

is undeniable that this type of poem was an important formal innovation. A more comprehensive look at the phenomenon of an Arabic dialogued style, however, will lead us not to love-poetry but to the archaic *qaṣīdah*-integrated theme of the *ʿādhilah* (termagant), with its own characteristic dialogue between the poet and his female interlocutor. The tone of this dialogue is understandably different from that of *ghazal.* It is one of reproach, irony, materialistic domesticity versus chivalrous abandon, and ultimately of stances not unlike those of Stoicism and Epicureanism. The formally most obvious antiposition in the *ʿādhilah* dialogue is, however, that of man to woman. This thus prepares it for its modal adjustment and stylistic transfer into the *ghazal.*

13. I discuss this problem more fully in my article "Sīnīyat Aḥmad Shawqī," pp. 16–17.

14. For a detailed review of the "pioneers" of the trend which culminated in Abū Nuwās, see Muḥammad Muṣṭafā Haddārah, *Ittijāhāt al-Shiʿr al-ʿArabī fī al-Qarn al-Thānī al-Hijrī,* 3d ed. (Cairo: Dār al-Maʿārif bi Miṣr, 1970), pp. 150–57.

15. Abū Nuwās al-Ḥasan Ibn Hāniʾ, *Dīwān,* ed. Aḥmad ʿAbd al-Majīd al-Ghazālī (Cairo: Maṭbaʿat Miṣr, 1953), p. 57.

16. Ibid., p. 37.

17. Gotthold Ephraim Lessing, *Nathan der Weise* (Stuttgart: Philip Reclam Jun., 1975), p. 100 (IV 4).

18. For a discussion of this short type of the *nasīb* as it appears in pre-Islamic poetry and as imitated by Ḥammād al-Rāwiyah, see Jacobi, *Studien zur Poetik der altarabischen Qaṣide,* pp. 7–18.

19. [Ḥassān Ibn Thābit], *Sharḥ Dīwān Ḥassān Ibn Thābit al-Anṣārī,* recension of ʿAbd al-Raḥmān al-Barqūqī (Cairo: Al-Maktabah al-Tijārīyah al-Kubrā, 1929), p. 11 (hereafter, Ḥassān Ibn Thābit, *Dīwān* [1929]).

20. Ibid., pp. 253–54.

21. The city of the Prophet, Medina.

22. Ḥassān Ibn Thābit. *Dīwān* (1929), p. 89.

23. Balāṭ is the area in Medina between the mosque and the marketplace. Gharqad is the old cemetery of Medina.

24. One of the three ritual stations of the "stoning."

25. Ibid., pp. 94–95.

26. When we pursue the development of this particular variety of the elegy-ode into the Abbasid period, we realize how much a poet like Diʿbil Ibn ʿAlī al-Khuzāʿī (d. 244/859 or 246/860) owes to Ḥassān Ibn Thābit. In particular, Diʿbil's *Al-Tāʾīyah al-Kubrā,* which sings the glory and the sorrows of the house of ʿAlī, is an example of formal and symbolic development and at the same time of preservation of a genre. See Diʿbil Ibn ʿAlī al-Khuzāʿī, *Shiʿr Diʿbil Ibn ʿAlī al-Khuzāʿī,* ed. ʿAbd al-Karīm al-Ashṭar (Damascus: Al-Majmaʿ al-ʿIlmī al-ʿArabī, 1964), pp. 71–77.

27. [Ghaylān Ibn ʿUqbah] Dhū al-Rummah, *Dīwān,* 2d ed. (Damascus: Al-

Maktabah al-Islāmīyah li al-Ṭibāʿah wa al-Nashr, 1384/1964), p. 182, poem 17, and p. 587, poem 67. See the discussion of this aspect of Dhū al-Rummah's poetry in Shawqī Ḍayf, *Al-Taṭawwur wa al-Tajdīd fī al-Shiʿr al-Umawī,* 2d ed. (Cairo: Dār al-Maʿārif bi Miṣr, 1959), p. 268.

28. Abū Nuwās, *Dīwān,* p. 3. An English translation of the first six verses of the poem can be found in Reynold A. Nicholson's *Translations of Eastern Poetry and Prose* (Cambridge: Cambridge University Press, 1922), p. 31. A German translation of the entire poem (twenty-five verses) is in Alfred von Kremer, *Dīwān des Abū Nuwās: des grössten lyrischen Dichters der Araber* (Vienna: W. Braumüller, 1855), pp. 26–31. Also see below, chap. 5, at n. 61, for my translation of up to v. 5.

29. Al-Anbārī, *Sharḥ al-Qaṣāʾid al-Sabʿ,* p. 188, v. 48.

30. Our understanding of the term "courtly" is throughout compatible with what C. S. Lewis understands as poetry recited in certain ceremonial surroundings, like festival poetry or forum poetry. Such poetry is then also "a poetry *about* nobles, made *for* nobles, and performed on occasion, by nobles" (my italics). See his *A Preface to Paradise Lost,* pp. 16 and 19.

31. Ḥassān Ibn Thābit, *Dīwān* (1929), pp. 234–35.

32. The *nasīb* is quoted by Usāmah Ibn Munqidh in *Al-Manāzil wa al-Diyār,* pp. 283–84, where it continues with four more verses.

33. This discussion of Abū al-ʿAtāhiyah's *qaṣīdah* was presented at the annual meeting of the American Research Center in Egypt (New York City, Apr. 1985), under the title "The Elegiac Landscape in the Late Classical Arabic *Qaṣīdah.*" Since the time I completed the manuscript of the present book, there has come to my attention an article on this *qaṣīdah* by Michael Zwettler. Although it covers some of the same ground, it is otherwise concerned with aspects of allusion which I did not intend to go into, so as not to diffuse my principal formal-symbolic focus. I consider of added interest, however, Zwettler's idea that the occurrence in the closing verse of the ode of the reference to Caliph al-Hādī as *kabīr* may be a Qurʾān-based allusion to Moses, which was also al-Hādī's given name. Such an allusion sheds light on the complex politics of caliphal succession between Hārūn al-Rashīd and al-Hādī. See Michael Zwettler, "The Poetics of Allusion in Abu l-ʿAtāhiya's Ode in Praise of al-Hādī," *Edebiyât,* n.s. 3, no. 1 (1989): 1–29.

34. Al-Iṣfahānī, *Al-Aghānī,* vol. 4, pp. 60–62. In v. 9, I have chosen A. J. Arberry's reading of *al-daqīq* instead of *al-dafīn* (buried). See his *Arabic Poetry: A Primer for Students* (Cambridge: Cambridge University Press, 1965), p. 49.

35. A. Richard Turner, *The Vision of Landscape in Renaissance Italy* (Princeton: Princeton University Press, 1966), p. 161.

36. On wine and other symbols of Paradise, see Suzanne Pinckney Stetkevych, "Intoxication and Immortality: Wine and Associated Imagery in al-Maʿarrī's Garden," in Fedwa Malti-Douglas, ed., *Critical Pilgrimages: Studies in the Arabic Literary Tradition,* in *Literature East and West* 25 (1989): 29–48.

37. See Byron's *Childe Harold's Pilgrimage,* Canto 4, lines 703–11.

38. The phrasing of the poem's closing verse points in the direction of the qur'ānic attribution of maturity and wisdom to Jesus while still in his cradle (Sūrat Āl ʿImrān, v. 46, and Sūrat al-Māʾidah, v. 110).

39. The Iraqi archeologist ʿAbd al-Sattār al-ʿIzzāwī, who excavated and did extensive archeological exploratory work in the area of Kufa and al-Ḥīrah, expressed in detailed conversations with me serious doubts regarding the likelihood of there ever having existed in the immediate vicinity of old al-Ḥīrah any structure of a magnitude that would even come close to the size of the legendary Khawarnaq. Al-Ḥīrah itself, as an "urban" settlement, is to him still a highly mystifying riddle precisely concerning the small size of its former structures, not to mention the, to him, hypothetical Khawarnaq. While working on the archeological remains of the Old Pilgrimage Road out of Kufa, he found no evidence to substantiate any so-called historical reports regarding the historicity of Khawarnaq ("Ṭarīq al-Ḥajj al-Qadīm: Darb Zubaydah—Maḥaṭṭat Umm al-Qurūn," *Sūmir* 44 [1985–86]: 199–213).

An important text about the state of al-Ḥīrah during the time of the persecution of the last Umayyads presents us with the image of a "ghost town" in which a fugitive would have chosen to hide, one like Ibrāhīm Ibn Sulaymān Ibn ʿAbd al-Malik, who, not knowing anyone in the vicinity, in Kufa, for instance, had to seek refuge in al-Ḥīrah's desolation. The text tells us that the "city" directly faced the desert; but it also tells us that at least some of its buildings must still have had roofs on which to hide and from which to overlook the "hostile" countryside. See Usāmah Ibn Munqidh, *Lubāb al-Ādāb,* ed. Aḥmad Shākir (Cairo: Dār al-Kutub al-Salafīyah, 1407/1987), p. 128.

40. For a discussion of the significance of the temple of Shīz and of *khvarne* as symbols of Iranian kingship, see Lars-Ivar Ringbom's *Graltempel und Paradies: Beziehungen zwischen Iran und Europa im Mittelalter* (Stockholm: Wahlstrom and Widstrand, 1951), esp. pp. 86ff., 112ff., 218–29.

41. Aside from the quite unsatisfactory treatment that Khawarnaq's historicity and etymology receive at the hand of Massignon in both editions of the *Encyclopaedia of Islam* (e.g., "old ed.," vol. 1, p. 585), there are lengthy and multifaceted discussions of *khvarne* by Lars-Ivar Ringbom in *Graltempel und Paradies;* and by H. W. Bailey in *Zoroastrian Problems in the Ninth-Century Books: Ratanbai Katrak Lectures* (Oxford: Clarendon Press, 1971), esp. the introduction and chaps. 1 and 2. On Khawarnaq, see Mohammad Moʿīn's Persian dictionary *Farhang-e Farsi* (Tehran: Amir Kabir Publications, 1966), vol. 1 (of the dictionary); vol. 5 (the encyclopedia) gives the word *khavarnaq* as the Arabicized version of *xoran-gāh* or *xoran-gah*. Niẓāmī's etymological understanding of Khawarnaq is to be derived from the way it occurs in his *Haft Paykar.* I am grateful to my student Franklin Lewis for his expert Persian lexicographical assistance.

42. The fullest version of Munakhkhal al-Yashkurī's poem appears in *Al-Aṣmaʿīyāt,* pp. 58–61, poem 14. In it the Khawarnaq motif falls wittily into a well-executed, fully form-conscious "closure." This approach to the poem's resolution is almost too "innovative" for an early *qaṣīdah,* however. Abū Tam-

mām's *Ḥamāsah* version of this poem is discussed in S. Stetkevych, *Abū Tammām and the Poetics of the ʿAbbāsid Age,* pp. 307–11.

43. Al-Aswad Ibn Yaʿfur al-Nahshalī's poem is no. 44 of *Al-Mufaḍḍalīyāt* (Lyall), p. 449, v. 9. See also Ibn Qutaybah, *Al-Shiʿr wa al-Shuʿarāʾ,* vol. 1, p. 44; the poet's *Dīwān,* ed. Nūrī Ḥamūdī al-Qaysī (Baghdad: Maṭbaʿat al-Jumhūrīyah, 1970), pp. 26–28; and *Averroes' Middle Commentary on Aristotle's Poetics,* trans. Charles Butterworth (Princeton: Princeton University Press, 1986), p. 135.

44. Ṭarafah Ibn al-ʿAbd, *Dīwān,* ed. Durrīyah al-Khaṭīb and Luṭfī al-Ṣaqqāl (Damascus: Maṭbaʿat Dār al-Kitāb, 1395/1975), p. 153.

45. See commentary on Ṭarafah's *Muʿallaqah* in al-Anbārī's *Sharḥ al-Qaṣāʾid al-Sabʿ,* p. 123.

46. Ibid., p. 118 (part of al-Anbārī's commentary on Ṭarafah's *Muʿallaqah*).

47. Luwīs Shaykhū, *Kitāb Shuʿarāʾ al-Naṣrānīyah,* 2d ed. (Beirut: Dār al-Mashriq, 1967), vol. 1, pp. 442–43.

48. Al-Aʿshā, *Dīwān,* p. 117.

49. The curious thing in this case is that Ibn Rushd assumes that Khawarnaq and Sadīr in that pre-Islamic poet's time were already *elegiac* relics of "lost kingdoms." The search of an *ubi sunt* illustration obviously prevails here over any need to think historically (*Averroes' Middle Commentary on Aristotle's Poetics,* p. 135).

50. Egyptologists recognize that the name of the temple complex of Karnak is not ancient Egyptian. It is wrong, however, to rest satisfied, as Kuentz does, with an etymologically uprooted and symbolically meaningless approximation and suggest that Karnak is merely "an old Arabic term" for a fortified village. See *Lexikon der Ägyptologie,* ed. Wolfgang Helck and Eberhard Otto (Wiesbaden: Otto Harrassowitz, 1975–86), vol. 3, p. 341, with reference to Paul Barquet, drawing upon Charles Kuentz, *Actes du Congrés international de toponymie et d'anthroponymie de juillet 1949 à Bruxelles,* (1951), p. 293. I owe my reference to the above entry in the *Lexikon* to Professor Edward F. Wente. Not very helpful and unrelated to Karnak (although one should be able to draw some symbolic inferences in very general terms) is the entry on *khawarnaq* by the geographer Shihāb al-Dīn Abū ʿAbd Allāh Yāqūt Ibn ʿAbd Allāh al-Ḥamawī in *Muʿjam al-Buldān* (Beirut: Dār Ṣādir/Dār Bayrūt, 1375/1956), vol. 3, pp. 401–4.

51. The ʿUdhrī version of the same motif comes from Majnūn's famous *Al-Muʾnisah:*

> I leave the house behind, perhaps
> At night, in solitude, I'll speak,
> with myself, of you. [174]

See Majnūn Laylā, *Qays Ibn al-Mulawwaḥ al-Majnūn wa Dīwānuh,* ed. Shawqīyah Inaljiq (Ankara: Maṭbaʿat al-Jamʿīyah al-Tārīkhīyah al-Turkīyah, 1967), p. 84. Ibn Rashīq tells us something of Dhū al-Rummah that gives theoretical backing to otherwise perfectly sufficient poetic testimony. The poet apparently practiced poetic solitude for creative purposes. Interestingly enough, however, most of the testimony introduced by Ibn Rashīq concerning solitude as a creative habit pertains to the Umayyad period (see *Al-ʿUmdah,* vol. 1, pp. 206–7).

52. Dhū al-Rummah, *Dīwān,* p. 706.

53. Al-Sharīf al-Raḍī, *Dīwān* (Beirut: Dār Sādir, 1961), vol. 1, p. 181. There is, however, an ancient tragic symbolism attached to "looking back," such as in the story of Lot's wife or in that of Orpheus and Euridice. The dangers of looking back were also part of Arabic lore. Thus in a fifteenth-century source we read: "As for 'looking back' [*al-iltifāt*], they maintained that if one went out on a journey but looked back, his journey would not come to fruition. Thus, if he looked back, they would practice augury in his behalf" (Muḥammad Ibn Aḥmad al-Khaṭīb al-Ibshīhī, *Al-Mustaṭraf min Kulli Fann Mustaẓraf* [Cairo: Būlāq, 1268 H.], vol. 2, pp. 90–91).

54. Quoted from Usāmah Ibn Munqidh, *Al-Manāzil wa al-Diyār,* p. 219. The poet's "remaining in body when the heart had left" also means that the poet sees himself "deposited in his grave," which is also the archaic poetic meaning of *muqīm*. *Al-shaṭṭ* (strand) may also be a place-name.

55. Al-Sharīf al-Raḍī, *Dīwān,* vol. 2, p. 107. The pastoral metaphor of the poet's "garden of the heart" is not uncommon in Arabic poetry. Usāmah Ibn Munqidh quotes some appropriate verses by Abū al-Ḥasan al-Tihāmī (*Al-Manāzil wa al-Diyār,* p. 220).

56. I choose to quote this verse as it appears in *Al-Manāzil wa al-Diyār* (p. 342). Cf. Mihyār al-Daylamī, *Dīwān* (Cairo: Dār al-Kutub al-Miṣrīyah, 1930), vol. 3, p. 327, v. 4, where, instead of the "decree" or "verdict" of love (*ḥukmu l-hawā*), we have the "preservation" of love (*ḥifẓu l-hawā*).

57. Ibrāhīm Ibn Abī al-Fatḥ Ibn Khafājah al-Andalusī, *Dīwān* (Alexandria: Munsha'at al-Maʿārif, 1960), p. 237. It is of interpretive significance that Ibn Khafājah's rather "pastoral" and idyll-like "as passion awakens passion" should in fact be a direct and conscious borrowing from a verse out of an elegy by Mutammim Ibn Nuwayrah which that *mukhaḍram* poet composed at the death of his brother Mālik. In it the poet answers his travel companion's rebuke for shedding copious tears over every grave he encounters:

"Passion awakens passion," I said to him,
"So let me be, for all these are Mālik's graves." [175]

See Abū Tammām, *Sharḥ Dīwān al-Ḥamāsah,* ed. Aḥmad Amīn and ʿAbd al-Salām Hārūn (Cairo: Lajnat al-Ta'līf wa al-Tarjamah wa al-Nashr, 1952), vol. 2, pp. 797–98, poem 265. To be noted is the circularity in the poetic use of the motifs of love-elegiac and threnodic passion and sorrow and of the remonstrating as well as consoling travel companion—once again both in the *nasīb* and in that particular early elegy. Also see the discussion of Mutammim Ibn Nuwayrah's elegy in S. Stetkevych, *Abū Tammām and the Poetics of the ʿAbbāsid Age,* pp. 319–20. Here we may also want to turn to al-Mutanabbī's evocation of the ʿUdhrī "martyr of love" ʿUrwah Ibn Ḥizām (see above, n. 8). Furthermore, if the general legend of Majnūn was responsible for much of the popularity of the cult of love in Ibn Khafājah's times, a close parallel motif is provided by Jamīl, the lover of Buthaynah:

> My young she-camel yearningly groaned, and I listened,
> At the sandy tract of Ludd, as she but dragged herself along. [176]

See Jamīl Ibn Maʿmar al-ʿUdhrī, ***Dīwān Jamīl Buthaynah*** (Beirut: Dār Ṣādir, 1966), p. 16.

The thematic antecedent of the pining Majnūn is the mythological Sicilian shepherd Daphnis, the disciple of Pan and originator of pastoral poetry. Entirely in the ʿUdhrī manner, he dies in sworn chastity for love of the nymph Xenea. All nature, animate and inanimate, first pines with him and then mourns over him. This, the most idealized version of the myth, was immortalized poetically by Theocritus:

> And Tityrus, beside me, will sing songs
> of Daphnis and his love for Xenea;
> and of the weeping of the hills around
> and of the oaks which sang a dirge for him
> beside Himera's waters, while he lay,
> pining, melting away like mountain snow
> on high Haemus, on Athos, Rhodope,
> on distant Caucasus. . . .

See Anthony Holden, trans., *Greek Pastoral Poetry,* Penguin Books, 1974, pp. 75–76.

58. Majnūn in his sorrow and Majnūn as poet resemble Orpheus, the Thracian poet who possessed the ability to charm animals and even inanimate nature and who, according to some scholars, may have been an archetypal and mythogenically efficacious personification. Not unlike Majnūn, that Thracian poet became a legendary, and then mythical, figure under whose name many poems were circulated. But as a "charmer" through song he was not an archaic Greek satirist—let's say an anthropological forerunner of Archilochus—nor was he an ancestor of Celtic charmer-poets who possessed the power to kill; or, at any rate, at some very early protomythological stage he must have developed from Orpheus the charmer-hunter and fisher to Orpheus the charmer or sympathetic gatherer of chthonic life and the opener of gates to the underworld. Thus Orpheus was closer to the broader "religious" poetic quality of Majnūn than to that of a "shaman" (*The Oxford Classical Dictionary,* 2d ed., ed. N. G. L. Hammond and H. H. Scullard [Oxford: Clarendon Press, 1970], p. 758; and esp. Robert Eisler, *Orpheus—The Fisher: Comparative Studies in Orphic and Early Christian Cult Symbolism* [London: J. M. Watkins, 1921], p. 16).

59. Wylie Sypher obviously follows Wölfflin when he states, "It is simply a matter of history that certain periods do reach a coherent style." But possessing a style does not automatically entail superior artistic quality, which may

manifest itself equally well in a period of stylization. If "academism" is a style, then "there is . . . nothing necessarily charismatic about a style, and in particular a classic style" (*Rococo to Cubism in Art and Literature* [New York: Vintage Books, 1960], pp. 154–55).

60. Ibn Khafājah, *Dīwān,* p. 128.

61. ʿUmar Ibn al-Fāriḍ, *Dīwān* (Beirut: Dār Ṣādir, 1957), pp. 177–78.

62. See above, p. 80.

63. Muḥyī al-Dīn Ibn ʿArabī, *Tarjumān al-Ashwāq* (Beirut: Dār Ṣādir, 1961), p. 47.

64. Ibn al-Fāriḍ, *Dīwān,* pp. 166–68. I have stayed with the reading of this poem's first line as it is in the Beirut edition. ʿAbd al-Khāliq Maḥmūd's edition of the *Dīwān* contains the name Salmā instead of Laylā (Ibn al-Fāriḍ, *Dīwān,* ed. ʿAbd al-Khāliq Maḥmūd [Cairo: Dār al-Maʿārif, 1984], p. 227). There are no further textual discrepancies.

65. See in Ibn al-Fāriḍ's *Dīwān,* p. 123, the poem beginning "*A wamīdu barqin,*" and p. 128, the poem beginning "*Hal nāru Laylā badat,*" and also a related opening of the poem on p. 117: "*Araju al-nasīmi sarā.*"

66. Jarīr [Ibn ʿAṭīyah], *Dīwān* (Beirut: Dār Ṣādir, 1964), p. 314.

67. Al-Buḥturī, *Dīwān,* vol. 3, p. 1927.

68. See above, at n. 60.

69. These verses of Majnūn Laylā sometimes appear preceded by one or two lines of somewhat discordant meaning, as in *Dīwān Majnūn Laylā,* ed. ʿAbd al-Sattār Aḥmad Farrāj (Cairo: Maktabat Miṣr, [1973]), pp. 292, 297; but they also open the poem, as in the Ankara edition, pp. 81, 90, 99.

70. Ibn al-Abbār Abū ʿAbd Allāh Muḥammad Ibn ʿAbd al-Quḍāʾī al-Andalusī, *Al-Muqtaḍab min Kitāb Tuḥfat al-Qādim,* ed. Ibrāhīm al-Abyārī (Cairo: Al-Maṭbaʿah al-Amīrīyah, 1957), pp. 51–52.

The place-name Laʿlaʿ, which already in its old, semantically multifaceted poetic usage is connected with ʿUdhayb, is, however, pre-Islamic in its earliest occurrences. See, for example, al-Ḥārith Ibn Ḥillizah, *Dīwān,* ed. Hāshim al-Ṭaʿʿān (Baghdad: Maṭbaʿat al-Irshād, 1969), pp. 17 and 26 (note). The true poetic distinction of this place-name is not pre-Islamic, however.

71. Émile Mâle, *The Gothic Image: Religious Art in France of the Thirteenth Century,* trans. Dora Nussey (New York: Harper and Row, Icon Editions, 1972), p. 22, n. 4.

72. Erich Auerbach, *Dante, Poet of the Secular World,* trans. Ralph Manheim (Chicago: University of Chicago Press, 1969), p. 20. Edgar Wind is less charitable in his reference to "vulgar spiritualism," which he traces through the humanistic revival of Orphism. Discussing Pico della Mirandola, he calls this phenomenon "less a 'revival of the classics' than a recrudescence of that ugly thing which has been called 'late-antique syncretism.'" But Edgar Wind recognizes that Pico della Mirandola "persistently claimed . . . that in the recondite and often monstrous decomposition which the classical heritage suffered

in the Hellenistic age, the genuine and permanent foundations of the classical achievement are laid bare." See his *Pagan Mysteries in the Renaissance,* rev. and enl. ed. (New York: W. W. Norton and Co., 1968), p. 22.

73. For a discussion of the problem of the *figura,* see Erich Auerbach, *Mimesis: The Representation of Reality in Western Literature,* trans. Willard R. Trask (Princeton: Princeton University Press, 1968), pp. 73ff., 116, 157–58, 195–96.

74. C. S. Lewis, *The Discarded Image: An Introduction to Medieval and Renaissance Literature* (Cambridge: Cambridge University Press, 1970), esp. chap. 4.

75. Mâle, *The Gothic Image,* p. vii.

76. Ibn ʿArabī, *Tarjumān.* Part of the commentary of this *Dīwān* has been translated into English by Reynold A. Nicholson (*The Tarjumān al-Ashwāq: A Collection of Mystical Odes, by Ibn ʿArabī* [London: Royal Asiatic Society, 1911]).

77. Ibn ʿArabī, *Tarjumān,* p. 101.

78. Ibid., p. 35.

79. Ibid., p. 75.

80. Ibid., p. 13.

81. Ibid., p. 20.

82. Ibid., p. 110.

83. Auerbach, *Mimesis,* p. 119.

84. This passage out of *De bestiis et aliis rebus* is quoted directly from Mâle, *The Gothic Image,* p. 30. Even if the source of the above "description" of the dove may not be the work of Hugh of St. Victor, it is nevertheless very much in the spirit and the style of what M.-D. Chenu calls Hugh of St. Victor's symbolically "valid poetico-theological 'demonstrations.'" See M.-D. Chenu, *Nature, Man, and Society in the Twelfth Century,* selected, ed., and trans. Jerome Taylor and Lester K. Little (Chicago: University of Chicago Pres, 1968), p. 104.

85. Ibn ʿArabī, *Tarjumān,* p. 15.

86. Ḥasan al-Būrīnī and ʿAbd al-Ghānī al-Nābulusī, *Sharḥ Dīwān Ibn al-Fāriḍ* (Cairo: Al-Maṭbaʿah al-ʿĀmirah al-Sharafīyah, 1306/1888).

87. On "absolute absence"/"absolute essence" (*al-ghayb al-muṭlaq*) see ʿAlī Ibn Muḥammad al-Jurjānī, *Kitāb al-Taʿrīfāt* (Cairo: Al-Maṭbaʿah al-Khayrīyah, 1306/1888), p. 70.

88. Al-Būrīnī and al-Nābulusī, *Sharḥ Dīwān Ibn al-Fāriḍ,* vol. 2, pp. 110–11.

89. The al-Būrīnī and al-Nābulusī commentary is based on a text which has here the name Salmā instead of Laylā (ibid., p. 110).

90. Quoted from Chenu's *Nature, Man, and Society in the Twelfth Century,* p. 99.

91. Such is also the title of one of the essays in ibid. (chap. 3).

92. See my discussion of Goethe's poem *Lied und Gebilde,* in "Arabic Poetry and Assorted Poetics," pp. 103–5.

93. Richard McKeon's essay "Poetry and Philosophy in the Twelfth Century: The Renaissance of Rhetoric" (in R. S. Crane, ed., *Critics and Criticism, Ancient and Modern* [Chicago: University of Chicago Press, 1968], pp. 297–

318) gives a concise but, in an exemplary way, problem-oriented review of the symbolic allegorical turn in medieval poetry during this crucial literary period.

94. See a somewhat more extensive discussion of the Sūrah of the Poets, with some literal repetition, however, in my article "Arabic Hermeneutical Terminology: Paradox and the Production of Meaning," *Journal of Near Eastern Studies* 48, no. 2 (Apr. 1989): 84.

95. Herbert Reed, *Icon and Idea: The Function of Art in the Development of Human Consciousness* (New York: Schocken Books, 1972). I am referring directly to p. 88, but chaps. 3 and 5 are relevant to the present discussion.

96. William Wordsworth, *The Prelude, or Growth of a Poet's Mind,* ed. Ernest de Selincourt, 2d rev. ed. by Helen Darbishire (Oxford: Clarendon Press, 1959), pp. 168–69, vv. 555–56 (1850 ed.) and vv. 578–79 (1805–6). It is interesting to note that in the 1805–6 text the entire phrase "their own sakes" appears in italics.

97. "Ponete mente almen com'io son bella!" Thus in the apostrophe-tornata of the canzone *Voi che 'ntendendo il terzo ciel movete* (*Il convivio,* Collezione di Classici Italiani, vol. 4 [Torino, 1927], pp. 35, 39).

98. In a somewhat broader sense, however, we should take notice of Dante's soundness of critical approach to this question in *Il convivio* (1.1). In his discussion of the four levels of meaning of a text, Dante concludes that "in thus expounding, the literal sense should always come first as the one in the meaning whereof the others are included, and without which it were impossible and irrational to attend to the others, and specifically to the allegorical." Translation quoted from *The Convivio of Dante Alighieri,* Temple Classics (London, 1903), pp. 64–65. Dante restates, and modulates, his exposition of the four levels of textual interpretation in his Latin *Epistle to Can Grande,* meant to introduce *Il paradiso* to that former patron, Can Grande della Scala. See Charles Sterrett Latham, *A Translation of Dante's Eleven Letters* (Boston and New York: Houghton Mifflin Co., 1891), pp. 193–94. For a discussion of the pertinent passage, see *The Comedy of Dante Alighieri the Florentine,* trans. Dorothy L. Sayers (New York: Basic Books, 1962), pp. 44–48. One ought to be able to link Dante's method of interpretation—and in certain respects the Arabic one as well—to the Stoic heremeneutical tradition, because that tradition rested primarily "on the recognition in texts or myths of three levels of meaning—literal, ethical, and metaphysical." See Robert Lamberton, *Homer the Theologian: Neoplatonist Allegorical Reading and the Growth of the Epic Tradition* (Berkeley and Los Angeles: University of California Press, 1989), p. 47.

Chapter Three

1. Al-Qāḍī al-Fāḍil [ʿAbd al-Raḥīm Ibn ʿAlī al-Baysānī], *Dīwān,* ed. Aḥmad Aḥmad Badawī (Cairo: Dār al-Maʿārif, 1961), vol. 1, p. 91. See also one of the earliest Islamic poetic references to Medina in Ibn Muqbil, *Dīwān,* ed. ʿIzzat Ḥasan (Damascus: Maṭbūʿāt Mudīrīyat Iḥyāʾ al-Turāth al-Qadīm, 1381/1962), p. 283, poem 37, v. 1 (rhyming in *mā*); as well as an equally early reference to

the Sassanid al-Madā'in by ʿAbdah Ibn al-Ṭayyib, in *Al-Mufaḍḍalīyāt* (Lyall), p. 268, poem no. 26, v. 2 (rhyming in *lū*).

2. Al-Qāḍī al-Fāḍil, *Dīwān,* vol. 2, pp. 494–95, no. 612. This poet's yearning for his native Syria is as close to his "unreserved" yearning for his adopted Egypt as it is to the connotatively *primary* ancient Bedouin yearning for the *awṭān*.

3. Manṣūr al-Namarī, *Shiʿr Manṣūr al-Namarī,* ed. al-Ṭayyib al-ʿAshshāsh (Damascus: Dār al-Maʿārif li al-Ṭibāʿah, 1401/1981), pp. 140–41, poem 52.

4. See the discussion of Abū Nuwās above, in chap. 2, section 1.

5. Cf. the appearance of the *ẓaʿāʾin* in Ṭarafah's *Muʿallaqah,* vv. 3–5. See al-Anbārī, *Sharḥ al-Qaṣāʾid al-Sabʿ,* pp. 135–38.

6. Manṣūr al-Namarī, *Shiʿr Manṣūr al-Namarī,* p. 116, poem 33.

7. Aḥmad Ibn Muḥammad al-Maqqarī al-Tilimsānī, *Nafḥ al-Ṭīb min Ghuṣn al-Andalus al-Raṭīb—wa Dhikr Wazīrihā Lisān al-Dīn Ibn al-Khaṭīb,* ed. Muḥammad Muḥyī al-Dīn Ibn al-Ḥamīd (Beirut: Dār al-Kitāb al-ʿArabī, [1967?]), vol. 1, p. 284.

8. Maud Bodkin, *Archetypal Patterns in Poetry: Psychological Studies of Imagination* (Oxford: Oxford University Press, 1968), pp. 105–6.

9. Marcel Proust, *À la recherche du temps perdu* (Paris: Gallimard, 1954), vol. 1, pp. 390–91 (*Swann III,* "Noms de pays: le nom").

10. John Stevens, *Medieval Romance,* pp. 148–49. Cf. also the discussion of the representation and the naming of space in Chrétien de Troyes, by Wolfram Völker, *Märchenhafte Elemente bei Chrétien de Troyes* (Bonn: Rheinische Friedrich-Wilhelm-Universität, 1972), pp. 74–105. In a direction that leads away from my genre-centered approach, André Miquel and Percy Kemp discuss place-names in the Majnūn Laylā material in terms of Roland Barthes's distinction between *atopie* and *utopie.* To them Majnūn's madness alone transforms reality, creating the *irréel,* not the *deréel.* See André Miquel and Percy Kemp, *Majnûn et Laylâ: l'amour fou* (Paris: Sindbad, 1984), pp. 81–90, esp. p. 88.

11. ʿAlī Ibn al-Jahm, *Dīwān,* 2d ed., ed. Khalīl Mardam (Beirut: Dār al-Āfāq al-Jādīdah, [1979?]), pp. 141–43.

12. On al-Ruṣāfah and al-Jisr with regard to the city of Baghdad, see Jacob Lassner, *The Topography of Baghdad in the Early Middle Ages: Text and Studies* (Detroit: Wayne State University Press, 1970), pp. 149–54.

13. The tradition of the Ruṣāfah of Hishām was continued in al-Andalus by ʿAbd al-Raḥmān I, who built himself a Ruṣāfah of his own where he could dream the nostalgic dreams of one who still saw himself as an exile. It should also be noted that ʿAbd al-Raḥmān's Ruṣāfah did not seek the river. Between it and the river lay the city. It yearned, as it were, toward the open countryside, toward the surrogate desert. Above all, interpretively and metaphorically valid in this context is the attribution to ʿAbd al-Raḥmān I of two elegiac epigrams in which Ruṣāfah and its lonely palm-tree are still primarily the exponents of Bedouinizing Umayyad nostalgia. See the varying texts and attributions of the

poems in Ibn al-Abbār [Abū ʿAbd Allāh al-Quḍāʾī], *Al-Ḥullah al-Sayrāʾ*, ed. Ḥusayn Muʾnis (Cairo: Al-Sharikah al-ʿArabīyah li al-Ṭibāʿah wa al-Nashr, 1963), vol. 1, p. 37; and Aḥmad Ibn Muḥammad al-Maqqarī al Tilimsānī, *Nafḥ al-Ṭīb min Ghuṣn al-Andalus al-Raṭīb,* vol. 2, pp. 716–18. For a comprehensive treatment of the subject of the Ruṣāfah of ʿAbd al-Raḥmān I and the palm-tree as the expression of his nostalgia, see H. Peres, "Le palmier en Espagne musulmane: notes d'après les textes arabes," *Mélanges Gaudefroy-Demombynes* (Cairo: Imprimerie de l'Institut Français, 1937), pp. 226–29.

14. As an echo of ʿAlī Ibn al-Jahm comes to us a contemplative elegy by al-Ruṣāfī al-Balansī (d. 572/1176) in which the poet's two imaginary companions are invoked to halt at Ruṣāfah and the Pont in the certainty that their thirst will be quenched by rains destined to fall over those privileged places:

Halt uncommanded and, assured of rain,
Thirst and invoke the drops to fall.

At the Pont of Maʿān, at Ruṣāfah—
surely,
Rain must fall on Ruṣāfah and the Pont! [177]

See [Abū ʿAbd Allāh Muḥammad Ibn Ghālib] al-Ruṣāfī al-Balansī, *Dīwān,* ed. Iḥsān ʿAbbāṣ (Beirut: Dār al-Thaqāfah, 1960), p. 69. In this poem we deal with a real place-name, the Ruṣāfah of Valencia, which was a garden-suburb that separated the city from the sea. As for the Jisr, which also existed, what intrigues us here are the various ways in which *bi jisri maʿānin* may be understood: from "abode," "halting-place," "inn," "tavern," "place of visibility," to "meanings" and "discreet intimations."

15. Al-Anbārī, *Sharḥ al-Qaṣāʾid al-Sabʿ,* pp. 15 and 20. Note al-Anbārī's comment explaining *fa* (and) *Ḥawmali* as implying *ilā* (toward) *Ḥawmali.*

16. Abū Bakr Muḥammad Ibn al-Ṭayyib al-Bāqillānī, *Iʿjāz al-Qurʾān,* ed. Aḥmad Ṣaqr (Cairo: Dār al-Maʿārif, 1963), pp. 160–221; and Gustave E. von Grunebaum, *A Tenth Century Document of Arabic Literary Theory and Criticism: The Sections on Poetry of al-Bāqillānī's Iʿjāz al-Qurʾān* (Chicago: University of Chicago Press, 1950), pp. 61–62, 93. I have appropriated much of von Grunebaum's phrasing.

17. See J. Stetkevych, "Arabic Hermeneutical Terminology," pp. 83–87.

18. For a discussion of the attempts to locate the paradise of Genesis by way of the four rivers flowing out of it, see Lars-Ivar Ringbom, *Graltempel und Paradies,* pp. 257, 266ff. For an interesting, etymology-based interpretation of the place-names in Imruʾ al-Qays's *nasīb,* see Adnan Haydar, "The Muʿallaqa of Imruʾ al-Qays: Its Structure and Meaning, I," *Edebiyât,* 2, no. 2 (1977): 238–41. I consider Adnan Haydar's method of viewing the place-names in this *nasīb* to be fully valid within given methodological restrictions and as long as the appropriate hermeneutical level of the total reading of the *nasīb* is observed. As such, the method should be analogically applicable to the reading of the *nasīb* from the pre-Islamic period through much of the Umayyad period.

19. Notice, for instance, the description of the stormy waters of the Euphrates in al-Nābighah al-Dhubyānī's *Yā dāra Mayyata,* vv. 45–47 (*Dīwān,* p. 36).

20. For references to other early-Arabic poetic occurrences of the ʿAqīq, see Ulrich Thilo, *Die Ortsnamen in der altarabischen Poesie* (Wiesbaden: Otto Harrassowitz, 1958), pp. 29–30. In poetically deeply rooted names such as al-ʿAqīq, it is hermeneutically helpful to be aware of their place within a broad spectrum of etymology, phonetic crossovers, and semantics. Thus J. C. Vadet's emphasis on the ritual function of *ʿaqīqah* (hair of a young just born) and its connection with the theme-premises of the classical Arabic *nasīb,* that is, with binding, pledging, and dedication. See the entry "*ḳalb*" in the *Encyclopaedia of Islam,* new ed., vol. 4, p. 488. For the ʿAqīq as the Prophet Muḥammad's "blessed valley," and for its *ḥimā*, see ibid., vol. 1, p. 336.

21. Imru' al-Qays, *Dīwān,* p. 169.

22. Al-Anbārī, *Sharḥ al-Qaṣā'id al-Sabʿ,* p. 437 (Al-Ḥārith Ibn Ḥillizah's *Muʿallaqah,* vv. 6–7).

23. Shaykhū, *Shuʿarā' al-Naṣrānīyah,* vol. 1, p. 767.

24. Al-Buḥturī, *Dīwān,* vol. 4, p. 2422.

25. Ibn al-Jahm, *Dīwān,* p. 37.

26. Quoted by Usāmah Ibn Munqidh (*Al-Manāzil wa al-Diyār,* p. 65) as attributed to Saydūk al-Wāsiṭī, and then also to al-Rustumī, it seems, in a bracketed addition. See ibid., the editor's footnote (n. 2).

27. Ibn Zaydūn, *Dīwān Ibn Zaydūn wa Rasā'iluh,* ed. ʿAlī ʿAbd al-ʿAẓīm (Cairo: Maktabat Nahḍat Miṣr bi al-Fajjālah, 1957), p. 131.

28. Ibn Khafājah, *Dīwān,* pp. 258–61. The paraphrased verses are 1–4, from p. 258.

29. Ibid., p. 116.

30. Al-Nuʿmān ʿAbd al-Mutaʿālī al-Qāḍī (*Shiʿr al-Futūḥāt al-Islāmīyah fī Ṣadr al-Islām* [Cairo: Dār al-Qawmīyah, 1965], p. 257) observes correctly that the motif of nostalgia for regions was not known in the pre-Islamic *qaṣīdah,* although the Jāhilīyah Arabs were departing continually, traveling from one place to another.

31. Arthur Heiserman, *The Novel before the Novel: Essays and Discussions about the Beginnings of Prose Fiction in the West* (Chicago: University of Chicago Press, 1977), pp. 4–10.

32. Ṭāhā Ḥusayn, *Ḥadīth al-Arbiʿā'* (Cairo: Dār al-Maʿārif bi Miṣr, 1954), vol. 1, pp. 216–18.

33. Thus the Najdi warrior-poet Qā'id Ibn Ḥakīm al-Rabʿī, as he faces death in distant Egypt, beseeches his "two companions" to carry his salute back to Najd:

Friends, if in Egypt my fate overtakes me
And you're resolved there to dig my grave,

Yet to the tamarisks, to Najd,
Forget not to send my salute,
never small, never scant. [178]

See Maḥmūd Shukrī al-Ālūsī, *Bulūgh al-Arab fī Maʿrifat Aḥwāl al-ʿArab* (Beirut: Dār al-Kutub al-ʿIlmīyah, n.d.), vol. 1, p. 201.

34. Majnūn Laylā, *Dīwān* (Ankara ed.), p. 36.

35. Ibid., p. 40; and Ibn al-Dumaynah, *Dīwān* (Cairo: Maktabat al-ʿUrūbah, 1959), p. 85. Ibn al-Dumaynah is said to have lived in southern Ḥijāz, in Yamāmah, as well as in Medina. His life span in not ascertained with precision either, but he may have died as late as the caliphate of Hārūn al-Rashīd (Sezgin, *Geschichte des arabischen Schrifttums,* vol. 2, *Poesie: bis ca. 430 H.*, pp. 445–46).

36. Majnūn Laylā, *Dīwān* (Ankara ed.), p. 14.

37. Abū Tammām, *Al-Ḥamāsah,* commentary by al-Tibrīzī, ed. Freytag (Bonn, 1828), p. 539. In the Cairo edition of the *Ḥamāsah,* with al-Marzūqī's commentary, p. 1216, this poem is joined to another fragment and v. 2 is missing.

38. Friedrich Rückert's title for the poem is "Abschied vom idyllischen Hochland." See his *Hamâsa, oder, die ältesten arabischen Volkslieder, gesammelt von Abû Temmâm* (Stuttgart: Samuel Gottlieb Liesching, 1846), vol. 2, p. 69.

39. In the Cairo edition of the al-Marzūqī recension (pp. 1240–41), this poem is attributed to al-Ṣimmah Ibn ʿAbd Allāh al-Qushayrī. The Freytag edition (p. 548), with commentary by al-Tibrīzī, introduces the poem by way of "*qāla ākharu.*"

40. Al-Maʿarrī, *Shurūḥ Saqṭ al-Zand,* vol. 1, pp. 390–91.

41. Ibn Khafājah, *Dīwān,* p. 294.

42. Ibn al-Fāriḍ, *Dīwān* (Beirut ed.), pp. 120–21.

43. Ibid., p. 117.

44. Ibn Khaldūn, *Al-Taʿrīf bi Ibn Khaldūn wa Riḥlatih Gharban wa Sharqan,* ed. Muḥammad Ibn Tāwīt al-Ṭanjī (Cairo: Lajnat al-Taʾlīf wa al-Tarjamah wa al-Nashr, 1370/1951), p. 48. According to the printed text, line 2 ends on the irregular rhyme *al-jurdu* instead of *al-jurdi.* The former would, of course, produce the charming reading "Did well-groomed steeds prance in its plains?"

45. Bruno Snell, *Die Entdeckung des Geistes: Studien zur Entstehung des europäischen Denkens bei den Griechen,* 4th ed. (Göttingen: Vandenhöck and Ruprecht, 1975), p. 273.

46. Margarethe Werner-Fädler, *Das Arkadienbild und der Mythos der goldenen Zeit in der französischen Literatur des 17. und 18. Jahrhunderts* (Salzburg: Institut für romanische Philologie der Universität Salzburg, 1972), p. 27.

47. Erwin Panofsky, "*Et in Arcadia Ego:* Poussin and the Elegiac Tradi-

tion," in idem, *Meaning in the Visual Arts* (Garden City, N.Y.: Doubleday, 1955), pp. 295–320; see also Werner-Fädler, *Das Arkadienbild,* p. 47, n. 1; regarding "misprision," see Harold Bloom, *Anxiety of Influence: A Theory of Poetry* (New York: Oxford University Press, 1973), pp. 19ff. Also see below, chap. 4, n. 28.

48. Especially as regards the geographical confines of Najd as traditionally viewed, see Al-Ālūsī, *Bulūgh al-Arab,* vol. 1, pp. 199–201.

49. For a historical overview of the kingdom of Kindah (a topic that needs more research), see *The Encyclopaedia of Islam,* new ed., s.v. "*Kinda,*" by I. Shahīd and A. F. L. Beaston. Reaching into the present, we may see in the Najd centricity of the kingdom of Saudi Arabia almost an ideological reenactment of the attempt of the Kindah dynasty to anchor in Najd their Arabian Peninsular idea of the state.

50. Aelian's association of the Arcadian Styx with the magic resiliency of the horns of the Scythian Asses (i.e., unicorns), the only "vessels" capable of holding those waters, add but one more jewel to Arcadia's symbolic crown. In its own way, however, it also *interprets.* See *On the Characteristics of Animals,* trans. A. F. Scholfield, Loeb Classical Library, vol. 2, pp. 335–37 (10.40).

51. *Paulys Realenzyclopädie der classischen Altertumswissenschaft,* ed. Georg Wissowa (Stuttgart: J. B. Metzlerscher Verlag, 1895), vol. 3, p. 1119.

52. The two quotations are from the eminently relevant book by Nicole Loroux, *The Invention of Athens: The Funeral Oration in the Classical City,* trans. Alan Sheridan (Cambridge: Harvard University Press, 1986), p. 442, n. 16.

53. Polybius, *The Histories,* trans. W. R. Paton, Loeb Classical Library, vol. 2, p. 349 (bk. 4, chap. 20).

54. J. M. Edmonds, trans., *The Greek Bucolic Poets,* Loeb Classical Library, pp. 102–3. References to Arcadia, although not necessarily by name, or to things Arcadian are numerous in the *Idylls* of Theocritus. See Thomas G. Rosenmeyer, *The Green Cabinet: Theocritus and the European Pastoral Lyric* (Berkeley and Los Angeles: University of California Press, 1969), pp. 232–46 ("Arcadia"). For the turning away from direct references to Arcadia in the pastoral idylls of post-Vergilian Greek and Latin literatures, see Herta Wendel, *Arkadien im Umkreis bukolischer Dichtung in der Antike und in der französischen Literatur,* (Giessen: Giessener Beiträge zur romanischen Philologie, 1933), pp. 30–46.

55. Polybius, *The Histories,* pp. 349, 351, 353.

56. A strong echo of this myth is found in the First Voyage of Sindbad the Seaman, in the *Arabian Nights,* in which "noble mares" are brought to the seashore "every month, about new-moon tide" to be impregnated by the "stallions of the sea." The translator of the *Nights,* Richard F. Burton, observes in a note to this story, "The myth of mares being impregnated by the wind was known to the Classics of Europe," although he does not identify the specific mythic character of the zephyr in this Helleno-Arabic mythopoeia. See Rich-

ard F. Burton, *A Plain and Literal Translation of the Arabian Nights' Entertainments, now entitled The Book of the Thousand Nights and a Night* (Burton Club for Private Subscribers, n.d.), vol. 6, pp. 7–9.

57. Denys Page, *Sappho and Alcaeus: An Introduction to the Ancient Lesbian Poetry* (Oxford: Clarendon Press, 1983), p. 269.

58. Edmonds, *The Greek Bucolic Poets,* pp. 30–31. We come close to the meaning and effect of the Arcadian plant "horse-madness" in the Arabian/Najdi "tangled, luxuriant grass" called *al-jamīm,* which "arouses," "bewitches," and "maddens" the wild ass/onager, as in *asʿalahū l-jamīmu,* "whom tangled, luxuriant grass has maddened" (i.e., has affected like a *ghūl* or *siʿlāh*). See *Al-Mufaḍḍalīyāt* (Lyall), poem 6, v. 12, by Salamah Ibn al-Khurshub al-Anmārī.

59. Jacopo Sannazaro, *Arcadia and Piscatorial Eclogues,* trans. Ralph Nash (Detroit: Wayne State University Press, 1966), pp. 108–9.

60. Willis Barnstone, trans., *Greek Lyric Poetry* (New York: Schocken Books, 1972), p. 165. The same line is translated by W. R. Paton in the Loeb Classics edition of the *Greek Anthology,* vol. 1, p. 327, as "Zephyr the richest of all winds."

61. Sannazaro, *Arcadia and Piscatorial Eclogues,* p. 165.

62. Ibid., p. 191.

63. Homer, *The Odyssey,* trans. R. Fitzgerald (Garden City, N.Y.: Doubleday, 1961), p. 81 (4.563–68). Instead of the translator's "West Wind," I have insisted on the original "Zephyr."

64. Ibid., p. 126. Here, too, rather than Fitzgerald's "West Wind," the literal reference to this wind is "Zephyr."

65. Shihāb al-Dīn Aḥmad Ibn ʿAbd al-Wahhāb al-Nuwayrī, *Nihāyat al-Arab fī Funūn al-Adab* (Cairo: Dār al-Kutub al-Miṣrīyah, 1923), vol. 1, p. 97.

66. Ibid., p. 95.

67. Abū al-ʿAbbās Muḥammad Ibn Yazīd al-Mubarrad, *Al-Kāmil fī al-Lughah wa al-Adab,* ed. Muḥammad Abū al-Faḍl Ibrāhīm (Cairo: Maktabat Nahḍat Miṣr, 1956), vol. 3, p. 62. It is worth speculating whether, and in what way, this anecdote ought to be related to v. 62 of Labīd's *Muʿallaqah* (*Dīwān,* p. 176), where it is the North Wind which drives the indigent clients to set claim to the poet's gallantry and generosity. Even if that verse were the source of the anecdote, however, once *rīḥu al-shamāli* becomes *al-ṣabā,* then, together with the manifest virtue of generosity, other positive qualities, too, are bound to attach themselves to the poet. The anecdote thus works within the semiotics of hagiography rather than of *fakhr.*

68. Lane, *Arabic-English Lexicon,* root *d-b-r.*

69. Cf. Genesis 41:6, 23, 27; Ezekiel 17:10, 19:12; Hosea 13:15; Jeremiah 18:17; Job 15:2. It should be of further interest to keep in mind that the word-term *ṣabā,* or one etymologically relatable to it, has no presence in the Hebrew lexicon.

70. Imru' al-Qays, *Dīwān,* pp. 170–71.

71. ʿAbīd Ibn al-Abraṣ, *Dīwān,* p. 41.

72. Shaykhū, *Shuʿarāʾ al-Naṣrānīyah,* vol. 1, p. 279.

73. Ibid., p. 443. In the *khabar* (report) that accompanies this poem we are given to understand, however, that the "lord of Khawarnaq and Sadīr" is not the Sassanid suzerain but the vassal king Nuʿmān of al-Ḥīrah. Furthermore, contrary to the tenor of the poem's elegiac reference to those palaces, it is the transitoriness of humans alone that is insisted upon in the *khabar.* This gives the impression of an attempt to save the verses themselves from appearing anachronistic. The time references of the poem, however, cannot be easily saved, for the poem is as confusing as its *khabar.* This contributes to substantive doubts about the textual authenticity of both. See the discussion of Khawarnaq with reference to Abū al-ʿAtāhiyah's *Lahfī ʿalā al-zamani al-qaṣīri* above, chap. 2, section 3.

74. Imruʾ al-Qays, *Dīwān,* p. 30.

75. This verse is found in al-Anbārī's *Sharḥ al-Qaṣāʾid al-Sabʿ,* p. 29, where it is v. 8; so, too, in al-Zawzanī's recension of the *Muʿallaqāt* (Abū ʿAbd Allāh al-Ḥusayn Ibn Aḥmad Ibn al-Ḥusayn al-Zawzanī, *Sharḥ al-Muʿallaqāt al-Sabʿ* [Cairo: Maktabat wa Maṭbaʿat Muḥammad ʿAlī Ṣabīḥ wa Awlādih, 1367/1948], p. 7). In Ahlwardt's *The Divans* (p. 146) it is v. 6. In the text of the *Muʿallaqah* in Imruʾ al-Qays's *Dīwān* (p. 15), its wording is slightly different and its placement in the poem is that of v. 29. On the whole, this verse suffers from a highly unstable placement in other recensions as well.

In the context of the analogy I am presently drawing between *al-ṣabā* and "zephyr," it is quite intriguing to note that in 1783, when Goethe translated the *nasīb* fragment of the *Muʿallaqah* of Imruʾ al-Qays through that ode's English rendition (1774) by William Jones, he nevertheless chose to change in our presently discussed verse Jones's "the eastern gale" to "*Westwind.*" What lies, one must ask, behind such a glaring departure from the philological authority of Jones? Was Goethe simply negligent or distracted by Jones's English archaism of calling the gentle *nasīm al-ṣabā* an "eastern gale"? Or was Goethe, the consummate classicist, simply another perpetrator of creative "misprision" precisely *because* he was a classicist, for whom the gentle Arabian wind from the east, in a compulsive poetic association, as it were, had become the zephyr, and thus *der Westwind?* For a convenient juxtaposition of both the Jones and the Goethe texts, see Katharina Mommsen, *Goethe und die arabische Welt* (Frankfurt am Main: Insel Verlag, 1988), p. 55. One more poem sheds further light on Goethe's complex understanding of the Arabian *al-ṣabā:* see below, n. 97.

76. Imruʾ al-Qays, *Dīwān,* p. 340.

77. *Al-Mufaḍḍalīyāt* (Lyall), p. 54, poem 8, v. 6. See a similar occurrence of *al-ṣabā* in a poem by Subayʿ Ibn al-Khaṭīm al-Taymī, in ibid., p. 731, poem 112, v. 21.

78. Ṭarafah Ibn al-ʿAbd, *Dīwān,* p. 83.

79. See above, at n. 35.

80. Abū Tammām, *Ḥamāsah* (Marzūqī), p. 1332, poem 532.

81. Abū Muḥammad Jaʿfar Ibn Aḥmad Ibn al-Ḥusayn al-Sarrāj, *Maṣāriʿ al-*

ʿUshshāq (Beirut: Dār Ṣādir, n.d.), vol. 2, p. 78. In the *Dīwān* of Majnūn (ed. ʿAbd al-Sattār Aḥmad Farrāj), pp. 113–14, the poem to which the above line belongs is poem 94 and is longer by two lines and has a different order of lines.

82. Abū Tammām, *Ḥamāsah* (Marzūqī), p. 918, poem 311.

83. Ibn Abī Rabīʿah, *Dīwān,* p. 146.

84. Ibid., p. 130.

85. Ibid., p. 294.

86. Muslim Ibn al-Walīd [Ṣarīʿ al-Ghawānī], *Sharḥ Dīwān Ṣarīʿ al-Ghawānī,* 2d ed., ed. Sāmī al-Dahhān (Cairo: Dār al-Maʿārif bi Miṣr, 1970), p. 132.

87. Ibn al-Jahm, *Dīwān,* pp. 56–57.

88. Al-Buḥturī, *Dīwān,* vol. 2, p. 1045. This being v. 2 of the elegy, my addition of the "halting place" is a reference to *maḥallun* in v. 1, which, importantly, also means "a funeral meeting."

89. [Abū Bakr Aḥmad al-Ḍabbī al-Anṭākī] al-Ṣanawbarī, *Dīwān,* ed. Iḥsān ʿAbbās (Beirut: Dār al-Thaqāfah, 1970), p. 454. For a full translation and discussion of this poem, see below, chap. 5, section 2.

90. Ibn Zaydūn, *Dīwān,* p. 144.

91. Ibn Khafājah, *Dīwān,* p. 116.

92. Ibid., p. 136.

93. Ibid., p. 125.

94. Ibid., p. 193.

95. Ibid., p. 137.

96. Ibn al-Abbār, *Al-Muqtaḍab min Kitāb Tuḥfat al-Qādim,* p. 51.

97. Aḥmad Shawqī, *Al-Shawqīyāt* (Cairo: Al-Maktabah al-Tijārīyah al-Kubrā, 1970), vol. 2, pp. 45–46. The motif of the East Wind/*al-ṣabā* is also admirably correctly identified by Goethe, who links it with the ultimate *locus amoenus* of the Islamic celestial Paradise. There he lets it carry a swarm of celestial maidens into the presence of those among the faithful who fell in the battle of Badr:

> Und nun bringt ein süsser Wind von Osten
> Hergeführt die Himmelsmädchenschar.

See Johann Wolfgang Goethe, *Gedichte,* ed. Stefan Zweig (Stuttgart: Philip Reclam, Jun., 1983), p. 172 (poem beginning "Seine Toten mag der Feind betrauern"). See, however, above, n. 75.

98. F. Max Müller, *Comparative Mythology,* ed. A. Smyth Palmer (New York: Dutton, 1909). See also Richard M. Dorson, ed., *Peasant Customs and Savage Myths: Selections from the British Folklorists* (Chicago: University of Chicago Press, 1968), vol. 1, pp. 66–119.

99. Although the Greek zephyr in its morphological configuration (*qālib*) resembles so closely the Arabic onomatopoeic *zafīr,* this does not preclude the validity—primary or associative—in the Greek as well as in the Latin case of another and broader onomatopoeic pool that includes *psóphein,* "to make a sound such as whistling," and *spirare,* "to blow" (wind), "to breathe."

Chapter Four

1. J. D. Carlyle, *Specimens of Arabian Poetry: From the Earliest Time to the Extinction of the Khaliphat,* 2d ed. (London: T. Cadell, 1810), p. 4.

2. Sir William Jones speaks of the *Muʿallaqah* of Labīd as "purely pastoral, and extremely like the *Alexis* of Vergil, but far more beautiful, because it is more agreeable to nature" (*Poems* [Oxford: Clarendon Press, 1772], p. 184).

3. Carlyle, *Specimens of Arabian Poetry,* p. 4.

4. This does not necessarily mean that the efficacy of the pastoral as a pervading literary type remains entirely unrecognized today. William Empson's *Some Versions of Pastoral* (New York: New Directions, 1968) alone would disprove such a categorical denial.

5. From Ovid's *Amores* (1.13.40), also translated by Marlowe himself (Ovid, *The Amours* [Philadelphia, 1902], pp. 134–35). Marlowe includes his adaptation of the less dramatically phrased Ovidian line in *Dr. Faustus,* 5.2.

6. See below, at n. 43.

7. Fray Luis de León appropriated Horace's *Epode* 2 twice, once through direct translation ("Dichoso el que de pleitos alejado, / cual los del tiempo antiguo, / labra sus heredades no obligado") and once in the freely assimilated, and considerably more influential *Canción de la vida solitaria:*

> !Qué descansada vida
> la del que huye el mundanal ruido
> y sigue la escondida
> senda, por donde han ido
> los pocos sabios que en el mundo han sido:
> . . . !

In this poem, too, there is still fresh the memory of "del sabio Moro, en jaspes sustentado." See Fray Luis de León, *Poesía completa,* ed. Guillermo Serés (Madrid: Clásicos Taurus, 1990), pp. 316 and 53 respectively. Also see Gilbert Highet, *The Classical Tradition: Greek and Roman Influences on Western Literature* (Oxford: Oxford University Press, 1970), p. 245.

8. Johan Huizinga, *Men and Ideas* (New York: Harper Torchbooks, 1970), pp. 84, 85. See also Empson, *Some Versions of Pastoral.*

9. In his own pastoral reflections, Wordsworth captures the idea of the unconsciousness of pastoral happiness:

> So that we love, not knowing that we love,
> And feel, not knowing whence our feeling comes,

only to awaken to the externality of his real perspective:

> This, alas!
> Was but a dream; the times had scattered all
> These lighter graces.

Pristine, pastoral happiness is therefore an existential state. It is perceived and understood only by the poet as onlooker, even as the witness to his own, recollected past. The poet is therefore no longer a pastor. He has already lost his happiness and his innocence: he knows, he is reflexive—and melancholy. See *The Prelude,* bk. 8, lines 170–71 and 203–5.

10. Homer, *Odyssey,* 4.561–68.

11. Panofsky, *Meaning in the Visual Arts,* p. 300. The "discovery of the evening," of course, is a rewording from Oscar Wilde's "The Decay of Lying" (1889): "At present people see fogs, not because there are fogs, but because poets and painters have taught them the mysterious loveliness of such effects." Vergil was in an eminent way such a poet. In Ovid's *Fasti* (5.315–24), A. Bartlett Giamatti notices a measure of the same melancholy in the neglect of what was an ideal garden. "To waste a garden is the proper external symbol of a man's interior disintegration and uneasiness" (*The Earthly Paradise and the Renaissance Epic* [Princeton: Princeton University Press, 1966], p. 42).

12. Alexander Heidel, *The Gilgamesh Epic and Old Testament Parallels* (Chicago: University of Chicago Press, 1965), p. 68.

13. This archaic concept is still alive in Isaiah 11:6–9. See also W. Robertson Smith, *The Religion of the Semites* (New York: Meridian Books, 1957), p. 307. We should also note here that it is out of the Edenic background that both the shamanistic "master of animals" and the master-pastor arise.

14. Song of Songs 4:12.

15. Giamatti, *The Earthly Paradise,* pp. 13–14 (also see n. 11 above); and Highet, *The Classical Tradition,* pp. 163–65.

16. As Giamatti observes, "Indeed, it would not be unfair to say that the Christian poets plundered Elysium to decorate the earthly paradise" (*The Earthly Paradise,* p. 15). Or, as Jean Seznec could add, through allegory, "all mythology is nothing more—or pretends to be nothing more—than a system of ideas in disguise, a 'secret philosophy.'" This gives allegory an unlimited dialectic dimension (Jean Seznec, *The Survival of the Pagan Gods: The Mythological Tradition and Its Place in Renaissance Humanism and Art,* trans. Barbara F. Sessions [Princeton: Princeton University Press, 1972], p. 321).

17. The translation of Claudian's *Epithalamium* used by Giamatti is from the Loeb edition. See his discussion in his *The Earthly Paradise,* pp. 50ff.

18. Giamatti, *The Earthly Paradise,* p. 53.

19. Ibid., p. 61.

20. "Je fui liez e bauz e joianz; / Et sachiez que je cuidai estre / Por voir en parevis terestre" (Guillaume de Lorris and Jean de Meung, *Le Roman de la Rose* [Paris: Librairie de Firmin-Didot et Cie., 1920], vol. 2, p. 33, vv. 634–36; translation in Giamatti, *The Earthly Paradise,* p. 62).

21. Thus Saint John of the Cross: "Yo no supe donde entraba, / pero, cuando allí me vi, / sin saber donde me estaba, / grandes cosas entendí; / no diré lo que sentí / que me quedé no sabiendo." See *Vida y obras de San Juan de la Cruz; biografía inédita del Santo por Crisógono de Jesús,* 3d ed., ed. Lucinio del SS. Sacramento and Matias del Niño Jesus (Madrid: Biblioteca de Autores Cristianos, 1955), p. 1311.

22. C. S. Lewis points out that, within such a distinction, the ideal of courtly love, too, must be "unreal" (*The Allegory of Love: A Study in Medieval Tradition* [New York: Oxford University Press, 1971], pp. 151–53).

23. The full title is *Paraiso cerrado para muchos, jardines abiertos para pocos,* published together with *Los fragmentos del Adonís* (1652) in *Obras de Don Pedro Soto de Rojas,* ed. Antonio Gallego Morell (Madrid, 1950), pp. 385–428. There is also a beautiful essay by García Lorca on the nature of the poetry of Granada which derives its tenor from Pedro Soto de Rojas and his suggestive title (Federico García Lorca, *Obras completas* [Madrid: Aguilar, 1954], pp. 3–7).

24. *Poems of Michael Drayton* (London: Routledge and Kegan Paul, 1953), vol. 1, p. 206, lines 101–4.

25. The great development of the theme connected with the discovery of the New World is only beginning to produce literary results.

26. Miguel de Cervantes Saavedra, *El ingenioso hidalgo Don Quijote de la Mancha,* Clásicos Castellanos, 8th ed. (Madrid: Espasa-Calpe, 1964), pt. 1, chaps. 11–14.

27. Vergil, *Eclogues,* ed. Robert Coleman (Cambridge: Cambridge University Press, 1977), p. 69 (Eclogue 10.35).

28. Erwin Panofsky, in his essay "*Et in Arcadia Ego:* Poussin and the Elegaic Tradition," develops the theme of the almost intentional mistake in interpretation of the favorite elegiac epigram (*Meaning in the Visual Arts,* pp. 295–320). I am tempted to suggest that the persistent misinterpretation of *Et in Arcadia ego* may have occurred under the influence of precisely the Vergilian *utinam ex vobis unus vestrique fuissem* (Eclogue 10.35), which demanded a coming true of the bucolic wish. It is also interesting to notice that in Persian miniature painting the almost identical treatment of the "true" *Et in Arcadia ego* exists. See, for example, the depiction of Majnūn at Laylā's tomb in the manuscript written for Iskandar, sultan at Shiraz (1410) (David Talbot Rice, *Islamic Art* [London: Thames and Hudson, 1965], p. 216).

29. It is significant that Cervantes should speak of the labyrinth precisely in the pastoral digression of the *Quijote* (pt. 1, chap. 11, pp. 253–54).

30. In Homer the labyrinth is represented as a dance floor. This may be the first attested literary representation of a symbolic labyrinth. It is from this dance along the path of the labyrinth that the Gothic cathedrals may have developed the so-called *chemins de Jerusalem.* Thus symbol and decorativeness blend with equal effectiveness in the tiled winding design on the floor of Chartres Cathedral, and similar labyrinths once existed in the naves of the cathedrals of Reims and Amiens. The labyrinth's center is formed by the mystic rose. The soul's progress through the maze to the rose is then also an evocative symbolic pilgrimage to the Holy Land. According to Hans Jantzen, however, we do not know with any degree of certainty whether these labyrinths really possessed any religious significance, "as is sometimes supposed." See his *High Gothic: The Classic Cathedrals of Chartres, Reims, Amiens,* trans. James Palmes (New York: Pantheon Books, 1962), pp. 83–85. Among those who "suppose" a symbolic—and ritually/religiously relevant—meaning for these labyrinths and a relationship to the Homeric occurrences is Dieter Hennebo, who relies on A. Griesbach. See Dieter Hennebo, *Gärten des Mittelalters* (Hamburg: Broscheck Verlag, 1962), p. 105. The most recent and, to my mind, the most comprehen-

sive treatment of these questions concerning the labyrinth is Penelope Reed Doob's *The Idea of the Labyrinth from Classical Antiquity through the Middle Ages* (Ithaca: Cornell University Press, 1990), see esp. chaps. 2 and 5.

31. Abū al-Faraj al-Iṣbahānī, *Kitāb al-Aghānī,* ed. Ibrāhīm al-Abyārī (Cairo: Dār al-Shaʿb, 1969), vol. 2, p. 429 (henceforth referred to as *Al-Aghānī* [Dār al-Shaʿb]); and Majnūn Laylā, *Dīwān* (Cairo ed.), p. 238. For a discussion of the "persona" and the story of Majnūn as reflected in *Al-Aghānī,* see Miquel and Kemp, *Majnûn et Laylâ,* esp. pp. 213–56.

32. Al-Iṣbahānī, *Al-Aghānī* (Dār al-Shaʿb), vol. 2, p. 430.

33. Majnūn, *Dīwān* (Ankara ed.), p. 45; and Majnūn, *Dīwān* (Cairo ed.), p. 164.

34. To give to this specific image its full due, we must not lose sight of the fact that especially an Umayyad poet's reference to his beloved as dwelling on a high, unscalable mountain evokes first of all the "pastoral" image of the beloved as a mountain antelope.

35. Ibn al-Dumaynah, *Dīwān,* pp. 97–98.

36. Ibid., p. 172.

37. Majnūn, *Dīwān* (Ankara ed.), p. 64. In the Cairo edition by Farrāj (pp. 85–87) this motif occurs in a slightly different version, aside from being expanded through a repetition of its variants both as topical and stylistic clusters. One more version in the form of "another" poem—as far as the arrangement of motifs is concerned—is given in al-Iṣbahānī, *Al-Aghānī* (Dār al-Shaʿb), vol. 9, p. 3403, where this motif forms the closure rather than the opening of the composition. There, however, it is not attributed to Majnūn but to "a Bedouin" and is said to have been favored by Caliph al-Wāthiq (p. 3402). My thanks to Professor ʿIzz al-Dīn Ismāʿīl for helping clarify these verses.

38. Ibn Khafājah, *Dīwān,* p. 333. The lyrical quality which Ibn Khafājah perceived in Majnūn's lines is in its own turn something the Majnūn poem owes to the topical refinement and stylization of phrasing of earlier poets, such as the "Companion" Mutammim Ibn Nuwayrah al-Yarbūʿī (*Al-Mufaḍḍalīyāt* [Lyall], pp. 541–42, poem 67):

41. No passion of three foster-nursing,
love-bonded she-camels is as strong—
When of their unweaned foal they find
the dragged trail and death-place.

42. The sorrowful, the sad one they remind of his great pain:
When plaintively the first one calls, the others groan in unison.

43. When the elder one among them lets resound her yearning moan,
Her anguish makes the whole resting herd moan too.

44. No, none was more stricken than I, on the day
When the herald of Mālik's death spoke his word
of the fatal parting.

In Mutammim Ibn Nuwayrah's poem, instead of an *aʿrābīyah* (a Bedouin maiden, but also, a desert-reared she-camel), we find three *aẓʾār* (she-camels trained to nurse unweaned camel-orphans). So, too, the poetess al-Khansāʾ, still characterized as pre-Islamic in spite of qualifying as *mukhaḍramah,* compares her own sorrow over the loss of her brother Ṣakhr with the sorrow of an *ʿajūl* (a she-camel pining over the loss of her newborn) and her perplexity over the taxidermically prepared mock-foal (*baww*) that is meant to secure the flow of her milk (Tumāḍir Bint ʿAmr Ibn al-Ḥārith Ibn ʿAmr al-Khansāʾ, *Dīwān,* redaction of al-Shaybānī, ed. Anwar Abū Suwaylim [Amman: Dār ʿAmmār, 1409/1988], pp. 381–85 [vv. 11–14]). Such "classical" precedents establish, in the first place, this motif's firm elegiac, even dirgelike roots, and it is this that explains the affinity of tone between Majnūn's idyllic *aʿrābīyah* and the inherently elegiac semantics of both the three *aẓʾār* and the *ʿajūl.* The Majnūn poem could thus build with ease on such empathetic she-camels of the older poets, albeit now transformed into a Bedouin maiden and transported to a new *nasīb-ghazal* context. As for Ibn Khafājah, he is a true interpreter of an entire tradition: he allows us to see clearly that already in the late pre-Islamic period and in the generation of the "companions," poets had spoken of their own souls through the symbol of the she-camel. The same motif, both topically and in its characteristic phrasing by way of the overstretched enjambment, may also be found in the *mukhaḍram* poet of the tribe of Hudhayl, Sāʿidah Ibn Juʾyah, where, instead of the bereft she-camel, we have a gazelle, "mother of a fawn" (*mughzil*) (*Dīwān al-Hudhalīyīn* [Cairo: Dār al-Qawmīyah li al-Ṭibāʿah wa al-Nashr, 1385/1965] [photo-offset of the Dār al-Kutub ed., 1945–50], vol. 2, pp. 211–14, vv. 5–14). As such it enters into the Umayyad motif repertory through the poet ʿAbd Allāh Ibn al-Dumaynah (*Dīwān,* p. 51). Returning to the she-camel, the motif with its specific phrasing appears in its simplest—and perhaps oldest—form in the *Muʿallaqah* of ʿAmr Ibn Kulthūm, v. 15 (Al-Anbārī, *Sharḥ al-Qaṣāʾid al-Sabʿ,* p. 384). Concerning the fullness of the elegiac semiotics of the "three *aẓʾār*" of Mutammim Ibn Nuwayrah and their strong symbolic linkage with the motif of *al-athāfī,* the "three hearthstones" of the "abandoned encampment," see my study, "Toward an Arabic Elegiac Lexicon: The Seven Words of the *Nasīb,*" in S. Stetkevych, ed., *Reorientations.*

39. I. Goldziher, "Bemerkungen zur neuhebräischen Poesie," *Jewish Quarterly Review* 14 (1902): 734–36.

40. In spite of being appreciative of the beauty and frequency of occurrence of this motif, Gustave E. von Grunebaum merely adds to Goldziher's textual references his own substantial listing of its instances. This addendum speaks for itself as far as the scholar's personal fascination with the motif is concerned. In critical terms, however, a remark like "Dieses Motiv hat vielleicht die verhältnismässig persönlichste Behandlung erfahren und ist, aus heidnischer wie aus islamischer Zeit, in einigen Passagen von bemerkenswerter Schönheit uns überliefert" fails to take us beyond the stage of an interest in the cataloguing of assorted motifs (*Kritik und Dichtkunst: Studien zur arabischen Literaturgeschichte* [Wiesbaden: Otto Harrassowitz, 1955], p. 31).

41. Luṭfī ʿAbd al-Badīʿ, *ʿAbqarīyat al-ʿArabīyah fī Ruʾyat al-Insān wa al-Ḥayawān wa al-Samāʾ wa al-Kawkab* (Cairo: Maktabat al-Nahḍah al-Miṣrīyah, 1976), pp. 113–14.

42. Nuṣrat ʿAbd al-Raḥmān, *Al-Ṣūrah al-Fannīyah fī al-Shiʿr al-Jāhilī fī Ḍawʾ al-Naqd al-Ḥadīth* (Amman: Maktabat al-Aqṣā, 1976), p. 38.

43. Al-Nābighah al-Dhubyānī, *Dīwān,* p. 9.

44. For Muhalhil Ibn Rabīʿah's elegy, see Shaykhū, *Shuʿarāʾ al-Naṣrānīyah,* vol. 1 (pre-Islamic), pp. 163–64.

45. Al-Khansāʾ, *Dīwān,* p. 290, vv. 2–3.

46. Ibid., p. 388.

47. Ibid. In v. 22, I have adopted the reading in which *ibn nahīk* is the direct object of *naʿā* and *akhū thiqah* is the subject of *naʿā.*

48. Abū Tammām, *Dīwān,* vol. 3, pp. 160–61.

49. Ḥassān Ibn Thābit, *Dīwān,* (Cairo, 1929), p. 18. The readings *taṣawwaba* (v. 1) and *taghayyaba* (v. 2) have been adopted in accordance with the edition of the poet's *Dīwān* by Walīd ʿArafāt (Beirut: Dār Ṣādir, 1974), vol. 1, p. 116.

50. Al-Buḥturī, *Ḥamāsah,* 2d ed. (Beirut: Dār al-Kitāb al-ʿArabī, 1967), p. 35, poem 150.

51. ʿAntarah Ibn Shaddād, *Dīwān* (Beirut: Dār al-Kutub al-ʿIlmīyah, 1405/1985), p. 29.

52. The motif of the Bier's Daughters (*banātu naʿshin*) occurs in all the periods of classical Arabic poetry. The stars called by that name are in the constellations of both the Large and the Small Dipper (i.e., Ursa Major and Ursa Minor). The latter points with its Bier's Daughters precisely toward the North Star, and it is in this visualization that it is used, for instance, by Waḍḍāḥ al-Yaman (d. 93/712) (Abū Tammām, *Ḥamāsah* [Marzūqī], vol. 2, p. 244, poem 212). Otherwise, as in al-Mutanabbī (*Dīwān,* vol. 1, p. 208), the Bier's Daughters are seen—much more explicitly than is the case in the line by Bishr Ibn Abī Khāzim—as "maidens (*ẓaʿāʾin*) in mourning." As illustrated in al-Rāzī al-Ṣūfī's *Kitāb Ṣuwar al-Kawākib al-Thamāniyah wa al-Arbaʿīn* (Beirut: Dār al-Āfāq al-Jadīdah, 1401/1981), pp. 27–40, in Ursa Major the *naʿsh* is the part of the "trunk" or "wagon" and the *banāt* are the three stars of the "tail" or "shaft." In Ursa Minor the *naʿsh* is once again the trunk or wagon (four stars), and the *banāt* are the three stars of the tail or shaft. Ursa Major, however, also has a group of stars in the front called *sarīr banāt al-naʿsh,* "the throne of the Bier's Daughters"; cf. the Iranian *hoptóringa,* the "seven enthroned-ones").

Essentially the same information is summed up in Paul Kunitzsh's *Untersuchungen zur Sternnomenklatur der Araber* (Wiesbaden: Otto Harrassowitz, 1961), p. 48. The only additional note of interest which he introduces is his quite perfunctory reference to Fritz Hommel's remark (*Zeitschrift der Deutschen morgenländischen Gesellschaft* 45 [1891]: 594ff.) that "die Auffassung von 'naʿsh' als 'Sarg' dürfte spätere Volksetymologie sein." Of seemingly quite indirect but nevertheless considerable interest is Robert Brown's reference in his *Semitic*

Influence in Hellenic Mythology (Clifton, N.J.: Reference Book Publishers, 1966), p. 63, to Bachofen's *Der Baer in den Religionen des Altertums* (1863), on which he bases his characterization of the bear cult in ancient Greece as a feminine cult: "the maternal, and hence fostering and kindly, aspect of the Bear, which in Greek is always feminine, . . . is the leading idea in the mythologico-religious treatment of the animal." Such a bear, Brown stresses (p. 63), is thus the *Ursa Matronalis,* "connected with the cult of the great non-Aryan Goddess-mother of Western Asia." He also points out (pp. 168–69) that the seven stars of Ursa Major were called in Sumerian and Akkadian the *Margidda* (the long-chariot), which "all the year is fixed around the pole." Thus the "Bear was the Mediterranean, the Wain the Euphratean name of the constellation." Hence the two names in Homer, for whom it "turns round [the pole] without moving away" (*Iliad* 18.488). Furthermore (pp. 188–89), the constellation "'Margidda' ('the Wain') was, in the Euphratean scheme, specially connected with the god Mul-lil" as his nocturnal manifestation, the "Lord-of-the-Ghost-world," which then leads to the Iranian "expanded" "ruler of the ghosts." These stars "were entrusted with the gate and passage of hell." The connection of the two Bears/Wains with the Biers, Brown suggests (pp. 189–90), may even have come from those constellations' slowness and solemnity of motion. As for the "Daughters" specifically, here the myth of Artemis of Braurôn, the patroness of the bear, should be of further significance, for the bear is one of that goddess's emblematic animals. Thus "acting the bear" was part of the ritual celebration of Artemis in ancient Greece in the city of Braurôn. There, as one of the rites of a festival, young girls, sometimes clad in bearskins, danced, gestured, growled, and otherwise mimicked "the bear." As Ginette Paris puts it in a somewhat too demystifying manner, "The bear cult and the rituals in honor of Artemis were occasions for girls to be together" (*Pagan Meditations: The Worlds of Aphrodite, Artemis, and Hestia,* trans. Gwendolyn Moore [Dallas: Spring Publications, 1986], pp. 151–52). Accordingly—also to be deduced from Brown and Bachofen—it should appear that "the girls of the bear" are none other than the mythological "daughters of the bier," in spite of the surface awkwardness of the pun. As much as "bier" is related etymologically to "to bear," it is, for other, potentially revealing reasons, also close semantically to the Arabic *naʿsh,* because, prima facie, it does not appear likely that *naʿsh* itself is of Arabic, or even Semitic, linguistic provenance, which ought to introduce at least a question mark into Brown's Semitic theory. Its true etymological connection ought to be with the Slavic *nesty* ("to carry," "to bear") and, more specifically, *noshi* ("bier"). In this respect, too, the form-coherent configuration of the constellation of the "Bear"/*dubb* as a "Wain"/"Wagon" is mythopoetically translatable into a "bier"/*noshi*/*naʿsh*. What nevertheless remains is the transition from the representational-mythopoetic to the tragic-mythical—and that is to be found in a poetically entirely persuasive manner in the praxis of Arabic poetry.

53. Ibn Abī Khāzim al-Asadī, *Dīwān,* pp. 61ff., esp. pp. 65–66.

54. In the *Ḥamāsah* of al-Buḥturī (p. 35, poem 149), in a poem of blood vengeance by Ashʿar Ibn Mālik al-ʿUdhrī, there is, however, an oblique evo-

cation of the motif of the pasturing of the stars. The obliqueness consists in a metathetic use of *aʿāra* ("to lend") instead of *raʿā* ("to pasture").

55. Ibn Abī Rabīʿah, *Dīwān,* p. 61.

56. Ibid., p. 204.

57. Ibid., p. 105. Repetitive occurrences of this motif in this poet's *Dīwān* are on pp. 160 and 313.

58. Dhū al-Rummah, *Dīwān,* p. 335.

59. Sezgin, *Geschichte des arabischen Schrifttums,* vol. 2, *Poesie,* p. 473.

60. Dhū al-Rummah, *Dīwān,* pp. 488–89.

61. Abū al-Hindī, *Dīwān Abī al-Hindī wa Akhbāruh,* ed. ʿAbd Allāh al-Jabūrī (Baghdad/Najaf: Maṭbaʿat al-Nuʿmān [Najaf], 1389/1969), p. 15.

62. [Abū ʿĀmir] Ibn Shuhayd al-Andalusī, *Dīwān,* ed. Yaʿqūb Zakī, rev. Maḥmūd ʿAlī Makkī (Cairo: Dār al-Kitāb al-ʿArabī li al-Ṭibāʿah wa al-Nashr, n.d.), pp. 143–44.

63. Ibid., p. 166.

64. Abū Tammām, *Dīwān,* vol. 3, pp. 160–61, poem 134.

65. [Abū al-Faraj Muḥammad Ibn Aḥmad al-Ghassānī] al-Waʾwāʾ al-Dimashqī, *Dīwān,* ed. Sāmī al-Dahhān (Damascus: Al-Majmaʿ al-ʿIlmī al-ʿArabī bi Dimashq, 1369/1950), p. 18.

66. Ibn Khafājah, *Dīwān,* p. 217.

67. Abū Muḥammad ʿAlī Ibn Aḥmad Ibn Saʿīd Ibn Ḥazm al-Andalusī, *Ṭawq al-Ḥamāmah fī al-Ilfah wa al-Ullāf,* 3d ed., ed. al-Ṭāhir Aḥmad Makkī (Cairo: Dār al-Maʿārif, 1400/1980), p. 30.

68. Ibn Ḥazm, *Ṭawq al-Ḥamāmah,* p. 30.

69. See above, at n. 45.

70. See above, at n. 49.

71. Lane, *Arabic-English Lexicon,* p. 816 (entry *kh-n-s*).

72. See below, chap. 5, section 2, and nn. 44 and 54.

73. For a mythological/mythopoetic connection between "hunter" and "herdsman," see Robert Eisler's discussion of Orpheus the "hunter" and Orpheus Eunomos/Euphrobos (the "Good Shepherd"/the "Good Herder") in *Orpheus—The Fisher,* pp. 16 and 51 note.

74. Note above (at n. 65) how al-Waʾwāʾ al-Dimashqī compares the "green hue" of the nightly firmament to a "tower of chrysolite."

75. Ibn Khafājah, *Dīwān,* p. 237.

76. Majnūn Laylā, *Dīwān* (Ankara ed.), p. 74. The Cairo edition (ed. Farrāj, pp. 90–91) adds to the poem one more line (v. 7). Furthermore, without its opening and closure and beginning instead with Majnūn's v. 4, together with other minor textual variants, this poem is also attributed to Nuṣayb Ibn Rabāḥ, who lived entirely during the high Umayyad period (d. 108/726) (*Shiʿr Nuṣayb Ibn Rabāḥ,* ed. Dāwūd Sallūm [Baghdad: Maṭbaʿat al-Irshād, 1976], p. 74).

77. Majnūn, *Dīwān* (Ankara ed.), p. 74.

78. This fidelity to the pastoral genre in the "romance" aspect of the *Dīwān* of Majnūn necessarily provokes comparison with the manner in which a pastoral, ecloguelike excursus is introduced in *Don Quijote,* where in part 1, at the end of chapter 10, Don Quijote and Sancho Panza, "desirous . . . of seeking a lodging for the night, . . . mounted and made what haste they could that they might arrive at a shelter before nightfall; but the sun failed them, and with it went the hope of attaining their wish. As the day ended they found themselves beside some goatherd's huts and they accordingly decided to spend the night there." We are then told how Don Quijote "was received by the herders with good grace" and how, in appreciation of the pastoral condition of things encountered, Don Quijote "took up a handful of acorns and, gazing at them attentively, fell into a soliloquy: 'Happy the age and happy those centuries. . . .'" From here on there follows an ironic but nonetheless "pure pastoral" in the manner of an eclogue (Miguel de Cervantes Saavedra, *The First Part of the Life and Achievements of the Renowned Don Quijote de la Mancha,* trans. Peter Motteux [New York: Random House, 1941], pp. 99ff.).

79. Qur'ān, Sūrat al-Ra'd, v. 2; Sūrat Luqmān, v. 10.

80. Al-Anbārī, *Sharḥ al-Qaṣā'id al-Sab',* p. 594. In Labīd's *Dīwān* (p. 180) this verse is no. 85.

81. Uno Holmberg, *Der Baum des Lebens,* Annales Academiae Scientiarum Fennicae, ser. B, vol. 16, (1922), p. 22.

82. Concerning references to *Himmelszelt, Himmelszelt der Welt,* and *Haus des Hirtenzeltes der Welt,* the star-studded *toga picta,* the "golden fleece," and other archetypally relevant *Spiegelbilder des Irdischen am Himmel,* see Robert Eisler, *Weltenhimmel und Himmelszelt: Religionsgeschichtliche Untersuchungen zur Urgeschichte des antiken Weltbildes* (Munich: C. H. Beck'sche Verlagsbuchhandlung, 1910), vol. 1, pp. 17–19, 41 (*toga picta*); 82 (the golden fleece); 214–17, 603ff. (*Spiegelbilder* . . .); vol. 2, p. 588 (cloth of heaven); 606–7 (*Himmelszelt der Welt, Haus des Hirtenzeltes der Welt*).

83. C. Kerenyi and C. G. Jung, *Essays on a Science of Mythology: The Myth of the Divine Child and the Mysteries of Eleusis,* Bollingen Series 22 (Princeton: Princeton University Press, 1973), p. 11. Kerenyi's argument is not disturbed by his philological awareness that *mundus* "may also derive from the Etruscan, in which case it is probably not identical with *mundus,* 'world.'"

84. Ovid, *Amores* 1.13.40.

85. Sannazaro, *Arcadia and Piscatorial Eclogues,* pp. 58–60.

86. We may do well to remember that in the *Dīwān* of Majnūn, with its romancelike *akhbār,* that poet, too, had first performed sacrificial rites (the spilled blood of a she-camel) over his father's grave and had intoned, conspicuously closely after that, his "O herders of the night" (*Dīwān* [Ankara ed.], p. 74).

87. Sannazaro, *Arcadia and Piscatorial Eclogues,* p. 61.

88. Friedrich Spee, *Trutznachtigall,* ed. Gustave Otto Arlt (Halle/Saale: Max Niemeyer Verlag, 1936), pp. 178–83 (no. 30), 228–34 (no. 39).

89. Gerhard H. Lemke, *Sonne, Mond und Sterne in der deutschen Literatur seit dem Mittelalter: Ein Bildkomplex im Spannungsfeld gesellschaftlichen Wandels* (Bern: Peter Lang, 1981), p. 117.

90. See further, ibid., pp. 117–18.

91. Spee, *Trutznachtigall,* pp. 178–80 (no. 30), 228–29 (no. 39).

92. Ibid., p. 234 (line 2). More in the Jungian, as well as the qur'ānic, vein is this eclogue's eliciting of the motif of *puer aeternus/walad mukhallad*/"ein Englisch Edel-knab" (p. 232, line 1). On *walad mukhallad,* see S. Stetkevych, "Intoxication and Immortality: Wine and Associated Imagery in al-Maʿarrī's Garden," pp. 40–41.

93. Luis de Góngora, *Antología poética, selección y poema de Rafael Alberti* (Buenos Aires: Editorial Pleamar, 1945), p. 89; also see, in Góngora, a recurrence of the motif of the *toro que pisa el cielo,* pp. 228–29.

94. The instant elegiac response, as one might call it, falls into place almost automatically when a star is invoked; and it is thus possible to find a connection between the elegiac evocations of the stars in pre-Islamic and later Arabic poetry, Walt Whitman's "When lilacs last in the dooryard bloom'd," and the tenuously implicit but nevertheless poetically effective nexus between Charmian's exclamation "O eastern star!" and the dying Cleopatra's reply (Shakespeare, *Antony and Cleopatra,* act 5, scene 2):

Peace, peace!
Dost thou not see my baby at my breast,
That sucks the nurse asleep?

95. Walt Whitman, *Leaves of Grass* (New York: Bantam Books, 1983), p. 266.

96. Miguel de Unamuno, *Andanzas y visiones españolas* (Madrid: Renacimiento, 1922), pp. 272–72.

97. Diane Ackerman, *The Planets: A Cosmic Pastoral* (New York: William Morrow and Co., 1976), p. 73.

Chapter Five

1. Gustave E. von Grunebaum, *Medieval Islam* (Chicago: University of Chicago Press, 1947), p. 82.

2. Consider Abū Nuwās's numerous travesties—more than parodies—of the *aṭlāl*-centered *nasīb,* as in his *Dīwān,* pp. 52, 65, 84, 90, 100–101, 109, 110–11, 132, 158, 185–86, where the poet begins by rejecting, or replacing, Bedouin poetic conventions, but in the end submits to their lyrical, not merely sentimental, hold on his own poetics. This poet's mannered pseudoattack on the traditional *nasīb* has been misunderstood by critics almost routinely. See also above, chap. 2, section 1.

3. The verses are found in al-Bāqillānī, *Iʿjāz al-Qurʾān,* p. 52; and in Mu-

ḥammad Ibn Mukarram Ibn Manẓūr al-Miṣrī, ***Akhbār Abī Nuwās: Ta'rīkhuh wa Nawādiruh, Shi'ruh, Mujūnuh,*** ed. Shukrī Maḥmūd Aḥmad (Baghdad: Maṭba'at al-Ma'ārif [1952?]), vol. 2, p. 53; see also Ibn al-Mu'tazz, ***Ṭabaqāt al-Shu'arā',*** 2d ed., ed. 'Abd al-Sattār Aḥmad Farrāj (Cairo: Dār al-Ma'ārif bi Miṣr, 1968), p. 207; and Abū Hiffān 'Abd Allāh Ibn Aḥmad Ibn Ḥarb al-Mihzamī, ***Akhbār Abī Nuwās,*** ed. 'Abd al-Sattār Aḥmad Farrāj (Cairo: Maktabat Miṣr, 1954), p. 68. In the last source, Abū Nuwās's first line appears with the inverted word order of ***rayḥānuhum * wujūhuhum.*** Al-Bāqillānī's reason for quoting these lines is a response to those who regard v. 14 of the Sūrah of Man as falling into the meter ***rajaz.*** For more qur'ānic echoes, including those of "the abode," in the poetry of Abū Nuwās, see A. M. Zubaidi, "The Impact of the Qur'ān and *Ḥadīth* on Medieval Arabic Literature," in A. F. L. Beeston et al., eds., ***The Cambridge History of Arabic Literature to the End of the Umayyad Period*** (Cambridge: Cambridge University Press, 1983), p. 328.

4. Al-Anbārī, ***Sharḥ al-Qaṣā'id al-Sab',*** p. 519 (Labīd's *Mu'allaqah*).

5. As quoted by Harry Levin in *The Myth of the Golden Age in the Renaissance* (New York: Oxford University Press, 1972), p. 186.

6. Quoted from Usāmah Ibn Munqidh, *Al-Manāzil wa al-Diyār,* pp. 290–91. For a convincing exposition of the circumstances of Ṣāliḥ Ibn 'Abd al-Quddūs's death, see J. van Ess, "Die Hinrichtung des Ṣāliḥ b. 'Abdalquddūs," in R. Roemer and Albrecht Noth, eds., ***Studien zur Geschichte und Kultur des vorderen Orients: Festschrift für Bertold Spuler zum siebzigsten Geburtstag*** (Leiden: E. J. Brill, 1981), pp. 53–66.

Ṣāliḥ Ibn 'Abd al-Quddūs is also the belated, but not last, link in the chain of appropriators of two verses of great traditional ascendancy which, in the manner understood by him, are relevant to us precisely because they could change greatly in their genre quality and connotation. The lines are:

> To die and find repose is not to die.
> The truly dead one is the agonizing
> among the living,
>
> His life in grief,
> his heart in darkness,
> his hope faint. [180]

See Yāqūt Ibn 'Abd Allāh al-Ḥamawī, ***Mu'jam al-Udabā'*** (Cairo: 'Īsā al-Bābī al-Ḥalabī, 1936), vol. 12, p. 9. Then, quite clearly as a quotation, the courtly litterateur and at times mannered poet Ibn 'Abd Rabbih will make use of the first one of the above lines by converting it into *ghazal*. This, however, only proves that, as much as early 'Udhrī love-poetry could become the idiom and the imagery of later *ṣūfī* poetry, ascetic and moralizing verse could with equal ease be found useful by poets of the *ghazal* genre. For Ibn 'Abd Rabbih's lines, see Abū Manṣūr 'Abd al-Malik [Ibn Muḥammad Ibn Ismā'īl] al-Tha'ālibī, ***Yatīmat al-Dahr fī Maḥāsin Ahl al-'Aṣr,*** ed. Mufīd Muḥammad Qamīḥah (Beirut: Dār al-Kutub al-'Ilmīyah, 1403/1983), vol. 2, p. 105. The "original" of this attractive poetic topos seems to be the pre-Islamic poet ʿAdī Ibn Raʿlāʾ al-Ghassānī, who, quite appropriately, has *dhalīlan* instead of Ṣāliḥ's sentimental *ka'iban,* and *sayyi'an* instead of *kāsifan.* See Muṭāʿ Ṣafadī and Īlīyā Ḥāwī, eds., *Mawsūʿat al-Shiʿr al-ʿArabī: Al-Shiʿr al-Jāhilī* (Beirut: Sharikat Khayyāṭ li al-Kutub wa al-Nashr, 1974), vol. 4, p. 163.

7. Ibn al-Rūmī, *Dīwān* (Cairo: Maṭbaʿat al-Hilāl, 1922), vol. 2, p. 107; also in Ibn al-Rūmī [Abū al-Ḥasan ʿAlī Ibn al-ʿAbbās Ibn Jarīḥ], *Dīwān,* ed. Ḥusayn Naṣṣār (Cairo: Maṭbaʿat Dār al-Kutub, 1974), vol. 2, p. 558, where v. 13 has *thamana* (price) instead of *thamara* (fruit). I chose the former reading.

8. Thus, for example, the motif of v. 3 of Ibn al-Rūmī's poem derives from such eminent sources as the *mukhaḍram* Ḥassān Ibn Thābit (*Dīwān,* eds. Sayyid Ḥanafī Ḥasanayn and Ḥasan Kāmil al-Ṣīrafī [Cairo: Al-Hay'ah al-Miṣrīyah ʿAmmah li al-Kitāb, 1974], p. 81, v. 5) and the early Abbasid Muslim Ibn al-Walīd [(*Sharḥ Dīwān Ṣarīʿ al-Ghawānī,* p. 192, poem 25)].

9. Giamatti, *The Earthly Paradise,* p. 6.

10. In his *Ḥadīth al-Sindibād al-Qadīm* (Cairo: Lajnat al-Ta'līf wa al-Tarjamah wa al-Nashr, 1943), pp. 336–45, Ḥusayn Fawzī discusses in detail the identification of Serendib as it figures in medieval Arabic geographic and related literature. For a comprehensive discussion of the name and the literary treatment of Serendib-Ceylon, see Schuyler V. R. Cammann, "Christopher the Armenian and the Three Princes of Serendip," in A. Owen Aldridge, ed., *Comparative Literature: Matter and Method* (Urbana: University of Illinois Press, 1969), pp. 227–56. See also André Miquel, *La géographie humaine du monde musulman jusqu'au milieu du 11ᵉ siècle,* vol. 2: *Geographie arabe et représentation du monde: la terre et l'étranger* (Paris–La Haye: Mouton and Co., 1975), pp. 78–79.

11. The Alexandrian Claudius Claudianus has in his *Epithalamium for Honorius Augustus and Maria, Daughter of Stilico* a description of the bower of Venus of great literary appeal: "A mountain casts its shadow over the western end of Cyprus: it faces Pharos and the mouths of the Nile; nothing can violate it. No man has climbed its slopes; it never has frost; the winds and the clouds do not attack its cliffs. It was made for pleasure and is a shrine to Venus. The climate never changes; the seasons are always the same; it enjoys the grandeur of eternal spring. The slopes become a level plain surrounded by a golden hedge which guards the meadows from the world" (Harold Isbell, trans., *The Last Poets of Imperial Rome* (Penguin Books, 1982), p. 109).

12. Dante's Earthly Paradise (*Purgatory* 28.19), too, has a "pineta," native to the poet's own landscapes.

13. The symbolic similarities between such medieval Arabic localizations of Earthly Paradise and Dante's broad design of the Mount of Purgatory are prominent. Particularly important in medieval topography of creation and salvation was the great height upon which Adam first stepped: it had to pierce the sublunar sphere. The fresco of Domenico di Michelino in Santa Maria del Fiore, with the city of Florence at the foot of the Mount of Purgatory, is not

very much different in conception from "the main city of Serendib," lying at the foot of Adam's mountain.

14. See John Gardner and John Maier, trans., *Gilgamesh: Translated from the Sîn-leqi-unninnī Version* (New York: Vintage Books, Random House, 1985), p. 205 (tablet 9, col. 5, lines 47–51). Also see above, chap. 4, n. 12. The bejeweled-garden motif has entered into descriptions of Paradise in the European Middle Ages more directly in connection with the river Pishon and the land of Havilah (Genesis 2:11–12), and also as it reappears in the representation of Celestial Jerusalem (Revelation 21:18–21). The bejeweled *locus amoenus* becomes the palace of Venus in Claudius Claudianus's *Epithalamium* (lines 84–94; see above, n. 11), and it finds its way even into Renaissance poetry, where one would normally expect purely vegetative elements to prevail. Thus in Sir Walter Raleigh's *The Passionate Man's Pilgrimage:*

And when our bottles and all we,
Are fild with immortalitie:
Then the holy paths weele trauell
Strewde with Rubies thicke as grauell,
Seelings of Diamonds, Saphire floores,
High walles of Corall and Pearle Bowres.

See *The Poems of Sir Walter Raleigh,* ed. Agnes M. C. Latham (Cambridge: Harvard University Press, 1962), p. 50.

15. The name of this imaginary island exhibits minor variations from text to text, hence "the Island of Wāq-wāq," "the Land of Wāq al-Wāq," etc. For an informal, perhaps, but highly informative and reliable discussion of the tree of Wāq al-Wāq and the Islands of the Women in Arabic literature of oddities, see Fawzī, *Ḥadīth al-Sindibād al-Qadīm,* pp. 93–119. See also Zakarīyā al-Qazwīnī, *ʿAjāʾib al-Makhlūqāt wa Gharāʾib al-Mawjūdāt,* 2d ed., ed. Fārūq Saʿd (Beirut: Dār al-Āfāq al-Jadīdah, 1977), pp. 154–55; and Sirāj al-Dīn Abū Ḥafṣ ʿUmar Ibn al-Wardī, *Kharīdat al-ʿAjāʾib wa Farīdat al-Gharāʾib* (Cairo: Al-Maṭbaʿah al-ʿĀmirah al-Malījīyah, 1324 H.), pp. 81–82. Miquel (*La géographie humaine du monde musulman,* vol. 1, p. 119, n. 2, and vol. 2, pp. 20, 80, 487, 490, 511, 513) provides an excellent survey of the pertinent textual sources, but without further interpretive intent.

16. Abū Bakr Ibn Ṭufayl, *Ḥayy Ibn Yaqẓān* (Beirut: Al-Maṭbaʿah al-Kāthūlīkīyah, 1963), pp. 26, 29, 89–90. The long-standing scholarly concern with Ibn Ṭufayl's text has for the most part been philosophico-theological and mystical or primarily explanatory in a manner that does not quite meet critical expectations. See a welcome exception in the literary-critical sense in Fedwa Malti-Douglas's *Woman's Body, Woman's Word: Gender and Discourse in Arabo-Islamic Writing* (Princeton: Princeton University Press, 1991), esp. pp. 67–84, but also pp. 85–110. Espousing a refreshing feminist perspective, Malti-Douglas's study is, however, less concerned than the present study with the archetype of the *locus amoenus* in Ibn Ṭufayl.

17. Al-Masʿūdī repeats chiefly the "geographical" commonplaces with reference to *bilād al-Wāq wāq*. To him it is the land of *kathīrat al-ʿajāʾib,* of many *mirabilia,* rich in gold and in pearls. See Abū al-Ḥasan ʿAlī Ibn al-Ḥusayn Ibn ʿAlī al-Masʿūdī, *Murūj al-Dhahab wa Maʿādin al-Jawhar,* 4th ed., ed. Yūsuf Asʿad Dāghir (Beirut: Dār al-Andalus li al-Ṭibāʿah wa al-Nashr, 1401/1981), vol. 1, pp. 123, 424–25. Of similar nature are the references in Ibn al-Faqīh al-Hamadhānī, *Abrégé du Livre des pays,* trans. Henri Massé (Damascus: Institut Français de Damas, 1973), pp. 4, 9. Again, a perceptive critical discussion is that of Malti-Douglas, *Woman's Body, Woman's Word,* pp. 71ff. and esp. chap. 5.

18. Cf. "the island of women" in Celtic folklore; also concerning Morgana, "a woman from a coral-tree," see Lucy Allen Paton, *Studies in the Fairy Mythology of Arthurian Romance* (New York: Burt Franklin, 1960), pp. 38ff.

19. Concerning such islands outside the Arabic tradition of *mirabilia,* be they the Fortunate Islands, the location of the Elysian Fields, the Islands of the Blest, etc., see Arthur O. Lovejoy and George Boas, *Primitivism and Related Ideas in Antiquity* (New York: Octagon Books, 1980), esp. chap. 11, pp. 287ff.

20. For a conceptual and cultural-historical discussion of the "strange" and the "marvelous" (i.e., the broad scope of *mirabilia* of the Arabo-Islamic Middle Ages), see Mohamed Arkoun, Jacques le Goff, Jacqueline Sublet, Tawfiq Fahd, and Maxime Rodinson, *L'étrange et le merveilleux dans l'Islam médiéval: Actes du colloque tenu au Collège de France à Paris, en mars 1974* (Paris: L'Institut du Monde arabe/Éditions J.A., 1978). Despite this colloquium's liberal theoretical scope, however, the anthropology and symbolism of Arabo-Islamic *loci amoeni* are conspicuously missing.

21. Sūrah 2:267.

22. Sūrah 3:12; also Sūrah 3:13, 36:55–57; 37:39–47; 52:17–24; 56:10–38; 76:5–22; 78:31–36; etc. We may remember that, if among the Epicureans *voluptas* comprised all levels of pleasure, the Neoplatonist Plotinus, too, advised that the understanding of earthly passions was a helpful point of reference in conveying "Heaven-passion": "And those to whom the Heaven-passion is unknown may make guess at it by the passion of earth" (*Enneads* 6.9.9). See Wind, *Pagan Mysteries in the Renaissance,* p. 55. The eagerness for bodily enjoyment of heavenly bliss appears also in Dante's *Paradiso* (14), and, not at all accidentally, in connection with Solomon, who, obviously, brings to the poet's mind all the corporeal sensuality of the Song of Songs. Solomon's exaltation of the "holy and glorious flesh" (*la carne gloriosa e santa*) (1.43) ends with the tercet:

> Nor shall that light have the power to do us wrong,
> Since for all joys that shall delight us then
> The body's organs will be rendered strong. (Lines 58–60)

After which assertion, the beatific choirs exclaim with a most eager "Amen" (lines 61–63) (*The Comedy of Dante Alighieri the Florentine,* Cantica 3, *Il Paradiso,* pp. 179–80). And then, to prove how right Plotinus was, but with all the vengeance of poetry, Wallace Stevens proclaims:

After death, the non-physical people, in paradise,
Itself non-physical, may, by chance, observe
The green corn gleaming and experience
The minor of what we feel.

See Wallace Stevens, *The Palm at the End of the Mind: Selected Poems and a Play by Wallace Stevens*, ed. Holly Stevens (New York: Alfred A. Knopf, 1971), p. 262 ("Esthetique du Mal," 15).

23. Composed in 1032, al-Maʿarrī's *Risālah* has one good modern edition by Bint al-Shāṭi' (Cairo: Dār al-Maʿārif bi Miṣr, 1950).

24. In its present form, Ibn Shuhayd's *Risālah* is much shorter than what its original length must have been. It has an Arabic edition by Buṭrus al-Bustānī (Beirut: Maktabat Ṣādir, 1951) and an English study and commented translation by James T. Monroe (*Risālat at-Tawābiʿ wa z-Zawābiʿ: The Treatise of Familiar Spirits and Demons by Abū ʿĀmir ibn Shuhaid al-Ashjaʿī, al-Andalusī* [Berkeley and Los Angeles: University of California Press, 1971]). According to Monroe (pp. 16–17), Ibn Shuhayd composed his *Risālah* between 1025 and 1027.

25. The broader Platonizing or, rather, Neoplatonic, aesthetics of Ibn Shuhayd is discussed incisively by Monroe in the introductory essay to his translation of the *Risālah* (*Risālat at-Tawābiʿ wa z-Zawābiʿ*, esp. p. 39).

26. Al-Maʿarrī, *Ghufrān*, pp. 15–16. 27. Ibid., p. 48.

28. "wa ahlu al-jannati adhkiyā'u lā yukhāliṭuhumu al-aghbiyā'u (ibid., p. 69).

29. Ibid., p. 84.

30. Ibid., pp. 102–5. 31. Ibid., pp. 169–73.

32. Not, perchance, the trees of Wāq al-Wāq?

33. Ibid., pp. 190–96. The above is a very free paraphrase of that particular episode in the *Risālah*.

34. Northrop Frye is centrally concerned with the difference between the undistorted flow of the symbolic imagination in "romance" and in popular literature as opposed to the "corrected" vision of demythologizing literature. He calls the process "displacement." See his *The Secular Scripture: A Study of the Structure of Romance* (Cambridge: Harvard University Press, 1982), pp. 36ff.

35. The material in this section is a revised form of my earlier discussion in "Spaces of Delight: A Symbolic Topoanalysis of the Classical Arabic *Nasīb*," *Literature East and West* 25 (1989): 5–28.

36. Gaston Bachelard, *The Poetics of Space*, trans. Maria Jolas (Boston: Beacon Press, 1972), p. 8.

37. Ibid., p. 9.

38. Al-Mutanabbī, *Dīwān*, vol. 1, p. 348. Al-Mutanabbī's masterfully achieved line is, however, only a felicitous rephrasing of a somewhat encumbered verse by Abū Tammām, where the "hearts" are still the more archaic

"bowels" (*aḥshā'*) (*Dīwān,* vol. 3, p. 21 poem 112). Cf. al-Qāḍī ʿAlī ʿAbd al-Azīz al-Jurjānī, who brings both verses together to illustrate al-Mutanabbī's plagiarisms (*Al-Wasāṭah bayna al-Mutanabbī wa Khuṣūmih* [Cairo: Maṭbaʿat ʿĪsā al-Bābī al-Ḥalabī, 1966], p. 314).

39. Bachelard, *The Poetics of Space,* chap. 10, esp. pp. 232, 234, and 240.

40. Gaston Bachelard, *The Poetics of Reverie, Childhood, Language, and the Cosmos,* trans. Daniel Russel (Boston: Beacon Press, 1971), p. 176.

41. Bachelard, *The Poetics of Space,* p. 55. The reference is to a verse by Jean Bourdeillette: "Pivoines et pavots paradis taciturnes!" (Peonies and poppies silent gardens of Paradise!).

42. Also see above, chap. 1, section 3, and esp. my "Toward an Arabic Elegiac Lexicon," in S. Stetkevych, ed., *Reorientations.*

43. Quoted from Usāmah Ibn Munqidh, *Al-Manāzil wa al-Diyār,* p. 220.

44. Ḥāzim al-Qarṭājannī, *Dīwān* (Beirut: Dār al-Thaqāfah, 1964), p. 36. This "external" quality of the garden as promenade is relatively rare in Arabic poetry, as is the externality of the concrete garden itself. But then even the Arabic poetic "outer" garden may be seen as tied to the pre-Islamic *rawḍah* (meadow) as a possible *locus amoenus,* which, however, is still in need of being further qualified as *conclusus* if such be its poetic function. See, for instance, ʿAntarah's *Muʿallaqah,* v. 15 (Al-Anbārī, *Sharḥ al-Qaṣā'id al-Sabʿ,* p. 311): "Or a garden secure . . ." (*aw rawḍatan unufan*); while in the so-called eighth *Muʿallaqah* by al-Aʿshā, on the other hand, this *rawḍah,* equally a metaphor for the beloved, is not explicitly *unuf* (secure or interdicted) but rather a uniquely luxuriant meadow. See al-Aʿshā [Maymūn], *Dīwān,* p. 145, vv. 14–16, corresponding to vv. 12–14 in al-Tibrīzī, *Sharḥ al-Qaṣā'id al-ʿAshr,* pp. 332–33.

The subsequent Arabic poetic references to the garden as *ḥadīqah* or *jannah* do imply enclosure of space with their transparent etymologies—philological-lexical in the case of the former (*ḥ-d-q*) and chthonic and symbolic-idealogical in that of the latter (*j-n-n*).

On the other hand, contrary to the closed-in space of the claustral garden of the European Middle Ages, the garden of the Renaissance is physically "externalized": it is the surrounding space rather than the enclosed one, and as such it is, in the words of Terry Comito, "a medium to be shaped and given form." In its own way, however, it, too, delimits space toward the interior (Terry Comito, *The Idea of the Garden in the Renaissance* [New Brunswick, N.J.: Rutgers University Press, 1978], pp. 152ff).

45. George Moore, *An Anthology of Pure Poetry* (New York: Liveright, 1973), p. 17.

46. Abū Tammām, *Dīwān,* vol. 2, p. 194.

47. In the edition of Iḥsān ʿAbbās, this poem has ten verses (al-Ṣanawbarī, *Dīwān,* p. 454). I have added the line occurring as no. 4 from the edition of Muḥammad Rāghib al-Ṭabbākh in *Al-Rawḍīyāt: Min Shiʿr al-Shāʿir al-Majīd Abī Bakr al-Ṣanawbarī al-Ḥalabī* (Aleppo: Al-Maṭbaʿah al-ʿIlmīyah, 1351/1932), p. 20.

48. Abū Tammām, *Al-Ḥamāsah* (Marzūqī), vol. 3, p. 1377, no. 568. Here, in the fragment's third line, the chosen but interdicted mountain spring is still another form of the internalized archetype of a "garden," easily recognized as such by al-Ṣanawbarī.

49. See Abū Tammām's *qaṣīdah* no. 71, vv. 1–21 (*Dīwān*, vol. 2, pp. 191–96). Also see above, at n. 46 (v. 23).

50. See above, chap. 4, at nn. 23 and 24.

51. Robertson Smith, *The Religion of the Semites*, p. 156.

52. Comito, *The Idea of the Garden in the Renaissance*, p. 164.

53. See above, n. 44.

54. There is an etymologically perceptible paradox already in the root-meaning, or meanings, of *rawḍah* alone. Being the open space of the meadow on the one hand, it is associated by true—or false—etymology with the idea of subduing, training, cultivating: thus of the mind as in mathematics and music, of untamed horses and their training, and of meadows turned into gardens, where cultivation implicitly means containment and enclosure. Also, to an Abbasid courtly poet-panegyrist such as ʿAlī Ibn al-Jahm, *rawḍatun unufun* becomes the "repose of truth," as caliphal proximity or presence (*Dīwān*, p. 141). The metaphoric and symbolic force of this *rawḍah*, or *rawḍ*, as a "privileged place" has made itself felt even in domains not directly poetic. Thus the Andalusian philologist Abū al-Qāsim (or Abū al-Ḥasan) al-Suhaylī (d. 581/1185) gives the title of *Al-Rawḍ al-Unuf* to his philological disquisition, which is also very much a poetic microanthology with a textual-exegetic purpose. See its discussion by Ḥāmid Muḥammad Amīn Shaʿbān, *Al-Buḥūth al-Lughawīyah fī al-Rawḍ al-Unuf* (Cairo: Maktabat al-Anjlū al-Miṣrīyah, 1404/1984). To the Andalusian philologist, his poetic language has become as much a *jardín cerrado para muchos* as the Granada of Pedro Soto de Rojas was to García Lorca (see above, chap. 4, n. 23). Also see Muṣṭafā Nāṣif (*Qirā'ah Thāniyah li Shiʿrinā al-Qadam* (Tripoli, Libya): Manshūrāt al-Jāmiʿah al-Lībīyah, Kullīyat al-Ādāb, n.d.], pp. 132–34), to whom the *rawḍatun unufun* of ʿAntarah's *Muʿallaqah*, more than being a metaphor for the beloved and her moist mouth, symbolizes the life-giving rain itself.

55. *Al-Mufaḍḍalīyāt* (Lyall), p. 337, poem 34, v. 6. The question may be put: How much does the new factor of possessing the scriptural backdrop of a *locus amoenus* flatten out the indispensable symbolic paradox or reduce the tension of polarization of planes of reality?

56. In the *Dīwān* of al-Sarī al-Raffā' these are vv. 39–41, of a poem of fifty-nine verses. Although a eulogy (*madḥ*) by intent, this poem's longest section presents a description of an idealized garden which is both a "courtly" place and a *locus amoenus*. See al-Sarī al-Raffā', *Dīwān*, ed. Ḥabīb Ḥusayn al-Ḥasanī (Baghdad: Al-Maktabah al-Waṭanīyah, 1981), vol. 1, pp. 324–29. I have also taken into account (v. 4) the reading of the first *al-malāʿib* of the *Dīwān* as *al-khamā'il* in Muṣṭafā al-Shakʿah's more carefully edited and printed *Funūn al-Shiʿr fī Mujtamaʿ al-Ḥamdānīyīn* (Cairo: Maktabat al-Anjlū al-Miṣrīyah, 1958), p. 357.

57. The richness of meaning of the carpet in Arabic poetry alone is an important ancillary avenue to the understanding of privileged poetic places and moods. In the present poem the emperor's carpet is the garden of delight itself. Evoked by the effective economy of the Arabic poem, too, an even more condensed image of kindred echoes comes to mind out of Spanish poetry. It is Diego de Saavedra Fajardo's (1584–1648) "epigrama español," which is one of the finest pastoral metaphors in European poetry relying on the association of water with the quality of purity, the place of refuge, and the pastoral time of the Golden Age:

Cuán sin malicia, cándida murmuras!
Oh sencillez de aquella edad primera!
Huyes del hombre y vives en las fuentes.

See Diego de Saavedra Fajardo, *República literaria* (Madrid: Atlas, Colección Cisneros, 1944), p. 4.

58. Al-Waʾwāʾ al-Dimashqī, *Dīwān,* pp. 136–37. These lines are also attributed to Ibn al-Muʿtazz (d. 296/908), in whose *Dīwān* (Beirut: Dār Ṣādir, 1961), p. 291, the first hemistich of the first verse is "narjisatun lā tazālu muḥaddiqatan," thus distorting the meter *al-munsariḥ*. I. Kratchkovsky finds reasons to hesitate before assigning this "fragment" to Ibn al-Muʿtazz. See his *Abū-l-Faradzh al-Vaʾva Damasskiy: Materialy dla Charakterystiki Poeticheskogo Tvorchestva* (St. Petersburg: Academy of Sciences, 1914), pp. 78–79.

59. Ibn Khafājah, *Dīwān,* pp. 124–25.

60. Ibid., p. 136.

61. Abū Nuwās, *Dīwān,* p. 3. For a full translation of the first two verses of the poem, see above, chap. 2, section 2 and n. 28.

62. Cf. Turner, *The Vision of Landscape in Renaissance Italy,* p. 161.

63. Al-Aṣmaʿī, *Al-Aṣmaʿīyāt,* pp. 58–61.

64. See above, chap. 2, section 3.

65. Al-Iṣfahānī, *Kitāb al-Aghānī* (Cairo: Al-Muʾassasah al-Miṣrīyah al-ʿĀmmah, 1974), vol. 4, pp. 60–62.

66. Al-Buḥturī, *Dīwān,* vol. 2, pp. 1152–62.

67. Al-Sharīf al-Murtaḍā, *Dīwān* (Cairo: ʿĪsā al-Bābī al-Ḥalabī wa Shurakāh, 1958), vol. 2, p. 160.

68. Ibid., p. 161.

69. ʿUbayd Allāh Ibn Qays al-Ruqayyāt, *Dīwān,* ed. Muḥammad Yūsuf Najm (Beirut: Dār Ṣādir/Dār Bayrūt, 1378/1958), p. 8, vv. 4 and 5.

70. Qurʾān, Sūrah 34:12.

71. Abū Tammām, *Dīwān,* vol. 2, pp. 101–2, vv. 1–3.

72. Ibid., p. 166. See a full discussion of this poem in S. Stetkevych, *Abū Tammām and the Poetics of the ʿAbbāsid Age,* chap. 6 and also chap. 5, for a pertinent discussion of Abū Tammām's poetic language.

73. Ibn Zaydūn, *Dīwān,* p. 139.

74. On the destruction of al-Zahrā', see Leopoldo Torres Balbás, "Arte califal," *Historia de España,* vol. 5: *España musulmana,* pt. 2, ed. Ramón Menéndez Pidal (Madrid: Espasa-Calpe, 1957), pp. 427–28 and ff.

75. Ibn Zaydūn, *Dīwān,* pp. 160-61.

76. Qur'ān, Sūrah 3:12, 13; 36:55–57; 78:31–36; 52:17–24; 76:5–22 (more specifically, 11–22); etc. Also see above, n. 22.

77. Qur'ān, Sūrah 20:115–18.

78. Before Ibn Zaydūn, Bashshār Ibn Burd (d. 167/783) had described a *locus amoenus* only to abandon it for the horror of war, into which he is carried on his steed (Bashshār Ibn Burd, *Dīwān,* ed. Muḥammad Shawqī Amīn [Cairo: Lajnat al-Ta'līf wa al-Tarjamah wa al-Nashr, 1950], vol. 1, pp. 334–35, vv. 24–28). By comparison, al-Mutanabbī's explicit reference to Earthly Paradise, using the same topos, also opts for an unmitigated directness of voice, rather in the manner of pathetic fallacy:

1. The abodes of this mountain cleft in delight's domain
Are as spring in the sway of time.

4. So invitingly they beckoned cavalier and steed,
That I feared restiveness would overbear nobility of breed.

17. In the canyon of Bawwān my steed thus utters:
"Am I to forsake this for spears' piercing thrusts?

18. Your father Adam bequeathed to you rebellion
And taught you to renounce Paradise." [181]

See Al-Mutanabbī, *Dīwān,* vol. 2, pp. 452, 454–55. Al-Mutanabbī's steed as the motif of the accusing animal (a case of pathetic fallacy or, rather, of a personified self-accusation, an allegorization) is again a specific adaptation to the ***nasīb*** of the motif as it figures in ʿAntarah's *Muʿallaqah* (vv. 71–72) (Al-Anbārī, *Sharḥ al-Qaṣā'id al-Sabʿ,* pp. 360–61), although that pre-Islamic poet avoids explicit pathetic fallacy, preferring a circumlocution. The closest model for al-Mutanabbī's talking, self-pitying horse, however, is found in a ***qaṣīdah*** of another pre-Islamic poet, al-Muthaqqib al-ʿAbdī, in which the animal is not a horse about to transport its rider out of a structurally and thematically identifiable ***nasīb*** but a she-camel placed fully in her structurally appropriate place, the ***raḥīl,*** in which the "garden" always lies behind:

35. When I strap the saddle girth she says:
"Will this forever be his wont and my fate?

36. Is life but camp and journey?
Will nothing pity and preserve me?" [182]

See *Al-Mafaḍḍalīyāt* (Lyall), p. 586, vv. 35–36; (Shākir), p. 292, vv. 36–37.

79. Khalīl Ibn Aybak al-Ṣafadī, *Tamām al-Mutūn fī Sharḥ Risālat Ibn Zaydūn,* ed. Muḥammad Abū al-Faḍl Ibrāhīm (Cairo: Dār al-Fikr al-ʿArabī, 1389/1969), p. 13.

80. Ibn Zaydūn, *Dīwān,* p. 145.

81. Ibid., p. 146. Of particular pathos is Ibn Zaydūn's reference to *zaqqūm* (Sūrah 56:52) and to *ghislīn* (Sūrah 69:36).

82. Ibid.

83. Thus in Abū al-Faraj ʿAbd al-Raḥmān Ibn al-Jawzī, *Dhamm al-Hawā,* ed. Muṣṭafā ʿAbd al-Wāḥid (Cairo: Dār al-Kutub al-Ḥadīthah, 1381/1962), pp. 147–48. But see also al-Mutanabbī's empathic elegiac threesome of the Bedouin poet, his camel, and the campsite ruin (*Dīwān,* vol. 2, p. 460), which, undoubtedly, was also at the back of the Andalusian poet's mind:

Be our third, for we, O campsite ruin,
  Weep, and under us our camels groan! [183]

84. "Je mettrois volontiers sur la porte du paradis le vers que Dante a mis sur celle de l'enfer: Lasciate ogni speranza voi ch'entrate" (N. Chamfort, *Oeuvres choisies* [Paris: Librairie des Bibliophiles, 1892], p. 30).

85. Ibn Zaydūn, *Dīwān,* p. 146.

86. Ibid., p. 132, stanza 3. For the archaic model of the topos, see above, chap. 4, section 2.

87. Ibn Zaydūn, *Dīwān,* p. 133, stanza 5.

88. Ibid., p. 135, stanza 12.

89. Indeed, only once in the poem is there a context which could be interpreted as containing the qur'ānic concept of bliss (*naʿīm*). See below, stanza X.

90. Ibid., p. 128.

91. Ibid., p. 131.

92. Ibid., p. 128.

93. The strophic structure of this poem contributes to the lyrical lightness and stylization of the idyll. The fifth line of each stanza comes close to being a refrain. It rounds off each stanza by changing the point of view or the point in time of its statement. It has an apostrophe-like effect. Above all, even a casual reader of the poem in its original cannot but realize that the fifth line breaks the monotony of rhythm in each stanza in a manner very much like syncopation, while at the same time carrying the entire composition's binding rhyme. This gives to the poem a rondeau-like definitiveness and lightness of progression from stanza to stanza.

The peculiar rhythmic effect in the poem is obtained by a shift from acatalectic *ṭawīl* meter in the first four lines of each stanza to catalectic *ṭawīl* in the fifth line. This means a shortening of the last line by one syllable, and, as a compounded effect throughout the poem, it means a general acceleration of the rhythmic pace. Further to be noticed is that the closing lines of the first and the last stanzas in Ibn Zaydūn's poem are an evocation of a *nasīb* by Abū Tammām, the first line being an almost literal quotation from the source's v. 7 and the last a clear allusion to its v. 1 (Abū Tammām, *Dīwān,* vol. 3, pp. 150–51). Furthermore, both Abū Tammām and Ibn Zaydūn make us think of a verse attributed to the pre-Islamic poet Aws Ibn Ḥajar (*Dīwān,* 2d ed., ed. Muḥammad Yūsuf Najm [Beirut: Dār Ṣādir, 1967], p. 74).

94. John Keats, *The Poetical Works of John Keats* (Oxford: Oxford University Press, 1930), p. 340 (On the Sonnet).

95. The theoretical relentlessness and immediacy of our modern understanding of all the formal and meaning-connotative aspects of artistic creation have undoubtedly contributed to our present aesthetic restlessness. The moment a form, subject, or symbol is used, it is also analytically understood in all its implications. Every repeated use of it then becomes a conscious imitation in depth. This we perceive as intolerable. At the most we cultivate it for a while only by attaching to it the suffix "ism" and building around it a closed circle of aesthetically generic, broader tolerance. True originality, however, becomes possible only when the circle is broken. A new circle is then initiated, which hastens to close even faster, and so forth.

BIBLIOGRAPHY

ʿAbbās, Iḥsān. *Tārīkh al-Naqd al-Adabī ʿind al-ʿArab: Naqd al-Shiʿr min al-Qarn al-Thānī ḥattā al-Qarn al-Thāmin al-Hijrī* (*sic*). 2d ed. Beirut: Dār al-Thaqāfah, 1398/1978.

ʿAbd al-Badīʿ, Luṭfī. *ʿAbqarīyat al-ʿArabīyah fī Ruʾyat al-Insān wa al-Ḥayawān wa al-Samāʾ wa al-Kawkab*. Cairo: Maktabat al-Nahḍah al-Miṣrīyah, 1976.

ʿAbd al-Raḥmān, Nuṣrat. *Al-Ṣūrah al-Fannīyah fī al-Shiʿr al-Jāhilī fī Ḍawʾ al-Naqd al-Ḥadīth*. Amman: Maktabat al-Aqṣā, 1976.

ʿAbīd Ibn al-Abraṣ. *Dīwān*. Ed. Karam al-Bustānī. Beirut: Dār Ṣādir/Dār Bayrūt, 1384/1964.

Abu-Deeb, Kamal. *Al-Jurjānī's Theory of Poetic Imagery*. Warminster, England: Aris and Phillips, 1979.

———. "Towards a Structural Analysis of Pre-Islamic Poetry (II): The Eros Vision." *Edebiyât* 1, no. 1 (1976): 3–69.

Abū al-Hindī. *Dīwān Abī al-Hindī wa Akhbāruh*. Ed. ʿAbd Allāh al-Jabūrī. Baghdad/Najaf: Maṭbaʿat al-Nuʿmān, 1389/1969.

Abū Nuwās, al-Ḥasan Ibn Hāniʾ. *Dīwān*. Ed. Aḥmad ʿAbd al-Majīd al-Ghazālī. Cairo: Maṭbaʿat Miṣr, 1953.

———. *Diwan des Abū Nuwās, des grössten lyrischen Dichters der Araber*. Vienna: W. Baumüller, 1855.

Abū Tammām. *Dīwān*. 3d ed. 4 vols. Recension of al-Khaṭīb al-Tibrīzī. Ed. Muḥammad ʿAbduh ʿAzzām. Cairo: Dār al-Maʿārif bi Miṣr, 1970.

———. *Al-Ḥamāsah*. Commentary by al-Tibrīzī. Ed. Freytag. Bonn, 1828.

———. *Sharḥ Dīwān al-Ḥamāsah*. 4 vols. Recension and commentary by Aḥmad Ibn Muḥammad al-Marzūqī. Ed. Aḥmad Amīn and ʿAbd al-Salām Hārūn. Cairo: Lajnat al-Taʾlīf wa al-Tarjamah wa al-Nashr, 1952.

Ackerman, Diane. *The Planets: A Cosmic Pastoral*. New York: William Morrow and Co., 1976.

Aelian. *On the Characteristics of Animals*. 3 vols. Trans. A. F. Scholfield. Loeb Classical Library. 1959.

Ahlwardt, Wilhelm. *The Divans of the Six Ancient Arabic Poets Ennabiga, ʿAntara, Tharafa, Zuhair, ʿAlqama, and Imruulqais*. London: Trübner, 1870.

Alldritt, Keith. *Eliot's "Four Quartets": Poetry as Chamber Music*. London: Woburn Press, 1978.

Altheim, Franz, and Ruth Stiehl. *Die Araber in der Alten Welt*. Vol. 1, *Bis zum Beginn der Kaiserzeit*. Berlin: Walter de Gruyter and Co., 1964.

al-Ālūsī, Maḥmūd Shukrī. *Bulūgh al-Arab fī Maʿrifat Aḥwāl al-ʿArab*. 3 vols. Beirut: Dār al-Kutub al-ʿIlmīyah, n.d.

al-Anbārī, Abū Bakr Muḥammad Ibn al-Qāsim. *Sharḥ al-Qaṣāʾid al-Sabʿ al-*

Ṭiwāl al-Jāhilīyāt. 2d ed., ed. ʿAbd al-Salām Muḥammad Hārūn. Cairo: Dār al-Maʿārif bi Miṣr, 1969.

ʿAntarah Ibn Shaddād. *Dīwān*. Beirut: Dār al-Kutub al-ʿIlmīyah, 1405/1985.

Arberry, A. J. *Arabic Poetry: A Primer for Students*. Cambridge: Cambridge University Press, 1965.

Aristotle. *Problems*. Loeb Classical Library. 1936.

Arkoun, Mohamed, Jacques le Goff, Jacqueline Sublet, Tawfiq Fahd, and Maxime Rodinson. *L'étrange et le merveilleux dans l'Islam médiéval: Actes du colloque tenu au Collège de France à Paris, en mars 1974*. Paris: L'Institut du Monde Arabe/Editions J.A., 1978.

al-Aʿshā [Maymūn]. *Dīwān*. Beirut: Dār Ṣādir, 1966.

al-ʿAskarī, Abū Hilāl. *Kitāb al-Ṣināʿatayn*. Istanbul: Maṭbaʿat Maḥmūd Bey, 1320/1902.

al-Aṣmaʿī, Abū Saʿīd ʿAbd al-Malik Ibn Qurayb Ibn ʿAbd al-Malik. *Al-Aṣmaʿīyāt*. 2d ed., ed. Aḥmad Muḥammad Shākir and ʿAbd al-Salām Hārūn. Cairo: Dār al-Maʿārif bi Miṣr, 1964.

ʿAṭwān, Ḥusayn. *Muqaddimat al-Qaṣīdah al-ʿArabīyah fī al-Shiʿr al-Jāhilī*. Cairo: Dār al-Maʿārif bi Miṣr, 1970.

Auerbach, Erich. *Dante, Poet of the Secular World*. Trans. Ralph Manheim. Chicago: University of Chicago Press, 1969.

———. *Mimesis: The Representation of Reality in Western Literature*. Trans. Willard R. Trask. Princeton: Princeton University Press, 1968.

Averroes. *Averroes' Middle Commentary on Aristotle's Poetics*. Trans. with introduction and notes by Charles Butterworth. Princeton: Princeton University Press, 1986.

Aws Ibn Ḥajar. *Dīwān*. 2d ed., ed. Muḥammad Yūsuf Najm. Beirut: Dār Ṣādir, 1967.

Bachelard, Gaston. *The Poetics of Reverie, Childhood, Language, and the Cosmos*. Trans. Daniel Russel. Boston: Beacon Press, 1971.

———. *The Poetics of Space*. Trans. Maria Jolas. Boston: Beacon Press, 1972.

Bailey, H. W. *Zoroastrian Problems in the Ninth-Century Books: Ratanbai Katrak Lectures*. 1943. Oxford: Clarendon Press, 1971.

al-Bāqillānī, Abū Bakr Muḥammad Ibn al-Ṭayyib. *Iʿjāz al-Qur'ān*. Ed. Aḥmad Ṣaqr. Cairo: Dār al-Maʿārif, 1963.

Barford, Philip. *The Keyboard Music of C. P. E. Bach: Considered in Relation to His Musical Aesthetic and the Rise of the Sonata Principle*. London: Barrie and Rockliff, 1965.

Barnstone, Willis, trans. *Greek Lyric Poetry*. New York: Schocken Books, 1972.

Bashshār Ibn Burd. *Dīwān*. 4 vols. Ed. Muḥammad Shawqī Amīn. Cairo: Lajnat al-Ta'līf wa al-Tarjamah wa al-Nashr, 1950.

Beeston, A. F. L., et al., eds. *The Cambridge History of Arabic Literature to the End of the Umayyad Period*. Cambridge; Cambridge University Press, 1983.

Bevan, Anthony Ashley, ed. *The Naḳā'iḍ of Jarīr and al-Farazdaḳ*. 3 vols. Leiden: E. J. Brill, 1905.

Bint al-Shāṭi' [ʿĀ'ishah ʿAbd al-Raḥmān]. *Al-Ḥayāh al-Insānīyah ʿind al-ʿArab*. Cairo: Al-Maʿārif, 1944.

Blachère, Régis. *Histoire de la littérature arabe des origines à la fin du XVe siècle de J.-C.* 3 vols. Paris: Librairie d'Amérique et d'Orient Adrien Maisonneuve, 1964–1980.

Bloch, Alfred. "Qaṣīda." *Asiatische Studien: Zeitschrift der Schweizerischen Gesellschaft für Asienkunde*. 2 (1948): 106–32.

Bloom, Harold. *Anxiety of Influence: A Theory of Poetry*. New York: Oxford University Press, 1973.

Bodkin, Maud. *Archetypal Patterns in Poetry: Psychological Studies of Imagination*. Oxford: Oxford University Press, 1968.

Bonebakker, Seeger A. "Poets and Critics in the Third Century A.H." In Gustave E. von Grunebaum, ed., *Logic in Classical Islamic Culture*, pp. 85–111. Wiesbaden: Otto Harrassovitz, 1970.

Bravmann, Meïr M. "Heroic Motives in Early Arabic Literature." *Der Islam: Zeitschrift für Geschichte und Kultur des islamischen Orients* 33 (1958): 256–79.

Brotman, D. Bosley. "T. S. Eliot: 'The Music of Ideas.'" *University of Toronto Quarterly* 8, no. 1 (Oct. 1948): 20–29.

Brown, Robert, Jr. *Semitic Influence in Hellenic Mythology*. 1898. Clifton, N.J.: Reference Book Publishers, 1966.

al-Buḥturī al-Ṭā'ī, Abū ʿUbādah al-Walīd Ibn ʿUbayd. *Dīwān*. 5 vols. Ed. Ḥusayn Kāmil al-Ṣīrafī. Cairo: Dār al-Maʿārif, 1963–1978.

———. *Al-Ḥamāsah*. 2d ed. Beirut: Dār al-Kitāb al-ʿArabī, 1967.

Bürgel, J. Christoph. "Die beste Dichtung ist die lügenreichste: Wesen und Bedeutung eines literarischen Streites des arabischen Mittelalters im Lichte komparatistischer Betrachtung." *Oriens* 23 (1974): 7–102.

al-Būrīnī, Ḥasan, and ʿAbd al-Ghānī al-Nābulusī. *Sharḥ Dīwān Ibn al-Fāriḍ*. 2 vols. Cairo: Al-Maṭbaʿah al-ʿĀmirah al-Sharafīyah, 1306/1888.

Burkert, Walter. *Greek Religion*. Cambridge: Harvard University Press, 1985.

Burton, Richard F. *A Plain and Literal Translation of the Arabian Nights' Entertainments, now entitled The Book of the Thousand Nights and a Night*. 12 vols. Burton Club for Private Subscribers, n.d.

Cammann, Schuyler V. R. "Christopher the Armenian and the Three Princes of Serendip." In A. Owen Aldridge, ed., *Comparative Literature: Matter and Method*, pp. 336–45. Urbana: University of Illinois Press, 1969.

Campbell, Joseph. *The Hero with a Thousand Faces*. Princeton: Princeton University Press, 1973.

Carlyle, J. D. *Specimens of Arabian Poetry: From the Earliest Time to the Extinction of the Khaliphat*. 2d ed. London: T. Cadell, 1810.

Cervantes Saavedra, Miguel de. *The First Part of the Life and Achievements of the Renowned Don Quijote de la Mancha*. Trans. Peter Motteux. New York: Random House, 1941.

———. *El ingenioso hidalgo Don Quijote de la Mancha.* Clásicos Castellanos. 8th ed. Madrid: Espasa-Calpe, 1964.

Chamfort, N. *Oeuvres choisies.* Preface, notes, and tables by M. de Lescure. Paris: Librairie des Bibliophiles, 1892.

Chenu, M.-D. *Nature, Man, and Society in the Twelfth Century*. Selected, ed., and trans. by Jerome Taylor and Lester K. Little. Chicago: University of Chicago Press, 1968.

Chrétien de Troyes [Kristian von Troyes]. *Erec und Enide*. 3d ed., ed. Wendelin Foerster. Halle/Saale: Max Niemeyer Verlag, 1934.

———. *The Knight with the Lion, or Yvain (Le Chevalier au Lion)*. Ed. and trans. William W. Kibler. New York and London: Garland Publishing, 1985.

Cicero. *De inventione. De optimo genere oratorum. Topica.* Loeb Classical Library. 1968.

Cohen, S. Marshall. "Music and Structure in Eliot's Quartets." *Dartmouth Quarterly* 5 (1950): 3–4.

Comito, Terry. *The Idea of the Garden in the Renaissance*. New Brunswick, N.J.: Rutgers University Press, 1978.

Crane, R. S., ed. *Critics and Criticism, Ancient and Modern*. Chicago: University of Chicago Press, 1968.

Curtius, Ernst Robert. *European Literature and the Latin Middle Ages*. Trans. Willard R. Trask. New York and Evanston: Harper and Row, Harper Torchbooks, 1963.

Dante Alighieri. *The Comedy of Dante Alighieri the Florentine*. Trans. Dorothy L. Sayers. New York: Basic Books, 1962.

———. *Il convivio*. Collezione di Classici Italiani, vol. 4. Torino, 1927.

———. *The Convivio of Dante Alighieri*. Temple Classics. London, 1903.

Darío, Rubén. *Poesias completas*. 2 vols. Madrid: Aguilar, 1967.

Ḍayf, Shawqī. *Al-Taṭawwur wa al-Tajdīd fī al-Shiʿr al-Umawī*. 2d ed. Cairo: Dār al-Maʿārif bi Miṣr, 1959.

Dhū al-Rummah [Ghaylān Ibn ʿUqbah]. *Dīwān*. 2d ed. Damascus: Al-Maktabah al-Islāmīyah li al-Ṭibāʿah wa al-Nashr, 1384/1964.

Diʿbil Ibn ʿAlī al-Khuzāʿī. *Shiʿr Diʿbil Ibn ʿAlī al-Khuzāʿī*. Ed. ʿAbd al-Karīm al-Ashṭar. Damascus: Al-Majmaʿ al-ʿIlmī al-ʿArabī, 1964.

Dīwān al-Hudhalīyīn. 3 vols. Cairo: Dār al-Qawmīyah li al-Ṭibāʿah wa al-Nashr, 1385/1965. [Photo-offset of Dār al-Kutub ed., 1945–50.]

Doob, Penelope Reed. *The Idea of the Labyrinth from Classical Antiquity through the Middle Ages*. Ithaca: Cornell University Press, 1990.

Dorson, Richard M., ed. *Peasant Customs and Savage Myths: Selections from the British Folklorists*. 2 vols. Chicago: University of Chicago Press, 1968.

Douglas, Mary. *Implicit Meanings: Essays in Anthropology*. London: Routledge and Kegan Paul, 1975.

———. *Purity and Danger: An Analysis of Concepts of Pollution and Taboo*. London: Routledge and Kegan Paul, 1966.

Drayton, Michael. *Poems of Michael Drayton*. 2 vols. London: Routledge and Kegan Paul, 1953.

Duerr, Hans Peter. *Dreamtime: Concerning the Boundary between Wilderness and Civilization*. Trans. Felicitas Goodman. Oxford: B. Blackwell, 1985.

Edmonds, J. M., trans. *The Greek Bucolic Poets*. Loeb Classical Library. 1912.

Eisler, Robert. *Orpheus—The Fisher: Comparative Studies in Orphic and Early Christian Cult Symbolism*. London: J. M. Watkins, 1921.

———. *Weltenhimmel und Himmelszelt: Religionsgeschichtliche Untersuchungen zur Urgeschichte des antiken Weltbildes*. 2 vols. Munich: C. H. Beck'sche Verlagsbuchhandlung, 1910.

Empson, William. *Some Versions of Pastoral*. New York: New Directions, 1968.

The Encyclopaedia of Islam. New ed., ed. H. A. R. Gibb et al. Leiden: E. J. Brill; London: Luzak and Co., 1960–80.

Ess, J. van. "Die Ḥinrichtung des Ṣāliḥ b. ʿAbdalquddūs." In R. Roemer and Albrecht Noth, eds., *Studien zur Geschichte und Kultur des vorderen Orients: Festschrift für Bertold Spuler zum siebzigsten Geburtstag*, pp. 53–66. Leiden: E. J. Brill, 1981.

Fawzī, Ḥusayn. *Ḥadīth al-Sindibād al-Qadīm*. Cairo: Lajnat al-Ta'līf wa al-Tarjamah wa al-Nashr, 1943.

Frankenberg, Lloyd. *Pleasure Dome: On Reading Modern Poetry*. Boston: Houghton Mifflin, 1949.

Frappier, Jean. "Chrétien de Troyes." In Roger Sherman Loomis, ed., *Arthurian Literature in the Middle Ages: A Collaborative History*, chap. 15. 2d ed. Oxford: Clarendon Press, 1961.

Frye, Northrop. *The Secular Scripture: A Study of the Structure of Romance*. Cambridge: Harvard University Press, 1982.

Frye, Prosser Hall. *Romance and Tragedy: A Study of Classical and Romantic Elements in the Great Tragedies of European Literature*. 1908. Lincoln: University of Nebraska Press, 1961.

García Lorca, Federico. *Obras completas*. Madrid: Aguilar, 1954.

Gardner, John, and John Maier. *Gilgamesh: Translated from the Sîn-leqi-unninnī Version*. New York: Vintage Books, Random House, 1985.

Gautier, Théophile. *Poésies Complètes*. 3 vols. Ed. René Jasinski. Paris: A. G. Nizet, 1970.

Giamatti, A. Bartlett. *The Earthly Paradise and the Renaissance Epic*. Princeton: Princeton University Press, 1966.

Gibb, Hamilton A. R. *Arabic Literature: An Introduction*. 2d rev. ed. Oxford: Clarendon Press, 1963.

Goethe, Johann Wolfgang. *Gedichte*. Ed. and with an introduction by Stefan Zweig. Stuttgart: Philip Reclam Jun., 1983.

Goldziher, Ignaz. *Abhandlungen zur arabischen Philologie*. 2 vols. Leiden: Buchhandlung und Druckerei vormals E. J. Brill, 1896–99.

———. "Bemerkungen zur neuhebräischen Poesie." *Jewish Quarterly Review* 14 (1902): 734–36.

Góngora, Luis de. *Antología poética, selección y poema de Rafael Alberti*. Buenos Aires: Editorial Pleamar, 1945.

The Greek Anthology. Loeb Classical Library. 1969.

Guillaume de Lorris and Jean de Meung. *Le Roman de la Rose*. 5 vols. Société des Anciens Textes Français, ed. Ernest Langlois. Paris: Librairie de Firmin-Didot/Librairie Ancienne Honoré/Édouard Champion, 1914–24.

Haddārah, Muḥammad Muṣṭafā. *Ittijāhāt al-Shiʿr al-ʿArabī fī al-Qarn al-Thānī al-Hijrī*. 3d ed. Cairo: Dār al-Maʿārif bi Miṣr, 1970.

Hagstrum, Jean H. *The Sister Arts: The Tradition of Literary Pictorialism and English Poetry from Dryden to Gray*. 1958. Chicago: University of Chicago Press, 1987.

Harrison, Thomas Perrin, Jr., ed. *The Pastoral Elegy: An Anthology*. Austin: University of Texas Press, 1939.

Ḥassān Ibn Thābit. *Dīwān*. 2 vols. Ed. Walīd ʿArafāt. Beirut: Dār Ṣādir, 1974.

———. *Dīwān*. Ed. Sayyid Ḥanafī Ḥasanayn and Ḥasan Kāmil al-Ṣīrafī. Cairo: Al-Hayʾah al-Miṣrīyah al-ʿĀmmah li al-Kitāb, 1974.

———. *Sharḥ Dīwān Ḥassān Ibn Thābit al-Anṣārī*. Recension of ʿAbd al-Raḥmān al-Barqūqī. Cairo: Al-Maktabah al-Tijārīyah al-Kubrā, 1929.

Ḥātim al-Ṭāʾī. *Dīwān*. *Shiʿr Ḥātim Ibn ʿAbd Allāh al-Ṭāʾī wa Akhbāruh*. Ed. ʿĀdil Sulaymān Jamāl. Cairo: Maṭbaʿat al-Madanī, 1395/1975.

al-Ḥātimī, Abū ʿAlī Muḥammad Ibn al-Ḥasan. *Ḥilyat al-Muḥāḍarah fī Ṣināʿat al-Shiʿr*. 2 vols. Ed. Jaʿfar al-Kattānī. Baghdad: Dār al-Rashīd li al-Nashr, 1979.

Havelock, Eric A. *The Muse Learns to Write: Reflections on Orality and Literacy from Antiquity to the Present*. New Haven: Yale University Press, 1986.

Haydar, Adnan. "The Muʿallaqa of Imruʾ al-Qays: Its Structure and Meaning, I." *Edebiyât* 2, no. 2 (1977): 227–61.

Heidegger, Martin. *Sein und Zeit*. 10th ed. Tübingen: Max Niemeyer Verlag, 1963.

Heidel, Alexander. *The Gilgamesh Epic and Old Testament Parallels*. Chicago: University of Chicago Press, Phoenix Books, 1965.

Heinrichs, Wolfhart. *Arabische Dichtung und griechische Poetik: Ḥāzim al-Qarṭāgannīs Grundlegung der Poetik mit Hilfe aristotelischer Begriffe*. Beirut: Deutsche Morgenländische Gesellschaft; Wiesbaden: F. Steiner, 1969.

Heiserman, Arthur. *The Novel before the Novel: Essays and Discussions about the*

Beginnings of Prose Fiction in the West. Chicago: University of Chicago Press, 1977.

Hennebo, Dieter. *Gärten des Mittelalters*. Hamburg: Broscheck Verlag, 1962.

Highet, Gilbert. *The Classical Tradition: Greek and Roman Influences on Western Literature*. Oxford: Oxford University Press, 1970.

Holden, Anthony, trans. *Greek Pastoral Poetry*. Penguin Books. 1974.

Holmberg, Uno. *Der Baum des Lebens*. Annales Academiae Scientiarum Fennicae, ser. B, vol. 16. 1922.

Homer. *The Iliad*. Trans. A. T. Murray. Loeb Classical Library. 1946.

———. *The Odyssey*. Trans. R. Fitzgerald. Garden City, N.J.: Doubleday, 1961.

Horace. *Satires, Epistles and Ars poetica*. Trans. H. Rushton Fairclough. Loeb Classical Library. 1966.

Huizinga, Johan. *Men and Ideas*. New York: Harper Torchbooks, 1970.

Ḥusayn, Ṭāhā. *Ḥadīth al-Arbiʿāʾ*. 3 vols. Cairo: Dār al-Maʿārif bi Miṣr, 1954–57.

———. *Tajdīd Dhikrā Abī al-ʿAlāʾ*. 5th ed. Cairo: Dār al-Maʿārif bi Miṣr, 1958.

al-Ḥuṭayʾah. *Dīwān*. Recension of Ibn al-Sikkīt. Ed. Nuʿmān Muḥammad Amīn Ṭāhā. Cairo: Maktabat al-Khānjī, 1987.

Ibn al-Abbār [Abū ʿAbd Allāh al-Quḍāʿī]. *Al-Ḥullah al-Sayrāʾ*. 2 vols. Ed. Ḥusayn Muʾnis. Cairo: Al-Sharikah al-ʿArabīyah li al-Ṭibāʿah wa al-Nashr, 1963.

———. *Al-Muqtaḍab min Kitāb Tuḥfat al-Qādim*. Redaction of Abū Isḥāq Ibrāhīm Ibn Muḥammad Ibn Ibrāhīm al-Bafiqī. Ed. Ibrāhīm al-Abyārī. Cairo: Al-Maṭbaʿah al-Amīrīyah, 1957.

Ibn Abī Khāzim al-Asadī, Bishr. *Dīwān*. 2d ed., ed. ʿIzzat Ḥasan. Damascus: Wizārat al-Thaqāfah, 1392/1972.

Ibn Abī Rabīʿah, ʿUmar. *Dīwān*. Beirut: Dār Ṣādir/Dār Bayrūt, 1385/1966.

Ibn ʿArabī, Muḥyī al-Dīn. *Tarjumān al-Ashwāq*. Beirut: Dār Ṣādir, 1961.

———. *The Tarjumān al-Ashwāq: A Collection of Mystical Odes by Ibn ʿArabī*. Trans. Reynold A. Nicholson. London: Royal Asiatic Society, 1911.

Ibn Aybak al-Ṣafadī, Khalīl. *Tamām al-Mutūn fī Sharḥ Risālat Ibn Zaydūn*. Ed. Muḥammad Abū al-Faḍl Ibrāhīm. Cairo: Dār al-Fikr al-ʿArabī, 1389/1969.

Ibn al-Dumaynah. *Dīwān*. Cairo: Maktabat al-ʿUrūbah, 1959.

Ibn al-Faqīh al-Hamadhānī. *Abrégé du Libre des pays*. Trans. Henri Massé. Damascus: Institut Français de Damas, 1973.

Ibn al-Fāriḍ, ʿUmar. *Dīwān*. Beirut: Dār Ṣādir, 1957.

———. *Dīwān*. Ed. ʿAbd al-Khāliq Maḥmūd. Cairo: Dār al-Maʿārif, 1984.

Ibn Ḥazm al-Andalusī, Abū Muḥammad ʿAlī Ibn Aḥmad Ibn Saʿīd. *Ṭawq al-Ḥamāmah fī al-Ilfah wa al-Ullāf*. 3d ed., ed. al-Ṭāhir Aḥmad Makkī. Cairo: Dār al-Maʿārif, 1400/1980.

Ibn Ḥillizah, al-Ḥārith. *Dīwān*. Ed. Hāshim al-Ṭaʿʿān. Baghdad: Maṭbaʿat al-Irshād, 1969.

Ibn al-Jahm, ʿAlī. *Dīwān*. 2d ed., ed. Khalīl Mardam. Beirut: Dār al-Āfāq al-Jadīdah, [1979?].

Ibn al-Jawzī, Abū al-Faraj ʿAbd al-Raḥmān. *Dhamm al-Hawā*. Ed. Muṣṭafā ʿAbd al-Wāḥid. Cairo: Dār al-Kutub al-Ḥadīthah, 1381/1962.

Ibn Khafājah al-Andalusī, Ibrāhīm Ibn Abī al-Fatḥ. *Dīwān*. Alexandria: Munshaʾat al-Maʿārif, 1960.

Ibn Khaldūn. *Al-Taʿrīf bi Ibn Khaldūn wa Riḥlatih Gharban wa Sharqan*. Ed. Muḥammad Ibn Tāwīt al-Ṭanjī. Cairo: Lajnat al-Taʾlīf wa al-Tarjamah wa al-Nashr, 1370/1951.

Ibn Manẓūr al-Miṣrī, Muḥammad Ibn Mukarram. *Akhbār Abī Nuwās: Taʾrīkhuh wa Nawādiruh, Shiʿruh, Mujūnuh*. 2 vols. Ed. Shukrī Maḥmūd Aḥmad. Baghdad: Maṭbaʿat al-Maʿārif, [1952?].

Ibn Munqidh, Usāmah. *Kitāb al-ʿAṣā*. Ed. Ḥasan ʿAbbās. Alexandria: Al-Hayʾah al-Miṣrīyah al-ʿĀmmah li al-Kitāb, 1978.

———. *Lubāb al-Ādāb*. Ed. Aḥmad Shākir. Cairo: Dār al-Kutub al-Salafīyah, 1407/1987 [1st ed. 1354 H.].

———. *Al-Manāzil wa al-Diyār*. Ed. Muṣṭafā Ḥijāzī. Cairo: Al-Majlis al-Aʿlā li al-Shuʾūn al-Islāmīyah, 1968.

Ibn Muqbil [Tamīm Ibn Ubayy]. *Dīwān*. Ed. ʿIzzat Ḥasan. Damascus: Maṭbūʿāt Mudīrīyat Iḥyāʾ al-Turāth al-Qadīm, 1381/1962.

Ibn al-Muʿtazz. *Dīwān*. Beirut: Dār Ṣādir, 1961.

———. *Ṭabaqāt al-Shuʿarāʾ*. 2d. ed., ed. ʿAbd al-Sattār Aḥmad Farrāj. Cairo: Dār al-Maʿārif bi Miṣr, 1968.

Ibn Qays al-Ruqayyāt, ʿUbayd Allāh. *Dīwān*. Ed. Muḥammad Yūsuf Najm. Beirut: Dār Ṣādir/Dār Bayrūt, 1378/1958.

Ibn Qutaybah. *Al-Shiʿr wa al-Shuʿarāʾ*. 2 vols. Ed. Aḥmad Muḥammad Shākir. Cairo: Dār al-Maʿārif bi Miṣr, 1966.

Ibn Rabāḥ, Nuṣayb. *Shiʿr Nuṣayb Ibn Rabāḥ*. Ed. Dāwūd Sallūm. Baghdad: Maṭbaʿat al-Irshād, 1976.

Ibn Rashīq al-Qayrawānī. *Al-ʿUmdah fī Maḥāsin al-Shiʿr wa Ādābih wa Naqdih*. 3d ed. 2 vols. Cairo: Al-Maktabah al-Tijārīyah al-Kubrā, 1963.

Ibn al-Rūmī. *Dīwān*. 2 vols. Cairo: Maṭbaʿat al-Hilāl, 1922.

——— [Abū al-Ḥasan ʿAlī Ibn al-ʿAbbās Ibn Jarīḥ]. *Dīwān*. 6 vols. Ed. Ḥusayn Naṣṣār. Cairo: Maṭbaʿat Dār al-Kutub, 1974.

Ibn Shuhayd al-Andalusī, Abū ʿĀmir. *Dīwān*. Ed. Charles Pellat. Beirut: Dār al-Makshūf, 1963.

———. *Dīwān*. Ed. Yaʿqūb Zakī. Revised by Maḥmūd ʿAlī Makkī. Cairo: Dār al-Kitāb al-ʿArabī li al-Ṭibāʿah wa al-Nashr, n.d.

———. *Risālat al-Tawābiʿ wa al-Zawābiʿ*. Ed. Buṭrus al-Bustānī. Beirut: Maktabat Ṣādir, 1951.

Ibn al-Taʿāwīdhī, Sibṭ. *Dīwān*. Beirut: Dār Ṣādir, 1967. [Photo-offset of Cairo ed., 1903.]

Ibn Ṭabāṭabā al-ʿAlawī, Muḥammad Ibn Aḥmad. *ʿIyār al-Shiʿr*. Ed. Ṭāhā al-Ḥājirī and Muḥammad Zaghlūl Sallām. Cairo: Al-Maktabah al-Tijārīyah al-Kubrā, 1955.

Ibn Ṭufayl, Abū Bakr. *Ḥayy Ibn Yaqẓān*. Beirut: Al-Maṭbaʿah al-Kāthūlīkīyah, 1963.

Ibn al-Wardī, Sirāj al-Dīn Abū Ḥafṣ ʿUmar. *Kharīdat al-ʿAjāʾib wa Farīdat al-Gharāʾib*. Cairo: Al-Maṭbaʿah al-ʿĀmirah al-Malījīyah, 1324 H.

Ibn Yaʿfur al-Nahshalī, al-Aswad. *Dīwān*. Ed. Nūrī Ḥamūdī al-Qaysī. Baghdad: Maṭbaʿat al-Jumhūrīyah, 1970.

Ibn Zaydūn. *Dīwān Ibn Zaydūn wa Rasāʾiluh*. Ed. ʿAlī ʿAbd al-ʿAẓīm. Cairo: Maktabat Nahḍat Miṣr bi al-Fajjālah, 1957.

Imruʾ al-Qays. *Dīwān*. 3d ed., ed. Muḥammad Abū al-Faḍl Ibrāhīm. Cairo: Dār al-Maʿārif bi Miṣr, 1969.

al-Iṣbahānī [al-Iṣfahānī], Abū al-Faraj. *Kitāb al-Aghānī*. 31 vols. Ed. Ibrāhīm al-Abyārī. Cairo: Dār al-Shaʿb, 1969–79.

———. *Kitāb al-Aghānī*. 24 vols. Cairo: Al-Muʾassasah al-Miṣrīyah al-ʿĀmmah li al-Taʾlīf wa al-Tarjamah wa al-Nashr, 1963/1970–74. [Photo-offset of Dār al-Kutub ed.]

Isbell, Harold, trans. *The Last Poets of Imperial Rome*. Penguin Books, 1982.

ʿIzz al-Dīn, Ḥasan al-Bannā. *Al-Ṭayf wa al-Khayāl fī al-Shiʿr al-ʿArabī al-Qadīm*. Cairo: Dār al-Nadīm li al-Nashr wa al-Tawzīʿ wa al-Ṣiḥāfah, 1988.

al-ʿIzzāwī, ʿAbd al-Sattār. "Ṭarīq al-Ḥajj al-Qadīm: Darb Zubaydah— Maḥaṭṭat Umm al-Qurūn." *Sūmir* 44 (1985–86): 199–213.

al-Jabūrī, Yaḥyā, ed. *Shiʿr ʿAbd Allāh Ibn Zabaʿrī*. Beirut: Muʾassasat al-Risālah, 1401/1981.

Jacobi, Renate. *Studien zur Poetik der altarabischen Qaṣide*. Wiesbaden: Franz Steiner Verlag, 1971.

———. "Time and Reality in *Nasīb* and *Ghazal*." *Journal of Arabic Literature* 16 (1985): 1–17.

Jaeger, Werner. *Paideia*. 3 vols. Trans. Gilbert Highet. New York: Oxford University Press, 1943.

al-Jāḥiẓ, ʿAmr Ibn Baḥr. *Al-Bayān wa al-Tabyīn*. 4 vols. 3d ed., ed. ʿAbd al-Salām Muḥammad Hārūn. Cairo: Maktabat al-Khānjī, 1388/1968.

———. *Kitāb al-Ḥayawān*. 8 vols. Ed. ʿAbd al-Salām Muḥammad Hārūn. Cairo: Dār al-Maʿārif, 1938.

Jamīl Ibn Maʿmar al-ʿUdhrī. *Dīwān Jamīl Buthaynah*. Beirut: Dār Ṣādir, 1966.

Jantzen, Hans. *High Gothic: The Classic Cathedrals of Chartres, Reims, Amiens*. Trans. James Palmes. New York: Pantheon Books, 1962.

Jarīr [Ibn ʿAṭīyah]. *Dīwān*. Beirut: Dār Ṣādir, 1964.

Jones, William. *Poems*. Oxford: Clarendon Press, 1772.

al-Jumaḥī, Ibn Sallām. *Ṭabaqāt Fuḥūl al-Shuʿarāʾ*. 2d ed. 2 vols. Ed. Maḥmūd Muḥammad Shākir. Cairo: Maṭbaʿat al-Madanī, 1974.

al-Jurjānī, ʿAbd al-Qāhir [Ibn ʿAbd al-Raḥmān]. *Dalāʾil al-Iʿjāz*. Ed. Maḥmūd Muḥammad Shākir. Cairo: Maktabat al-Khānjī, 1404/1984.

———. *Die Geheimnisse der Wortkunst (Asrār al-Balāghah) des ʿAbdalqāhir al-Curcānī*. Trans. Helmut Ritter. Wiesbaden: Franz Steiner Verlag, 1959.

al-Jurjānī, al-Qāḍī. ʿAlī ʿAbd al-ʿAzīz. *Al-Wasāṭah bayna al-Mutanabbī wa Khuṣūmih*. Cairo: Maṭbaʿat ʿIsā al-Bābī al-Ḥalabī, 1966.

al-Jurjānī, ʿAlī Ibn Muḥammad. *Kitāb al-Taʿrīfāt*. Cairo: Al-Maṭbaʿah al-Khayrīyah, 1306/1888.

Kaʿb Ibn Zuhayr. *Sharḥ Dīwān Kaʿb Ibn Zuhayr*. Ed. Abū Saʿīd al-Ḥasan Ibn al-Ḥusayn Ibn ʿAbd Allāh al-Sukkarī. Cairo: Al-Dār al-Qawmīyah li al-Ṭibāʿah wa al-Nashr, 1385/1965. [Photo-offset of Dār al-Kutub ed., 1369/1950.]

Keats, John. *The Poetical Works of John Keats*. Oxford: Oxford University Press, 1930.

Kennedy, George A. *Greek Rhetoric under Christian Emperors*. Princeton: Princeton University Press, 1983.

Kerenyi, C., and C. G. Jung. *Essays on a Science of Mythology: The Myth of the Divine Child and the Mysteries of Eleusis*. Bollingen Series 22. Princeton: Princeton University Press, 1973.

al-Khansāʾ, Tumāḍir Bint ʿAmr Ibn al-Ḥārith Ibn ʿAmr. *Dīwān*. Commentary by Thaʿlab Abū al-ʿAbbās Aḥmad Ibn Yaḥyā Ibn Sayyār al-Shaybānī. Ed. Anwar Abū Suwaylim. Amman: Dār ʿAmmār, 1409/1988.

al-Khaṭīb al-Ibshīhī, Muḥammad Ibn Aḥmad. *Al-Mustaṭraf min Kulli Fann Mustaẓraf*. 2 vols. Cairo: Būlāq, 1268 H.

al-Khuḍarī, Muḥammad, ed. *Muhadhdhab al-Aghānī*. 9 vols. Cairo: Maṭbaʿat Miṣr, 1925.

Kratchkovsky, Ignatius. *Abū-l-Faradzh al-Vaʾva Damasskiy: Materialy dla Charakterystiki Poeticheskogo Tvorchestva*. St. Petersburg: Academy of Sciences, 1914.

Kremer, Alfred von. *Dīwān des Abū Nuwās: des grössten lyrischen Dichters der Araber*. Vienna: W. Braumüller, 1855.

Kunitzsh, Paul. *Untersuchungen zur Sternnomenklatur der Araber*. Wiesbaden: Otto Harrassowitz, 1961.

Kuthayyir ʿAzzah. *Dīwān*. Ed. Iḥsān ʿAbbās. Beirut: Dār al-Thaqāfah, 1971.

Labīd Ibn Rabīʿah al-ʿĀmirī. *Dīwān*. Beirut: Dār Ṣādir, n.d.

———. *Sharḥ Dīwān Labīd Ibn Rabīʿah al-ʿĀmirī*. Ed. Iḥsān ʿAbbās. Kuwait: Al-Turāth al-ʿArabī, 1962.

Lamberton, Robert. *Homer the Theologian: Neoplatonist Allegorical Reading and the Growth of the Epic Tradition*. Berkeley and Los Angeles: University of California Press, 1989.

Lane, E. W. *Arabic-English Lexicon*. New York: Frederick Unger Publishing Co., 1955–56.

Lassner, Jacob. *The Topography of Baghdad in the Early Middle Ages: Text and Studies*. Detroit: Wayne State University Press, 1970.

Latham, Charles Sterrett. *A Translation of Dante's Eleven Letters*. Boston and New York: Houghton Mifflin Co.; Cambridge: Riverside Press, 1891.

Lemke, Gerhard H. *Sonne, Mond und Sterne in der deutschen Literatur seit dem Mittelalter: Ein Bildkomplex im Spannungsfeld gesellschaftlichen Wandels*. Bern: Peter Lang, 1981.

Leon, Fray Luis de. *Poesía completa*. Ed. Guillermo Serés. Madrid: Clàsicos Taurus, 1990.

Lesky, Albin. *A History of Greek Literature*. Trans. James Willis and Cornelis de Heer. New York: Crowell, 1966.

Lessing, Gotthold Ephraim. *Nathan der Weise*. Stuttgart: Philip Reclam Jun., 1975.

Levin, Harry. *The Myth of the Golden Age in the Renaissance*. New York: Oxford University Press, 1972.

Lévi-Strauss, Claude. *L'homme nu*. Paris: Plon, 1971.

Lewis, C. S. *The Allegory of Love: A Study in Medieval Tradition*. New York: Oxford University Press, 1971.

———. *The Discarded Image: An Introduction to Medieval and Renaissance Literature*. Cambridge: Cambridge University Press, 1970.

———. *A Preface to Paradise Lost*. 1942. New York: Oxford University Press, 1969.

Lexikon der Ägyptologie. 6 vols. Ed. Wolfgang Helck and Eberhard Otto. Wiesbaden: Otto Harrassowitz, 1975–86.

Lohner, Edgar, ed. *Interpretationen zum West-östlichen Divan*. Darmstadt: Wissenschaftliche Buchgesellschaft, 1973.

Loomis, Roger Sherman, ed. *Arthurian Literature in the Middle Ages: A Collaborative History*. Oxford: Clarendon Press, 1959–61.

Loroux, Nicole. *The Invention of Athens: The Funeral Oration in the Classical City*. Trans. Alan Sheridan. Cambridge: Harvard University Press, 1986.

Lovejoy, Arthur O., and George Boas. *Primitivism and Related Ideas in Antiquity*. With supplementary essays by W. F. Albright and P. E. Dumont. New York: Octagon Books, 1980.

al-Maʿarrī, Abū al-ʿAlāʾ. *Risālat al-Ghufrān*. Ed. Bint al-Shāṭiʾ. Cairo: Dār al-Maʿārif bi Miṣr, 1950.

———. *Shurūḥ Saqṭ al-Zand*. 5 vols. Cairo: Dār al-Kutub al-Miṣrīyah, 1945–48.

Majnūn Laylā. *Dīwān Majnūn Laylā*. Ed. ʿAbd al-Sattār Aḥmad Farrāj. Cairo: Maktabat Miṣr, [1973].

———. *Qays Ibn al-Mulawwaḥ al-Majnūn wa Dīwānuh*. Ed. Shawqīyah Inaljiq. Ankara: Maṭbaʿat al-Jamʿīyah al-Tārīkhīyah al-Turkīyah, 1967.

Mâle, Émile. *The Gothic Image: Religious Art in France of the Thirteenth Century*. Trans. Dora Nussey. New York: Harper and Row, Icon Editions, 1972.

Malti-Douglas, Fedwa. *Woman's Body, Woman's Word: Gender and Discourse in Arabo-Islamic Writing*. Princeton: Princeton University Press, 1991.

Mandūr, Muḥammad. *Fī al-Mīzān al-Jadīd*. 3d ed. Cairo/al-Fajjālah: Maktabat Nahḍat Miṣr wa Maṭbaʿatuhā, [1963].

al-Maqqarī al-Tilimsānī, Aḥmad Ibn Muḥammad. *Nafḥ al-Ṭīb min Ghuṣn al-Andalus al-Raṭīb—wa Dhikr Wazīrihā Lisān al-Dīn Ibn al-Khaṭīb*. 10 vols. Ed. Muḥammad Muḥyī al-Dīn Ibn al-Ḥamīd. Beirut: Dār al-Kitāb al-ʿArabī, [1967?] [Photo-offset of Cairo ed., Al-Maktabah al-Tijārīyah al-Kubrā, 1949.]

al-Masʿūdī, Abū al-Ḥasan ʿAlī Ibn al-Ḥusayn Ibn ʿAlī. *Murūj al-Dhahab wa Maʿādin al-Jawhar*. 4th ed. 4 vols. Ed. Yūsuf Asʿad Dāghir. Beirut: Dār al-Andalus li al-Ṭibāʿah wa al-Nashr, 1401/1981.

Meisami, Julie Scott. *Medieval Persian Court Poetry*. Princeton: Princeton University Press, 1987.

Mihyār al-Daylamī. *Dīwān*. 4 vols. Cairo: Dār al-Kutub al-Miṣrīyah, 1344/1925.

al-Mihzamī, Abū Hiffān ʿAbd Allāh Ibn Aḥmad Ibn Ḥarb. *Akhbār Abī Nuwās*. Ed. ʿAbd al-Sattār Aḥmad Farrāj. Cairo: Maktabat Miṣr, 1954.

Miquel, André. *La géographie humaine du monde musulman jusqu'au milieu du 11e siècle*. 2 vols. Paris–La Haye: Mouton and Co., 1967, 1975.

Miquel, André, and Percy Kemp. *Majnûn et Laylâ: l'amour fou*. Paris: Sindbad, 1984.

Moʿīn, Mohammad. *Farhang-e Farsi*. 6 vols. Tehran: Amir Kabir Publications, 1966.

Mommsen, Katharina. *Goethe und die arabische Welt*. Frankfurt am Main: Insel Verlag, 1988.

———. *Goethe und die Moallakat*. Berlin: Akademie Verlag, 1961.

Monroe, James T. *Risālat at-Tawābiʿ wa z-Zawābiʿ: The Treatise of Familiar Spirits and Demons by Abū ʿĀmir ibn Shuhaid al-Ashjaʿī, al-Andalusī*. Berkeley and Los Angeles: University of California Press, 1971.

Moore, George. *An Anthology of Pure Poetry*. 2d ed. New York: Liveright, 1973.

Mubārak, Zakī. *Al-Madāʾiḥ al-Nabawīyah fī al-Adab al-ʿArabī*. Cairo: Dār al-Shaʿb, n.d.

al-Mubarrad, Abū al-ʿAbbās Muḥammad Ibn Yazīd. *Al-Kāmil fī al-Lughah wa al-Adab*. 4 vols. Ed. Muḥammad Abū al-Faḍl Ibrāhīm. Cairo: Maktabat Nahḍat Miṣr, 1956.

al-Mufaḍḍal Ibn Muḥammad al-Ḍabbī, Abū al-ʿAbbās. *Dīwān al-Mufaḍḍalīyāt*. Commentary by Abū Muḥammad al-Qāsim Ibn Muḥammad Ibn Bashshār al-Anbārī. Vol. 1, *Arabic Text*. Ed. Charles James Lyall. Beirut: Maṭbaʿat al-Ābāʾ al-Yasūʿiyyīn, 1920.

———. *Al-Mufaḍḍalīyāt*. 5th ed., ed. Aḥmad Muḥammad Shākir and ʿAbd al-Salām Muḥammad Hārūn. Cairo: Dār al-Maʿārif bi Miṣr, 1976.

Muḥammad, Ibrāhīm ʿAbd al-Raḥmān. *Ibn Qays al-Ruqayyāt: Ḥayātuh wa Shiʿruh*. Cairo: Dār al-Nahḍah, 1965.

Müller, F. Max. *Comparative Mythology*. Ed. A. Smyth Palmer. New York: Dutton, 1909.

Murphy, James J. *Rhetoric in the Middle Ages: A History of Rhetorical Theory from St. Augustine to the Renaissance*. 1974. Berkeley and Los Angeles: University of California Press, 1981.

Muslim Ibn al-Walīd [Ṣarīʿ al-Ghawānī]. *Sharḥ Dīwān Ṣarīʿ al-Ghawānī*. 2d ed., ed. Sāmī al-Dahhān. Cairo: Dār al-Maʿārif bi Miṣr, 1970.

al-Mutanabbī, Abū al-Ṭayyib Aḥmad Ibn Ḥusayn. *Al-ʿArf al-Ṭayyib fī Sharḥ Dīwān Abī al-Ṭayyib*. 2 vols. Ed. Nāṣīf al-Yāzijī. Beirut: Dār Ṣādir/Dār Bayrūt, 1964.

al-Nābighah al-Dhubyānī. *Dīwān*. Ed. Karam al-Bustānī. Beirut: Dār Ṣādir, n.d.

Nagy, Gregory. *The Best of the Achaeans: Concepts of the Hero in Archaic Greek Poetry*. Baltimore: John Hopkins University Press, 1979.

al-Namarī, Manṣūr. *Shiʿr Manṣūr al-Namarī*. Ed. al-Ṭayyib al-ʿAshshāsh. Damascus: Dār al-Maʿārif li al-Ṭibāʿah, 1401/1981.

Nāṣif, Muṣṭafā. *Qirāʾah Thāniyah li Shiʿrinā al-Qadīm*. [Tripoli, Libya]: Manshūrāt al-Jāmiʿah al-Lībīyah, Kullīyat al-Ādāb, n.d.

Nicholson, Reynold A. *Translations of Eastern Poetry and Prose*. Cambridge: Cambridge University Press, 1922.

al-Nuwayrī, Shihāb al-Dīn Aḥmad Ibn ʿAbd al-Wahhāb. *Nihāyat al-Arab fī Funūn al-Adab*. 18 vols. Cairo: Dār al-Kutub al-Miṣrīyah, 1923.

Ovid. *The Amours*. Philadelphia, 1902.

The Oxford Classical Dictionary. 2d ed., ed. N. G. L. Hammond and H. H. Scullard. Oxford: Clarendon Press, 1970.

Page, Denys. *Sappho and Alcaeus: An Introduction to the Ancient Lesbian Poetry*. Oxford: Clarendon Press, 1983.

Panofsky, Erwin. *Meaning in the Visual Arts*. Garden City, N.Y.: Doubleday, 1955.

Paris, Ginette. *Pagan Meditations: The Worlds of Aphrodite, Artemis, and Hestia*. Trans. Gwendolyn Moore. Dallas: Spring Publications, 1986.

Paton, Lucy Allen. *Studies in the Fairy Mythology of Arthurian Romance*. New York: Burt Franklin, 1960.

Peres, H. "Le palmier en Espagne musulmane: notes d'après les textes arabes." In *Mélanges Gaudefroy-Demombynes*, pp. 226–29. Cairo: Imprimerie de l'Institute Français, 1937.

Pettit, Philip. *The Concept of Structuralism: A Critical Analysis*. Dublin: Gill and Macmillan, 1975.

Peyre, Henry. *Literature and Society*. New Haven: Yale University Press, 1969.

Plutarch. *Moralia*. Trans. Frank Cole Babbitt. Loeb Classical Library. 1936.

Polybius. *The Histories*. 6 vols. Trans. W. R. Paton. Loeb Classical Library. 1922.

Proust, Marcel. *À la recherche du temps perdu*. Paris, Gallimard, 1954.

Al-Qāḍī al-Fāḍil [ʿAbd al-Raḥīm Ibn ʿAlī al-Baysānī]. *Dīwān*. 2 vols. Ed. Aḥmad Aḥmad Badawī. Cairo: Dār al-Maʿārif, 1961.

al-Qāḍī, al-Nuʿmān ʿAbd al-Mutaʿālī. *Shiʿr al-Futūḥāt al-Islāmīyah fī Ṣadr al-Islām*. Cairo: Dār al-Qawmīyah, 1965.

al-Qālī, [Ismāʿīl Ibn al-Qāsim] Abū ʿAlī. *Kitāb al-Amālī*. 3d ed. 2 vols. Cairo: Al-Maktabah al-Tijārīyah al-Kubrā, 1373/1953.

al-Qarṭājannī, [Abū al-Ḥasan] Ḥāzim. *Dīwān*. Beirut: Dār al-Thaqāfah, 1964.

———. *Manāhij al-Bulaghā᾽ wa Sirāj al-Udabā᾽*. Ed. Muḥammad al-Ḥabīb Ibn al-Khūjah. Tunis: Dār al-Kutub al-Sharqīyah, 1966.

al-Qazwīnī, Zakarīyā. *ʿAjā᾽ib al-Makhlūqāt wa Gharā᾽ib al-Mawjūdāt*. 2d ed., ed. Fārūq Saʿd. Beirut: Dār al-Āfāq al-Jadīdah, 1977.

Qudāmah Ibn Jaʿfar, Abū al-Faraj. *Naqd al-Shiʿr*. 3d ed., ed. Kamāl Muṣṭafā. Cairo: Maktabat al-Khānjī, 1979.

al-Qurashī, Abū Zayd Muḥammad Ibn Abī al-Khaṭṭāb. *Jamharat Ashʿār al-ʿArab fī al-Jāhilīyah wa al-Islām*. 2 vols. Ed. ʿAlī Muḥammad al-Bijāwī. Cairo: Dār Nahḍat Miṣr li al-Ṭibāʿah wa al-Nashr, 1387/1967.

al-Rāʿī al-Numayrī. *Dīwān*. Ed. Reinhard Weipert. Beirut and Wiesbaden: Steiner Verlag, 1980.

Raleigh, Walter. *The Poems of Sir Walter Raleigh*. Ed. Agnes M. C. Latham. Cambridge: Harvard University Press, 1962.

al-Rāzī al-Ṣūfī. *Kitāb Ṣuwar al-Kawākib al-Thamāniyah wa al-Arbaʿīn*. Beirut: Dār al-Āfāq al-Jadīdah, 1401/1981.

Reed, Herbert. *Icon and Idea: The Function of Art in the Development of Human Consciousness*. New York: Schocken Books, 1972.

Rice, David Talbot. *Islamic Art*. London: Thames and Hudson, 1965.

Richter, Gustav. "Zur Entstehungsgeschichte der altarabischen Qaṣīde." *Zeitschrift der Deutschen morgenländischen Gesellschaft* 92, n.s. 17 (1938): 554–55.

Ringbom, Lars-Ivar. *Graltempel und Paradies: Beziehungen zwischen Iran und Europa im Mittelalter*. Stockholm: Wahlstrom and Widstrand, 1951.

Rojas, Pedro Soto de. *Paraiso cerrado para muchos, jardines abiertos para pocos* and *Los fragmentos del Adonís* (1652). In *Obras de Don Pedro Soto de Rojas*. Ed. Antonio Gallego Morell. Madrid, 1950.

Rolland, Romain. *Beethoven the Creator: The Great Creative Epochs, from the Eroica to the Appassionata*. New York: Dover Publications, 1964.

Rosen, Charles. *The Classical Style: Haydn, Mozart, Beethoven*. New York and London: W. W. Norton and Co., 1972.

———. *Sonata Forms*. Rev. ed. New York and London: W. W. Norton and Co., 1988.

Rosenmeyer, Thomas G. *The Green Cabinet: Theocritus and the European Pastoral Lyric*. Berkeley and Los Angeles: University of California Press, 1969.

al-Rūbī, Ilfat Kamāl. *Naẓarīyat al-Shiʿr ʿind al-Falāsifah al-Muslimīn (min al-Kindī ḥattā Ibn Rushd)*. Beirut: Dār al-Nashr li al-Ṭibāʿah wa al-Nashr, 1983.

Rückert, Friedrich. *Hamāsa, oder, die ältesten arabischen Volkslieder, gesammelt von Abū Temmām*. 2 vols. Stuttgart: Samuel Gottlieb Liesching, 1846.

al-Ruṣāfī al-Balansī, [Abū ʿAbd Allāh Muḥammad Ibn Ghālib]. *Dīwān*. Ed. Iḥsān ʿAbbās. Beirut: Dār al-Thaqāfah, 1960.

Saavedra Fajardo, Diego de. *República literaria*. Madrid: Atlas, Colección Cisneros, 1944.

Ṣafadī, Muṭāʿ, and Īlīyā Ḥāwī, eds. *Mawsūʿat al-Shiʿr al-ʿArabī: Al-Shiʿr al-Jāhilī*. 4 vols. Beirut: Sharikat Khayyāṭ li al-Kutub wa al-Nashr, 1974.

Saint John of the Cross. *Vida y obras de San Juan de la Cruz; biografía inédita del Santo por Crisógono de Jesús*. 3d ed., ed. Lucinio del SS. Sacramento and Matias del Niño Jesus. Madrid: Biblioteca de Autores Cristianos, 1955.

al-Ṣanawbarī [Abū Bakr Aḥmad al-Ḍabbī al-Anṭākī]. *Dīwān*. Ed. Iḥsān ʿAbbās. Beirut: Dār al-Thaqāfah, 1970.

Sannazaro, Jacopo. *Arcadia and Piscatorial Eclogues*. Trans. Ralph Nash. Detroit: Wayne State University Press, 1966.

al-Sarī al-Raffāʾ. *Dīwān*. 2 vols. Ed. and introduction by Ḥabīb Ḥusayn al-Ḥasanī. Baghdad: Al-Maktabah al-Waṭanīyah, 1981.

al-Sarrāj, Abū Muḥammad Jaʿfar Ibn Aḥmad Ibn al-Ḥusayn. *Maṣāriʿ al-ʿUshshāq*. 2 vols. Beirut: Dār Ṣādir, n.d.

Seifer, Wylie. *Rococo and Cubism in Art and Literature*. New York: Vintage Books, 1960.

Seybold, John. "The Earliest Demon Lover: *The Ṭayf al-Khayāl* in *al-Mufaḍḍalīyāt*. In S. Stetkevych, ed., *Reorientations*.

Sezgin, Fuat. *Geschichte des arabischen Schrifttums*. Vol. 2, *Poesie: bis ca. 430 H*. Leiden: E. J. Brill, 1975.

Seznec, Jean. *The Survival of the Pagan Gods: The Mythological Tradition and Its Place in Renaissance Humanism and Art*. Trans. Barbara F. Sessions. Princeton: Princeton University Press, 1972.

Shaʿbān, Ḥāmid Muḥammad Amīn. *Al-Buḥūth al-Lughawīyah fī al-Rawḍ al-Unuf*. Cairo: Maktabat al-Anjlū al-Miṣrīyah, 1404/1984.

al-Shakʿah, Muṣṭafā. *Funūn al-Shiʿr fī Mujtamaʿ al-Ḥamdānīyīn*. Cairo: Maktabat al-Anjlū al-Miṣrīyah, 1958.

al-Shammākh Ibn Ḍirār al-Dhubyānī. *Dīwān*. Ed. Ṣalāḥ al-Dīn al-Hādī. Cairo: Dār al-Maʿārif bi Miṣr, 1968.

al-Shanfarā. *Qaṣīdat Lāmīyat al-ʿArab wa yalīhā Aʿjab al-ʿAjab fī Sharḥ Lāmīyat al-ʿArab*. Commentary by Muḥammad Ibn ʿUmar al-Zamakhsharī. Istanbul: Al-Jawāʾib, 1300 H.

al-Sharīf al-Murtaḍā [ʿAlī Ibn al-Ḥusayn Ibn Mūsā]. *Dīwān*. 3 vols. Cairo: ʿĪsā al-Bābī al-Ḥalabī wa Shurakāh, 1958.

al-Sharīf al-Raḍī [Muḥammad Ibn Abī Ṭāhir al-Ḥusayn]. *Dīwān*. 2 vols. Beirut: Dār Ṣādir, 1961.

Shawqī, Aḥmad. *Al-Shawqīyāt*. 4 vols. Cairo: Al-Maktabah al-Tijārīyah al-Kubrā, 1970.

Shaykhū, Luwīs. *Kitāb Shuʿarāʾ al-Naṣrānīyah*. 2d ed. 2 vols. Beirut: Dār al-Mashriq, 1967.

Shepherd, Dorothy G. "Banquet and Hunt in Medieval Islamic Iconography." In Ursula E. McCracken, Lilian M. C. Randall, and Richard A. Randall, Jr., eds., *Gatherings in Honor of Dorothy E. Miner*. Baltimore: Walters Art Gallery, 1974.

Slochower, Harry. *Mythopoesis: Mythic Patterns in the Literary Classics*. Detroit: Wayne State University Press, 1970.

Smith, Grover. *T. S. Eliot's Poetry and Plays: A Study in Sources and Meaning*. 1950. Chicago: University of Chicago Press, 1967.

Smith, W. Robertson. *The Religion of the Semites*. New York: Meridian Books, 1957.

Snell, Bruno. *Die Entdeckung des Geistes: Studien zur Entstehung des europäischen Denkens bei den Griechen*. 4th ed. Göttingen: Vandenhöck and Ruprecht, 1975.

Spearing, A. C. *Readings in Medieval Poetry*. Cambridge: Cambridge University Press, 1989.

Spee, Friedrich. *Trutznachtigall*. Ed. Gustave Otto Arlt. Halle/Saale: Max Niemeyer Verlag, 1936.

Staiger, Emil. *Grundbegriffe der Poetik*. Zurich: Atlantis Verlag, 1946.

Stetkevych, Jaroslav. "Arabic Hermeneutical Terminology: Paradox and the Production of Meaning." *Journal of Near Eastern Studies* 48, no. 2 (Apr. 1989): 81–95.

———. "Arabic Poetry and Assorted Poetics." In Malcolm H. Kerr, ed., *Islamic Studies: A Tradition and Its Problems*, pp. 103–23. Malibu, Calif.: Undena Publications, 1980.

———. "Ibn Qutaybah wa mā baʿdah: al-Qaṣīdah al-ʿArabīyah al-Kilāsīkīyah." Trans. from English. *Fuṣūl* 6, no. 2 (1986): 71–78.

———. "Name and Epithet: The Philology and Semiotics of Animal Nomenclature in Early Arabic Poetry." *Journal of Near Eastern Studies* 45, no. 2 (Apr. 1986): 89–124.

———. "Sīnīyat Aḥmad Shawqī wa ʿIyār al-Shiʿr al-ʿArabī al-Kilāsīkī." *Fuṣūl* 7, nos. 1/2 (Oct. 1986/Mar. 1987): 12–29.

———. "Toward an Arabic Elegiac Lexicon: The Seven Words of the *Nasīb*." In S. Stetkevych, ed., *Reorientations*.

Stetkevych, Suzanne Pinckney. *Abū Tammām and the Poetics of the ʿAbbāsid Age*. Leiden: E. J. Brill, 1991.

———. "Archetype and Attribution in Early Arabic Poetry: al-Shanfarā and the Lāmiyyat at-ʿArab." *International Journal of Middle East Studies* 18 (1986): 361–90.

———. "Intoxication and Immortality: Wine and Associated Imagery in al-Maʿarrī's Garden." In Fedwa Malti-Douglas, ed., *Critical Pilgrimages: Studies in the Arabic Literary Tradition. Literature East and West* 25 (1989): 29–48.

———. *The Mute Immortals Speak: Pre-Islamic Poetry and the Poetics of Ritual*. Myth and Poetics Series. Ithaca: Cornell University Press, 1993.

———. "Pre-Islamic Panegyric and the Poetics of Redemption: *Mufaḍḍalīyah* 119 of ʿAlqamah ibn ʿAbadah and *Bānat Suʿād* of Kaʿb ibn Zuhayr." In idem, ed., *Reorientations*.

———. "Al-Qaṣīdāh al-ʿArabīyah wa Ṭuqūs al-ʿUbūr: Dirāsah fī al-Bunyah al-Namūdhajīyah." *Majallat Majmaʿ al-Lughah al-ʿArabīyah bi Dimashq* 60, no. 1 (1985): 55–85.

———, ed. *Reorientations/Arabic and Persian Poetry*. Bloomington: Indiana University Press, 1993.

———. "The Rithāʾ of Taʾabbaṭa Sharran: A Study of Blood-Vengeance in Early Arabic Poetry." *Journal of Semitic Studies* 31, no. 1 (1986): 27–45.

———. "Ritual and Sacrificial Elements in the Poetry of Blood-Vengeance: Two Poems by Durayd Ibn al-Ṣimmah and Muhalhil Ibn Rabīʿah." *Journal of Near Eastern Studies* 45, no. 1 (1986): 31–43.

———. "Structuralist Interpretations of Pre-Islamic Poetry: Critique and New Directions." *Journal of Near Eastern Studies* 42, no. 2 (1983): 85–107.

———. "The Ṣuʿlūk and His Poem: A Paradigm of Passage Manqué." *Journal of the American Oriental Society* 104, no. 4 (1984): 661–78.

Stevens, John. *Medieval Romance: Themes and Approaches*. New York: Norton Library, 1974.

Stevens, Wallace. *The Palm at the End of the Mind: Selected Poems and a Play by Wallace Stevens*. Ed. Holly Stevens. New York: Alfred A. Knopf, 1971.

Sullivan, J. W. N. *Beethoven: His Spiritual Development*. New York: Alfred A. Knopf, 1964.

al-Ṭabbākh, Muḥammad Rāghib. *Al-Rawḍīyāt: Min Shiʿr al-Shāʿir al-Majīd Abī Bakr al-Ṣanawbarī al-Ḥalabī*. Aleppo: Al-Maṭbaʿah al-ʿIlmīyah, 1351/1932.

Ṭarafah Ibn al-ʿAbd. *Dīwān*. Commentary by al-Shantamarī. Ed. Durrīyah al-Khaṭīb and Luṭfī al-Ṣaqqāl. Damascus: Maṭbaʿat Dār al-Kitāb, 1395/1975.

———. *Dīwān*. Damascus: Majmaʿ al-Lughah al-ʿArabīyah, 1975.

al-Thaʿālibī, Abū Manṣūr ʿAbd al-Malik [Ibn Muḥammad Ibn Ismāʿīl]. *Yatīmat al-Dahr fī Maḥāsin Ahl al-ʿAṣr.* 5 vols. Ed. Mufīd Muḥammad Qamīḥah. Beirut: Dār al-Kutub al-ʿIlmīyah, 1403/1983.

Thilo, Ulrich. *Die Ortsnamen in der altarabischen Poesie.* Wiesbaden: Otto Harrassowitz, 1958.

al-Tibrīzī, Abū Zakarīyā Yaḥyā Ibn ʿAlī. *Sharḥ Dīwān Ashʿār al-Ḥamāsah.* 4 vols. in 2. Cairo: Būlāq, 1296/1879.

———. *Sharḥ al-Qaṣāʾid al-ʿAshr.* Ed. ʿAbd al-Sallām al-Ḥūfī. Beirut: Dār al-Kutub al-ʿIlmīyah, 1405/1985.

Torres Balbás, Leopoldo. "Arte califal." *España musulmana, pt. 2. Historia de España,* vol. 5. Ed. Ramón Menéndez Pidal. Madrid: Espasa Calpe, 1957.

Turner, A. Richard. *The Vision of Landscape in Renaissance Italy.* Princeton: Princeton University Press, 1966.

Turner, Victor. *Dramas, Fields, and Metaphors: Symbolic Action in Human Society.* Ithaca: Cornell University Press, 1975.

———. *The Ritual Process: Structure and Anti-structure.* Ithaca: Cornell University Press, 1977.

Unamuno, Miguel de. *Andanzas y visiones españolas.* Madrid: Renacimiento, 1922.

Valle-Inclán, Ramón del. *Sonatas: memorias del Marqués de Bradomín.* Madrid: Espasa-Calpe, 1969.

van Gelder, G. J. H. *Beyond the Line: Classical Arabic Literary Critics on the Coherence and Unity of the Poem.* Leiden: E. J. Brill, 1982.

van Gennep, Arnold. *The Rites of Passage.* Trans. Monika B. Vizedom and Gabrielle L. Caffee. 1909. Chicago: University of Chicago Press, 1960.

Vergil/Virgil. *The Aeneid of Virgil.* 2 vols. Ed. with introduction and notes by T. E. Page. London: Macmillan; New York: St. Martin's Press, 1967.

———. *Eclogues.* Ed. Robert Coleman. Cambridge: Cambridge University Press, 1977.

Vico, Giovanni Battista. *La scienza nuova.* 2 vols. Ed. Fausto Nicolini. Bari: Gius. Laterza and Figli, 1928.

Vidal-Naquet, Pierre. "The Black Hunter and the Origin of the Athenian *Ephebeia.*" In R. L. Gordon, ed., *Myth, Religion and Society: Structuralist Essays by M. Detienne, L. Gernet, J.-P. Vernant and P. Vidal-Naquet,* pp. 147–72. Cambridge: Cambridge University Press, 1981.

———. "Sophocles' *Philoctetes* and the Ephebeia." In Jean-Pierre Vernant and Pierre Vidal-Naquet, *Myth and Tragedy in Ancient Greece,* pp. 161–79. Trans. Janet Lloyd. New York: Zone Books, 1988.

Völker, Wolfram. *Märchenhafte Elemente bei Chrétien de Troyes.* Bonn: Rheinische Friedrich-Wilhelm-Universität, 1972.

von Franz, Marie-Louise. *Number and Time: Reflections Leading towards a Uni-*

fication of Depth Psychology and Physics. Trans. Andrea Dykes. Evanston: Northwestern University Press, 1974.

von Grunebaum, Gustave E. *Kritik und Dichtkunst: Studien zur arabischen Literaturgeschichte*. Wiesbaden: Otto Harrassowitz, 1955.

———. *Medieval Islam*. Chicago: University of Chicago Press, 1947.

———. *A Tenth Century Document of Arabic Literary Theory and Criticism: The Sections on Poetry of al-Bāqillānī's Iʿjāz al-Qurʾān*. Chicago: University of Chicago Press, 1950.

al-Waʾwāʾ al-Dimashqī, [Abū al-Faraj Muḥammad Ibn Aḥmad al-Ghassānī]. *Dīwān*. Ed. Sāmī al-Dahhān. Damascus: Al-Majmaʿ al-ʿIlmī al-ʿArabī bi Dimashq, 1369/1950.

Wellek, René, and Austin Warren. *Theory of Literature*. 3d ed. New York: Harcourt, Brace and World, 1956.

Wendel, Herta. *Arkadien im Umkreis bukolischer Dichtung in der Antike und in der französischen Literatur*. Giessener Beiträge zur romanischen Philologie. Giessen, 1933.

Werner-Fädler, Margarethe. *Das Arkadienbild und der Mythos der goldenen Zeit in der französischen Literatur des 17. und 18. Jahrhunderts*. Salzburg: Institut für romanische Philologie der Universität Salzburg, 1972.

Wheelwright, Philip. *The Burning Fountain: A Study in the Language of Symbolism*. Rev. ed. Bloomington: Indiana University Press, 1968.

Whitman, Walt. *Leaves of Grass*. 1892 ed. New York: Bantam Books, 1983.

Wimsatt, William K., Jr., and Cleanth Brooks. *Literary Criticism: A Short History*. New York: Knopf, 1965.

Wind, Edgar. *Pagan Mysteries in the Renaissance*. Rev. and enl. ed. New York: W. W. Norton and Co., 1968.

Wissowa, Georg, ed. *Paulys Realenzyclopädie der classischen Altertumswissenschaft*. Stuttgart: J. B. Metzlerscher Verlag, 1895.

Wollheim, Richard, ed. *The Image in Form: Selected Writings of Adrian Stokes*. New York: Harper and Row, Icon Editions, 1972.

Wordsworth, William. *The Prelude, or Growth of a Poet's Mind*. Ed. Ernest de Selincourt. 2d rev. ed. by Helen Darbishire. Oxford: Clarendon Press, 1959.

Wright, W. *A Grammar of the Arabic Language*. 3d ed. 2 vols. Cambridge: Cambridge University Press, 1971.

Yāqūt Ibn ʿAbd Allāh al-Ḥamawī, Shihāb al-Dīn Abū ʿAbd Allāh. *Muʿjam al-Buldān*. 5 vols. Beirut: Dār Ṣādir/Dār Bayrūt, 1374–76/1955–57.

———. *Muʿjam al-Udabāʾ*. 20 vols. Cairo: ʿĪsā al-Bābī al-Ḥalabī, 1936.

al-Zawzanī, Abū ʿAbd Allāh al-Ḥusayn Ibn Aḥmad Ibn al-Ḥusayn. *Sharḥ al-Muʿallaqāt al-Sabʿ*. Cairo: Maktabat wa Maṭbaʿat Muḥammad ʿAlī Ṣabīḥ wa Awlādih, 1367/1948.

Zeitlin, Froma I. "The Dynamics of Misogyny: Myth and Mythmaking in the Oresteia." *Arethusa* 11, nos. 1/2 (Spring and Fall 1978): 7–21, 149–89.

Zuhayr Ibn Abī Sulmā. *Dīwān*. Recension of Abū al-ʿAbbās Aḥmad Ibn Yaḥyā Ibn Zayd al-Shaybānī Thaʿlab. Cairo: Dār al-Kutub al-Miṣrīyah, 1363/1944.

Zwettler, Michael. "The Poetics of Allusion in Abu l-ʿAtāhiya's Ode in Praise of al-Hādī." *Edebiyât*, n.s. 3, no. 1 (1989): 1–29.

INDEX

ʿAbbās, Iḥsān, on *naẓm,* 236n.8
ʿAbd al-Badīʿ, Luṭfī, 147
ʿAbd al-Malik Ibn Marwān, 13
ʿAbīd Ibn al-Abraṣ, 23, 33, 126
Abligh (inform!), 10
Abū al-ʿAtāhiyah, 64, 66, 72–73, 78, 190
Abu-Deeb, Kamal: on *naẓm,* 236n.8; binary opposition in *qaṣīdahs* of Labīd and Imruʾ al-Qays, 248n.67
Abū al-Hindī, 153
Abū Nuwās, 57, 153, 189; banquet scene, 169; pseudo-*nasīb,* 58, 63–64, 66, 79
Abū Qamqām al-Asadī, 185
Abū Tammām, 31, 48, 155, 183, 185, 192
Ackerman, Diane, 167
ʿĀdhilah (censuress), 14; and tone of voice in the *nasīb,* 244n.48
ʿAdī Ibn Zayd, 72, 126, 150
Alan of Lille, 98
Alceus, 5
Aleppo, 186; as enclosure for flowers, 185
Allegory, 90–91, 139
ʿAlqamah Ibn ʿAbadah, 34, 46
ʿAnazah (short spear), as Muḥammad's *Vortragslanze,* or as the staff of Achilles, 240n.27
Al-Andalus, 76, 122, 130, 154
ʿAntarah, 21, 151; pastoral meadow, 186
Apostrophe, Bedouin, 80
ʿAqīq, 111–13, 198
Arabian Nights, 174; Abū Muḥammad the Lazy, 174; Ḥasan al-Baṣrī, 174–75
Arcadia/Arcady, 117, 120, 122–24, 133, 137–38, 142, 148; dream, 146
Aristotelian mimesis, 4, 244n.53
al-Aʿshā Maymūn, 14–15, 72
al-ʿAskarī, Abū Hilāl, 2
Astronomy, animistic, 147
Aṭlāl/ṭalal (ruins/ruin), 12, 20, 22, 24–27, 29, 31, 54–55, 61, 88, 149; double meaning, 84; metaphoric openness, 64
Auerbach, Erich, 90, 94
Āyah, between pre-Islamic ("missive") and Islamic ("qurʾānic verse"), 242n.36

Bachelard, Gaston, 180–81
Baghdad, 105–6, 109, 122
Bahrām, Gūr, 71–72
Bakchylides, 124
Banquet, 33, 65, 170, 253n.93
al-Bāqillānī, 110
Barford, Philip, the "sonata principle" behind the sonata form, 245n.54
Baroque. *See* Sonata: *sonata da chiesa*
Bashshār Ibn Burd, renounced Paradise, 295n.78
Bayt (house, tent), 33
Beethoven, Ludwig van, idiosyncratic first movements, 248n.68
Beowulf, 235n.1
Biblia pauperum, 90
Bier's Daughters, 151–52; in al-Mutanabbī, 259n.74; their mythology, 282n.52
Bishr Ibn Abī Khāzim, 23, 151
Blachère, Régis, the *qaṣīdah* as "une 'suite' ou plutôt un 'mouvement,'" 248n.59
Bloch, Alfred, 10, 243n.41; indictment of Arabic *qaṣīdah* theorists as "philologists," 239n.22
Bodkin, Maud, 108

Boethius, 91
Boon-companion, 64–65
al-Buḥturī, Abū ʿUbādah, 3, 53, 86, 113, 129, 190
Bürgel, J. Christoph, on truth in poetry, 236 n.9
al-Būrīnī, Ḥasan, 95–96
Burkert, Walter, anathema and votive offering, 243 n.41
Byzantine iconography, 77

Campbell, Joseph, 31
Captatio benevolentiae, 9, 241 n.28
Carlyle, Joseph Dacre, 135
Cervantes, Miguel de, pseudo-Arcady, 142
Chamfort, N., 196
Chenu, M.-D., 98
Chrétien de Troyes, 34, 36–37, 109
Church fathers, 99
Cicero, forensic speech, 9
Cincinnatus, 138
Claude Lorrain, 69, 135
Claudian (Claudius Claudianus), *Epithalamium,* 139–40, 185, 288 n.11
Coleridge, Samuel Taylor, 30
Cordova, Umayyad grandeur, 193, 197–99
Ctesiphon, 70, 190–91
Curtius, Ernst Robert, 235 n.1

Dalí, Salvador, 74
Damascus, 121–22
D'Annunzio, Gabriele, 74
Dante, Alighieri, 100, 176, 196, 268
Daphnis and Chloe, 143
Dār (abode), 27, 31–32, 66; as either Paradise or Hell, 171; as repository of ancestral glory, 33; round abode, 119, 181
Ḍaw', as "light upon light," 34
Deconstruction, 30
Development, Sonata-form/*nasīb,* 19, 65, 172
Dhū al-Rummah, 63, 74, 153
Diʿbil Ibn ʿAlī al-Khuzāʿī, his indebtedness to Ḥassān Ibn Thābit, 260 n.26
Diyār (domain, abodes), 12, 24, 180, 186
Douglas, Mary, 42
Drayton, Michael, 141, 185

East Wind. See *Ṣabā*
Epideictic strategy of poem, 6–16
Erec, 34–36
Euphrates, 47–48, 104, 111
Exekias, 69
Exordium, 9
Exposition, 19

Fakhr (boast), 2, 12, 45
al-Farazdaq, 55–56; *shahādah* of originality for al-Kumayt, 259 n.10
Ferdowsī, 71
Fisher King, 48
Forensic oratory, 13
Form and content, 2–5
Frappier, Jean, 35–36
Frye, Northrop, flow of symbolic imagination in "romance," 291 n.34
Frye, Prosser Hall, 26

Garden, 137, 142; Belvedere gardens of the Vatican, 186; of Eden, 138, 173, 196, 198; of Gethsemane, 164; qur'ānic concreteness, 171–72; woman as garden, 189
Gavain, 35
Ghazal (erotic verse, or poem), 145, 172, 200; in dialogue form, 56, 259 n.12; Umayyad, 25, 57, 74, 80, 128, 152
Giamatti, A. Bartlett, 141, 173
Gilgamesh, 138, 174
Giorgione, 69
Goethe, Johann Wolfgang, 16, 42, 120; a correct identification of *al-ṣabā,* 276 n.97; hermeneutical "misprision," 275 n.75

Golden Age, 137–38, 141, 174
Goldziher, Ignaz, 146; on *qāfiyah* in archaic invective, 241 n.33
Góngora, Luis de, 165
Guillaume de Lorris, 140–41

al-Hādī, 70
al-Ḥādirah, 127
Ḥadīth, 32
Ḥafṣ al-Umawī, 65–66
Hārūn al-Rashīd, 57, 64, 171
Ḥassān Ibn Thābit, 11, 33, 59–63, 65, 77, 80, 150, 157, 166
Ḥātim al-Ṭā'ī, 14–15
al-Ḥātimī, Abū ʿAlī Muḥammad Ibn al-Ḥasan: *qaṣīdah,* analogy with the human body, 5
Haydar, Adnan, place-names and the etymological method, 270 n.18
Haydn, Josef, elegiac formal dictates, 248 n.60
Heidegger, Martin, on the allegory of "Cura"/*hamm,* 249 n.69
Heinrichs, Wolfhart, 235 n.1
Hellenistic rhetorical theory, 9
Hermogenes, 235 n.1
Herodotus, 122
Hesiod, 124, 137
Hijā' (invective), 2, 127
Ḥijāz, 81–82, 115–16, 118–19, 121, 161, 182
al-Ḥijr, 43
Ḥimā, 32–33, 47, 81–82, 106, 114; Mount Carmel, 186, 199; of the Thamūd, 252 n.90
Himerius, 8
al-Ḥīrah, 68, 71–72, 126
Homer, 124, 137; the labyrinth as a dance floor, 279 n.30
Hoplite, 47
Horace, 5, 17, 136; Horatian simile, 3
Horse, 34; statuary of the T'ang dynasty, 251 n.82
Hortus conclusus, 136, 139, 142, 158, 185
Hugo of St. Victor, 94
Huizinga, Johan, 136
Humūm/himmah (cares/aspiration), 21, 23, 27, 30, 35, 40
Hunt, chivalrous, 45, 47
Ḥusayn, Ṭāhā, 115
al-Ḥuṭay'ah, 32–33

Ibn ʿAbbād, al-Ḥārith, 126
Ibn ʿAbd al-Quddūs, Ṣāliḥ, 171
Ibn Abī Rabīʿah, ʿUmar, 55–57, 128–29, 152
Ibn al-ʿAlā', Abū ʿAmr, 44
Ibn ʿAmr, Bashāmah, 11–12
Ibn ʿArabī, 80, 92; mystical commentary, 93–95, 97
Ibn Barṣā' al-Murrī, Shabīb, 186
Ibn al-Dumaynah, 116, 128, 144–45
Ibn al-Fāriḍ, ʿUmar, 61, 63, 73, 79–81, 84–91, 95, 101–2, 132; archaic Bedouinity, 118; wine, 173
Ibn Ḥazm, Abū Muḥammad ʿAlī Ibn Aḥmad Ibn Saʿīd, 157–58, 160
Ibn Ḥillizah, al-Ḥārith, 112
Ibn al-Jahm, ʿAlī, 108–9, 113, 129
Ibn Jandal, ʿUbayd Ibn Ḥuṣayn. *See* al-Rāʿī al-Numayrī
Ibn Khafājah, 80, 86, 113–14, 130–32, 145, 160; desert of lovers, 76–77; myth of Atlas, 156, 187, 189
Ibn Khaldūn, 119
Ibn Khidhām, 54
Ibn Munqidh, Usāmah, 51–53; his *Al-Manāzil wa al-Diyār,* 51
Ibn Naṣr, Abū Muḥammad ʿAbd al-Wahhāb Ibn ʿAlī, 75
Ibn Nuwayrah, Mutammim, elegy influencing pastoral idyll, 264 n.57, 280 n.38
Ibn Qays al-Ruqayyāt, ʿUbayd Allāh, 191
Ibn Qutaybah, 5–9, 18, 26, 28; ternary structure, 7, 16, 238 n.20
Ibn Rashīq al-Qayrawānī, 3, 236 n.7; Umayyad poets' search for solitude, 263 n.51
Ibn al-Rayb, Mālik, 11
Ibn al-Rūmī, 172–73

Ibn Rushd, Khawarnaq as elegiac as the Bedouin *aṭlāl,* 72
Ibn Saʿd al-Khayr al-Balansī, 86, 132
Ibn Shuʿayb, Abū al-ʿAbbās Aḥmad, 119
Ibn Shuhayd, Abū ʿAmir, 154–55, 166; "literary republic," 177; *Risālat al-Tawābiʿ wa al-Zawābiʿ,* 176
Ibn al-Ṣimmah, Durayd, 112
Ibn Sīnah, 10
Ibn al-Taʿāwīdhī, Sibṭ, 48
Ibn Ṭabāṭabā al-ʿAlawī, 2, 7
Ibn al-Ṭabīb, ʿAbdah, 45–46
Ibn Ṭufayl, Abū Bakr, 175
Ibn Umāmah, ʿAmr, 72
Ibn ʿUmayrah al-Makhzūmī, 106
Ibn al-Walīd, Muslim, 129
Ibn Zaydūn, 113, 192, 193–94, 197–99; *Nūnīyah,* 130, 195, 199–201; qurʾānic concept of bliss, 296n.89; strophic structure, 296n.93
Ibn al-Zabaʿrā, 11
Ibn al-Zubayr, ʿAbd Allāh, 13
Icon, 31
Iltifāt ("looking back"), elegiac and tragic symbolism, 264n.53
Imru' al-Qays, 12, 21, 29, 34, 54, 70, 78, 81, 110–12, 126–27, 178; and Ovid's "horses of the night," 250n.71
Irony, 55, 180; in Paradise, 178–79
Isidor of Seville, 91
Iʿtidhār (apology, plea), 13
Īwān Kisrā, 70, 190
al-ʿIzzāwī, ʿAbd al-Sattār, doubts about the historicity of Khawarnaq, 262n.39

Jāhilīyah (Age of Ignorance), 2
al-Jāḥiẓ, ʿAmr Ibn Baḥr, 2, 5
Jamīl Ibn Maʿmar al-ʿUdhrī, 115
Jarīr Ibn ʿAṭīyah Ibn al-Khaṭafā, 74, 85
Jean de Meung, 140–41
Jisr, 109
Johnson, Samuel, 236n.6
Jones, William, 135
Journey, 38–39
Jung, C. G., the "triadic numbers" and the principle of movement, 254n.113
al-Jurjānī, ʿAbd al-Qāhir, 3, 235n.1; on *naẓm,* 236n.8

Kaʿb Ibn Zuhayr, 11
Kaʿbah, 33
Karnak, as Khawarnaq, 73
Kawthar, 111, 178, 195, 198
Keats, John, 201
Kennedy, George A., 8
Khalīṭ (seasonal medley of transhumant clans), 24
al-Khansāʾ, 148–49, 157, 159, 166, 198
Khawarnaq, 67–73, 126, 189; as Arabicized version of *xoran-gāh,* 262n.41
Kulayb, 54–55, 148
Kuthayyir ʿAzzah, 48
Khvarne, 71

Labīd Ibn Rabīʿah, 20, 33, 39, 43, 46–47, 125, 135, 143, 163, 177
Lamberton, Robert, the Stoic hermeneutical tradition, 268n.98
Laylā, 76
Lemke, Gerhard H., 165
León, Fray Luis de, 136
Lesky, Albin, 6
Lessing, Gotthold Ephraim, 59
Lévi-Strauss, Claude, 30, 41; conceptualization of symmetry, 252n.84
Lewis, C. S., "discarded image," 90; primary epic, 235n.1; definition of courtly poetry, 261n.30
Liminality, 41; liminal rights, 40; arrested liminality, 45
Lincoln, Abraham, 165
Locus amoenus, 72, 143, 175; Serendib, 174

*Ma*ʿ*ānī* (motifs, ideas), 2, 235 n.1
Maʿarrat al-Nuʿmān, 53
al-Maʿarrī, Abū al-ʿAlāʾ, 118; Parnassus, 177; *Risālat al-Ghufrān,* 176
al-Madāʾin, 70
Madḥ (praise), courtly, 13
Madīḥ (panegyric), 2–3, 19, 45, 47, 68
Majnūn, 76, 86, 115–16, 128, 143–45; his Orphism, 265 n.58; pasturing of stars, 161–62
Mâle, Émile, 89
Malḥamah (Battle Lay), 13
Malraux, André, 171
Malti-Douglas, Fedwa, *Ḥayy Ibn Yaqẓān* and Wāq al-Wāq in feminist perspective, 289 n.16
Mandūr, Muḥammad, on *naẓm,* 236 n.8
Marlowe, Christopher, 136
Martianus Capella, 91
al-Masʿūdī, Abū al-Ḥasan, 175
Mecca, 76, 89, 191; Mother of Cities, 81–82, 88, 95
Medina, 111, 119
Meisami, Julie Scott, on Ibn Qutaybah's rhetorical *qaṣīdah* theory, 241 n.28
Mihyār al-Daylamī, 76
Moore, George, imagism, 183
Morgana, 290 n.18
Mozart, Wolfgang A., 17–18
*Mu*ʿ*allaqāt* (celebrated odes of pre-Islamic Arabia), 7
Muhalhil Ibn Rabīʿah, 54–55, 57–58, 148–49
Müller, Max, 133
al-Munakhkhal al-Yashkurī, 72, 189–90
Mundus, 163
al-Mutalammis, 72
al-Mutanabbī, Abū al-Ṭayyib, 51, 114, 177, 180; binary structure of the courtly *qaṣīdah,* 238 n.20; renounced Paradise, 295 n.78
al-Muthaqqib al-ʿAbdī, 22–23; complaining riding animal (*nāqah*), 295 n.78
Muwashshaḥah (strophic poem of al-Andalus), 57
Mystical poetry, Arabic, 62. *See also* Ibn ʿArabī; Ibn al-Fāriḍ, ʿUmar
Mythopoesis, 38

al-Nābighah al-Dhubyānī, 11–13, 39, 43–44, 47–48, 136, 148–49, 198
al-Nābulusī, ʿAbd al-Ghānī, 95–96
Nagy, Gregory, 253 n.93
al-Nahshalī, Aswad Ibn Yaʿfur, 72
Najd, 81–82, 106–7, 115–19, 123, 125, 133, 142–43, 145–46, 161, 271 n.33; autochthony, 120–22, 128, 273 n.49
al-Namarī, Manṣūr, 105
Nāqah (she-camel), as mediator, 27; as structural icon, 31; the She-Camel of Ṣāliḥ, 252 n.90
Narratio, 9
Nasīb (opening section of the *qaṣīdah*), 2, 63; Bedouin symbolism, 200; cosmic metaphor, 148; erotic, 80; figurative understanding, 62; *ghazal*-like alternative, 151; landscape, 107; lyrical validity, 50; with nightly apparition, 86; nucleus, 84; pervasive in the structurally dominant *madīḥ,* 241 n.30; as poem, 197; poetic time, 24–25; pseudo-*nasīb,* 105; as sonata form, 16; symbolic idiom, 187; thematic modulation, 21; theme sequence, 22; as time of loss, 28; under the cloak of *ghazal,* 145
Naẓm (arrangement; aspectual formulation of expression, or speech), 236 n.8
Neo-Platonism, 90
Nile, 103–4
Niẓāmī, 71
Nöldeke, Theodor, 71

al-Nuʿmān Ibn al-Mundhir, 47–48, 71
Nūr, as "light within darkness," 34

Odyssey, 125
Oratory, adversary, 10
Oryx, 30
Ovid, 136, 163

Pan, 122–23, 136–37
Panegyric, Abbasid courtly, 7
Panofsky, Erwin, 120, 138
Paradise, 63, 67 142; descriptive *paradeisoi*, 139; earthly, 68, 139, 185; lost, 106; not a self-referential subject in the Qurʾān, 169; qurʾānic heavenly, 73, 176, 195, 198; Taoist, 31
Parallelism, 84
Parceval, 36
Passage, 37, 40; manqué, 42–43
Pastor of the stars, 146
Pastoral, 136, 138; cosmic projection, 147, 151, 164; ecloguelike excursus in *Don Quijote*, 285 n.78; Greek and Latin, 146; melancholy, 150; stylized elegy, 145; tent of the world, 163
Peloponnesus, 122, 132
Persona, poetic, 9
Pindar, 8
Place-names, 103, 114
Plato/Platonism, 3; language of the souls, 16; Platonic analogy, 17; Platonic matrix, 90; Platonic paradox, 98–99
Polybius, 122
Poussin, Nicolas, his Arcadies, 69, 142
Prophet, 60–63, 81; Sūrah of the Poets, 99; supported by *al-ṣabā*, 125
Proust, Marcel, 74, 107–8

al-Qāḍī al-Fāḍil, 103–4
Qāfiyah (rhyme, invective), 10
al-Qālī, Abū ʿAlī, 31
al-Qarṭājannī, Ḥāzim, 182; conditioned by the post-Mutanabbian *qaṣīdah*, 238 n.20
Qaṣīdah (archaic paradigm), canon, 67; epideictic, 8, 13; formal continuity, 1, 87; formal delivery, 8; like a human body, 5; meaning of main sections, 2; as missive, 12; organic form, 5; as rite of passage, 40–43; rhetorical intent, 9; rhetorical function, 12; schematized, 19; as sonata, 16; ternary structure, 26, 38; three theories, 6; Umayyad period, 13
Quijote, Arcadian shepherds, 141
Qudāmah Ibn Jaʿfar, 2
Quintilian, 236 n.1
Qurʾān, 168–69, 176; dome of the sky, 163; *iʿjāz*, 110; lofty halls, 191; Paradise as *theme* only in a cumulative sense, 170; qurʾānic subject of Paradise as *motif*, 169

Rabʿ (vernal encampment), 27
Raḥīl (journey section), 2, 9, 15, 39, 44–45, 68; as time of breaking away, 28; as vision of the past, 88; as *nasīb*-subservient, 129; pure/brackish water, 256 n.126
al-Rāʿī al-Numayrī, 13–16; variants of his *Malḥamah*, 243 nn.45, 46
Raleigh, Walter, bejeweled garden, 289 n.14
Rawḍah (meadow), 158; *rawḍatun unufun*, 186, 292 n.44, 293 n.54
Reed, Herbert, 100
Reverie, 21
Rhetorical strategy of poem, 6–16
Richter, Gustav, on Ibn Qutaybah as philologist, 239 n.22
Risālah (epistle), 7
Rite of passage, 40–43
Ritter, Helmut, truth in poetry, 237 n.10

Rojas, Pedro Soto de, 141, 185
Roland, Romain, 18
Roman de la Rose, 139–41, 185
Rose, 76
Rosen, Charles, multiplicity of sonata forms, 246n.55
Rückert, Friedrich, 117
Ruṣāfah, 108–9; of Hishām, 109

Saavedra Fajardo, Diego de, his pastoral "epigrama español," 294n.57
Ṣabā (East Wind), 123, 125–27, 130–33, 142–43; full poetic identity, 128; lyric-erotic code, 129
Sadīr, 67–73, 126, 189
al-Salūlī, ʿUjayr, 128
al-Ṣanawbarī, Abū Bakr Aḥmad al-Ḍabbī al-Anṭākī, 130, 184–85
Sannazaro, Jacopo, 51, 120, 124, 164
Santiago de Compostela, 88
al-Sarī al-Raffāʾ, 186
"Setting out," formulaic tradition of *wa qad aghtadī,* 257n.130
Seznec, Jean, allegory as a "secret philosophy," 278n.16
Shakespeare, William, 3
Sharīʿah (way to water, Islamic legal code), pastoral/heroic, 257n.134
al-Sharīf al-Murtaḍā, 190
al-Sharīf al-Raḍī, 75–76
Shawqī, Aḥmad, 132
She-camel. See *Nāqah*
Shepherd, G. Dorothy, on Sassanian iconography of the hunt, 253n.93
Shīz, 71
Signal, stylistic, 10–11, 21
al-Ṣimmah Ibn ʿAbd Allāh al-Qushayrī, 117, 120
Simonides of Ceos, "painting inarticulate poetry and poetry articulate painting," 236n.7, 245n.53
Sindbad, 174, 180
Slochower, Harry, 38–41; Oriental pattern of mythopoesis, 251n.81
Smith, W. Robertson, 186
Snell, Bruno, 120
Sonata, 17; *Kreutzer Sonata,* 247n.58; pre-Beethoven, 18; *sonata da chiesa,* 18–19; sonata form, 16–24, 246n.55, 247n.58
Sparta, 124
Spee, Friedrich, 164–66
Staiger, Emil, lyrical poetry as Heideggerian *Erinnerung,* 250n.76
Stetkevych, Suzanne P., 41–42; liminal feralization/humanization, 256n.127; *walad mukhallad/puer aeternus,* 286n.92
Stevens, John, 108
Stevens, Wallace, ironic twist to Plotinus and Dante, 290n.22
Stylization in Arabic poetry, 77
Ṣuʿlūk (brigand), 42, 45
Symbolism, Egyptian river, 48
Symphony, 17

Taʾabbaṭa Sharran, 151
Taḥrīḍ (instigation to blood vengeance), 10
Takhalluṣ (intersectional, or final, closure), 36
Ṭalal (ruin). See *Aṭlāl*
Ṭarafah, 20–21, 31, 33, 65, 72, 78, 127; complaining mount, 295n.78
Ṭayf al-khayāl (nightly phantom, dream phantom), 15, 85, 152
Tempi, 17
Thamūd, 44
Thaʾr (blood vengeance), 10
Theocritus, 123–24, 137
al-Tibrīzī, Abū Zakarīyā Yaḥyā Ibn ʿAlī, the love theme of the *nasīb* as originally part of the "desolate encampment scene," 250n.77
Tigris, 105, 109
Tihāmah, 114, 116, 118
al-Tihāmī, Abū al-Ḥasan, 182
Titian, 69
Tolkien, J. R. R., 235n.1

Topoanalysis, 180
Turner, Victor, 42

ʿUdhrī, *ghazal,* 251 n.78; martyr of love, 265 n.57; poets, 74, 115; topical pool, 86
Uḥud, battle of, 11
Umayyad, desert lyricism, 144; period of sensibility, 31
Unamuno, Miguel de, 166

Van Gelder, G. J. H., on al-Ḥātimī's *qaṣīdah*/body analogy, 237 n.17
Van Gennep, Arnold, 40–43
Valencia, 76, 78, 106–7
Venus, bower of love, 76, 139
Vergil, 120, 123, 136–37, 142, 148, 165–66; his bucolic wish, 279 n.28
Vico, Giambattista, 4
Vincent of Beauvais, 91
Von Grunebaum, Gustave E., subject of Paradise, 168

Waḍḍāḥ al-Yaman, dialogued *ghazal,* 259 n.12
Wallādah, 193
Wāq al-Wāq, 175
Wasteland, 36
al-Waʾwāʾ al-Dimashqī, 156, 187
Whitman, Walt, 165
Wilde, Oscar, "the discovery of fog," 278 n.11
Wordsworth, William, 100
Wuqūf (halting): of arrival, 29; of apotheosis, 29, 34

Yemen, 86
Yvain, 34–36

al-Zahrāʾ, idea of Paradise, 193–94, 198
Zamzam, 88
Ẓaʿn/*ẓaʿīnah* (departure of clan and beloved/departing beloved), 20, 22–25, 44, 151; pseudo-*ẓaʿn,* 106
Zephyr, 123, 125; Zephyros, 124, 131; *zophos,* 132–33
Zuhayr Ibn Abī Sulmā, 11, 33, 43, 46
Zwettler, Michael, al-Hādī/Moses allusion, 261 n.33

www.ingramcontent.com/pod-product-compliance
Lightning Source LLC
Chambersburg PA
CBHW050856300426
44111CB00010B/1277
9780226773360